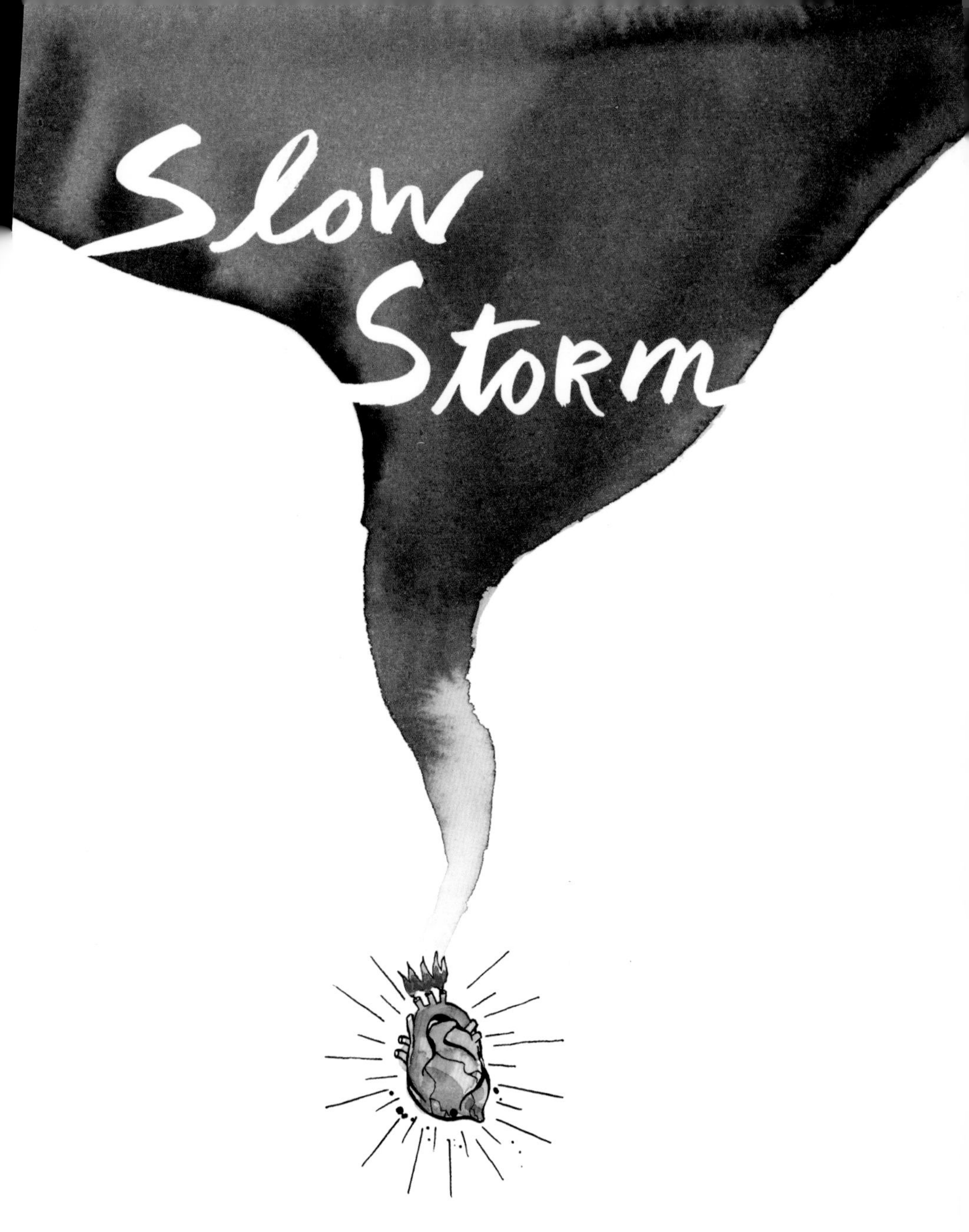
Slow
Storm

Slow Storm

Danica Novgorodoff

First Second
NEW YORK & LONDON

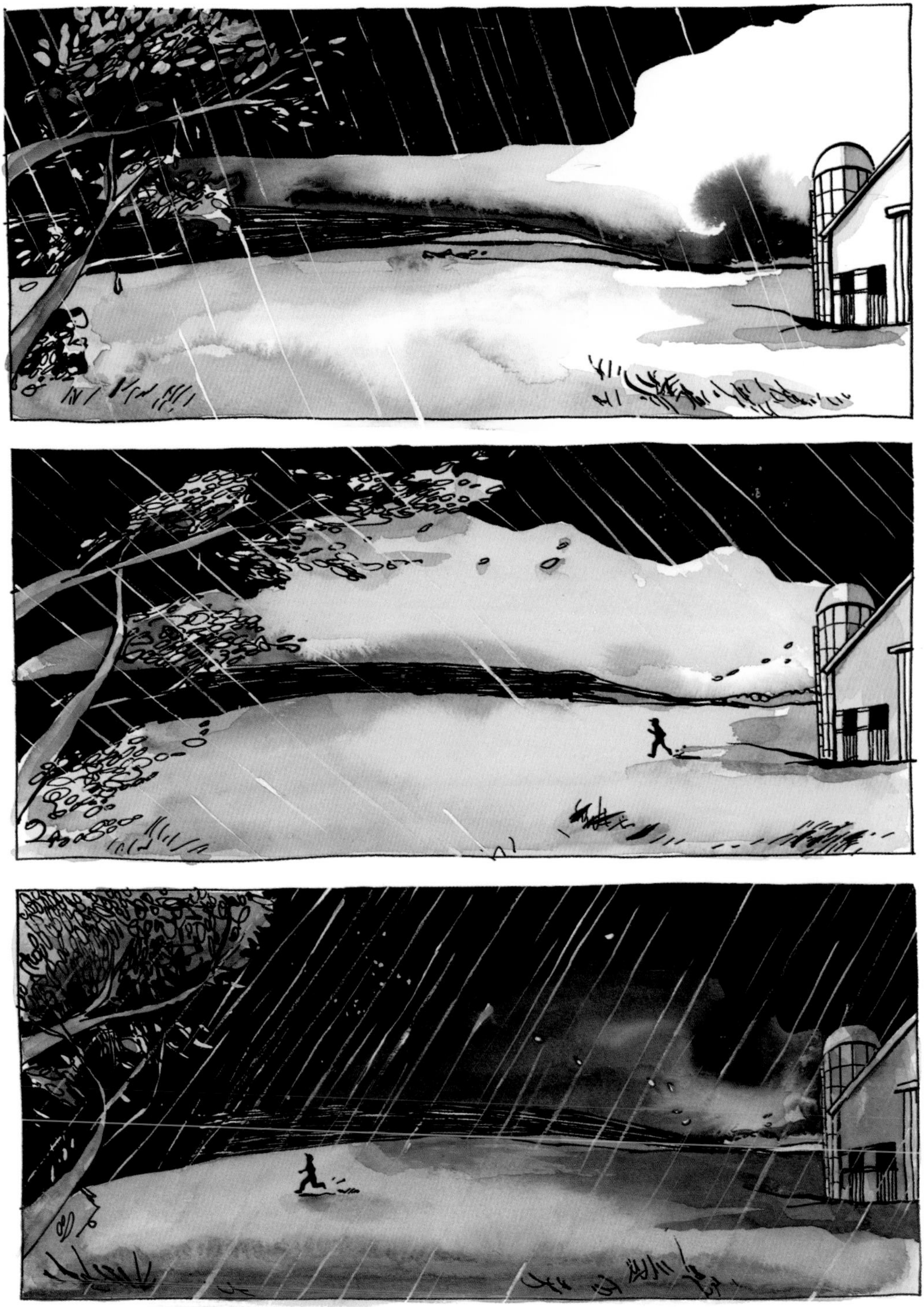

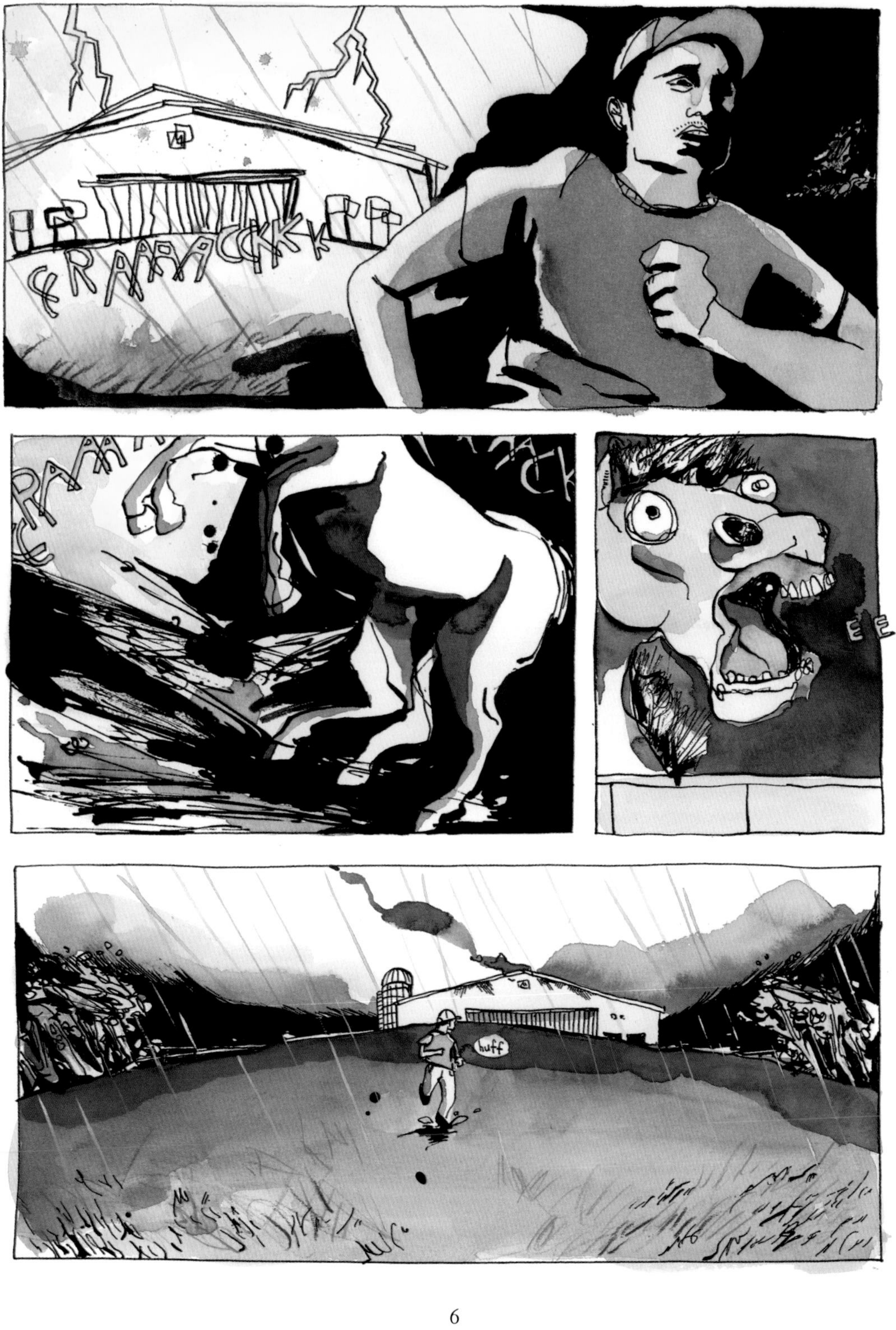
CRAAAACCKKK
huff

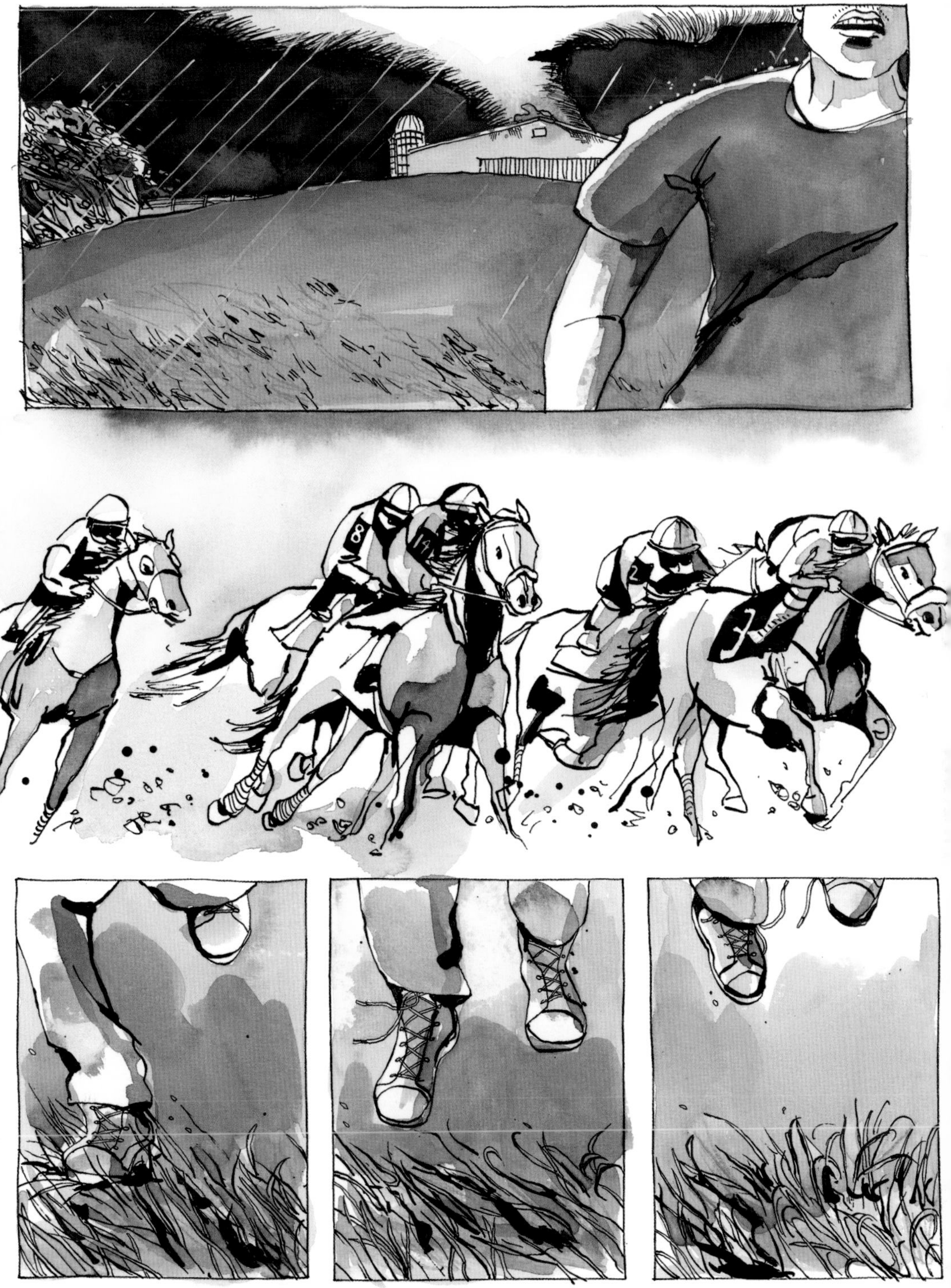

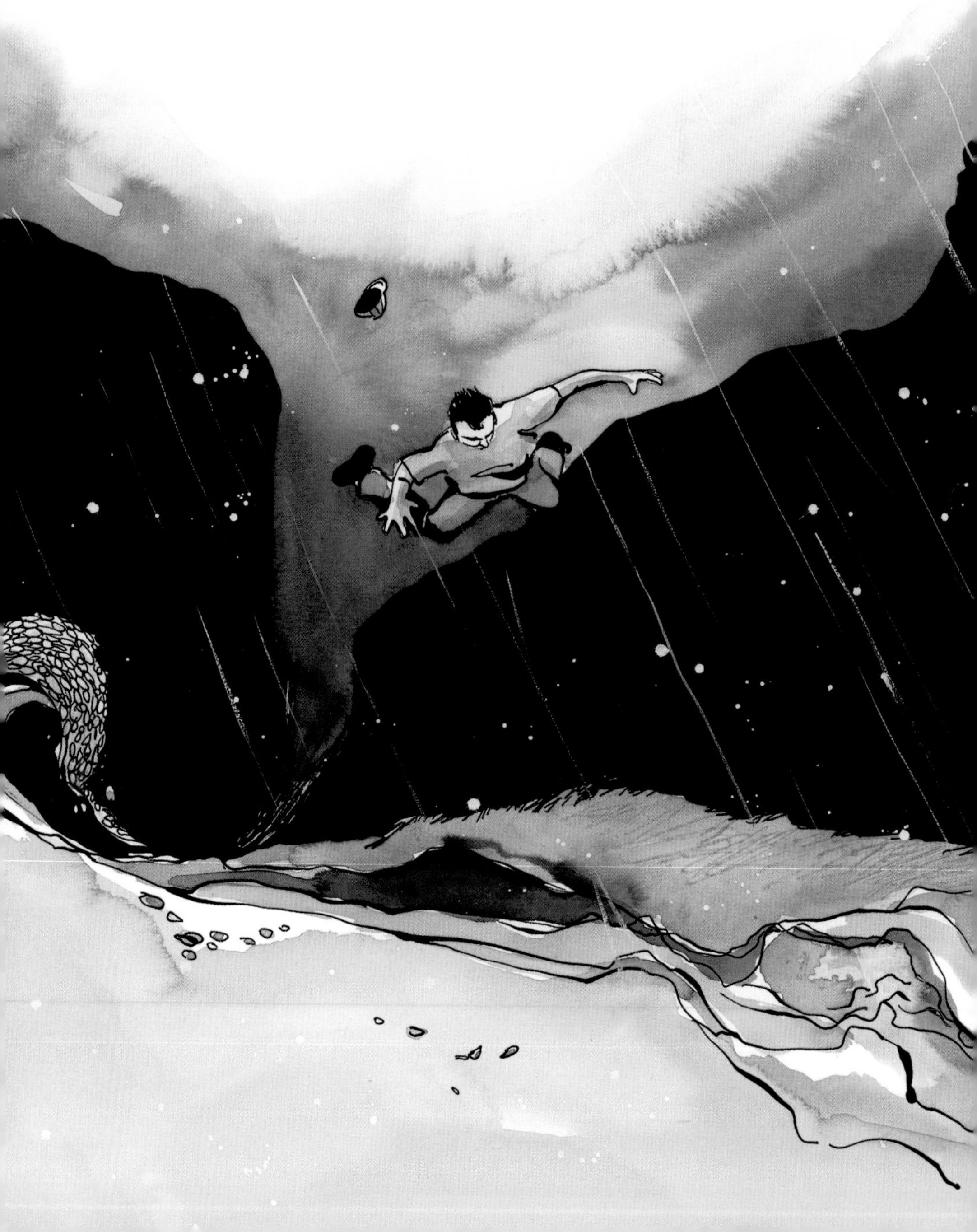

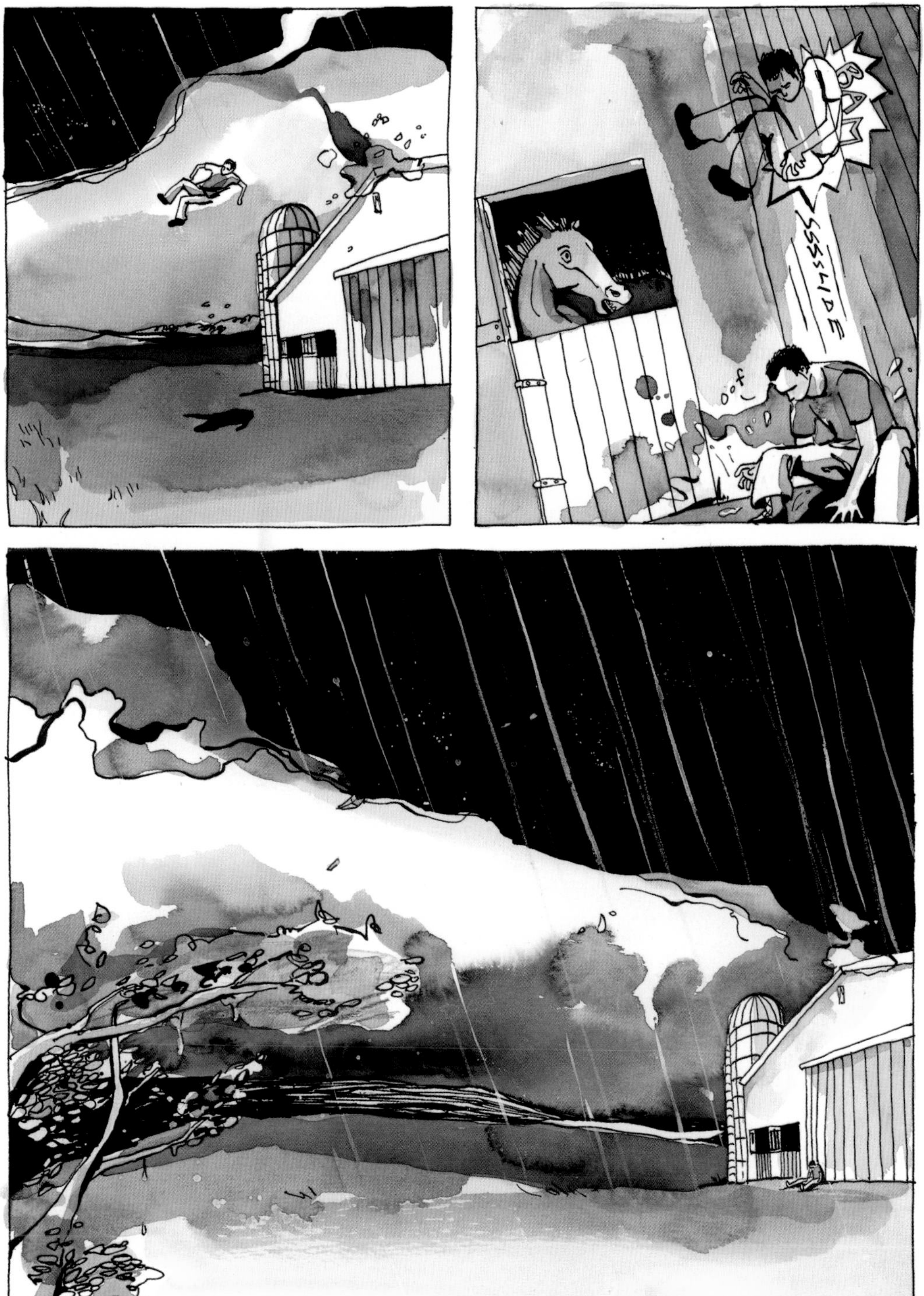
BAM
SSSSLIDE
oof

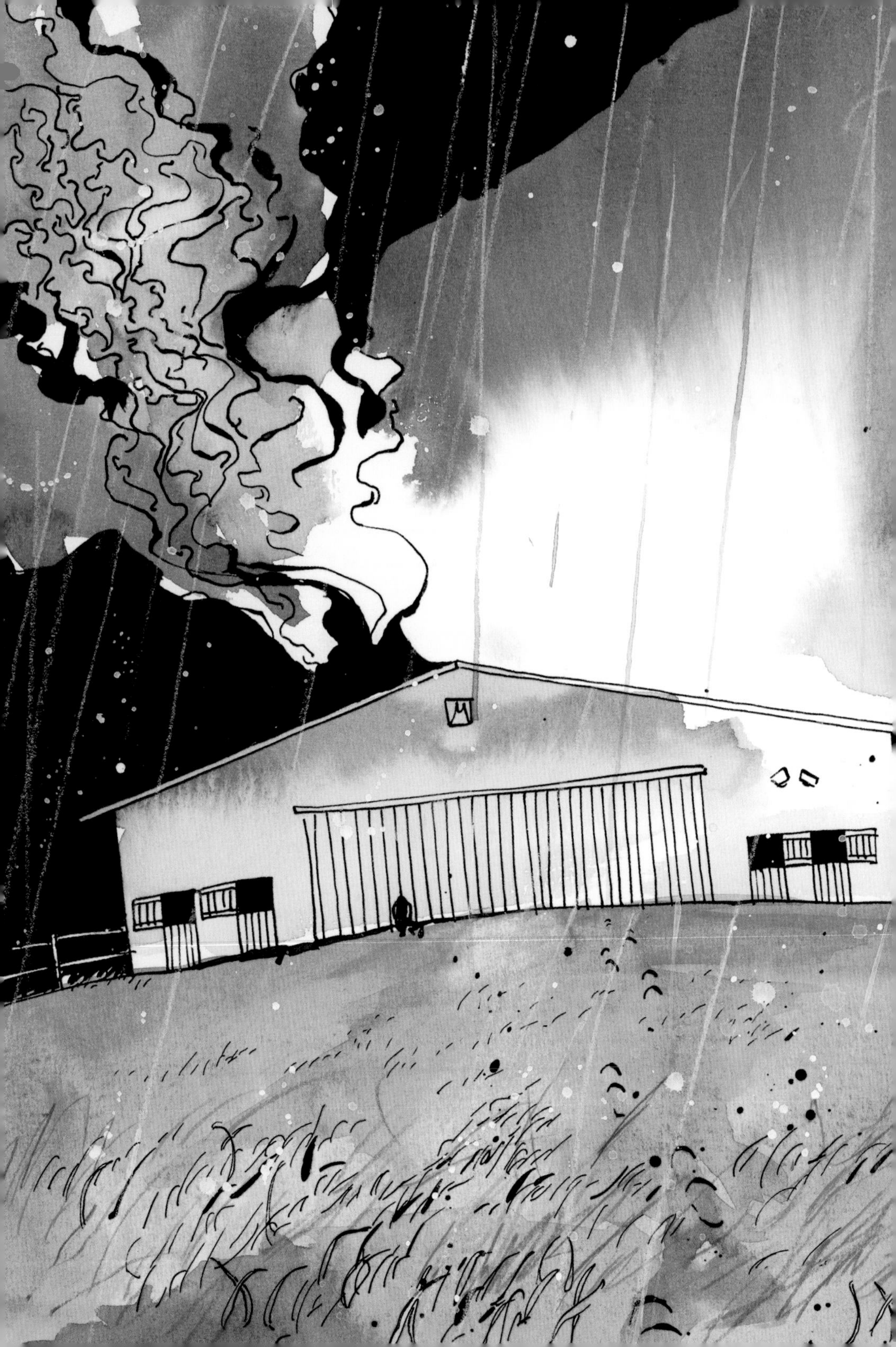

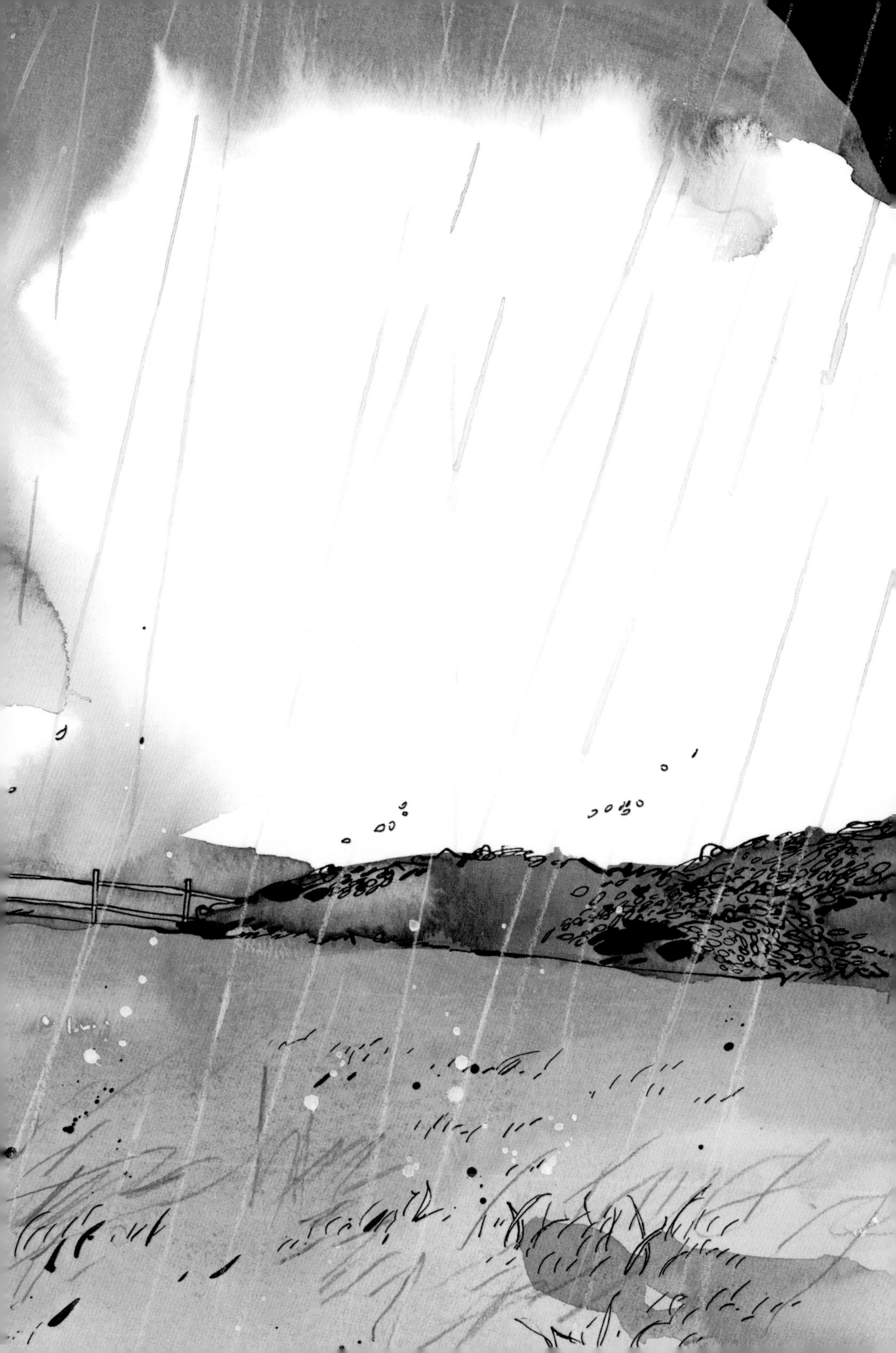

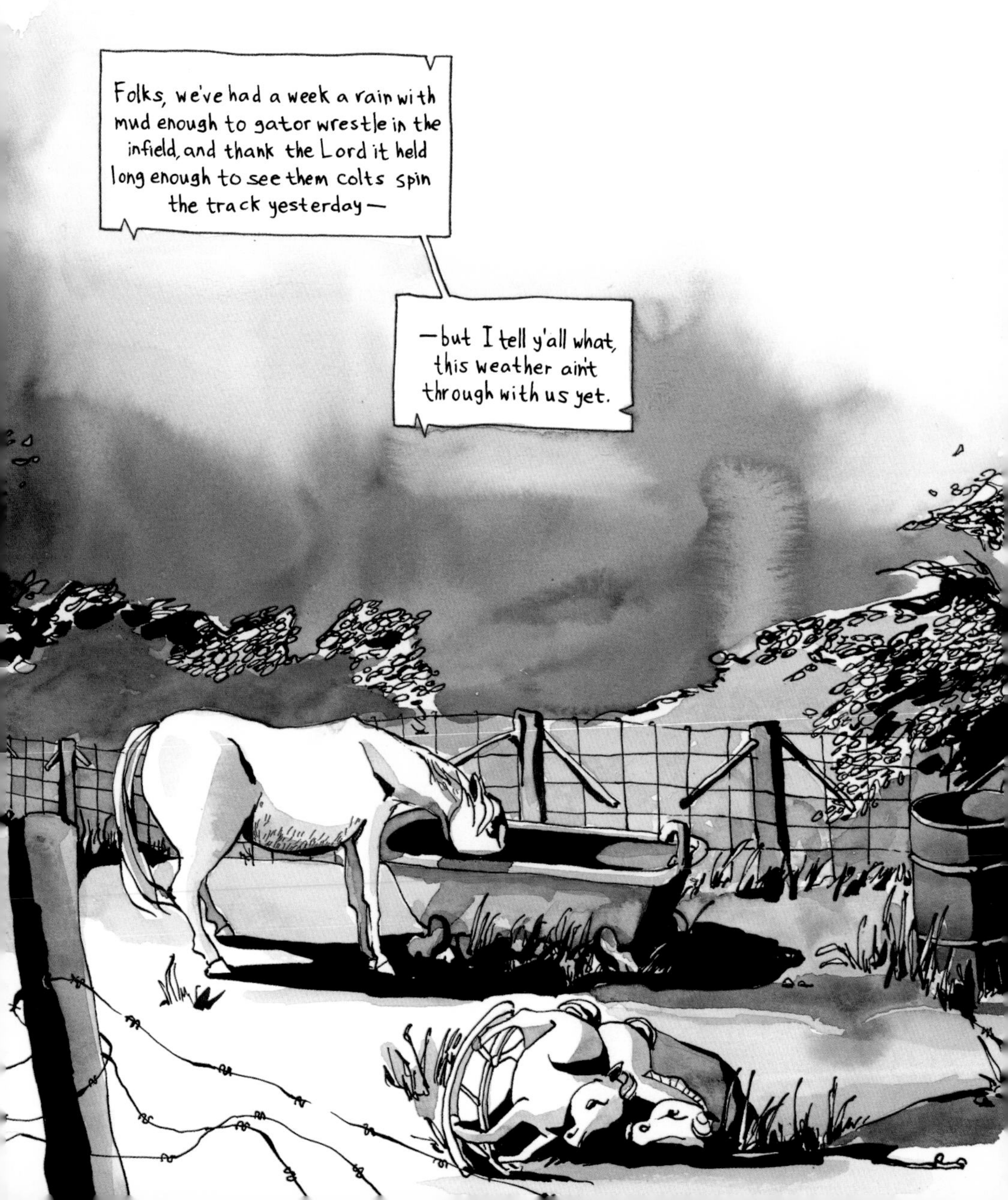
Folks, we've had a week a rain with mud enough to gator wrestle in the infield, and thank the Lord it held long enough to see them colts spin the track yesterday—
—but I tell y'all what, this weather ain't through with us yet.

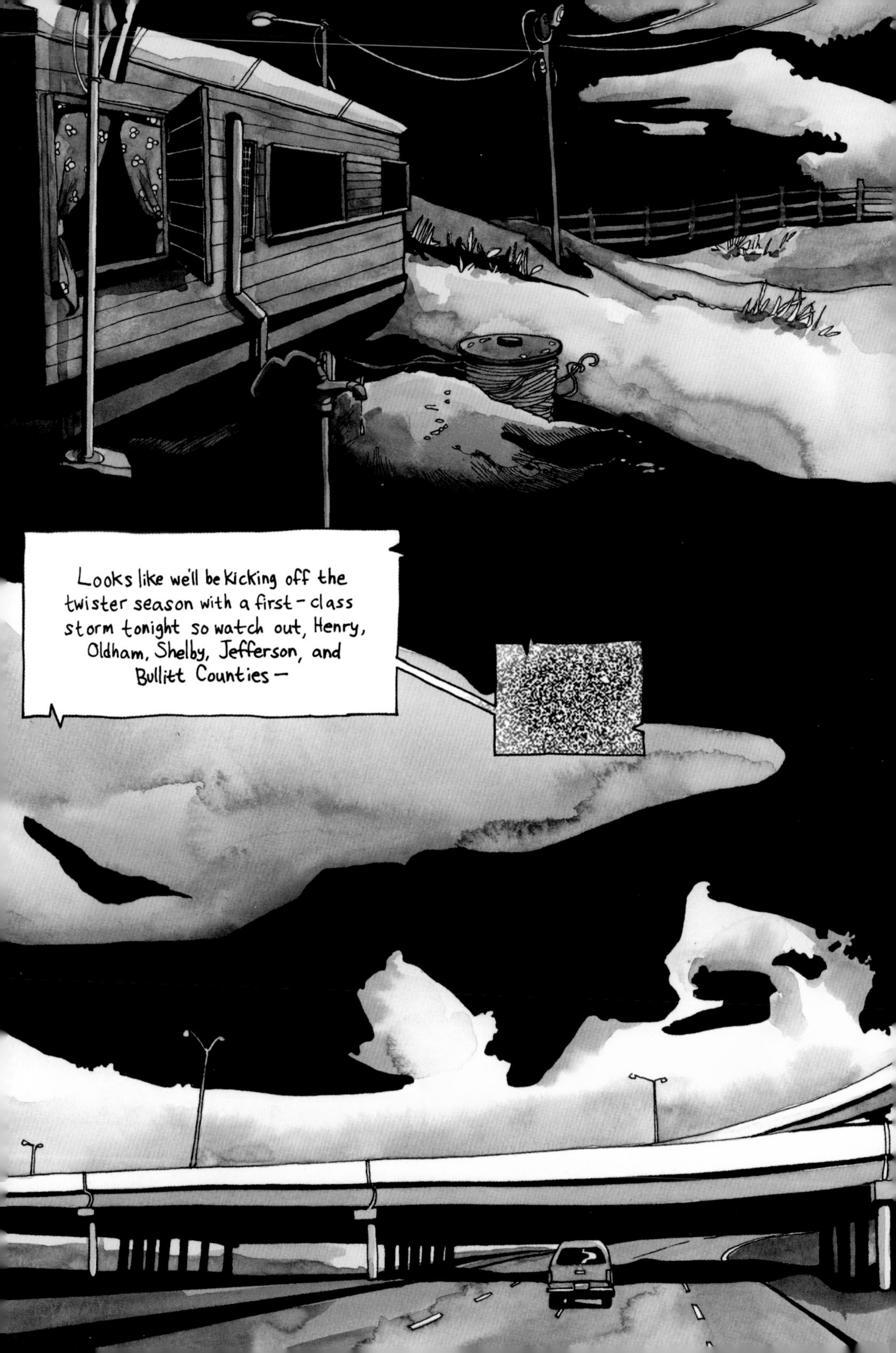
Looks like we'll be kicking off the twister season with a first-class storm tonight so watch out, Henry, Oldham, Shelby, Jefferson, and Bullitt Counties —

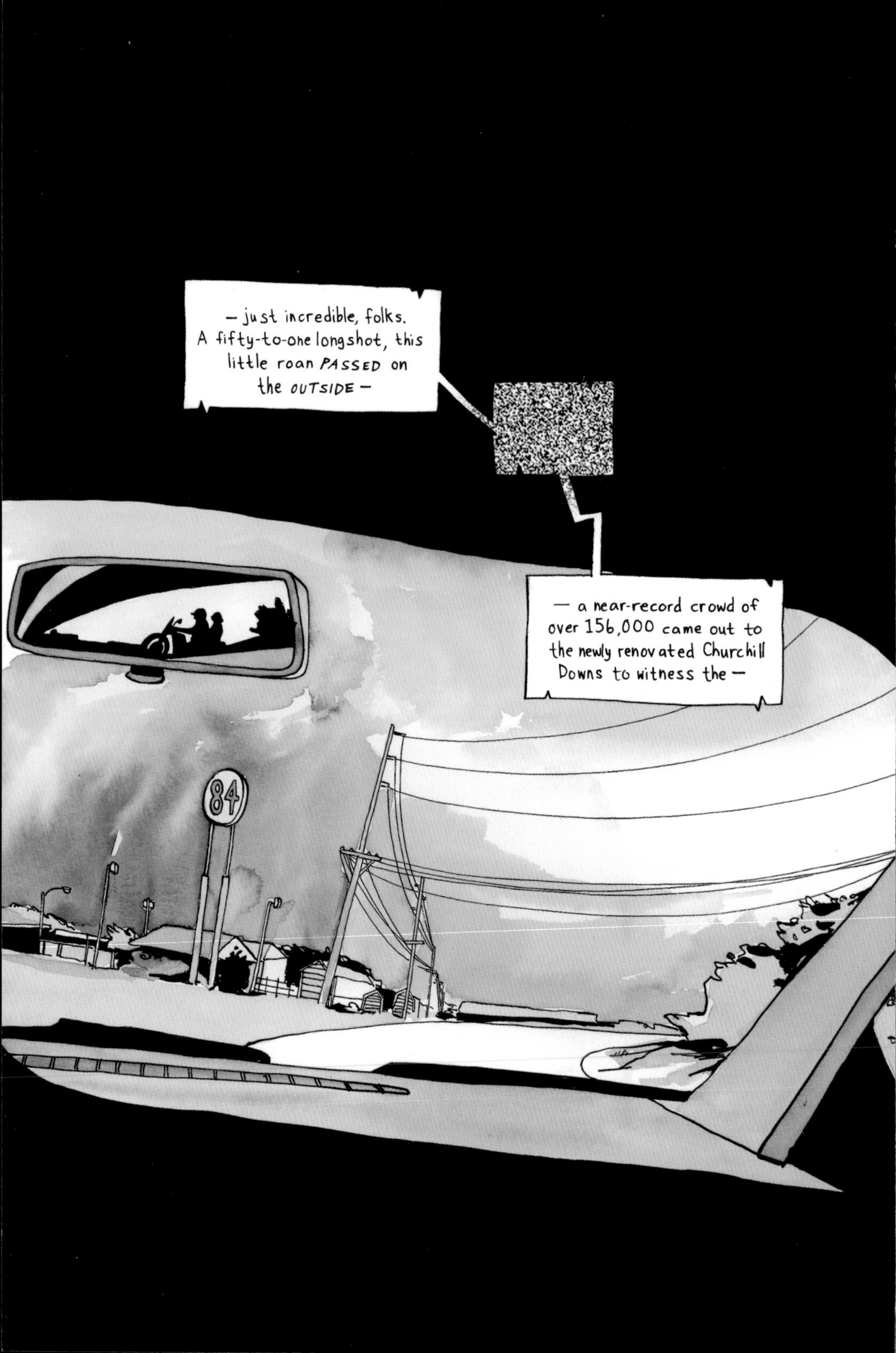

— just incredible, folks. A fifty-to-one longshot, this little roan PASSED on the OUTSIDE —
— a near-record crowd of over 156,000 came out to the newly renovated Churchill Downs to witness the —
84

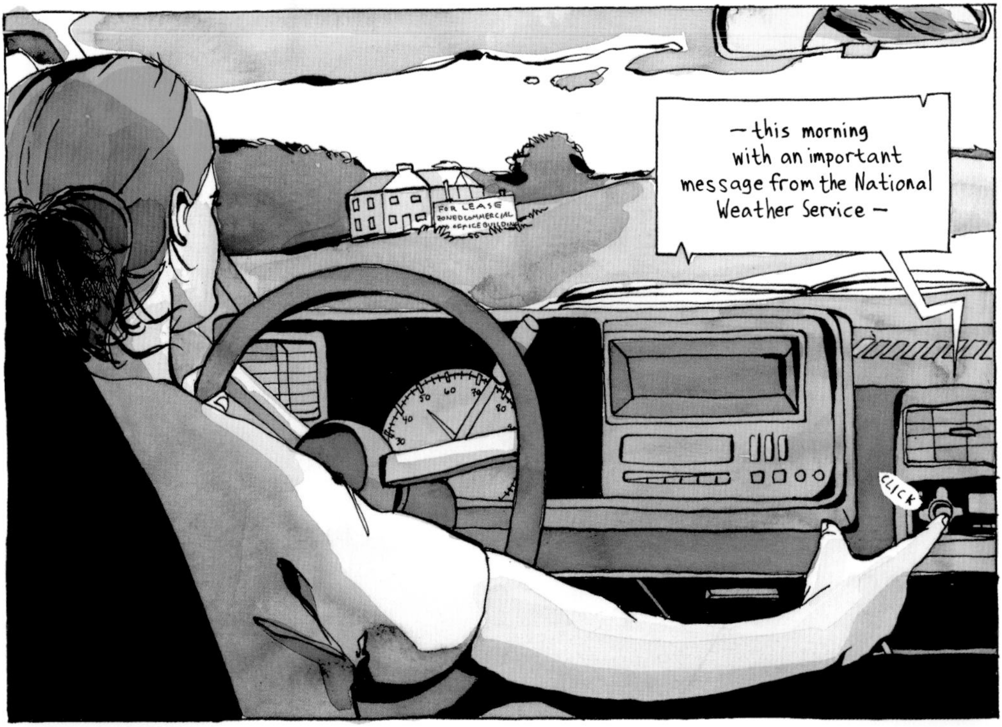
FOR LEASE
ZONED COMMERCIAL
OFFICE BUILDING
—this morning with an important message from the National Weather Service—
CLICK

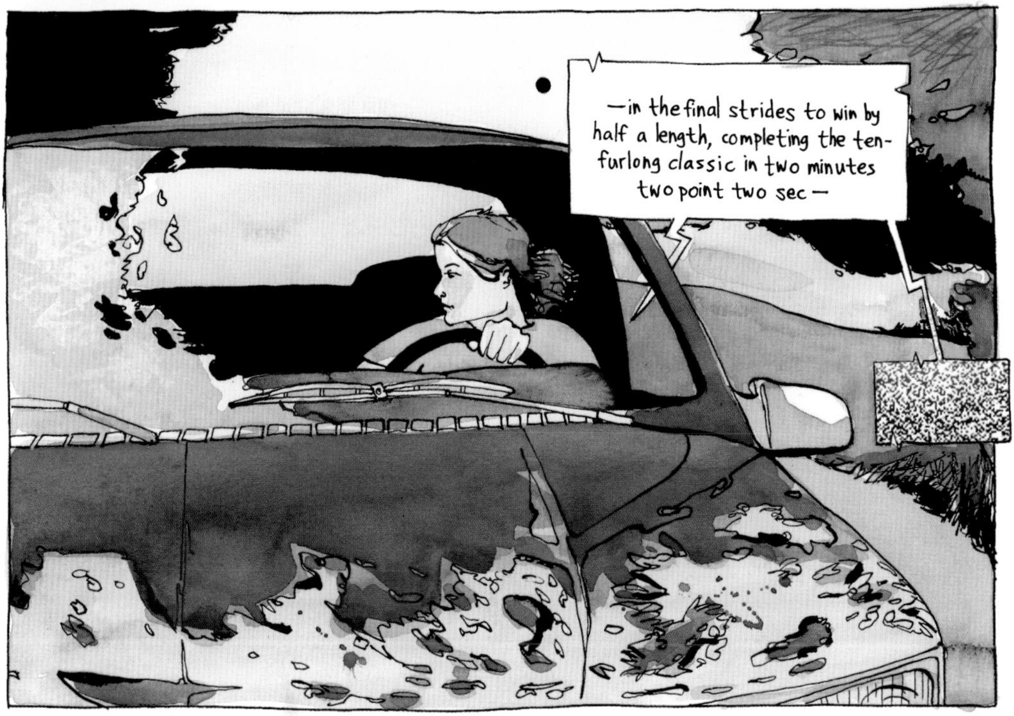
—in the final strides to win by half a length, completing the ten-furlong classic in two minutes two point two sec—

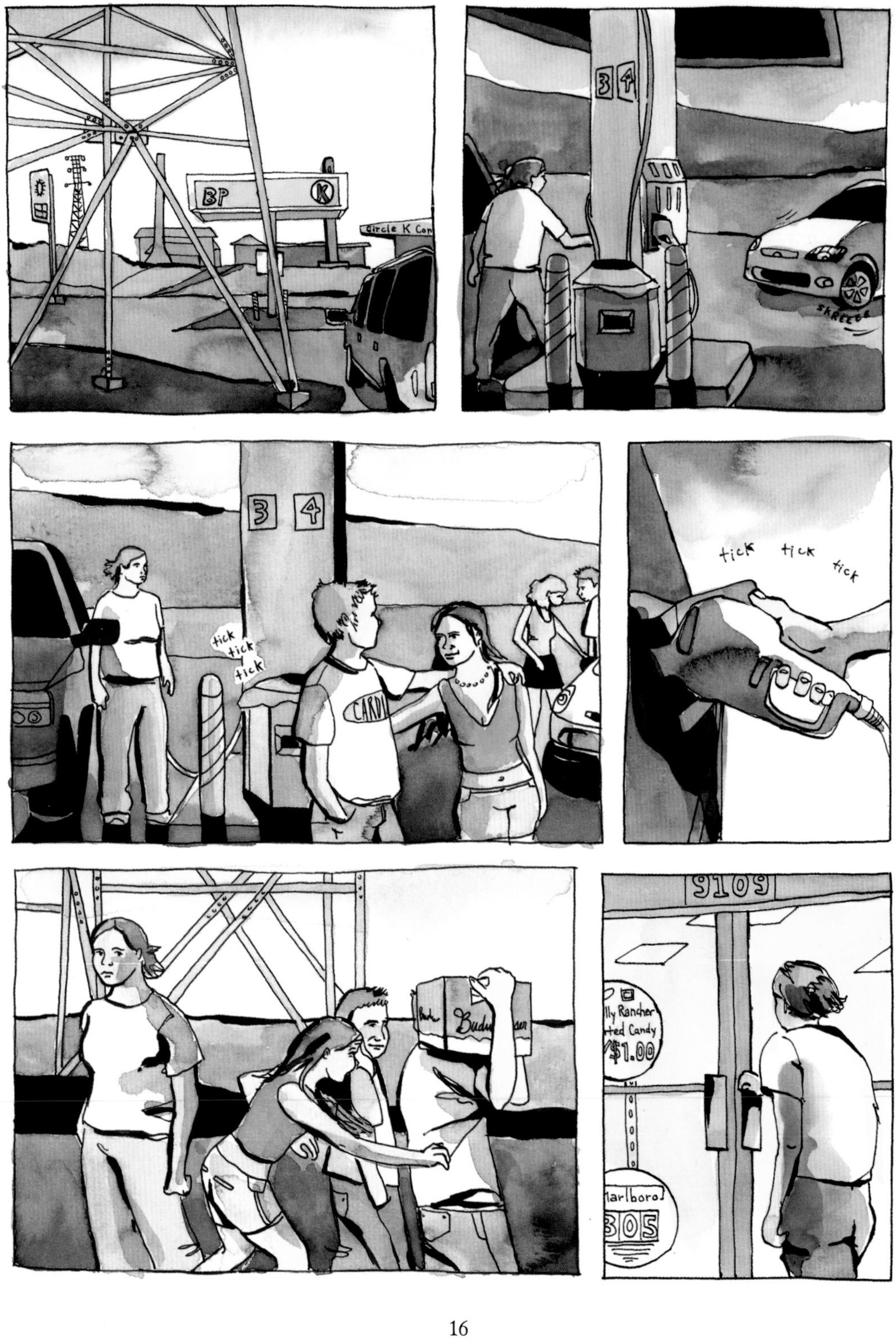
BP
K
Circle K Con
3 4
SKREEEE
3 4
tick
tick
tick
CARDI
tick tick tick
Budweiser
9109
lly Rancher
rted Candy
$1.00
Marlboro
305

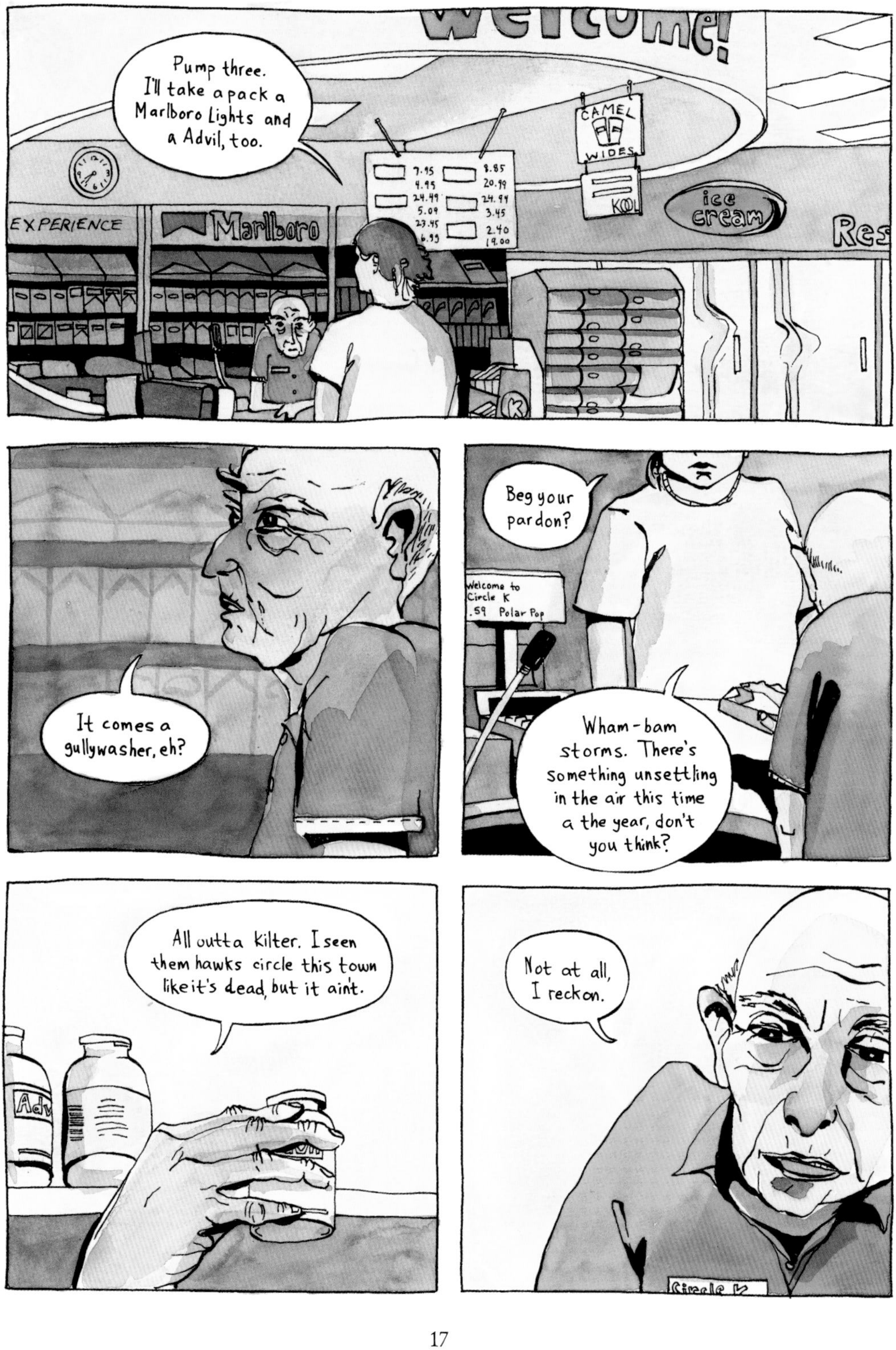
EXPERIENCE
Marlboro
CAMEL WIDES
KOOL
ice cream
Pump three. I'll take a pack a Marlboro Lights and a Advil, too.
It comes a gullywasher, eh?
Beg your pardon?
Welcome to Circle K .59 Polar Pop
Wham-bam storms. There's something unsettling in the air this time a the year, don't you think?
All outta kilter. I seen them hawks circle this town like it's dead, but it ain't.
Not at all, I reckon.

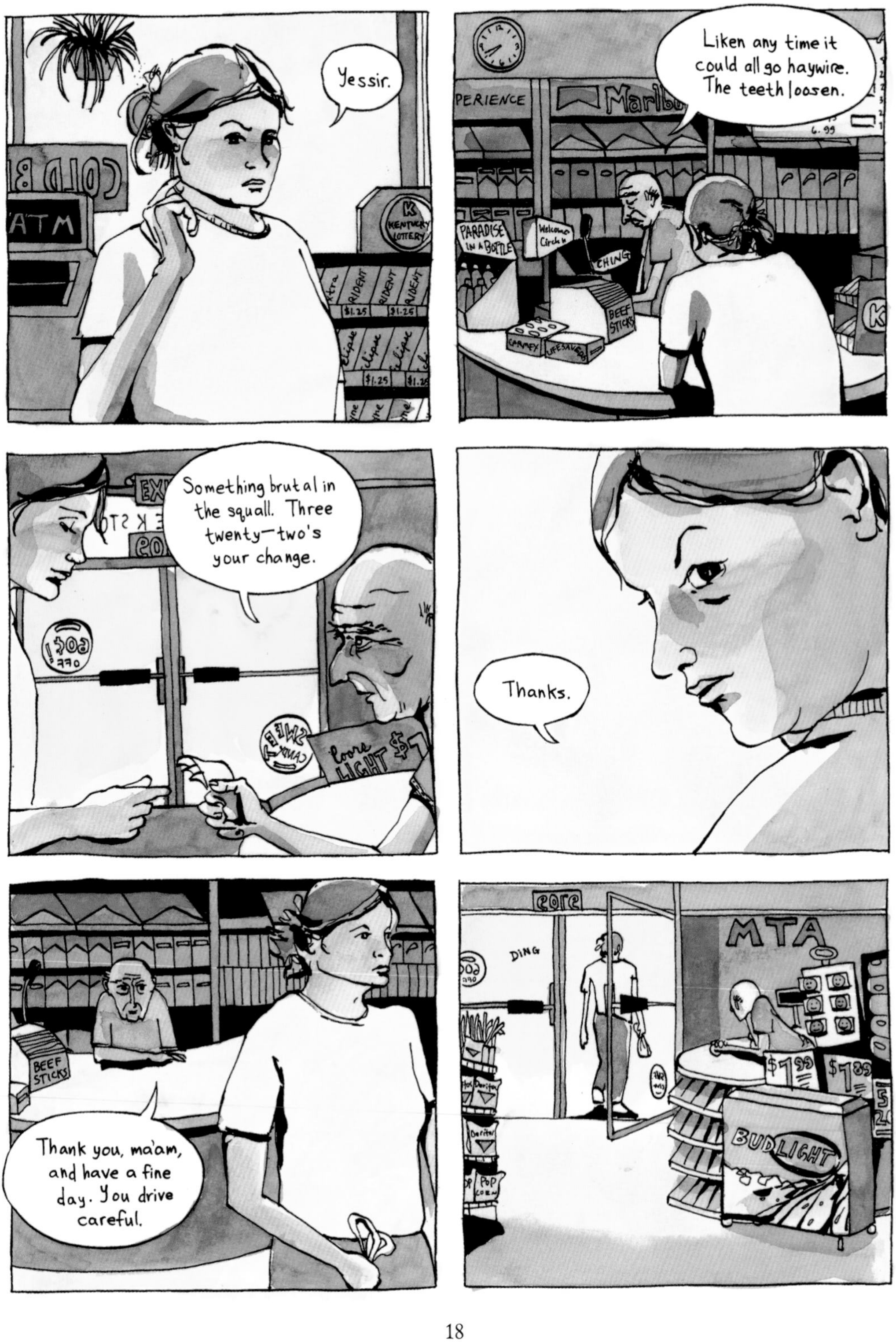
Yessir.
Liken any time it could all go haywire. The teeth loosen.
PARADISE IN A BOTTLE
CHING
BEEF STICKS
Something brutal in the squall. Three twenty-two's your change.
Thanks.
Thank you, ma'am, and have a fine day. You drive careful.
DING
MTA
BUDLIGHT

squee

squee

EXPERIENCE

CLICK

SNICKERS

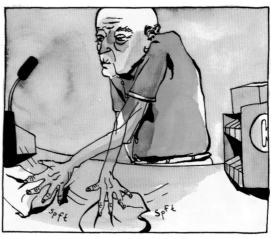

spft

spft

Sure enough,
it comes a
gullywasher...

$1⁹⁹

$1

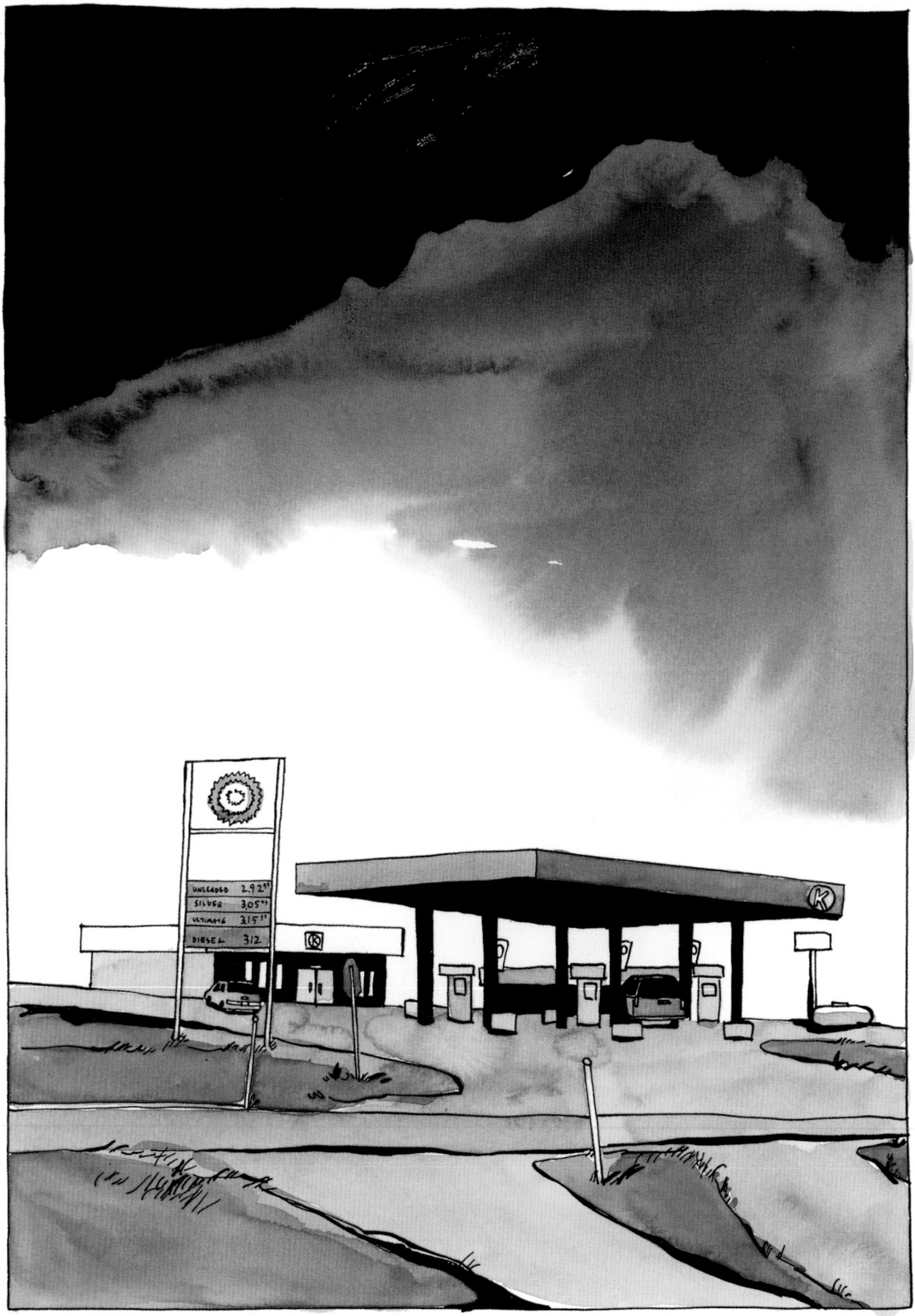
UNLEADED 2.92
SILVER 3.05
ULTIMATE 3.15
DIESEL 312

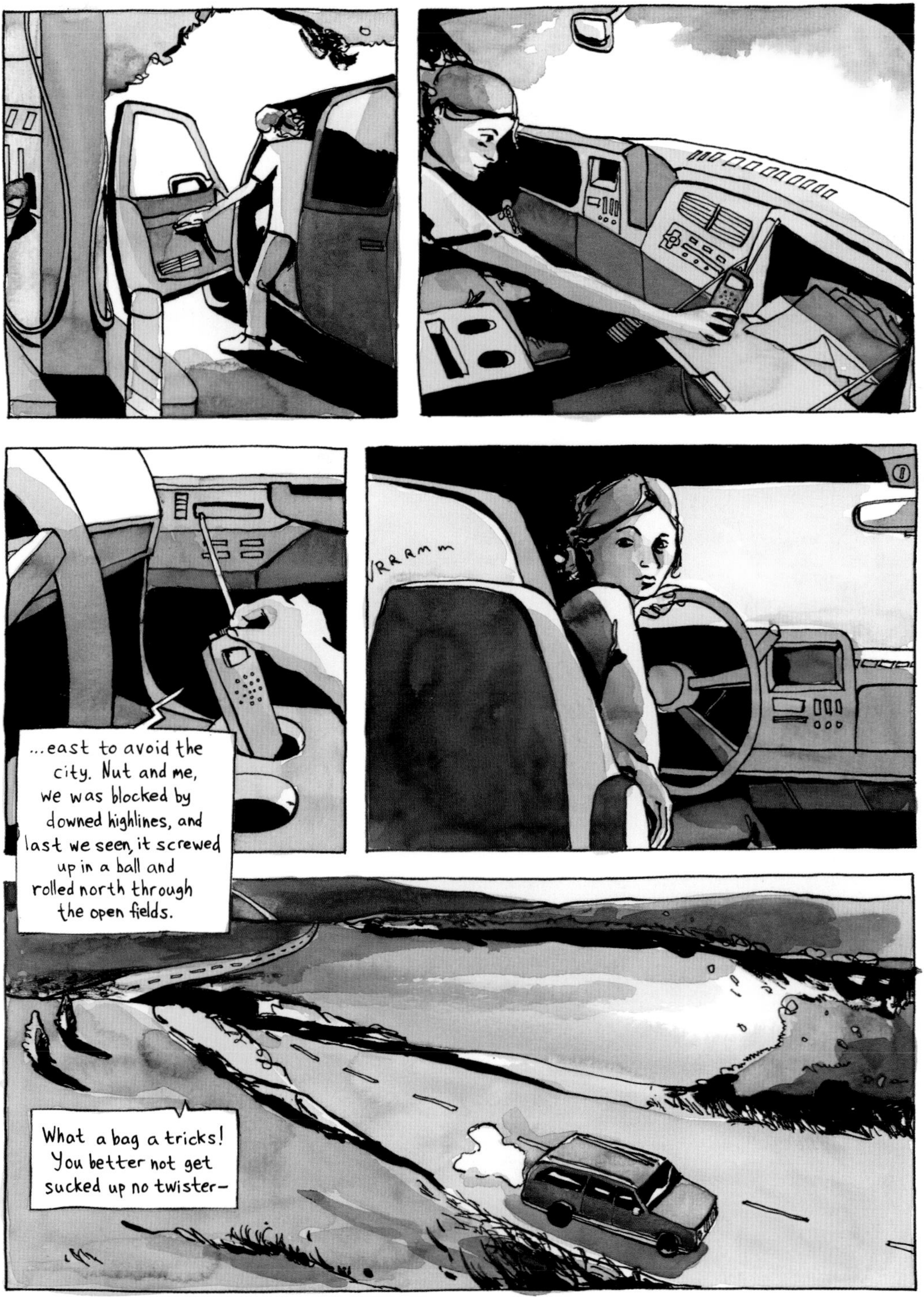
VRRAMM
...east to avoid the city. Nut and me, we was blocked by downed highlines, and last we seen, it screwed up in a ball and rolled north through the open fields.
What a bag a tricks! You better not get sucked up no twister—

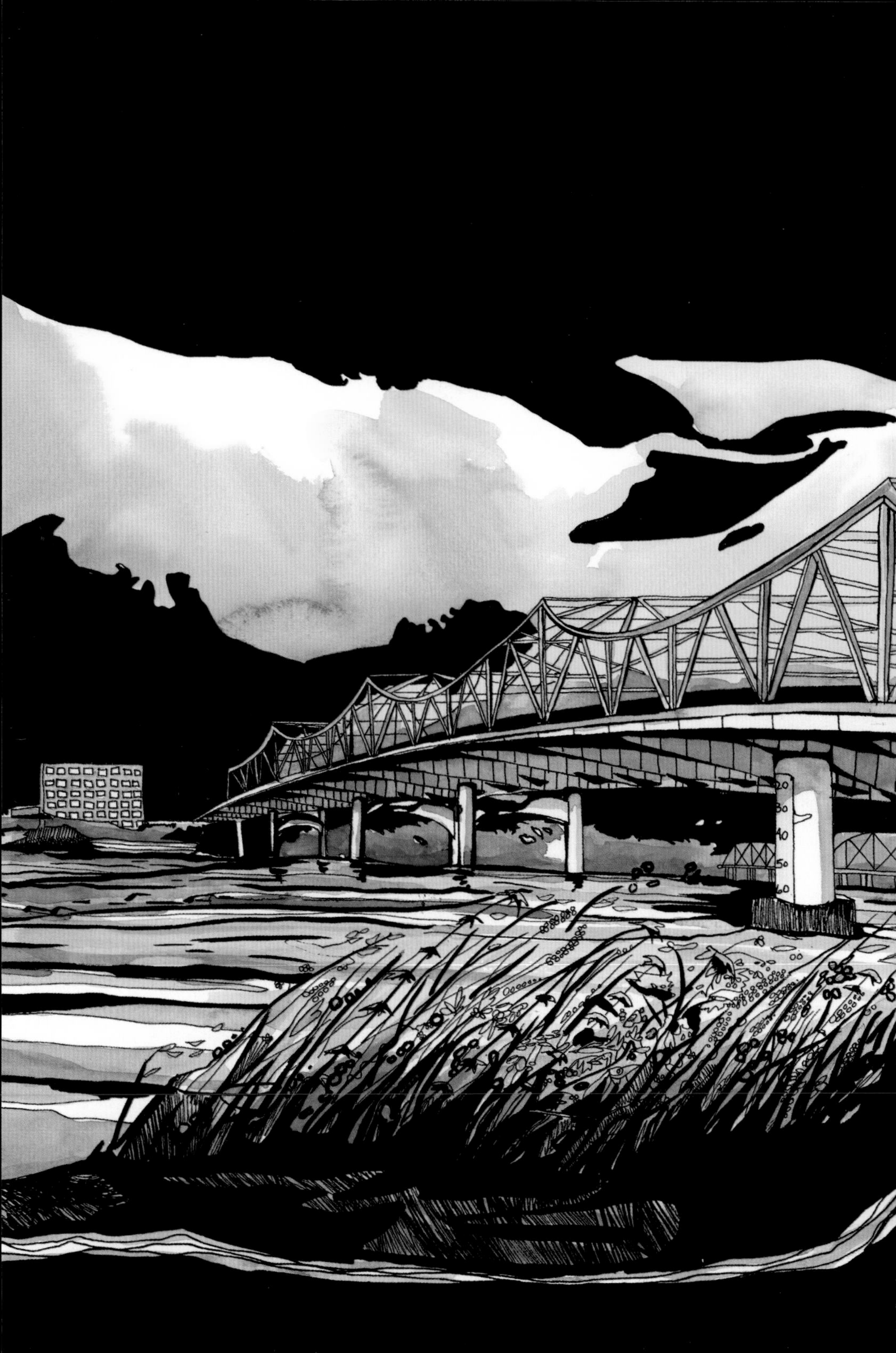
20
30
40
50
60

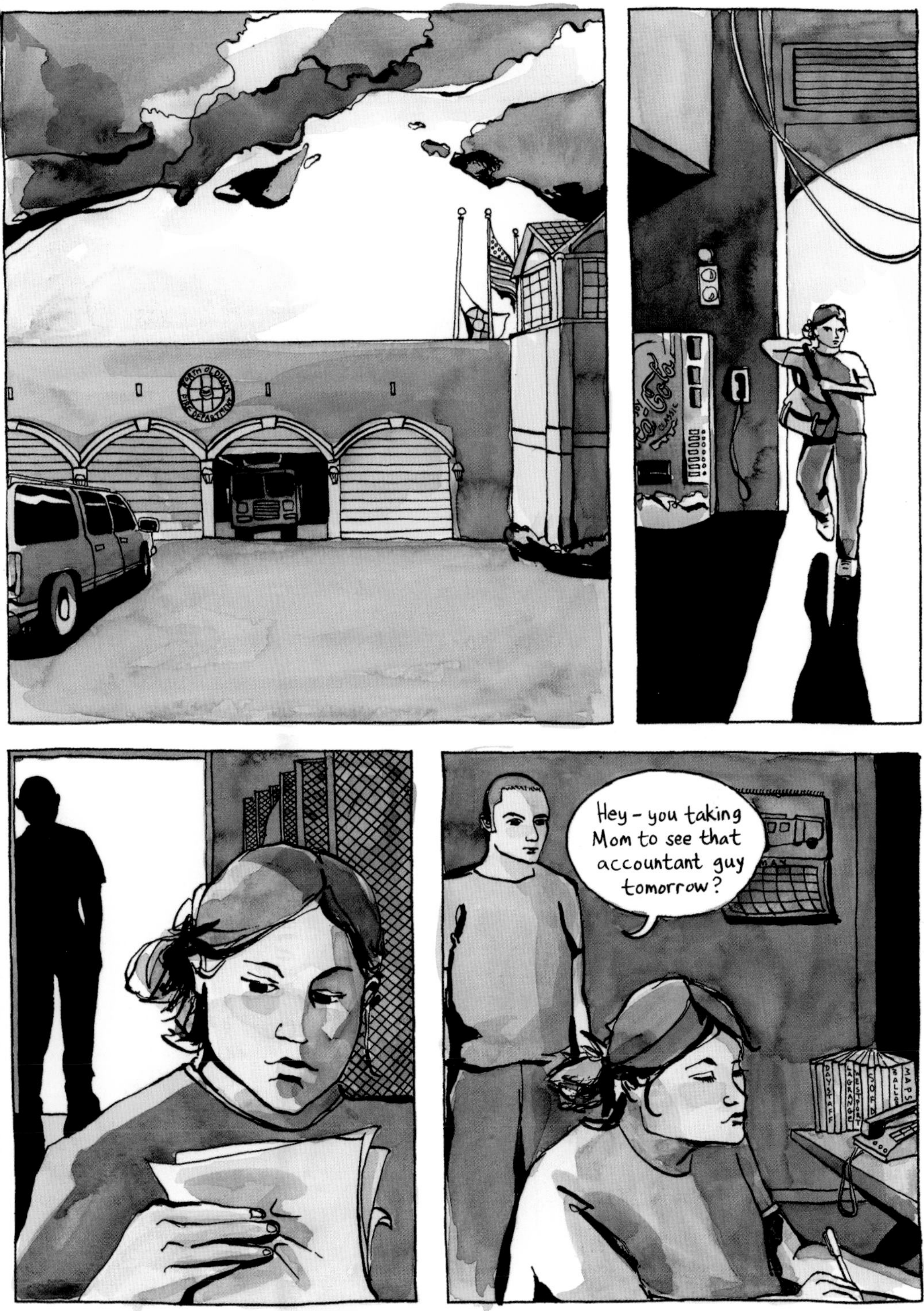
Hey – you taking Mom to see that accountant guy tomorrow?

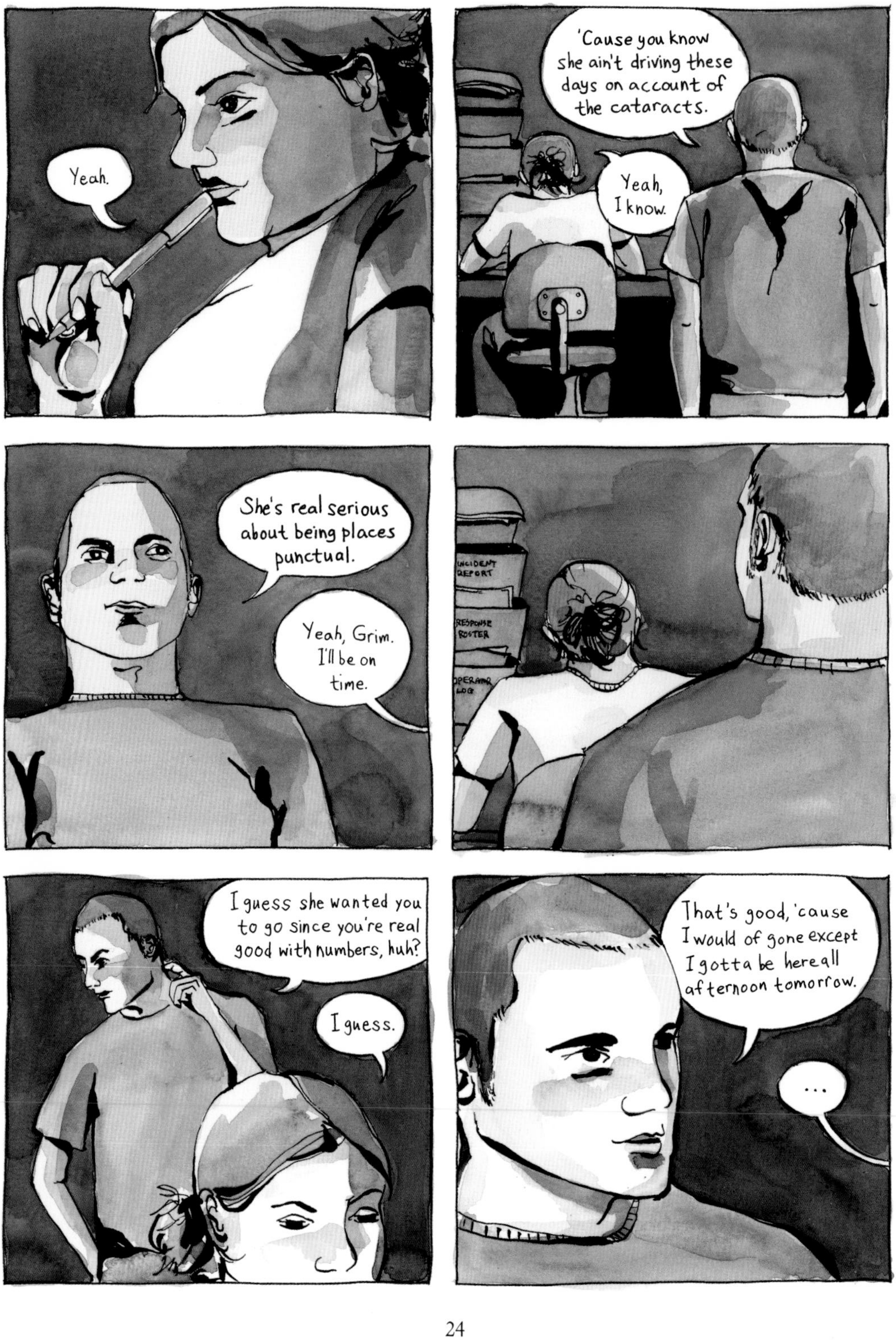
Yeah.
'Cause you know she ain't driving these days on account of the cataracts.
Yeah, I know.
She's real serious about being places punctual.
Yeah, Grim. I'll be on time.
INCIDENT REPORT
RESPONSE ROSTER
I guess she wanted you to go since you're real good with numbers, huh?
I guess.
That's good, 'cause I would of gone except I gotta be here all afternoon tomorrow.
...

'Cause I gotta lead swiftwater rescue training.

Shit! I can't take Mom — I'm sposed to lead swiftwater!

Oh, it's OK, I told Chief I'd fill in.

What are you talking about? You ain't certified to teach yet.

Yeah, but Chief says I'm doing real good.

Anyway, just because you pass some test doesn't mean you can teach good.

I don't need a college education to be a serious firefighter, you know.

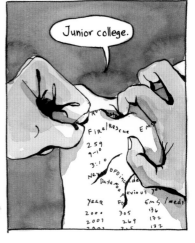

Junior college.

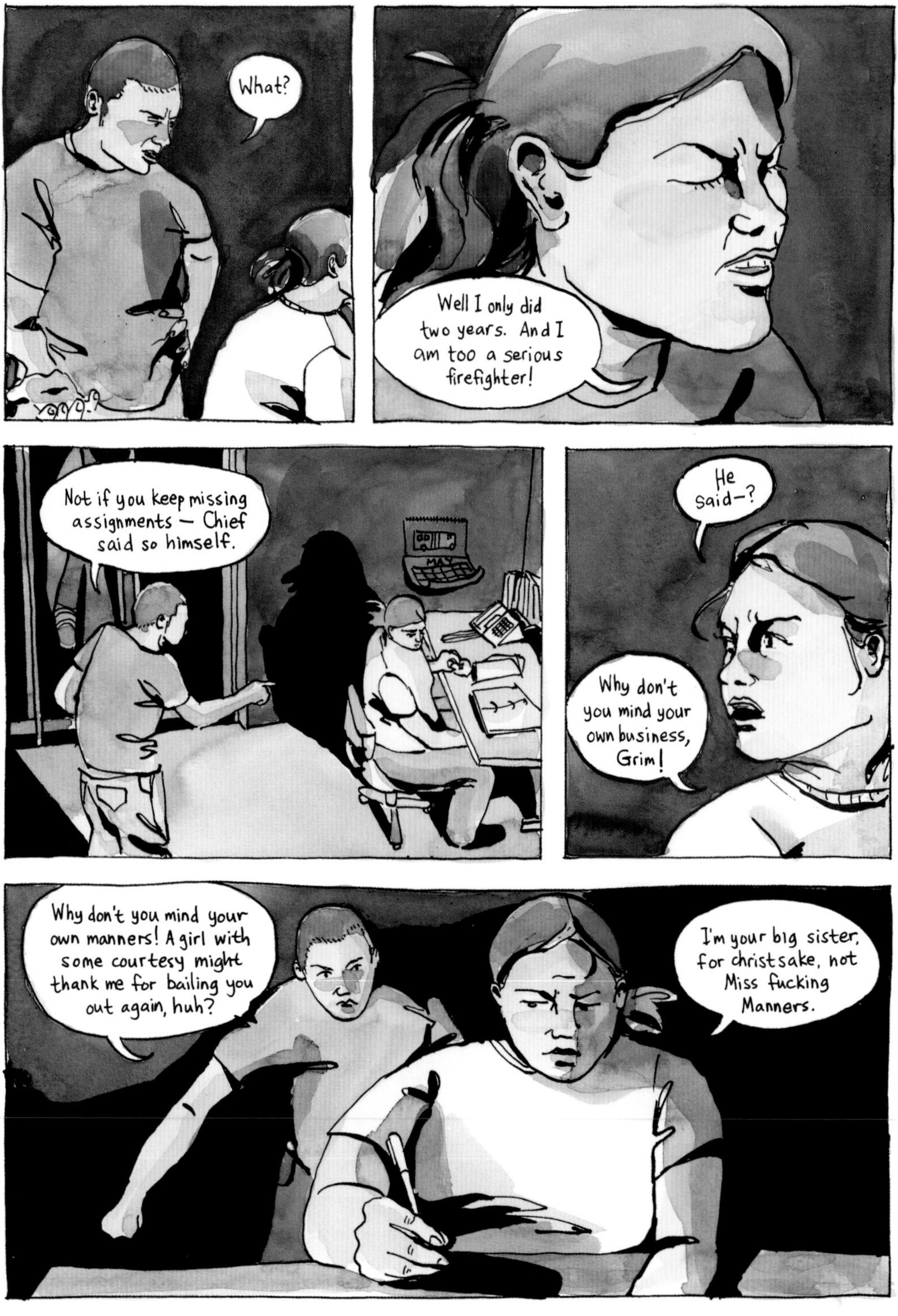
What?
Well I only did two years. And I am too a serious firefighter!
Not if you keep missing assignments — Chief said so himself.
MAY
He said—?
Why don't you mind your own business, Grim!
Why don't you mind your own manners! A girl with some courtesy might thank me for bailing you out again, huh?
I'm your big sister, for christsake, not Miss fucking Manners.

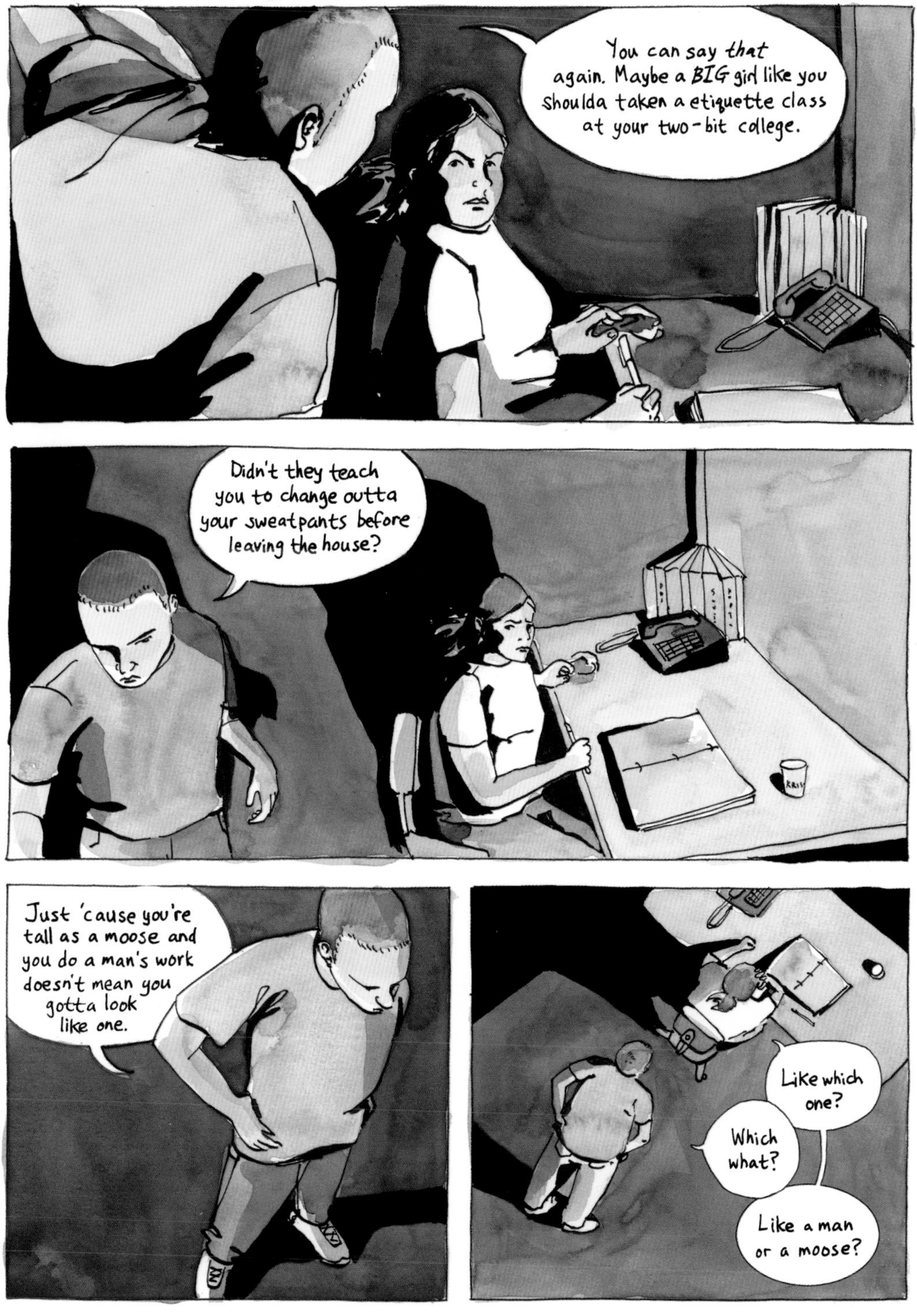
You can say *that* again. Maybe a *BIG* girl like you shoulda taken a etiquette class at your two-bit college.
Didn't they teach you to change outta your sweatpants before leaving the house?
KRIS
Just 'cause you're tall as a moose and you do a man's work doesn't mean you gotta look like one.
Like which one?
Which what?
Like a man or a moose?

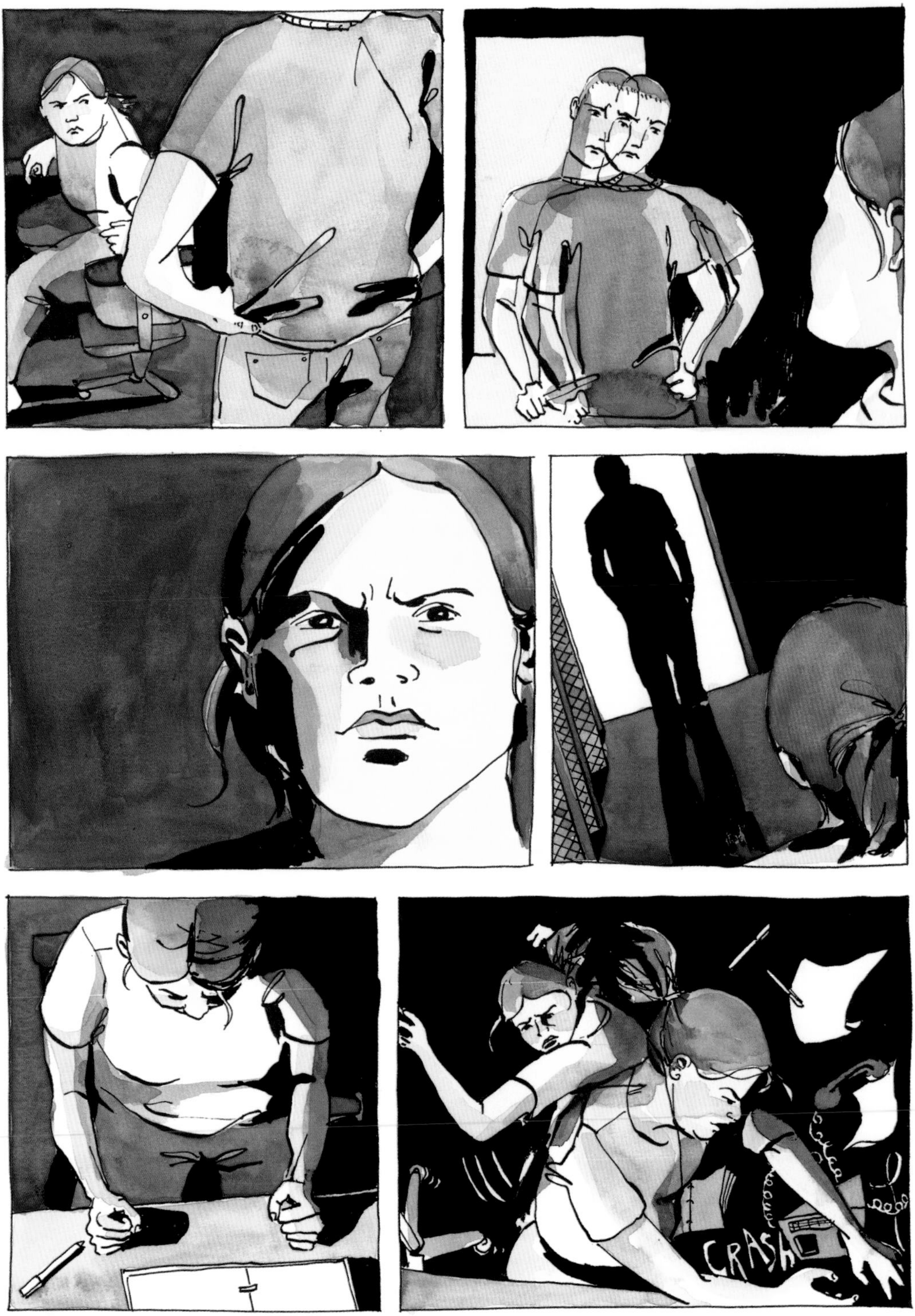
CRASH

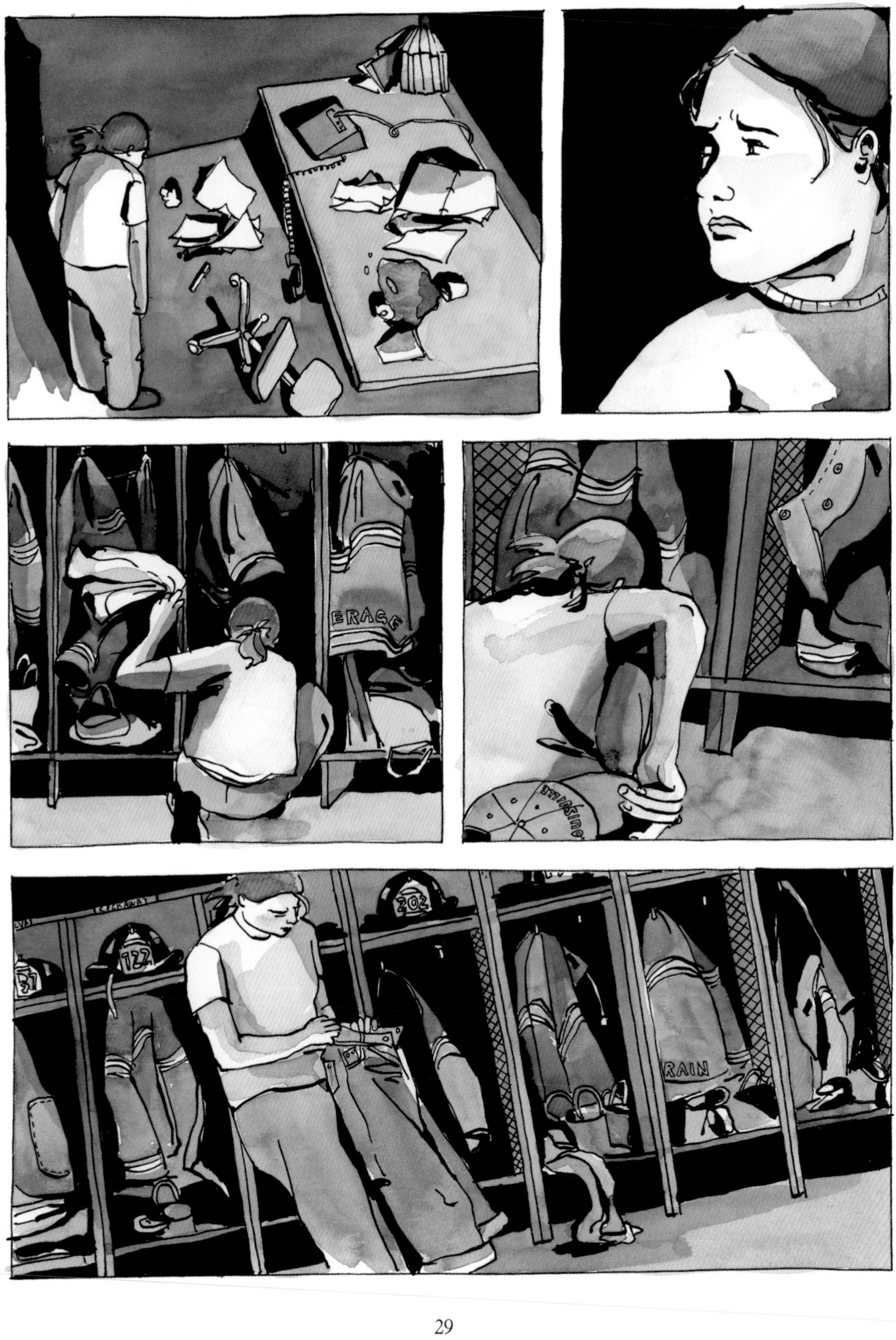
31
122
202
RAIN

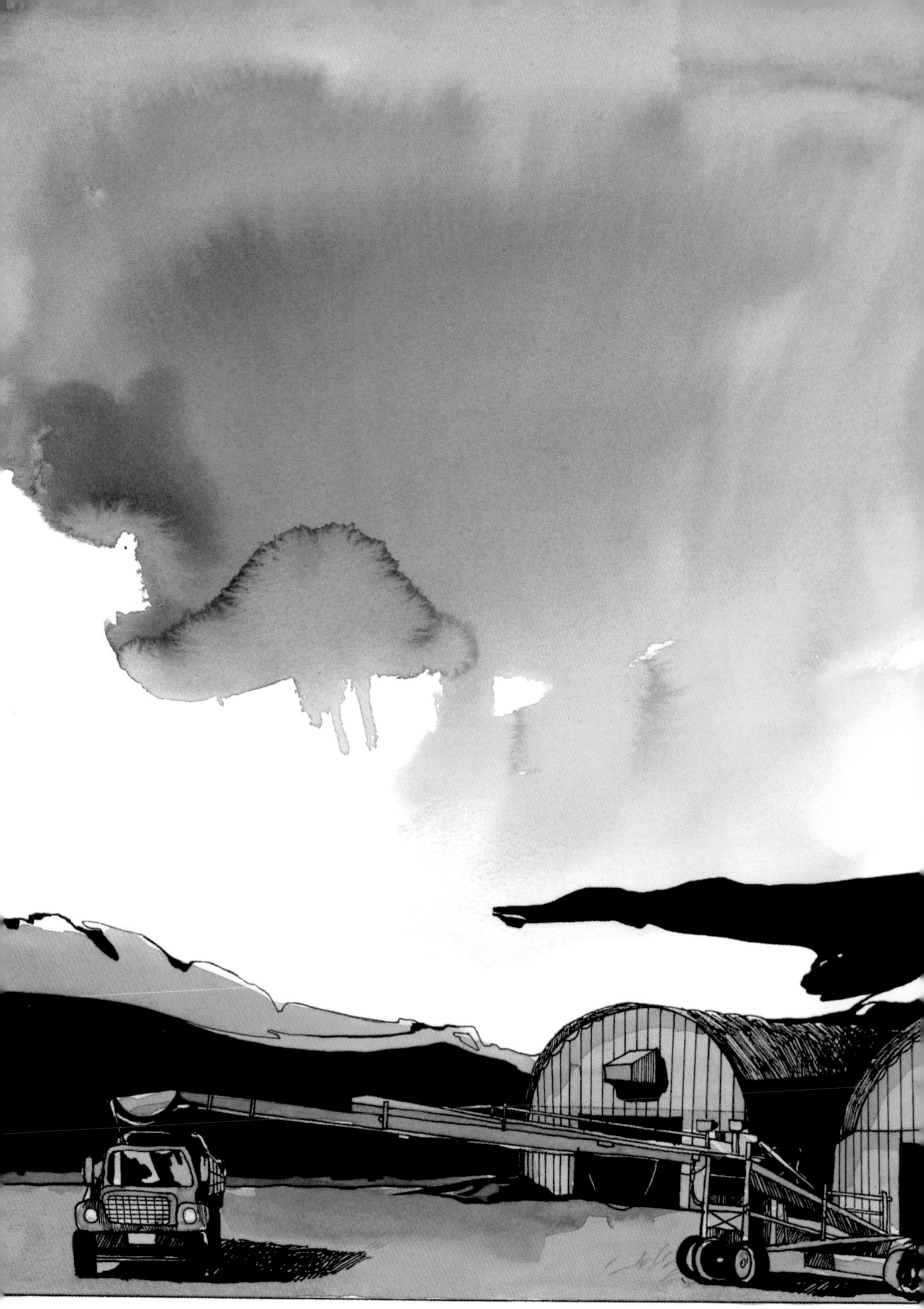

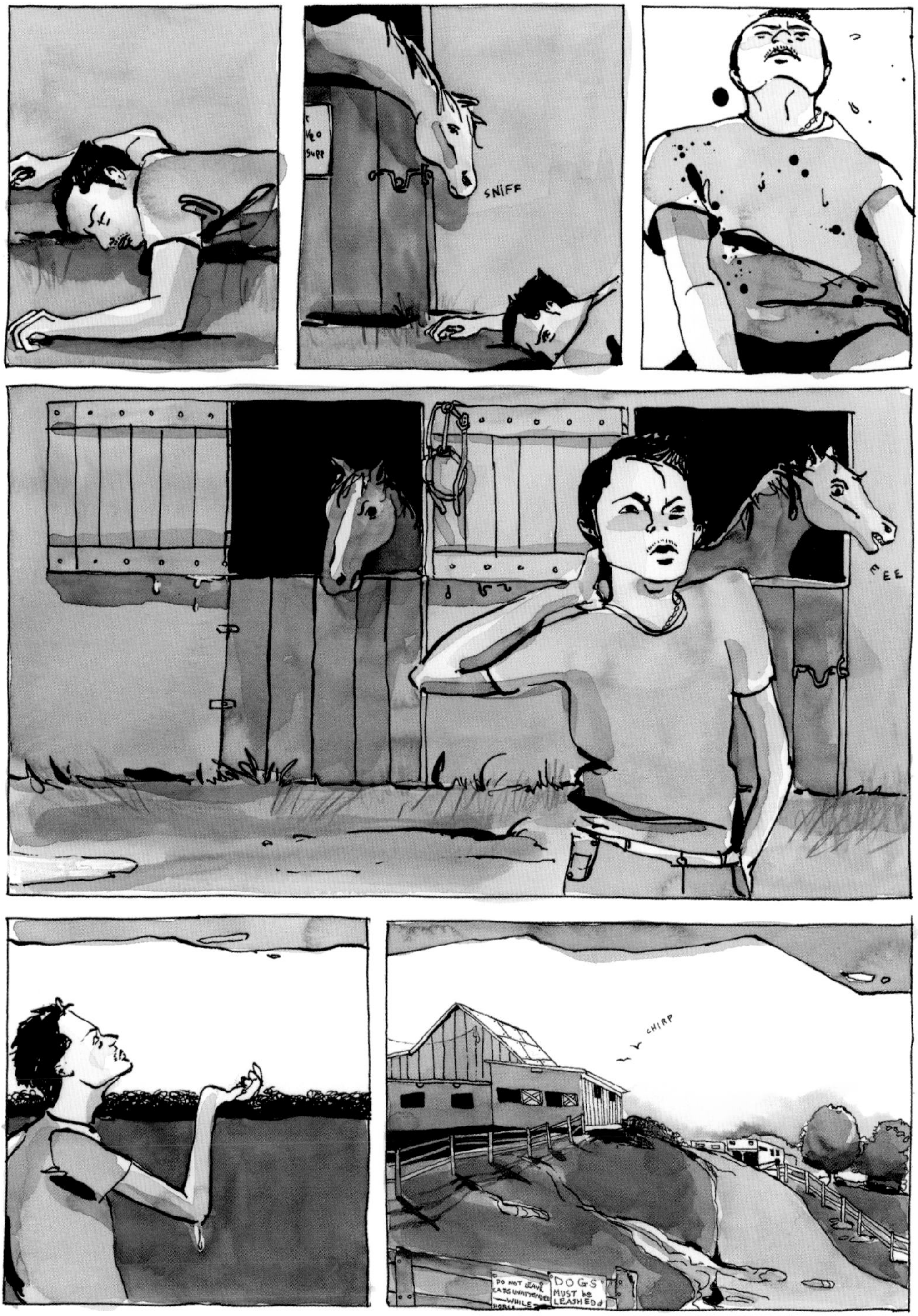
SNIFF
EEE
CHIRP
DOGS MUST be LEASHED!

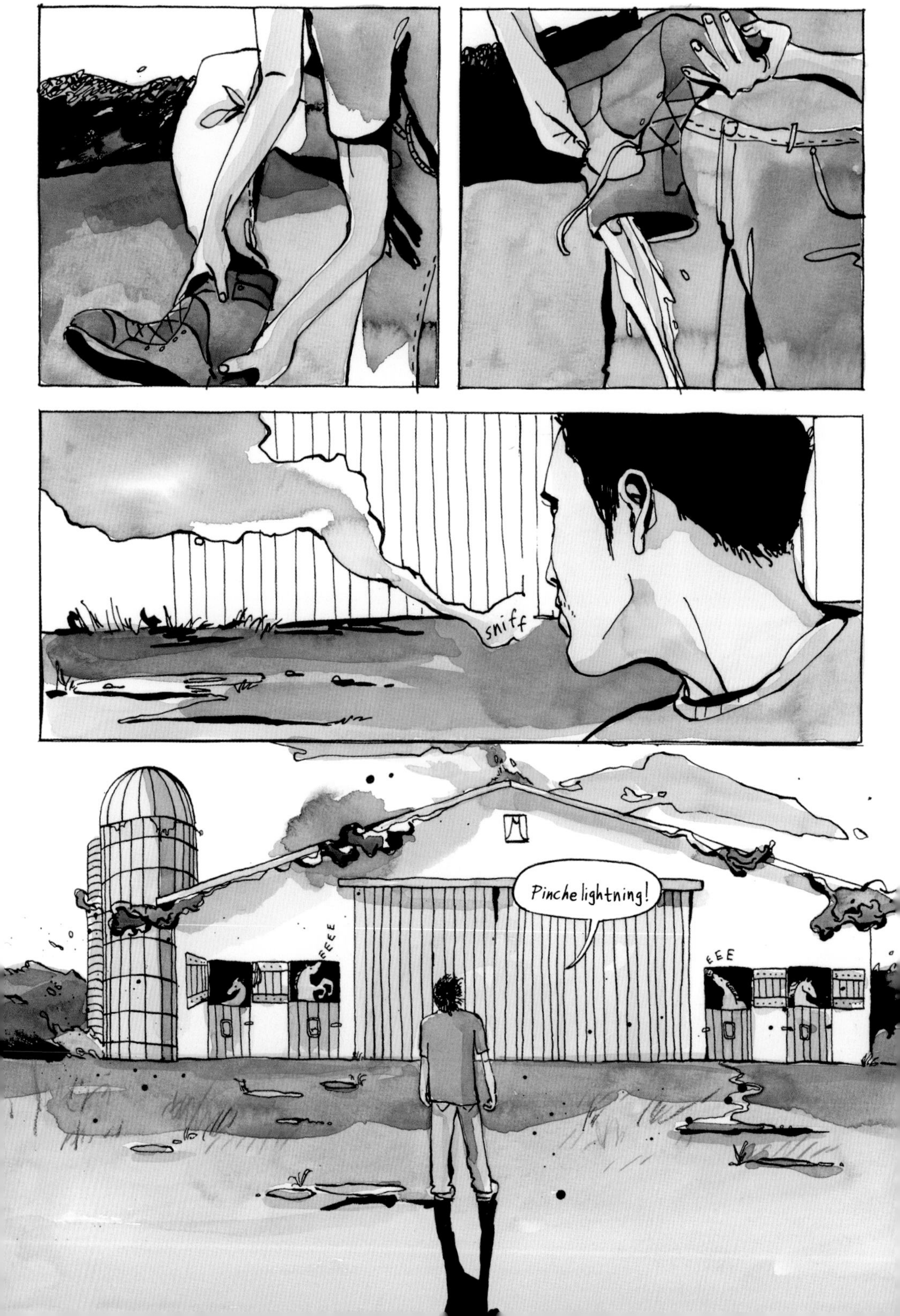
sniff
EEEE
Pinche lightning!
EEE

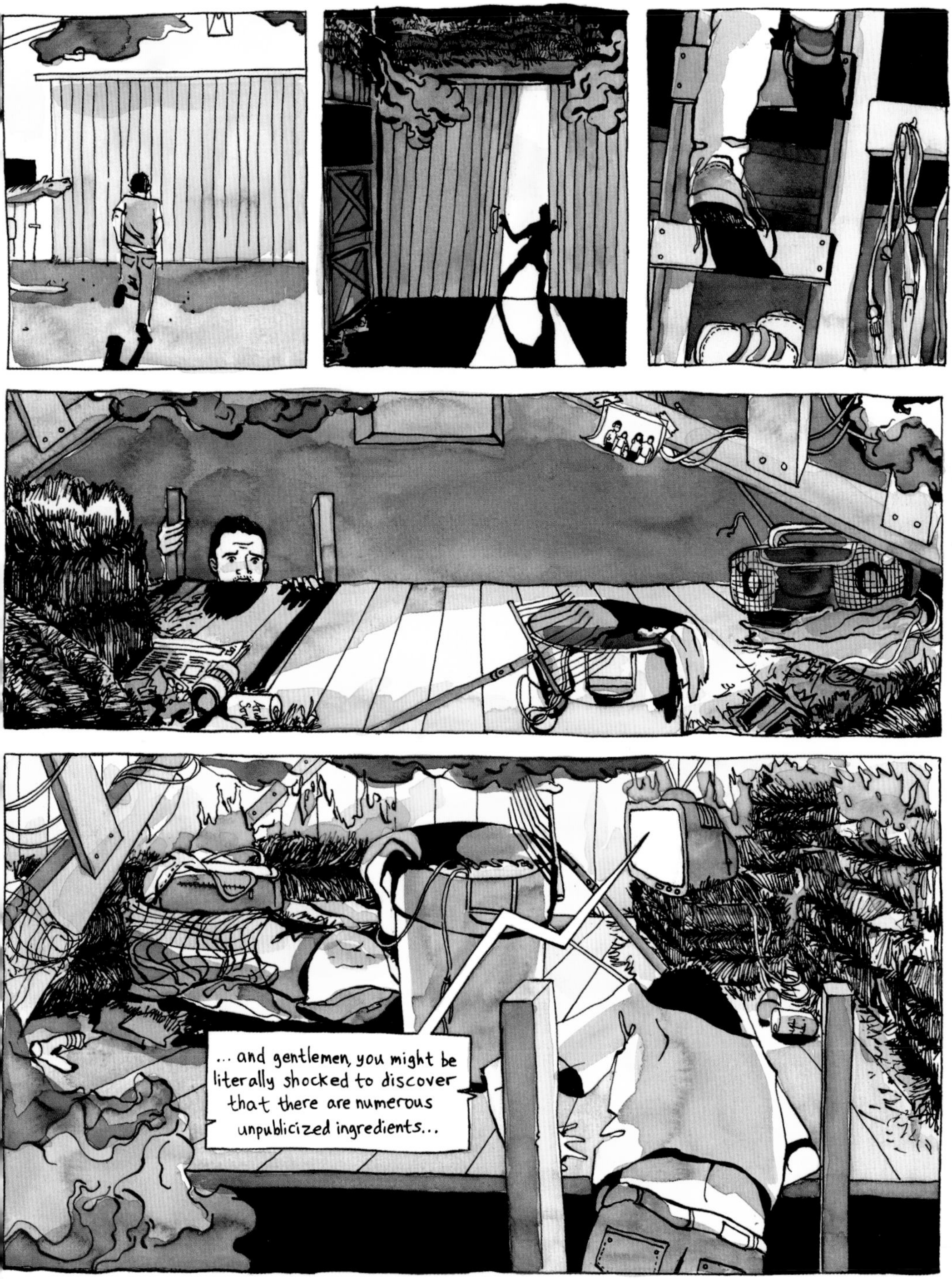
... and gentlemen, you might be literally shocked to discover that there are numerous unpublicized ingredients...

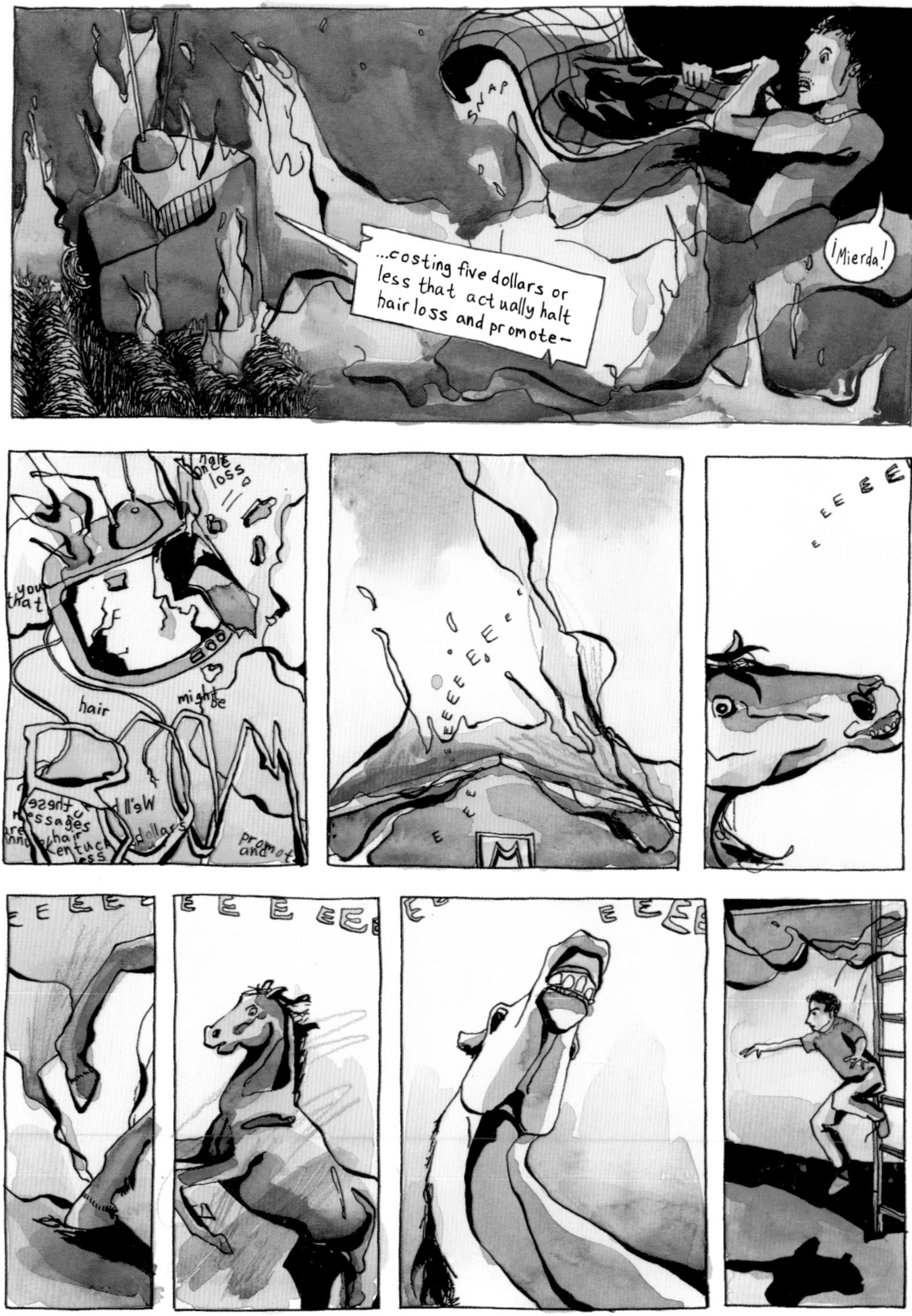
SNAP
...costing five dollars or less that actually halt hair loss and promote—
¡Mierda!
you that
hair
might be
We'll
messages
dollars
promot and

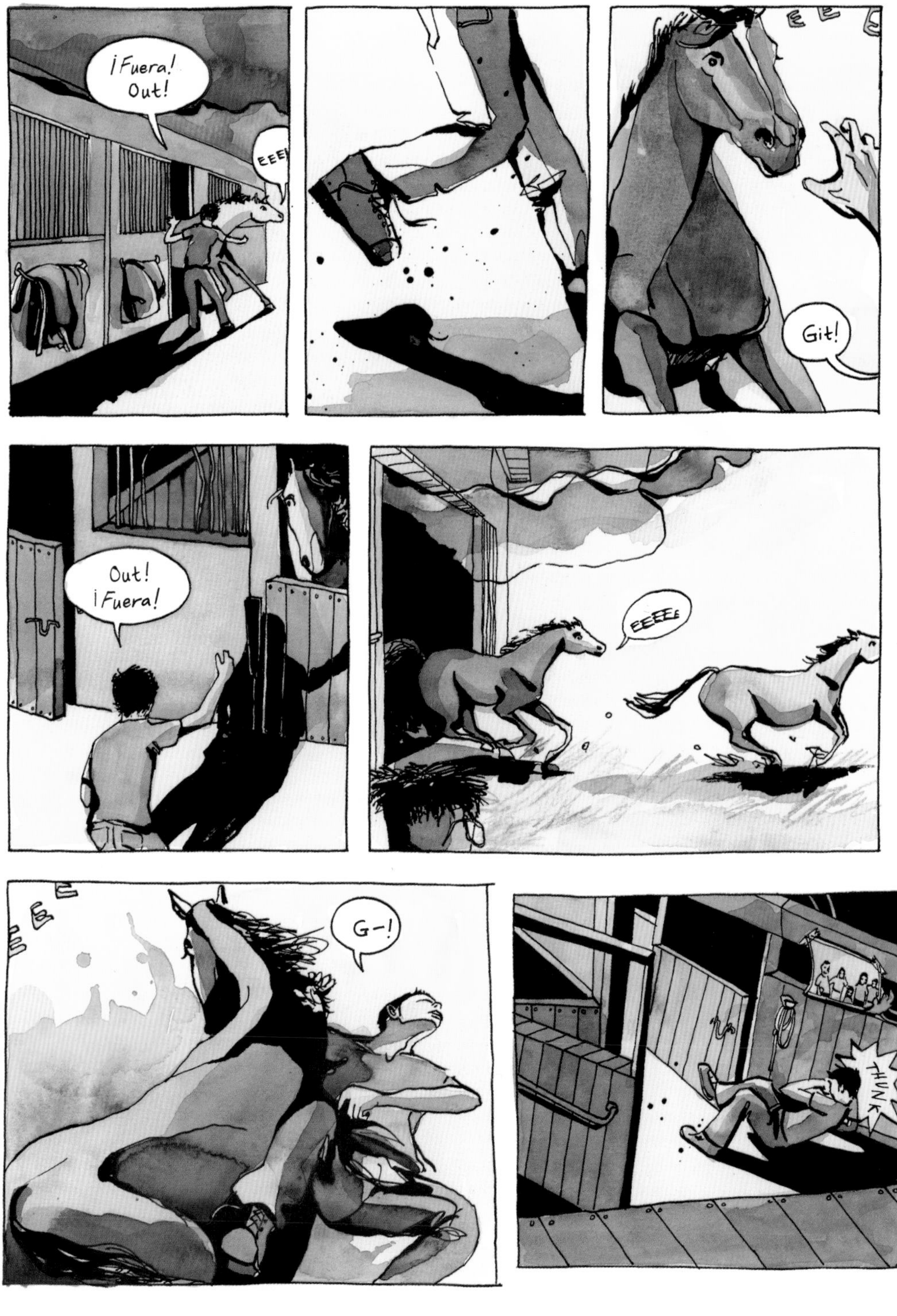
¡Fuera! Out!
EEE
EEE
Git!
Out! ¡Fuera!
EEEEE
EEE
G—!
THUNK

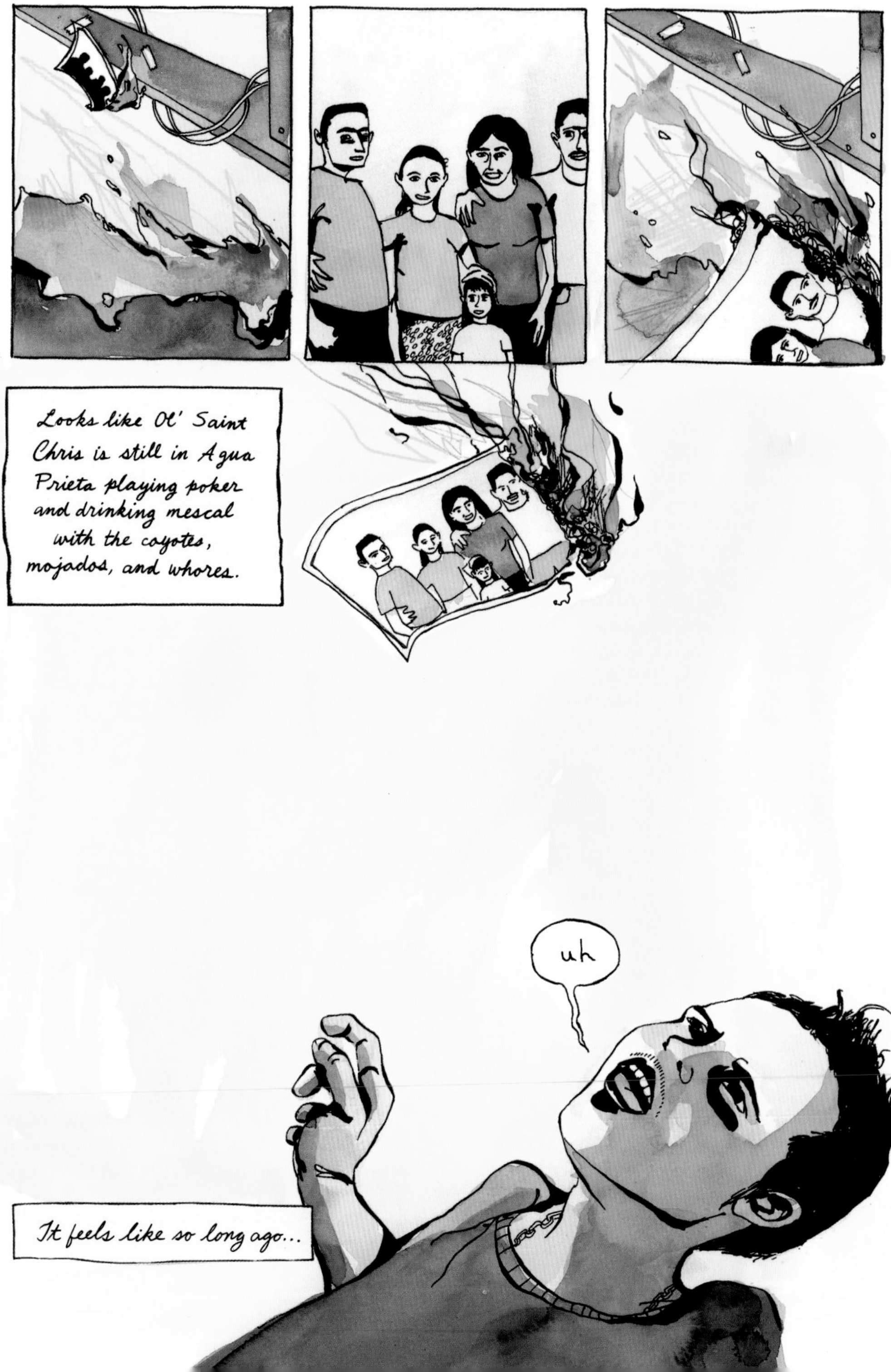
Looks like Ol' Saint Chris is still in Agua Prieta playing poker and drinking mescal with the coyotes, mojados, and whores.
uh
It feels like so long ago...

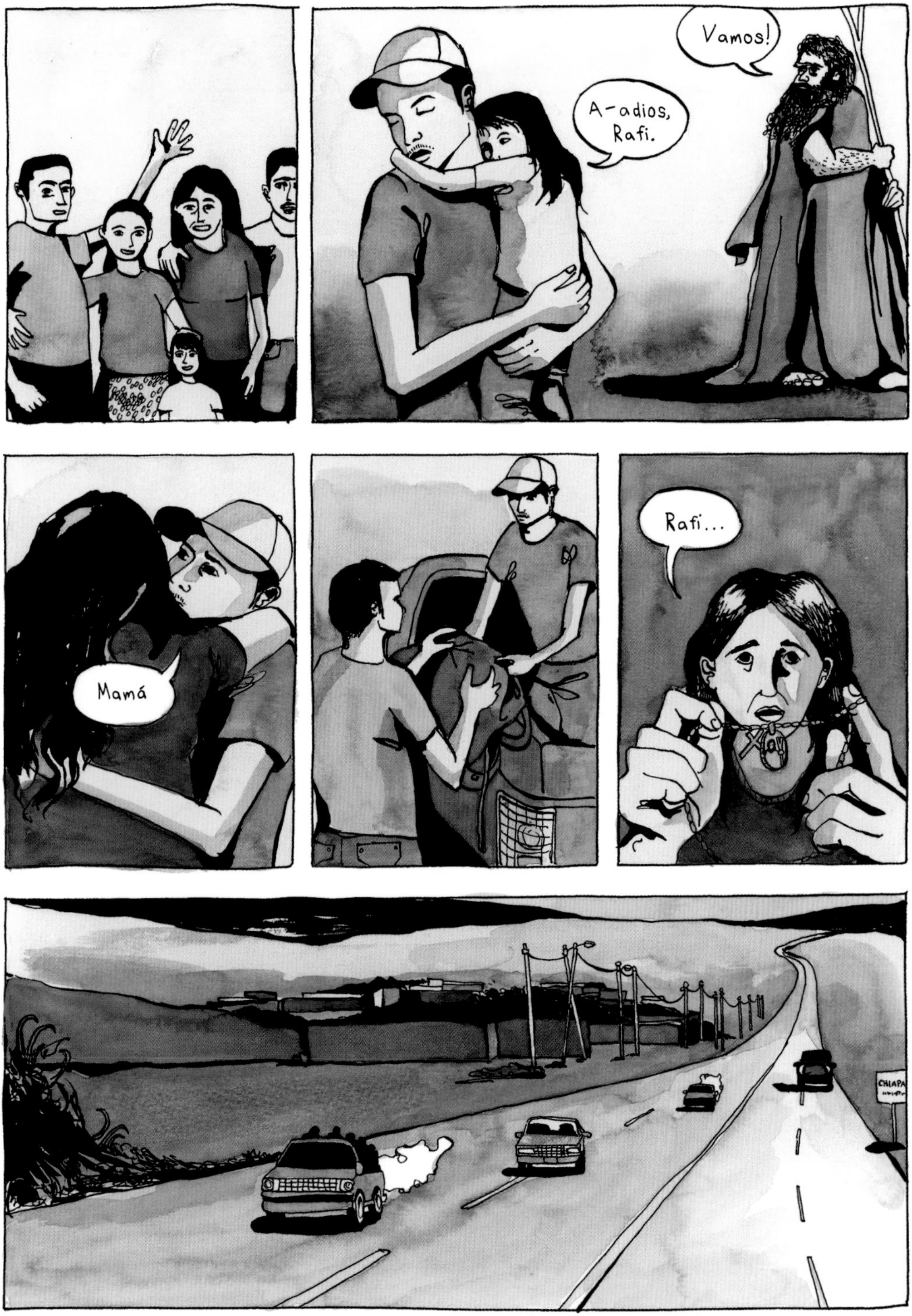
A-adios, Rafi.
Vamos!
Mamá
Rafi...
CHIAPA

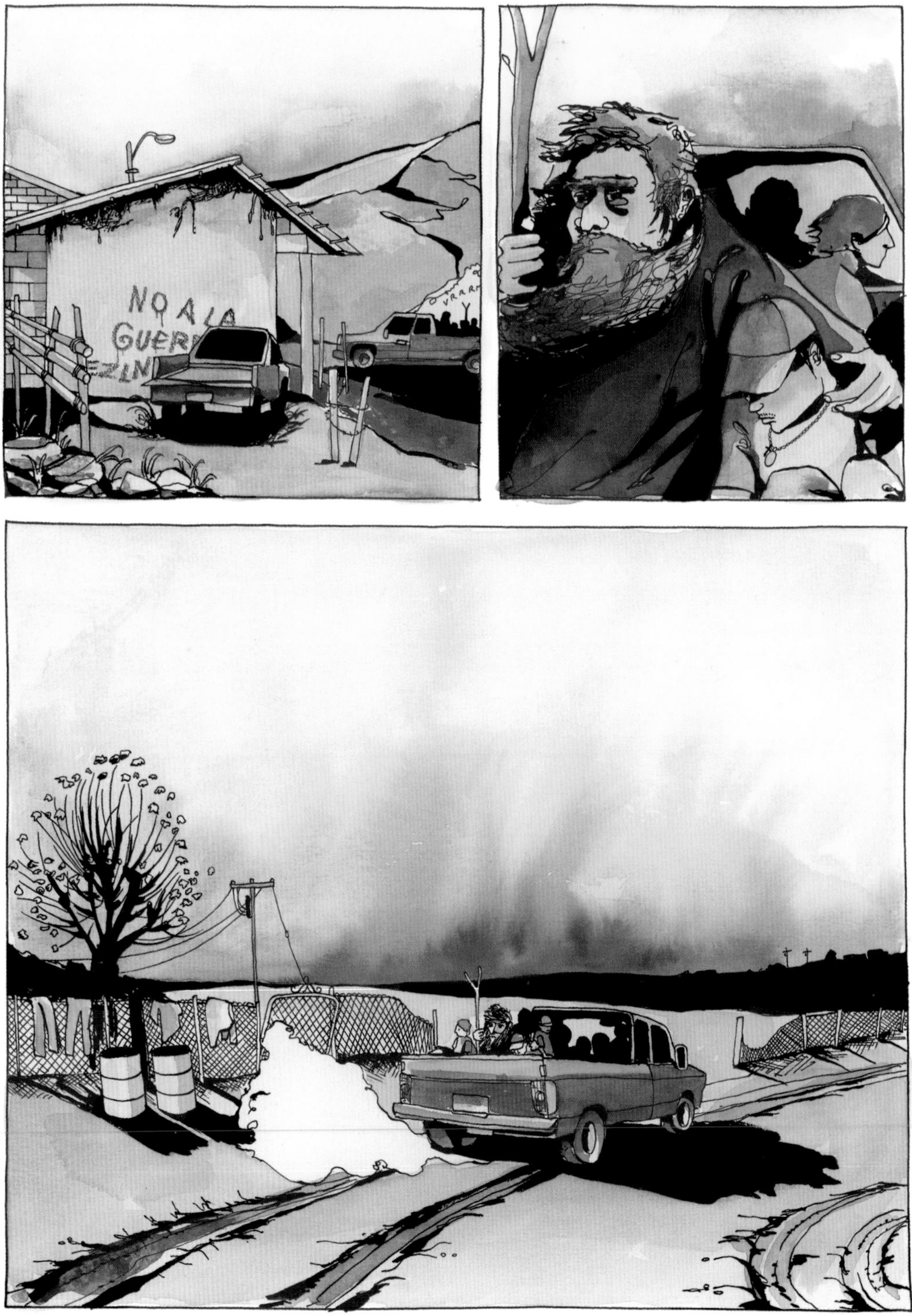
NO A LA
GUERR
EZLN
VRRRM

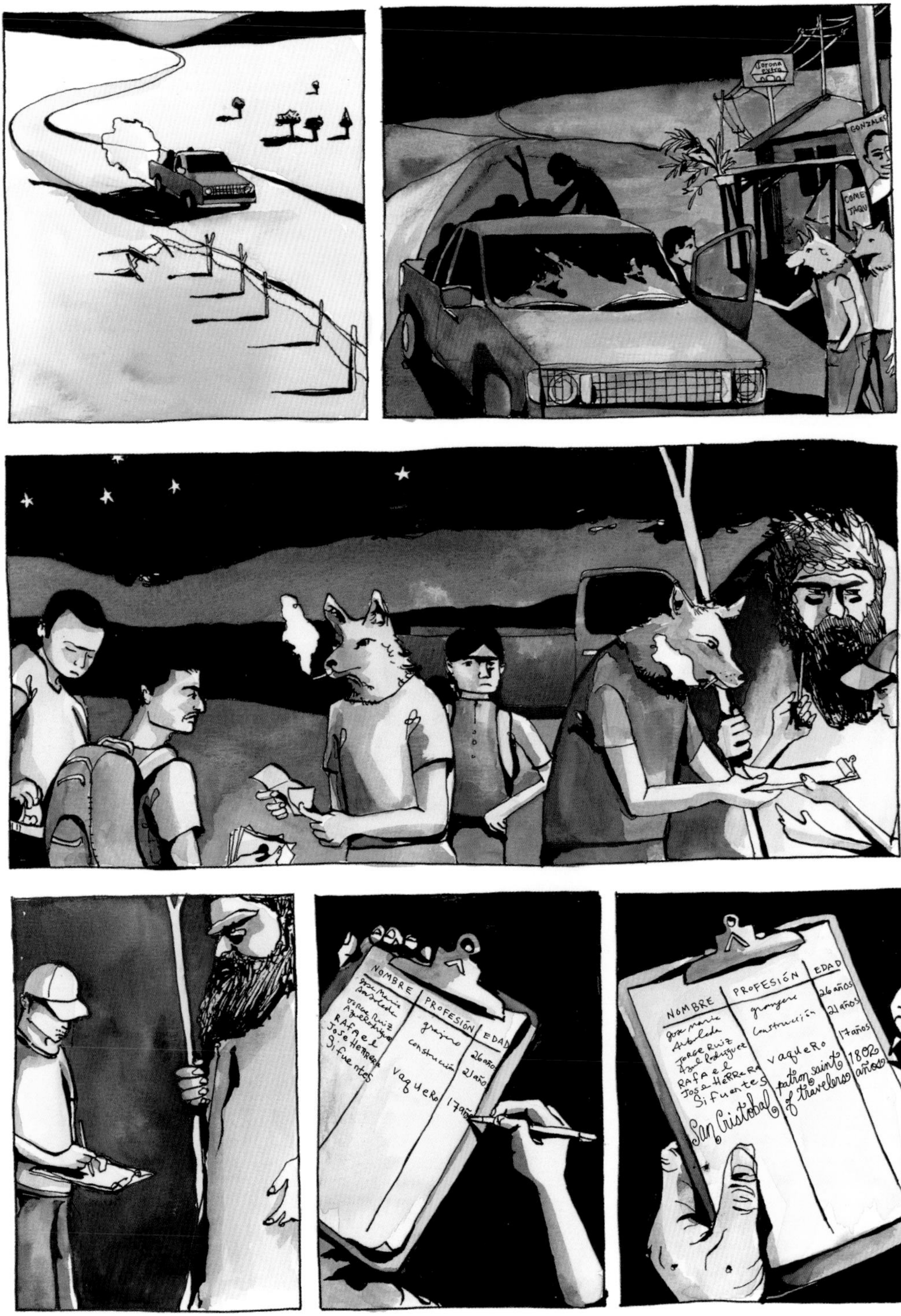
Corona extra
NOMBRE
PROFESIÓN
EDAD
NOMBRE
PROFESIÓN
EDAD
26 años
21 años
17 años
JORGE Ruiz
construcción
VAQUERO
RAFAEL
JOSE HERRERA
SIFUENTES
patron saint
of travelers
1802
años
San Cristobal

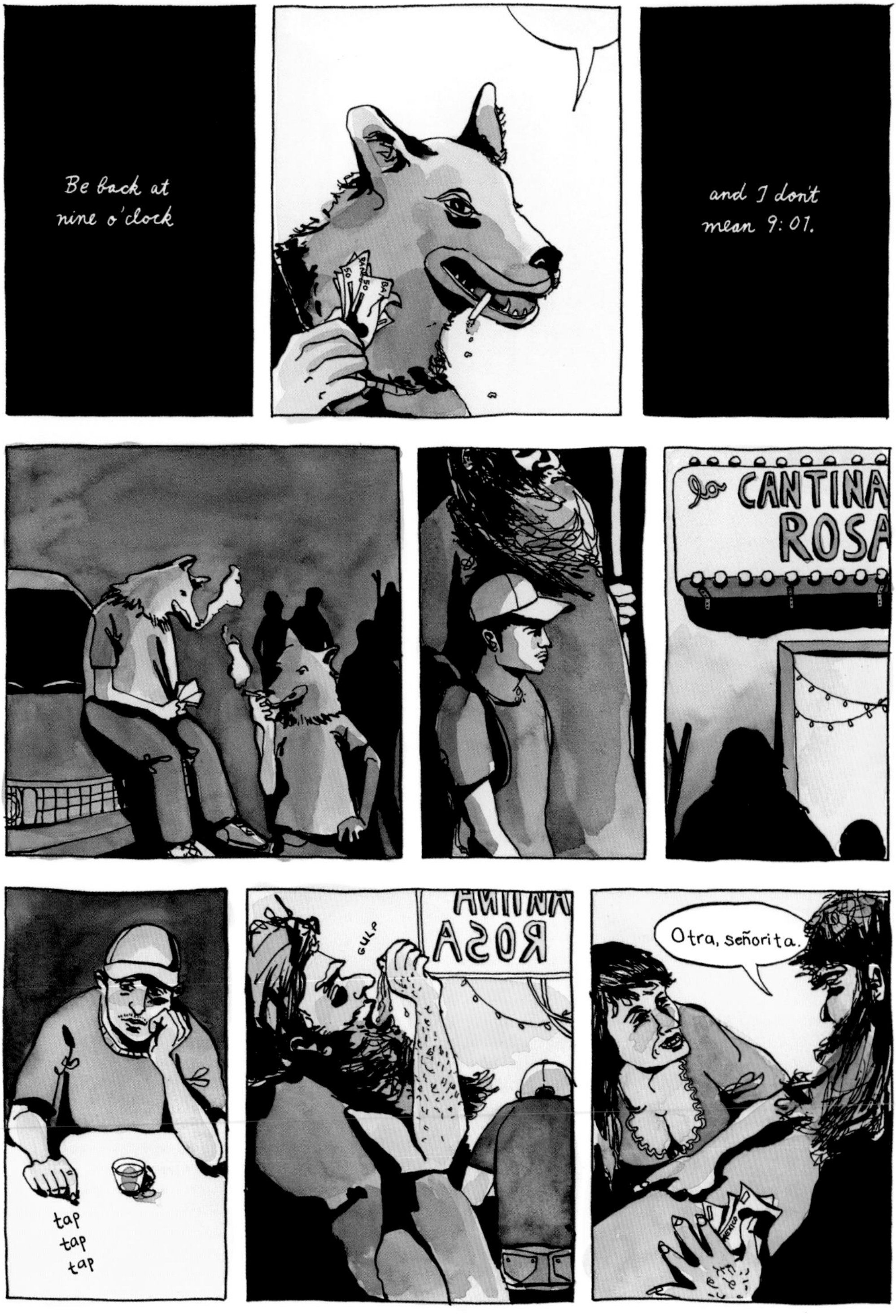
Be back at nine o'clock
and I don't mean 9:01.
la CANTINA ROSA
tap tap tap
GULP
Otra, señorita.

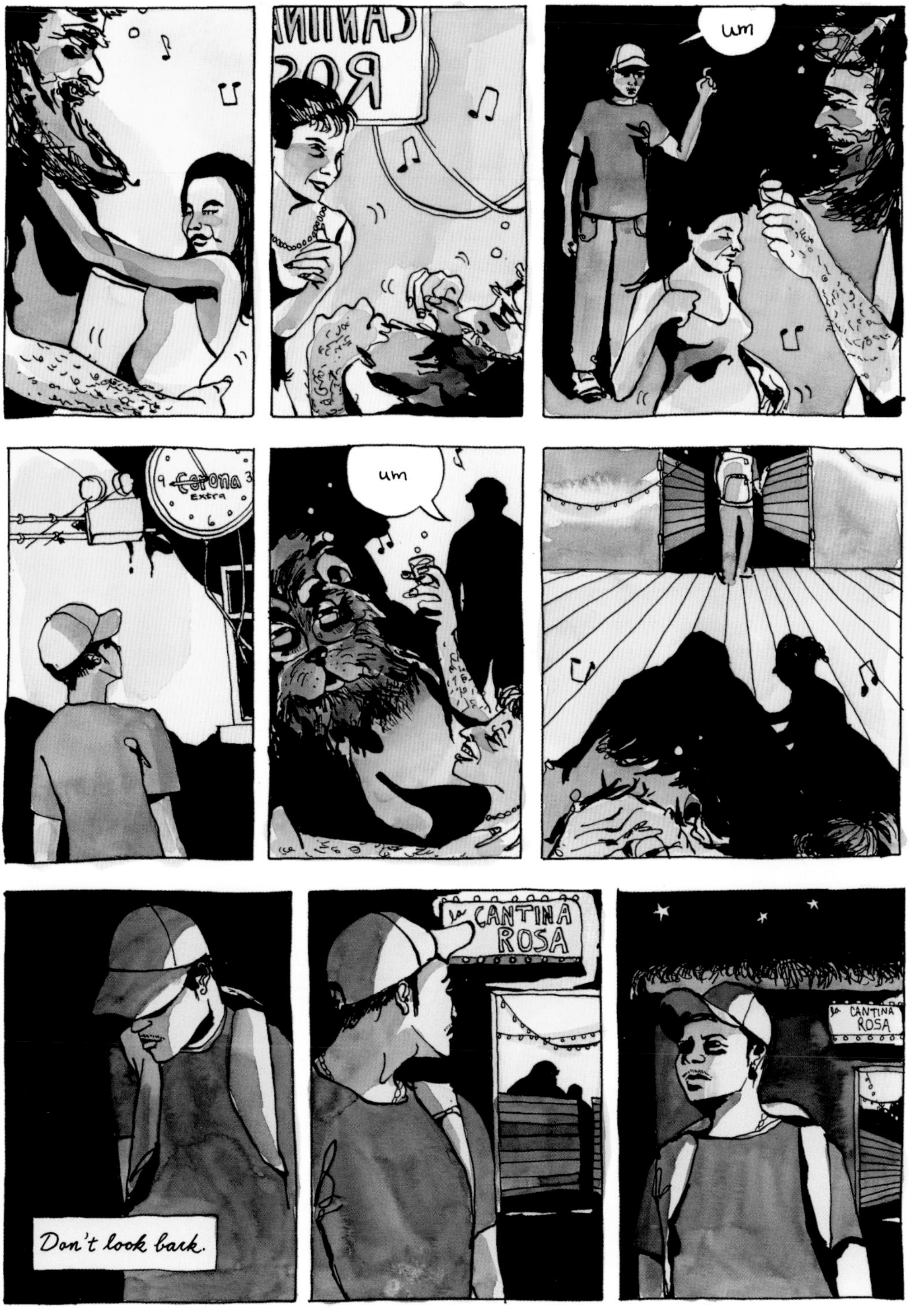
um
um
Corona
Extra
La CANTINA ROSA
Don't look back.
La CANTINA ROSA

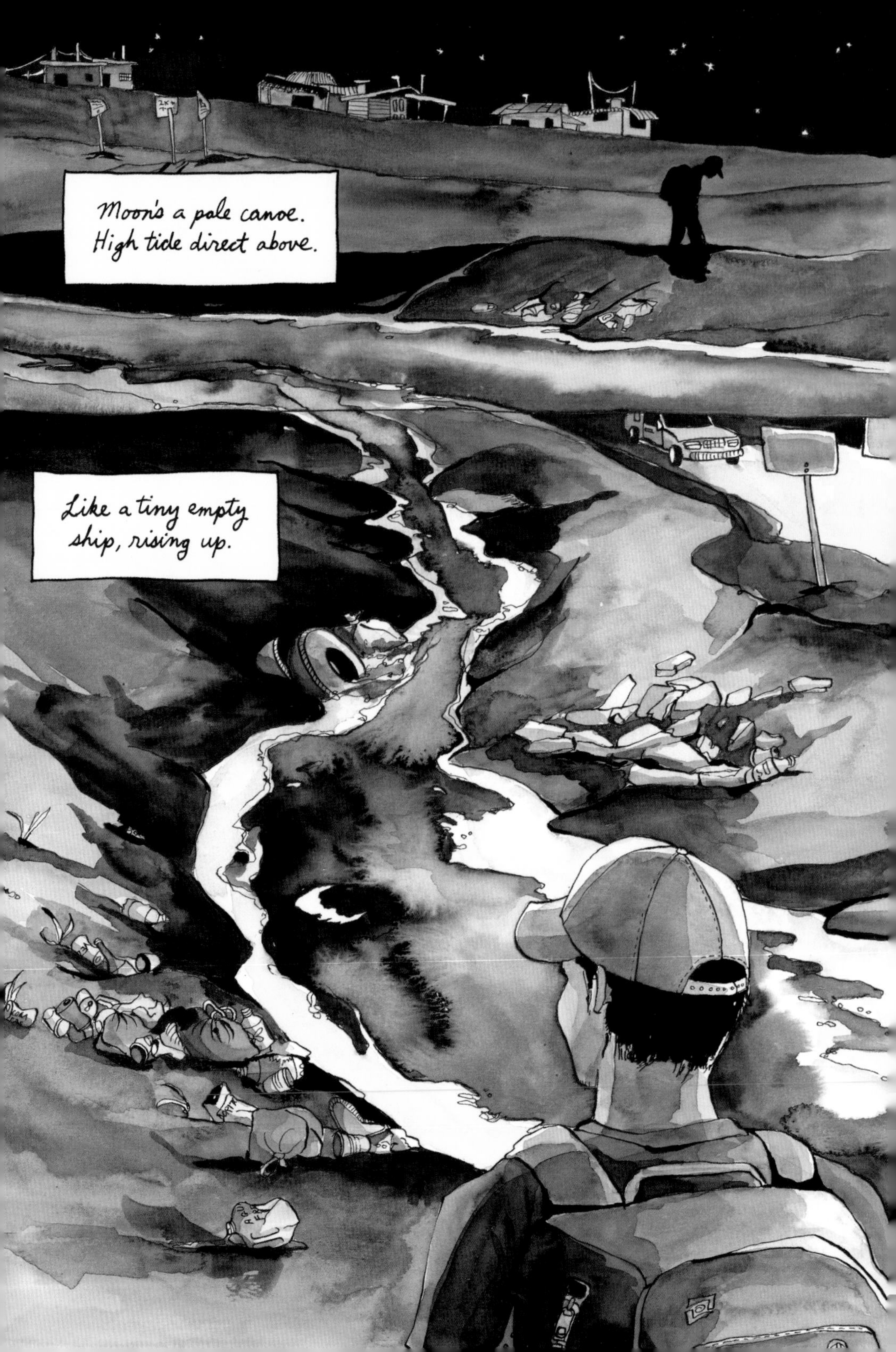
Moon's a pale canoe.
High tide direct above.
Like a tiny empty
ship, rising up.

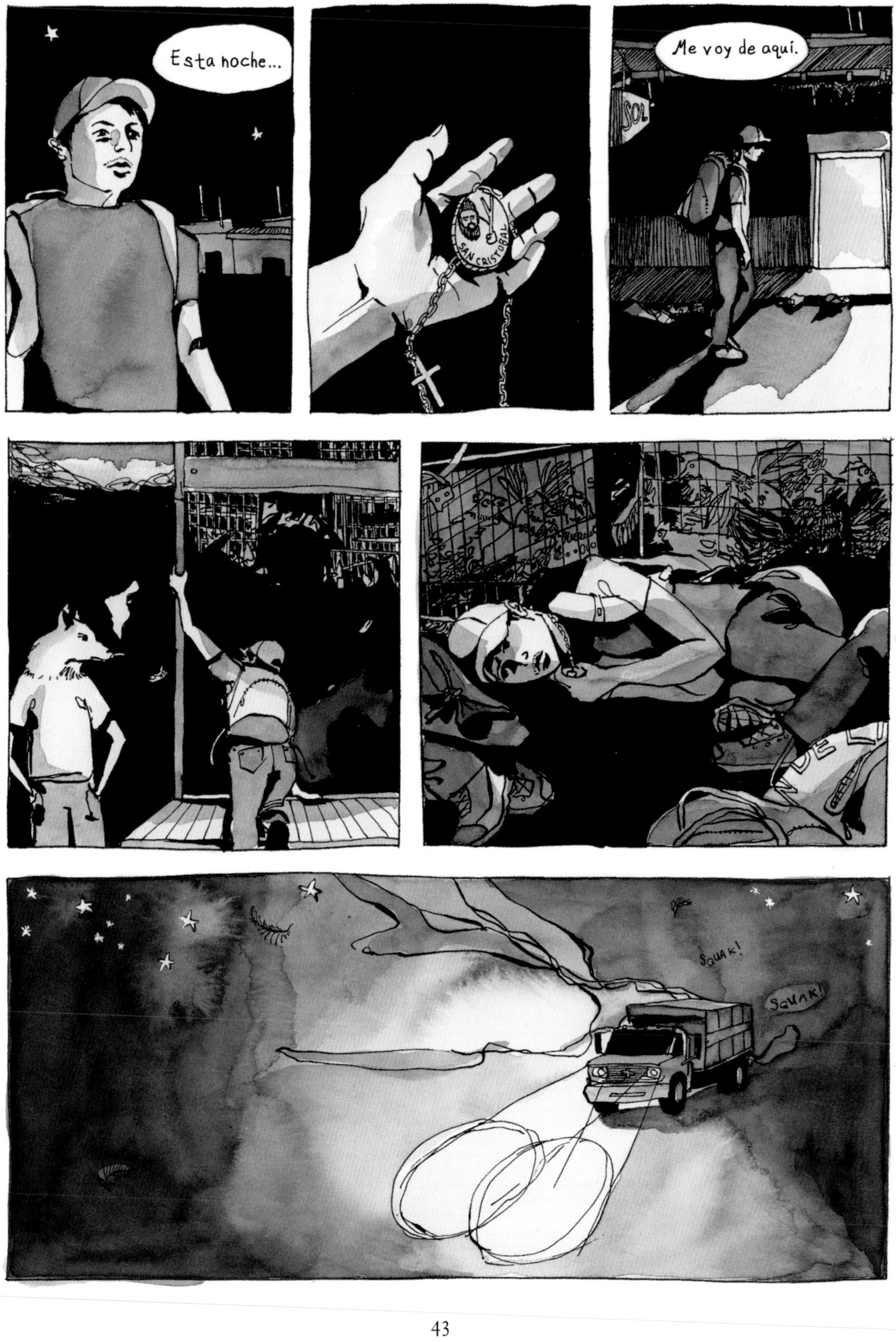
Esta noche...
SAN CRISTOBAL
Me voy de aquí.
SOL
SQUAK!
SQUAK!

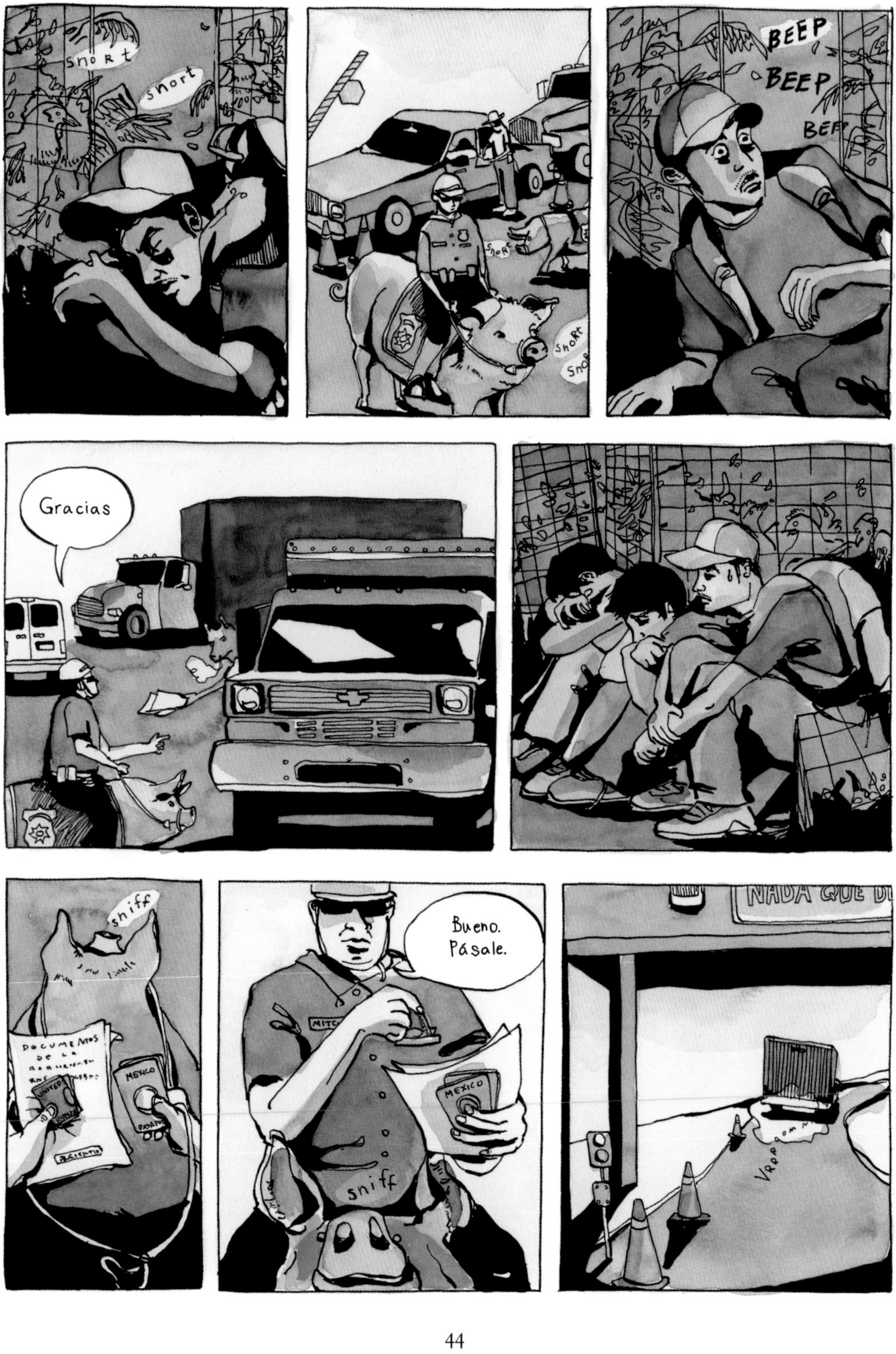
snort
snort
snort
snort
BEEP
BEEP
Gracias
sniff
DOCUMENTOS DE LA
UNITED
MEXICO
Bueno. Pásale.
MEXICO
sniff
NADA QUE

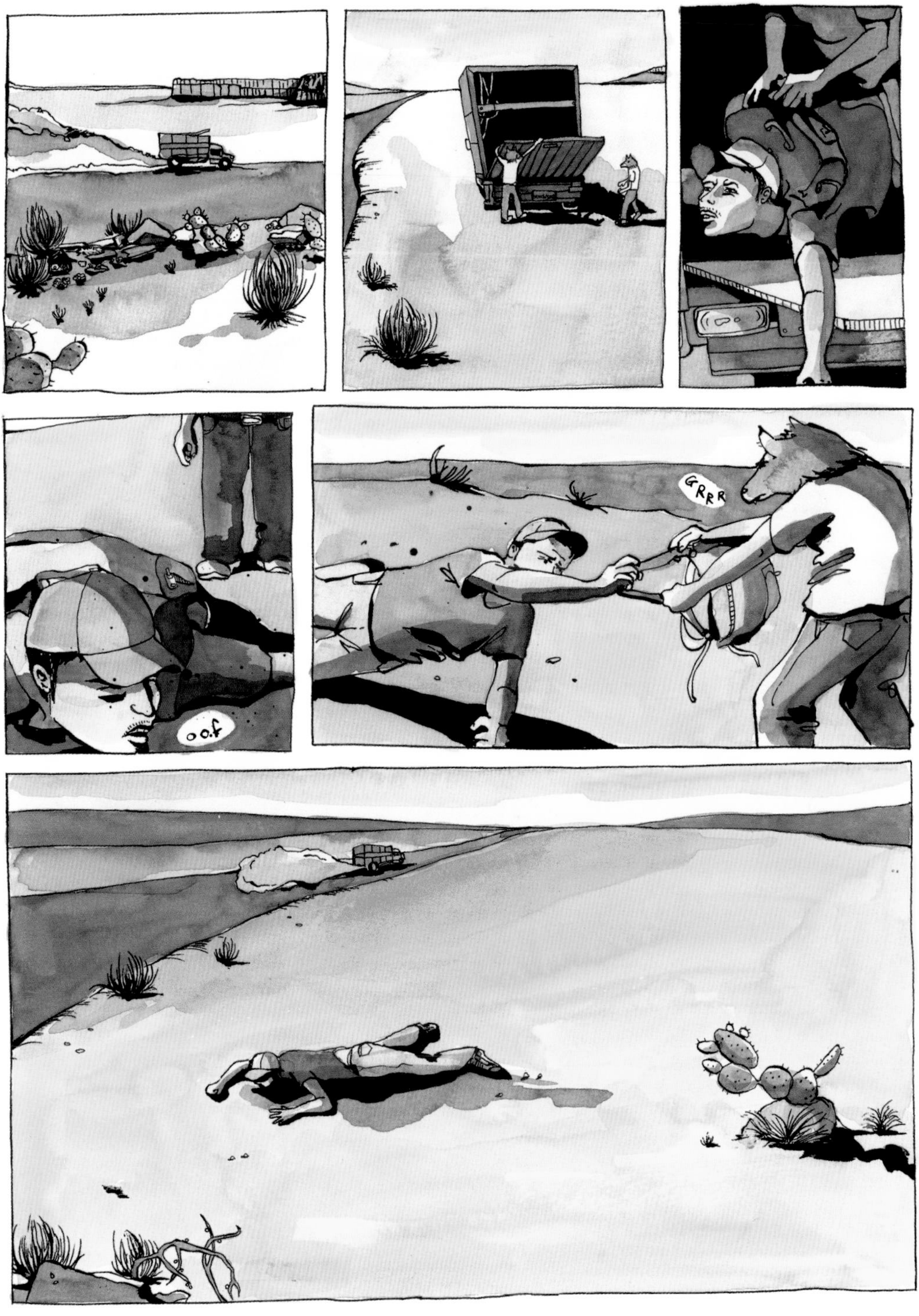
oof
GRRR

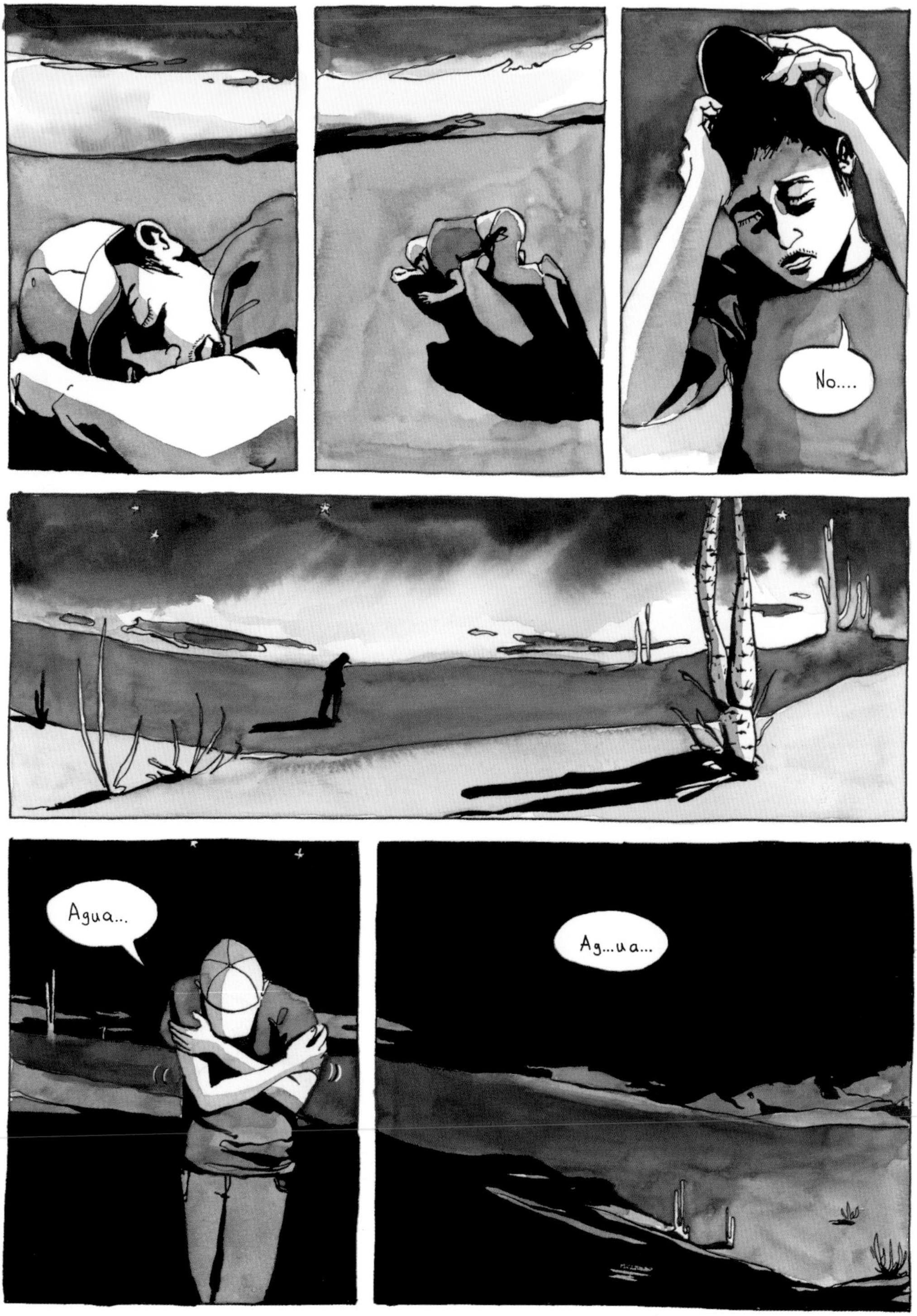
No....
Agua...
Ag...ua...

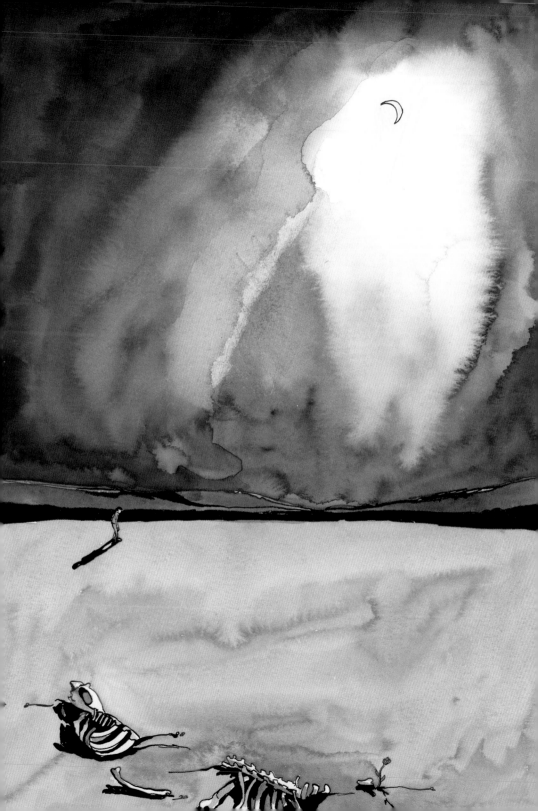

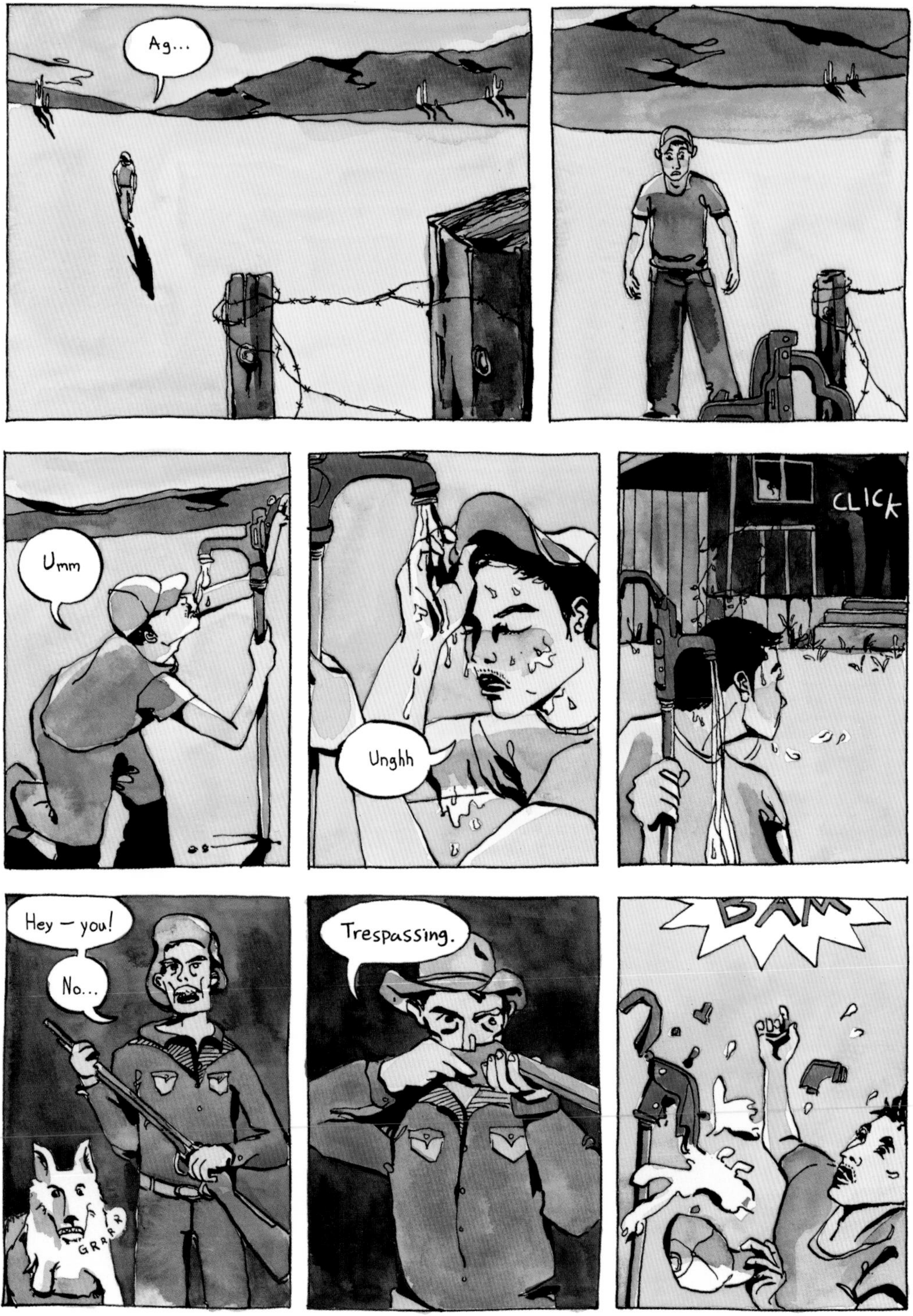
Ag...
Umm
Unghh
CLICK
Hey — you!
No...
GRRRR
Trespassing.
BAM

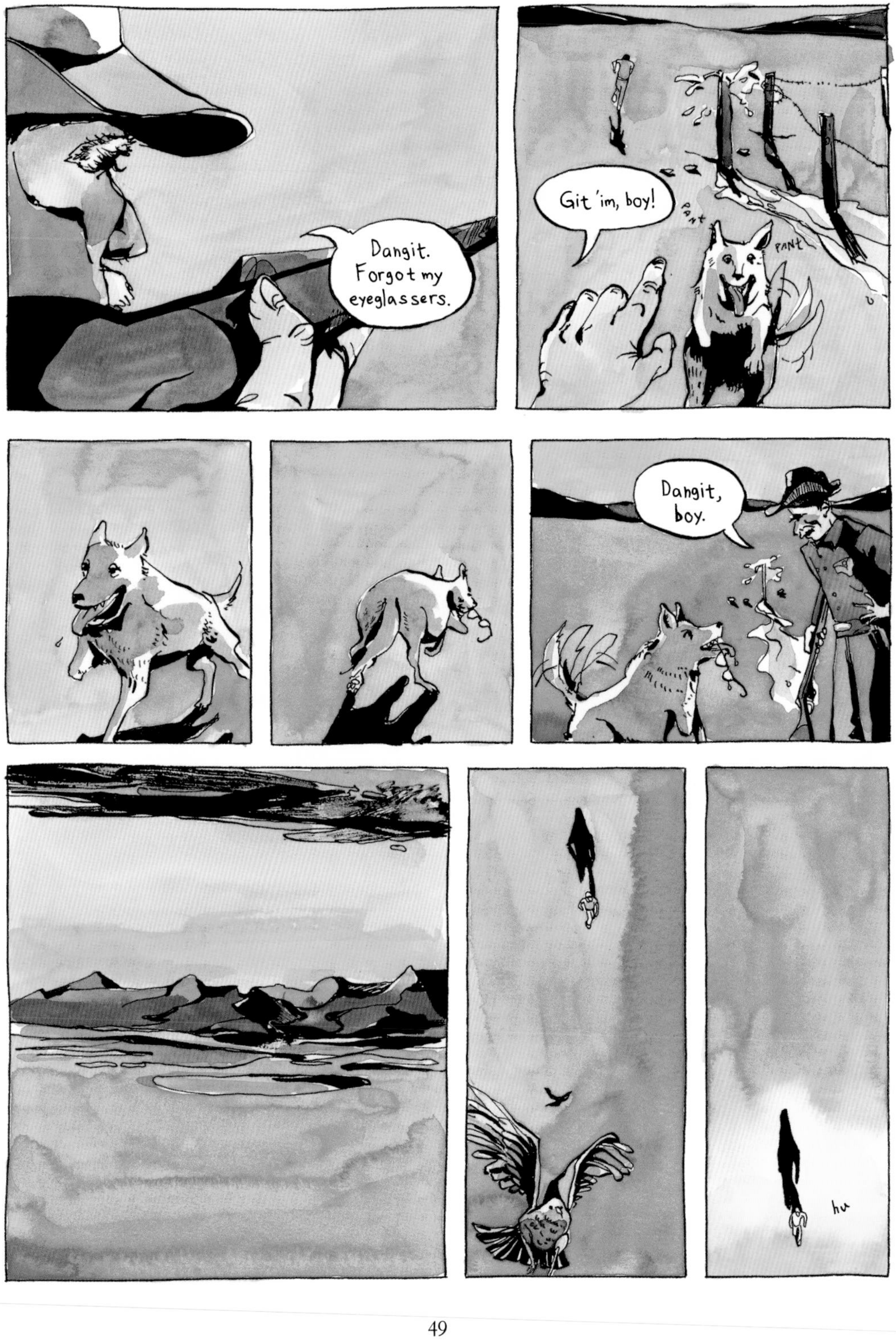
Dangit.
Forgot my
eyeglassers.
Git 'im, boy!
PANT
PANT
Dangit,
boy.
hu

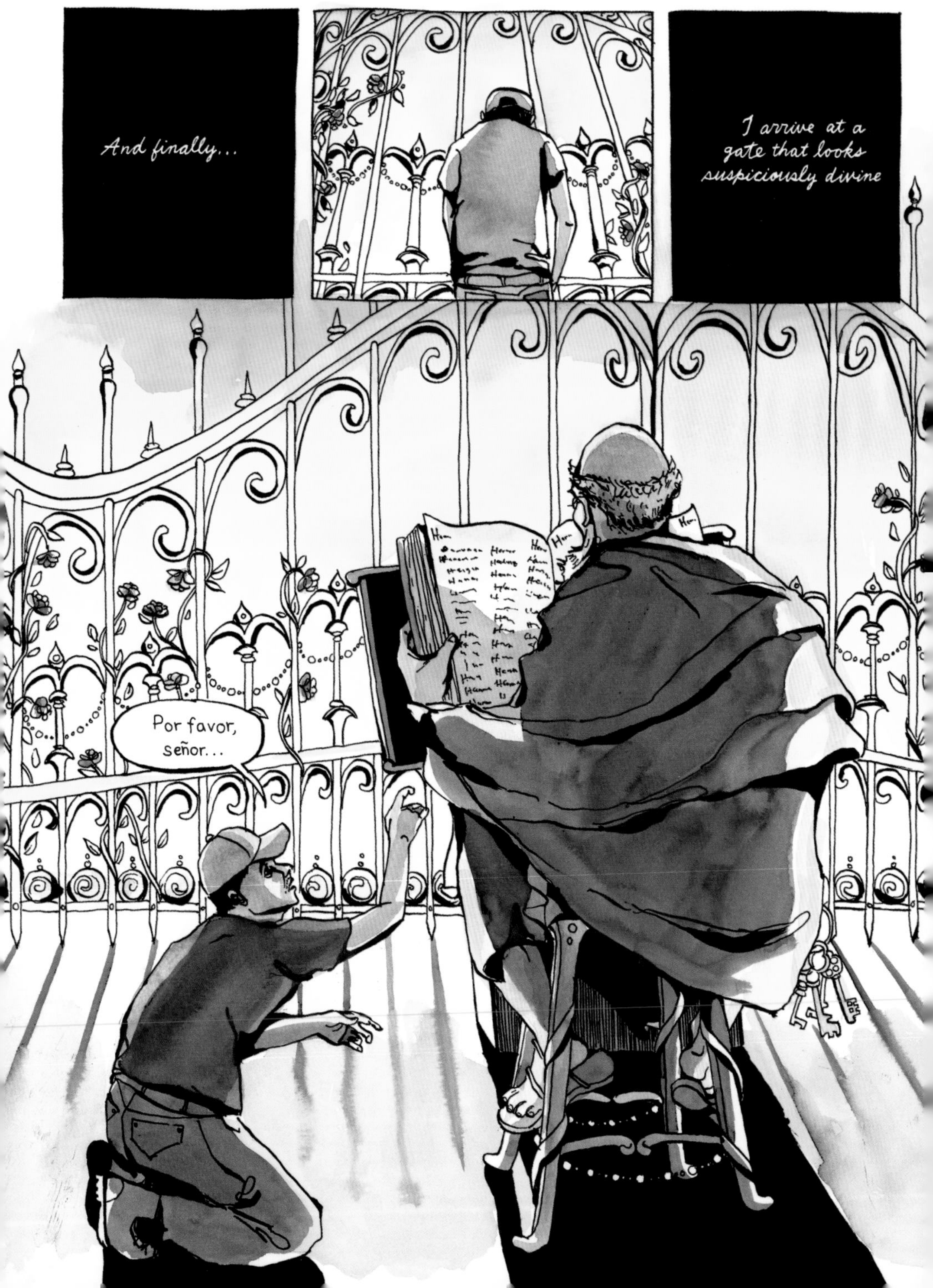

And finally...
I arrive at a gate that looks suspiciously divine
Por favor, señor...

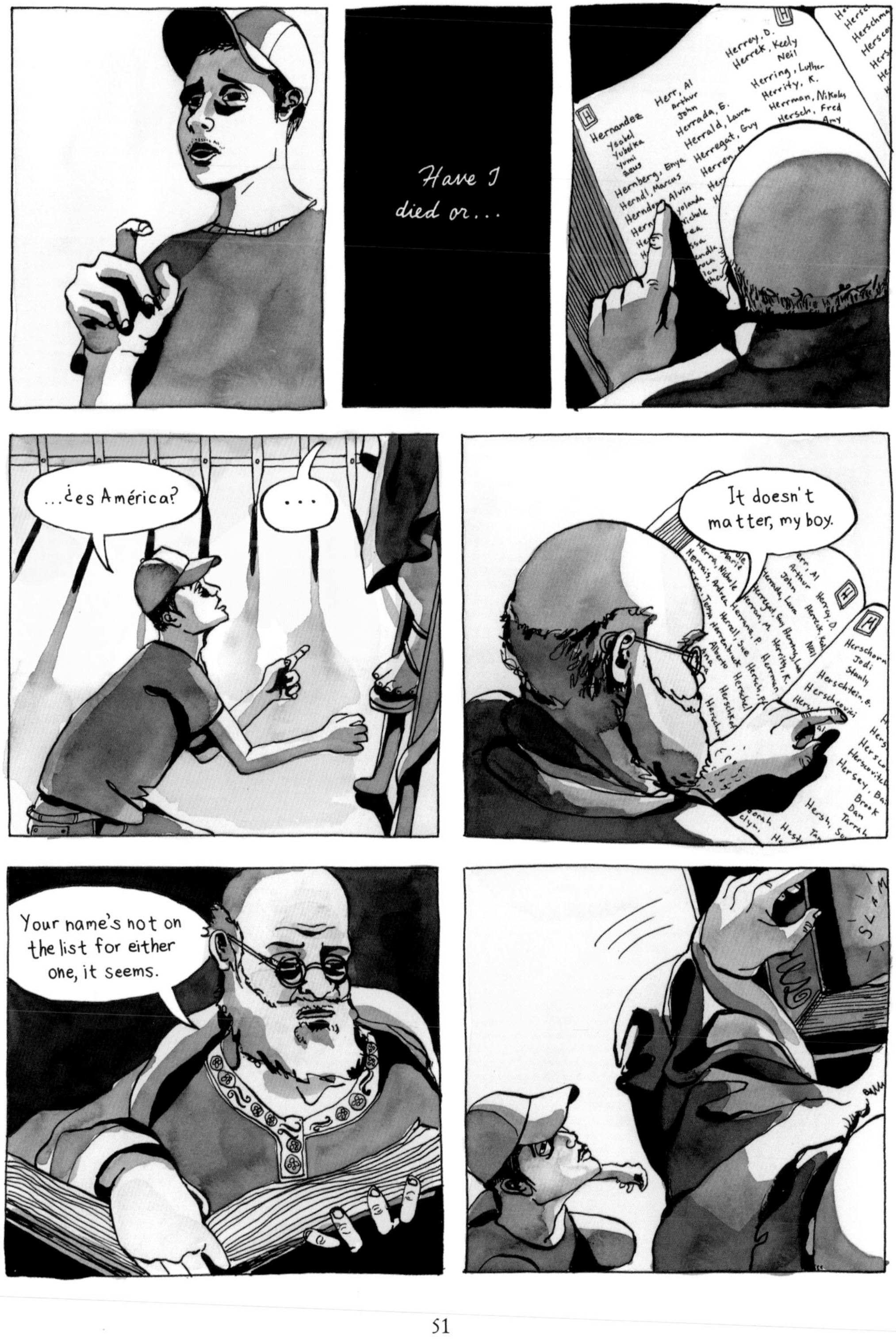
Have I died or...
...¿es América?
...
It doesn't matter, my boy.
Your name's not on the list for either one, it seems.
SLAM

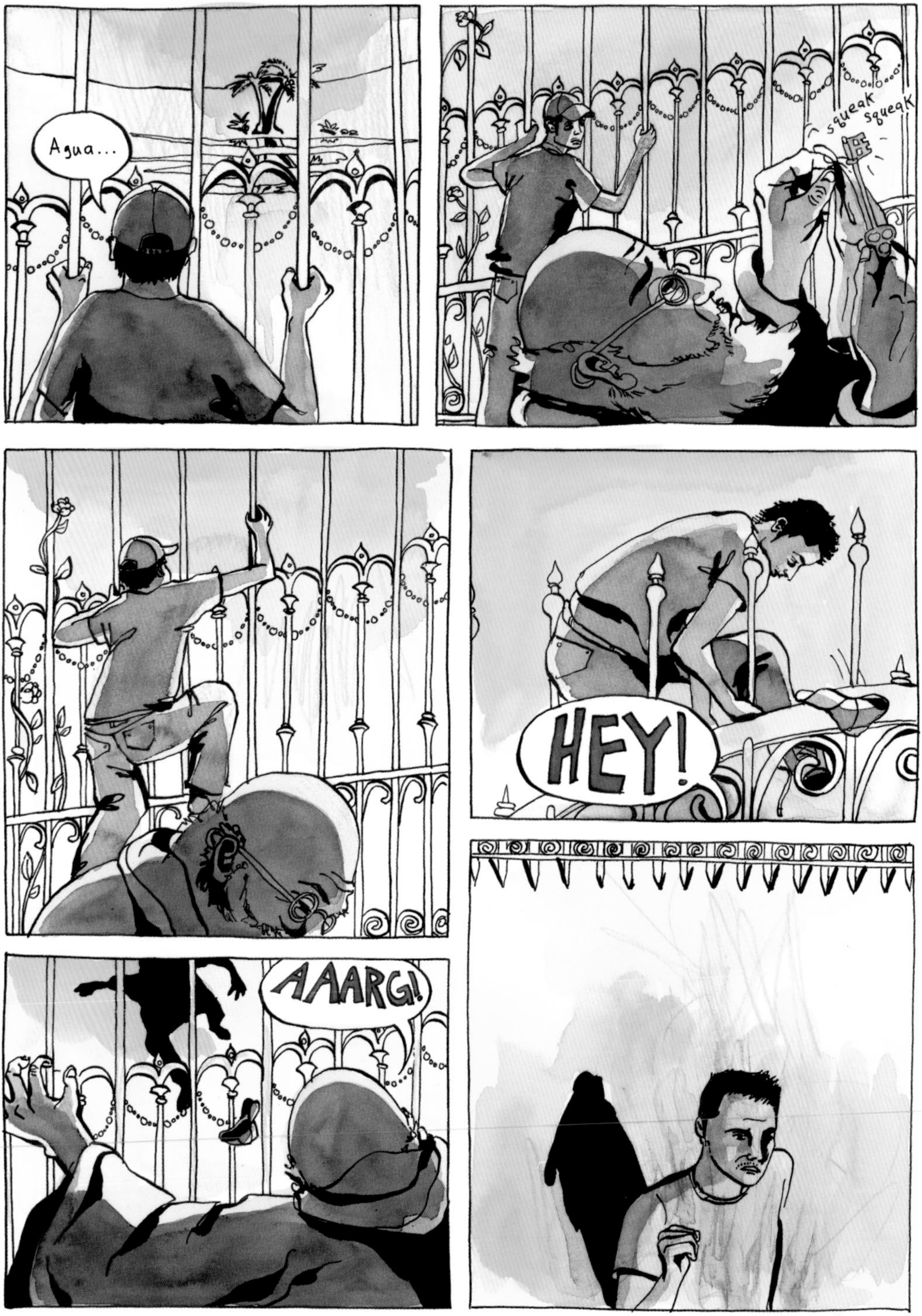
Agua...
squeak
squeaK
HEY!
AAARG!

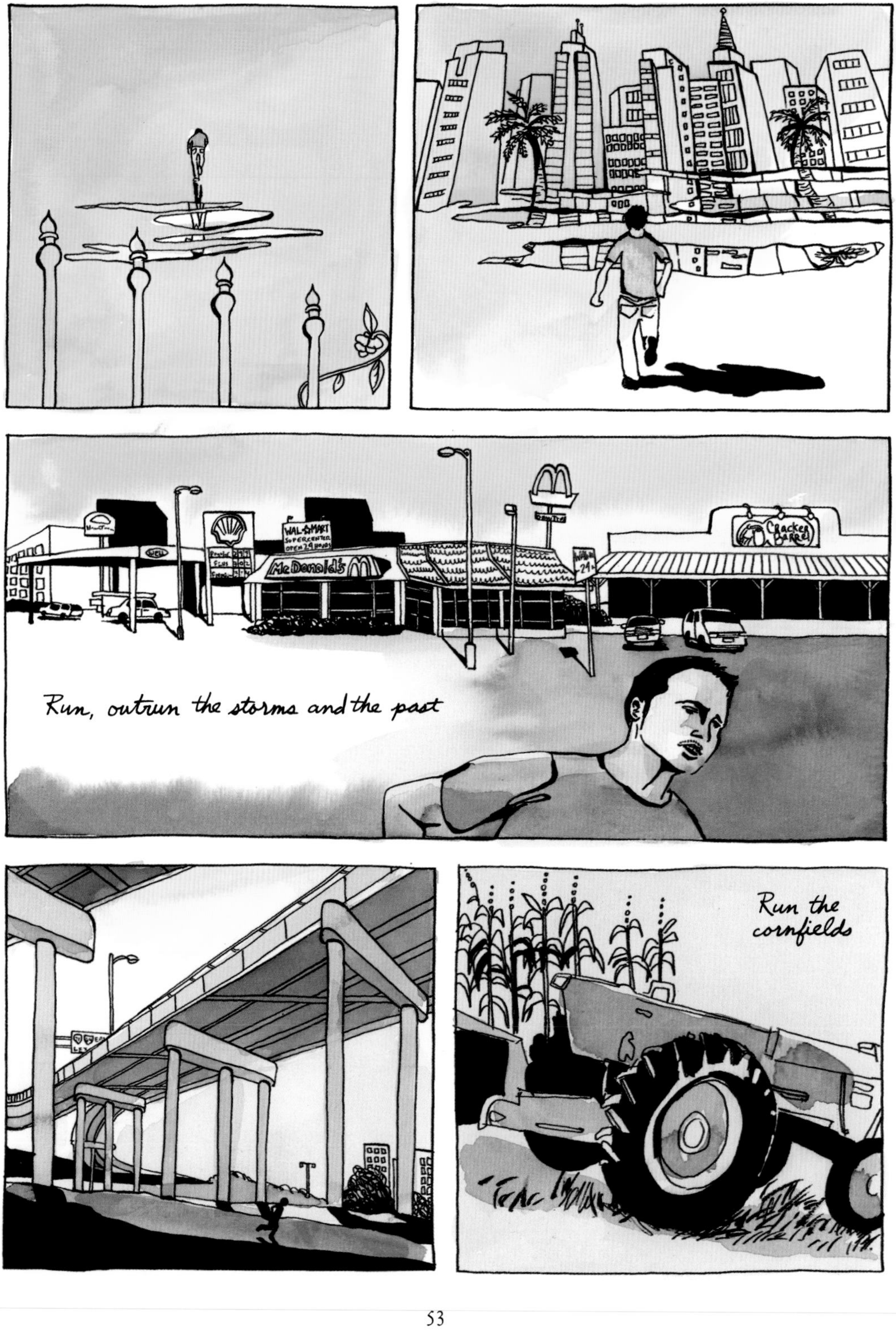
WAL-MART
SUPERCENTER
OPEN 24 HOURS
McDonald's
Cracker Barrel
Run, outrun the storms and the past
Run the cornfields

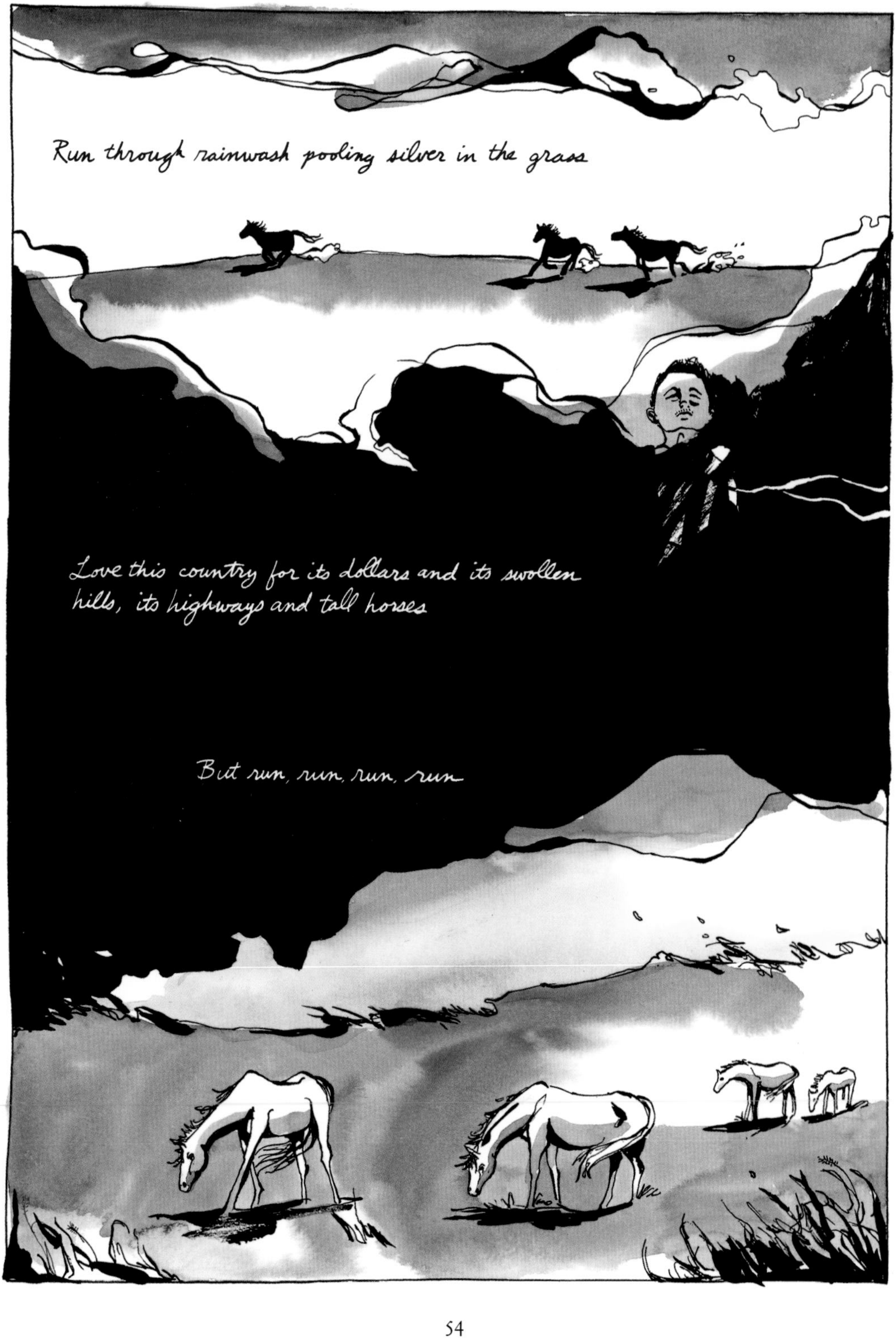
Run through rainwash pooling silver in the grass
Love this country for its dollars and its swollen hills, its highways and tall horses
But run, run, run, run

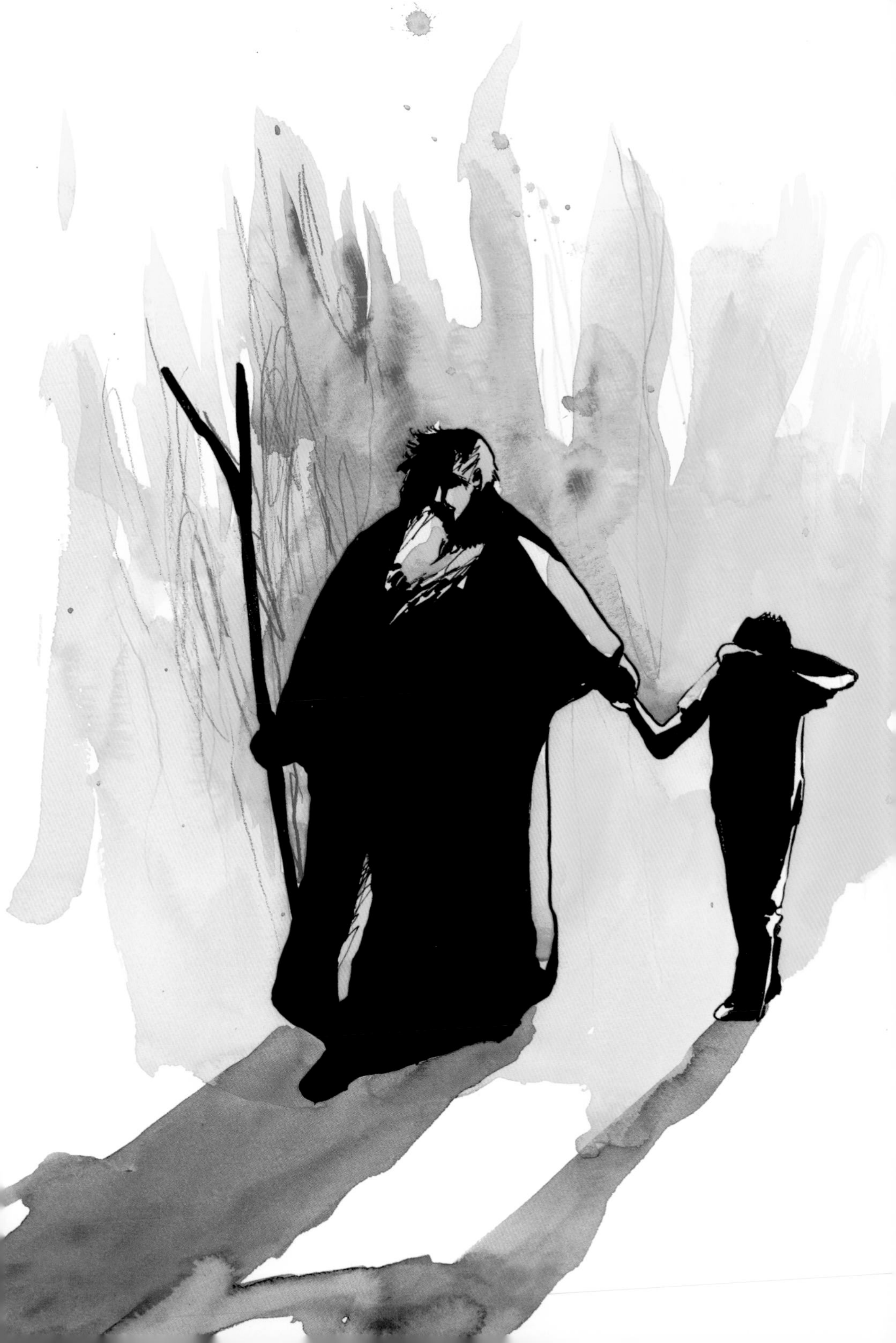

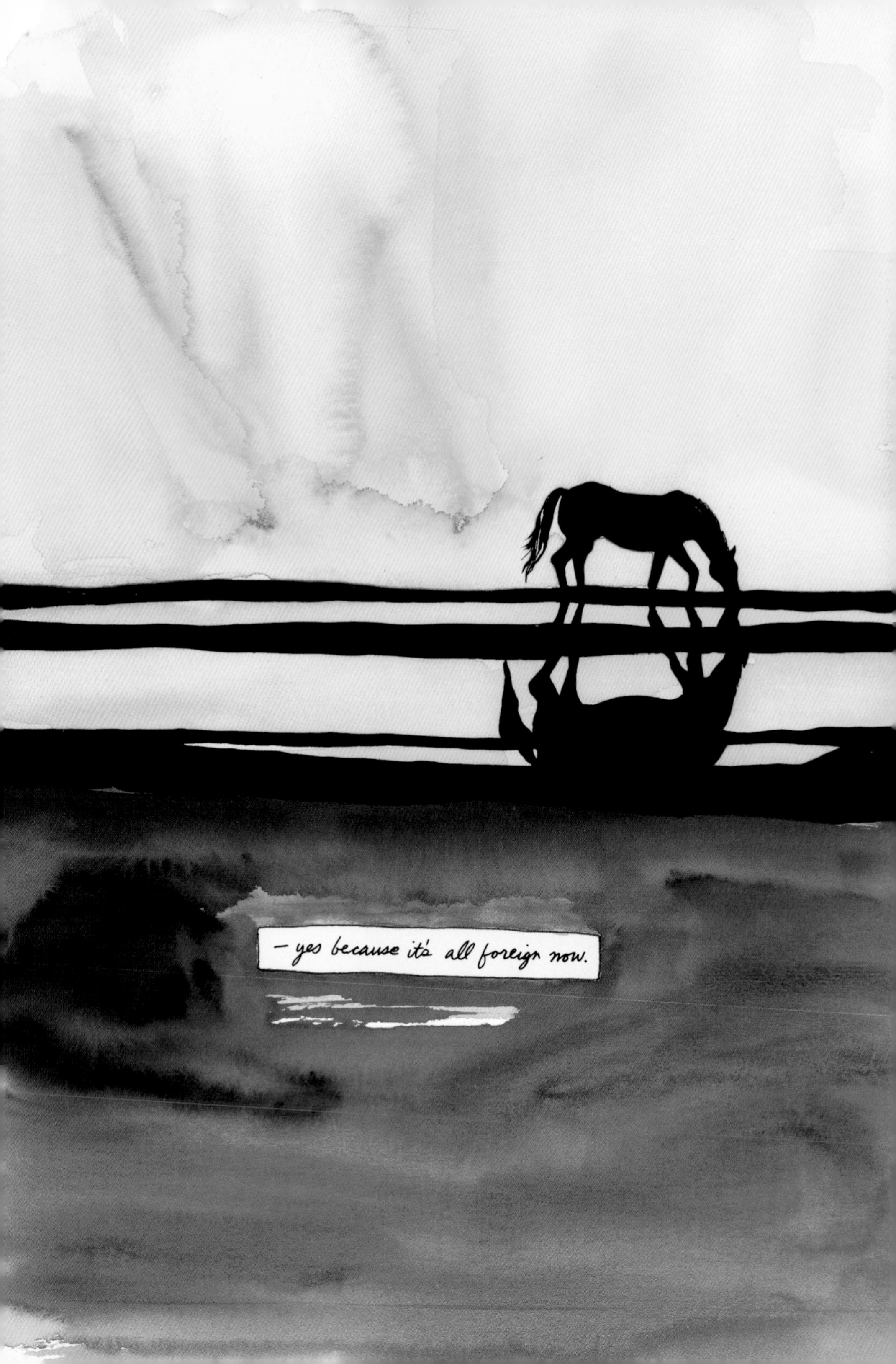
– yes because it's all foreign now.

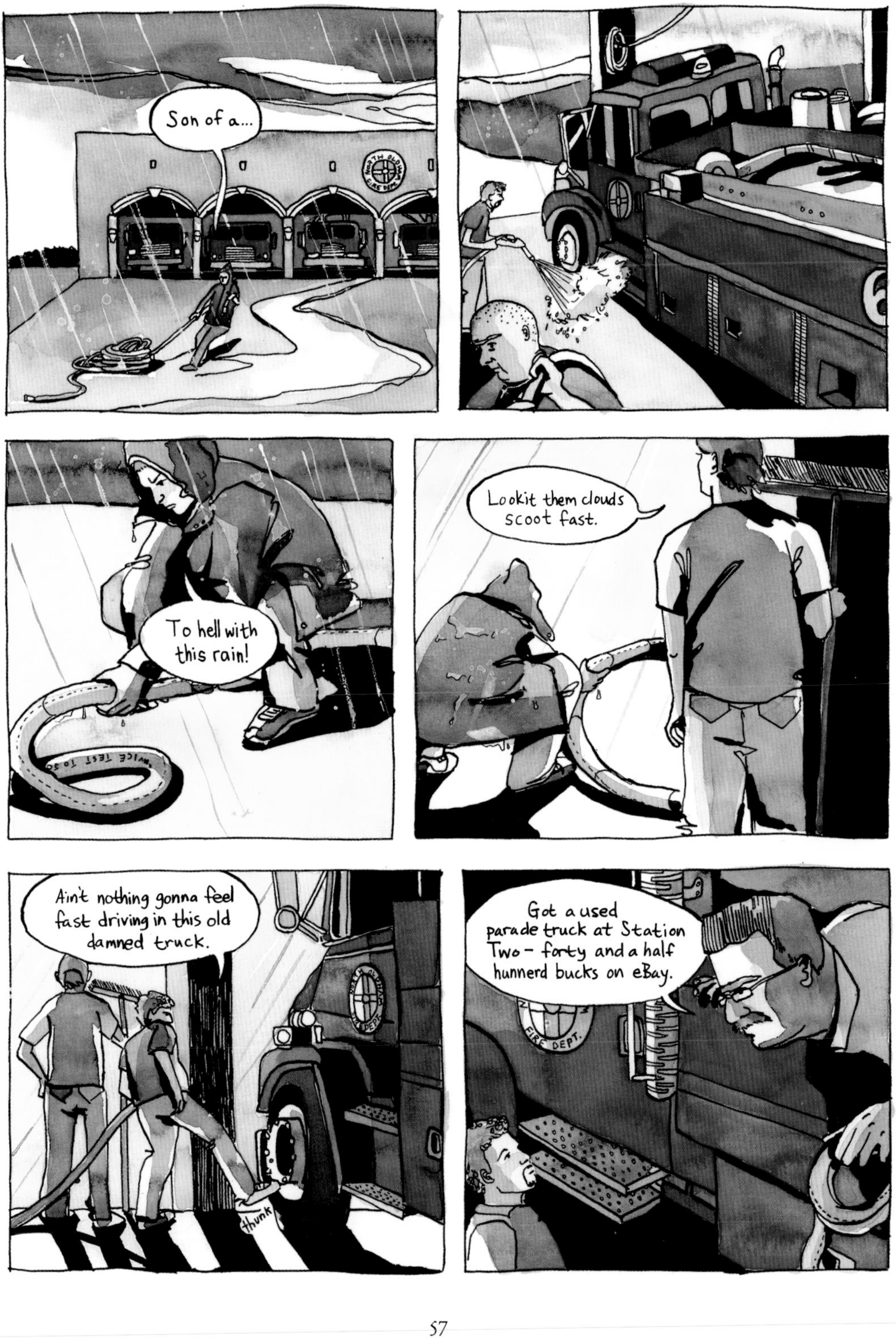
Son of a...
To hell with this rain!
Lookit them clouds scoot fast.
Ain't nothing gonna feel fast driving in this old damned truck.
thunk
Got a used parade truck at Station Two – forty and a half hunnerd bucks on eBay.
FIRE DEPT.

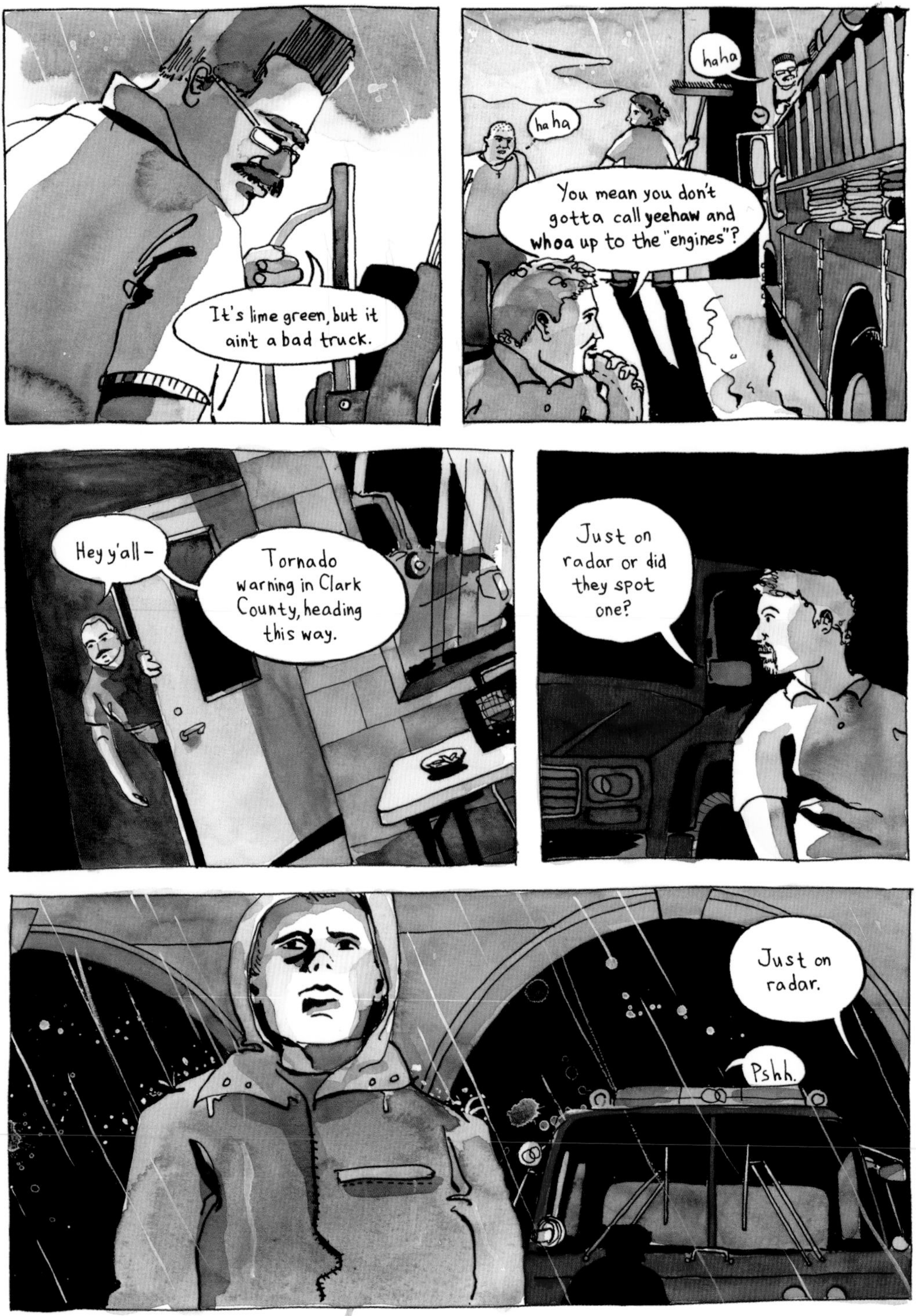
It's lime green, but it ain't a bad truck.
haha
ha ha
You mean you don't gotta call yeehaw and whoa up to the "engines"?
Hey y'all –
Tornado warning in Clark County, heading this way.
Just on radar or did they spot one?
Just on radar.
Pshh.

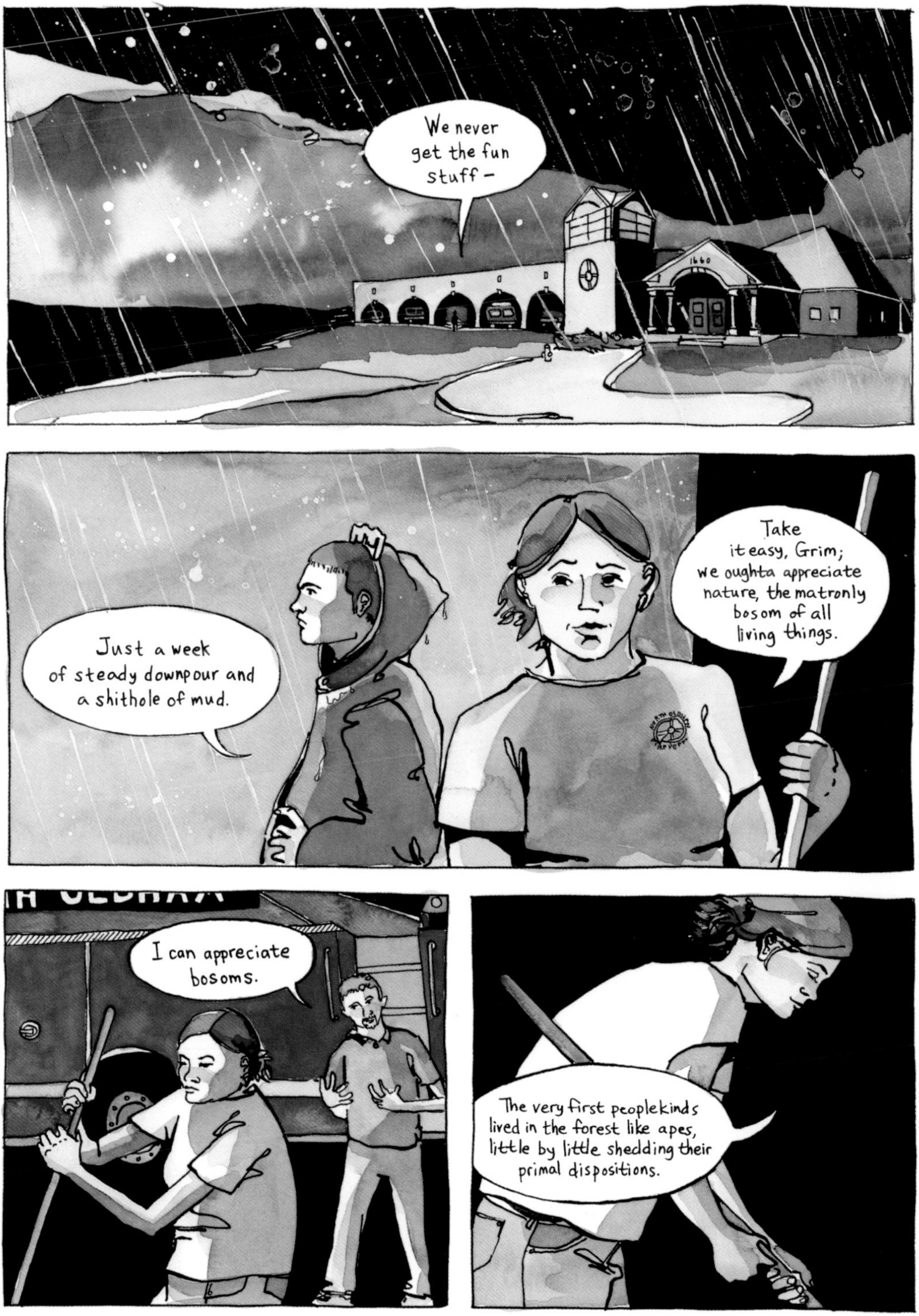
We never get the fun stuff –
Just a week of steady downpour and a shithole of mud.
Take it easy, Grim; we oughta appreciate nature, the matronly bosom of all living things.
I can appreciate bosoms.
The very first peoplekinds lived in the forest like apes, little by little shedding their primal dispositions.

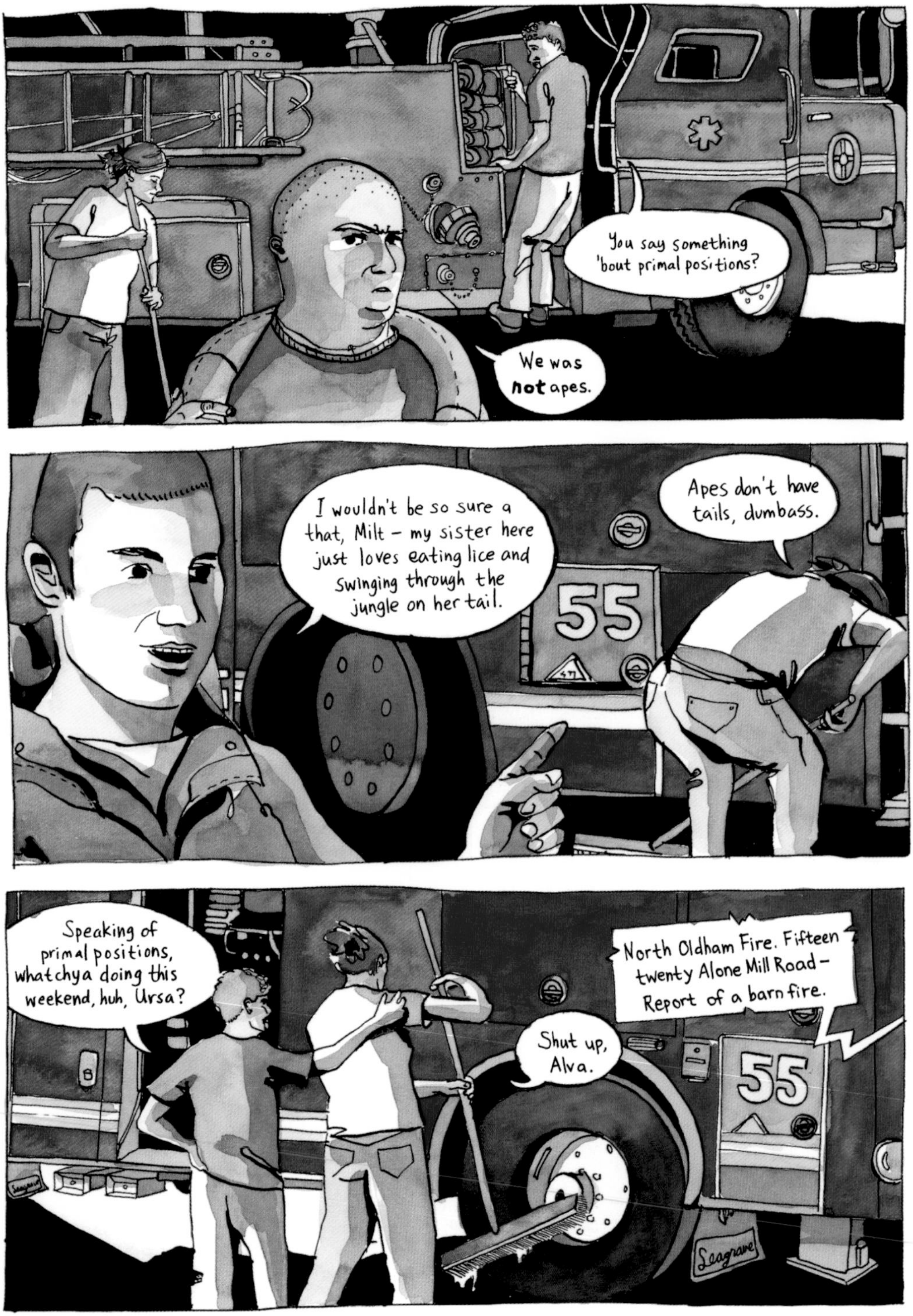
You say something 'bout primal positions?
We was **not** apes.
I wouldn't be so sure a that, Milt – my sister here just loves eating lice and swinging through the jungle on her tail.
Apes don't have tails, dumbass.
55
Speaking of primal positions, whatchya doing this weekend, huh, Ursa?
Shut up, Alva.
North Oldham Fire. Fifteen twenty Alone Mill Road – Report of a barn fire.
55
Seagrave

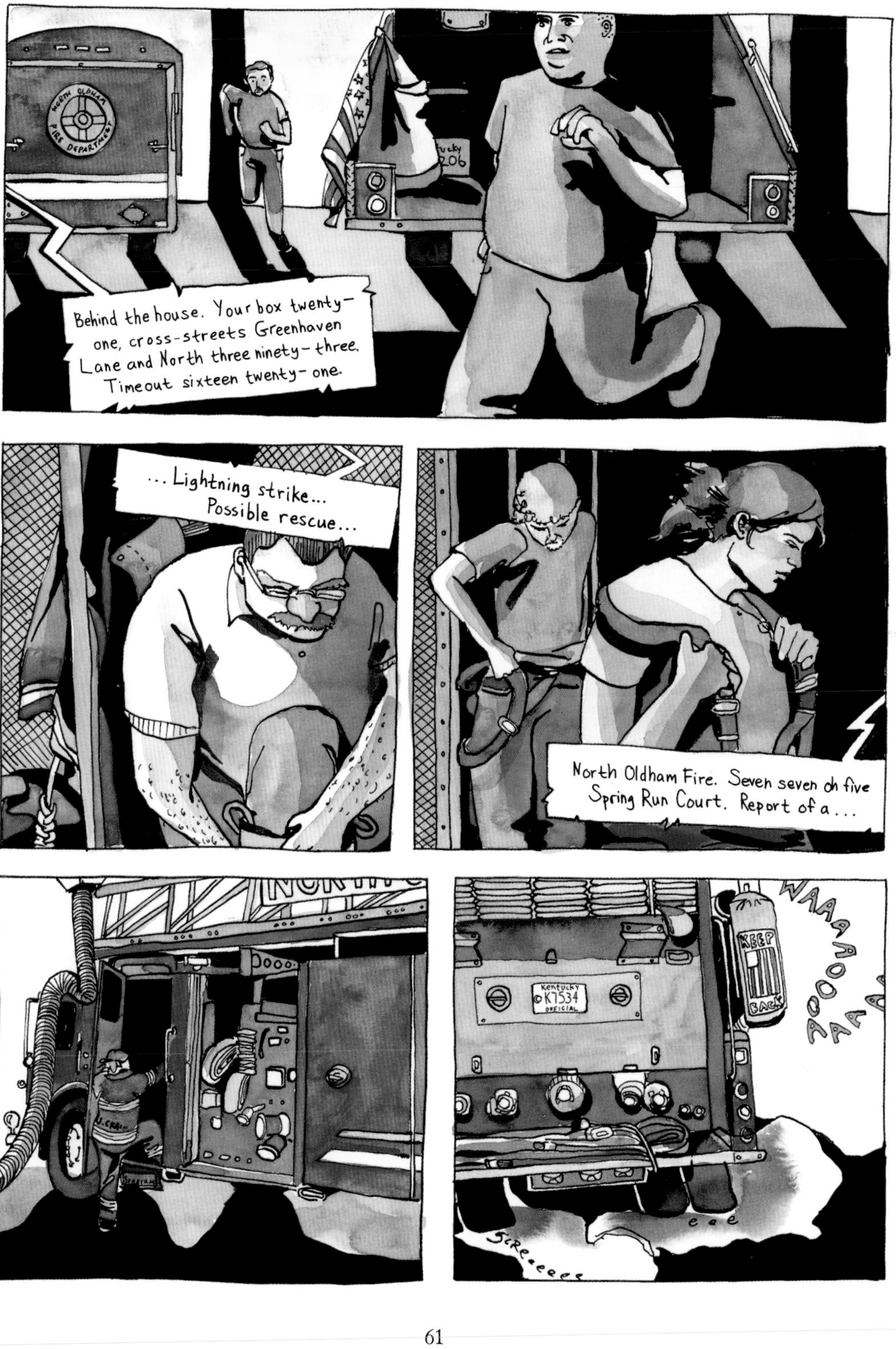
NORTH OLDHAM FIRE DEPARTMENT
Behind the house. Your box twenty-one, cross-streets Greenhaven Lane and North three ninety-three. Timeout sixteen twenty-one.
... Lightning strike... Possible rescue...
North Oldham Fire. Seven seven oh five Spring Run Court. Report of a . . .
Kentucky K7534 OFFICIAL
KEEP BACK
WAAAAOOOOAAAA
Screeeeeee
eee

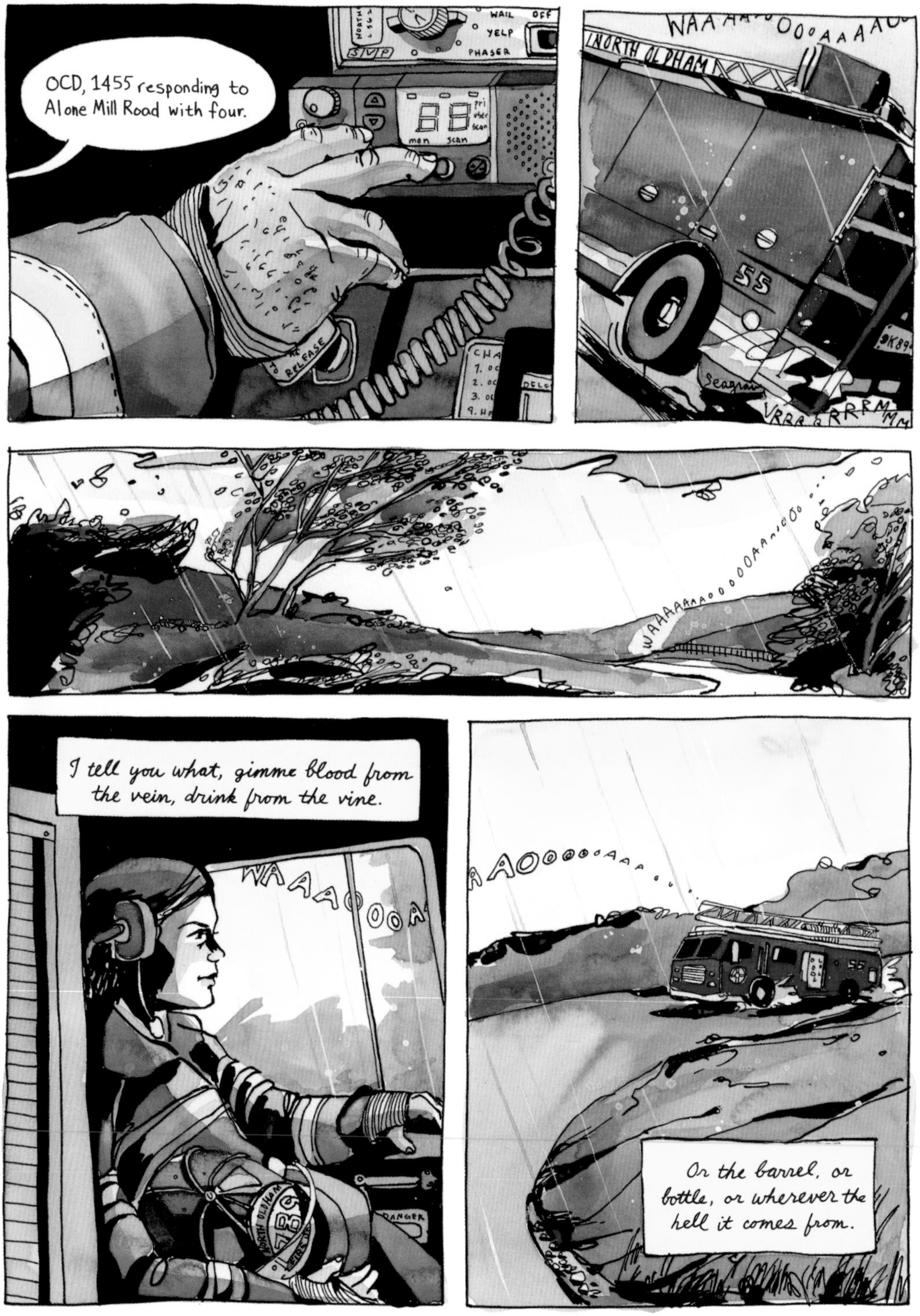
OCD, 1455 responding to Alone Mill Road with four.
WAIL
YELP
PHASER
OFF
WAAAAOOOOAAAAO
NORTH OLDHAM
VRRRRRRRMMM
WAAAAAAAOOOOAA
I tell you what, gimme blood from the vein, drink from the vine.
WAAAOOOA
AAOOOOOAAA
Or the barrel, or bottle, or wherever the hell it comes from.

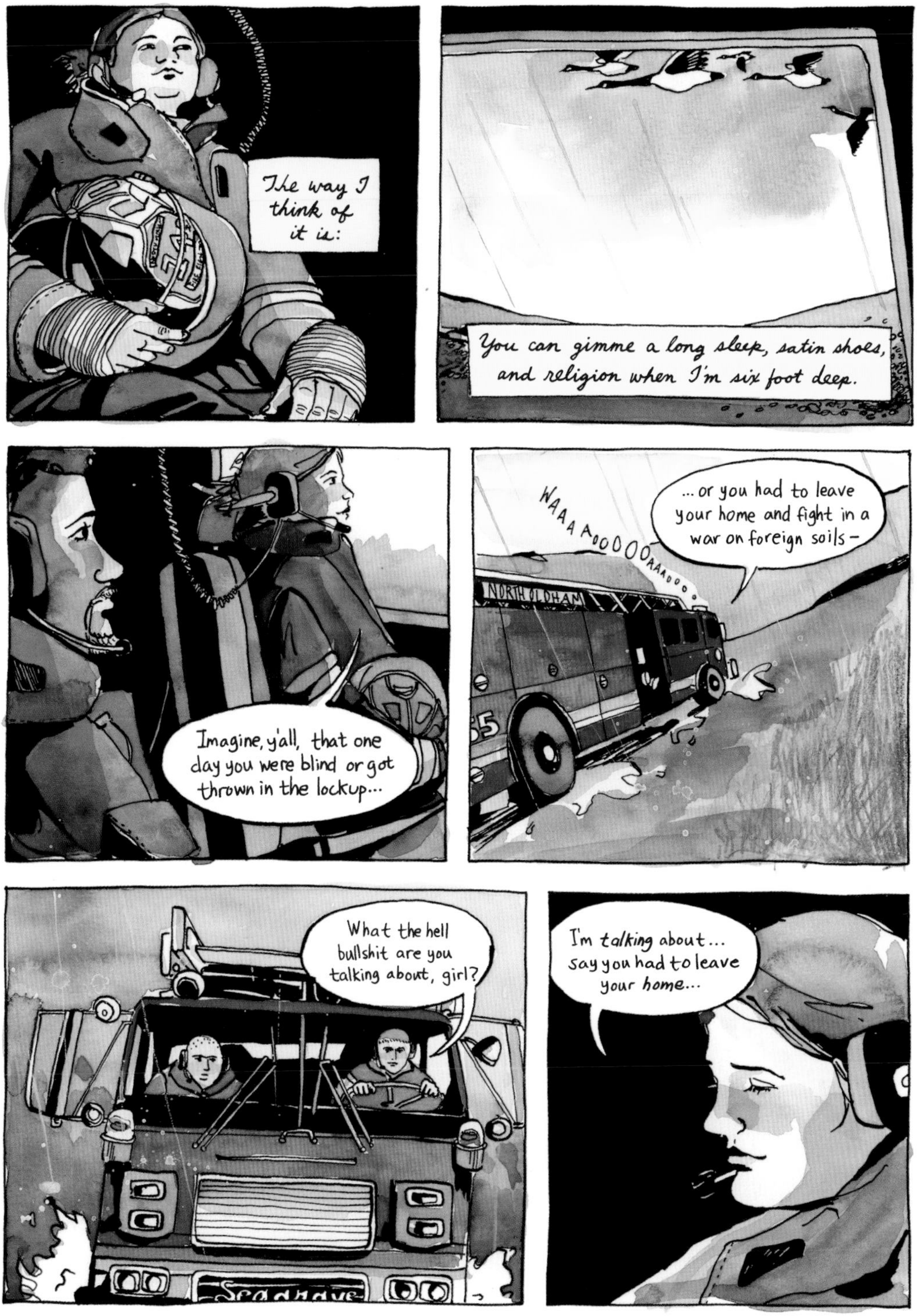
The way I think of it is:
You can gimme a long sleep, satin shoes, and religion when I'm six foot deep.
Imagine, y'all, that one day you were blind or got thrown in the lockup...
WAAAAAOOOOOAAAOOOO
...or you had to leave your home and fight in a war on foreign soils–
NORTH OLDHAM
What the hell bullshit are you talking about, girl?
I'm *talking* about... say you had to leave your *home*...

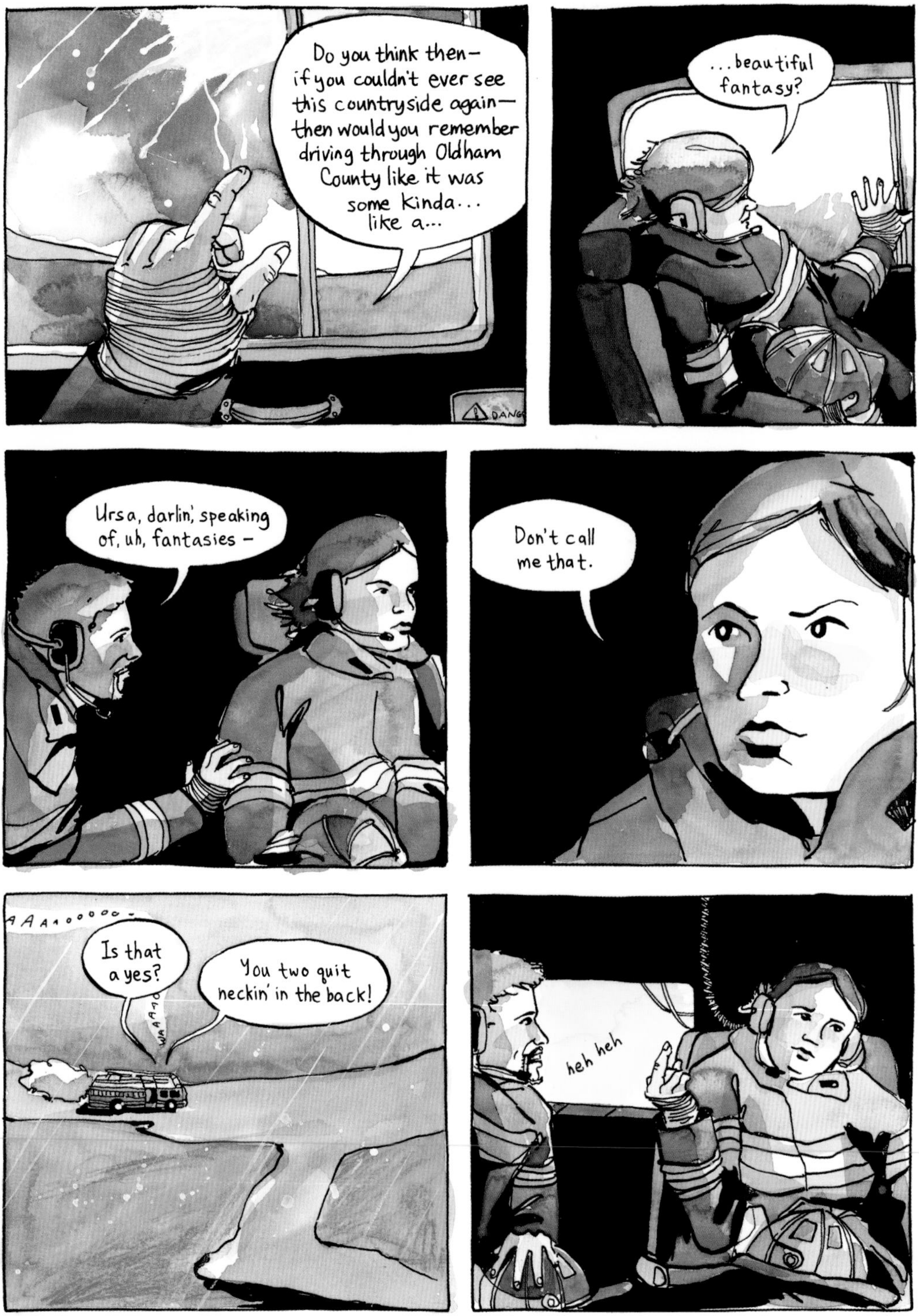

Do you think then– if you couldn't ever see this countryside again– then would you remember driving through Oldham County like it was some Kinda... like a...
...beautiful fantasy?
Ursa, darlin', speaking of, uh, fantasies –
Don't call me that.
AAAAooooo-
WAAAO
Is that a yes?
You two quit neckin' in the back!
heh heh

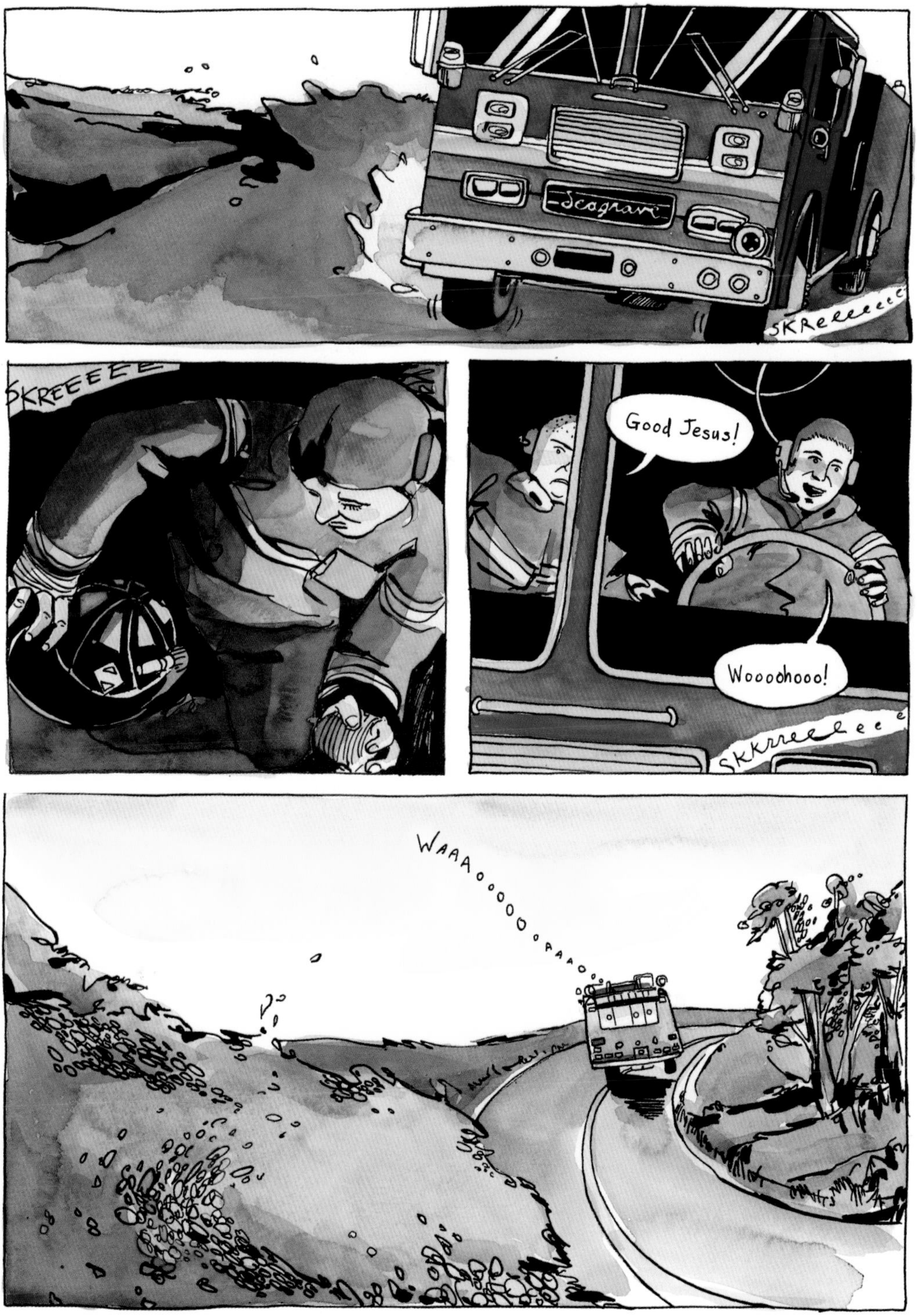

SKReeeeeee
SKREEEEEE
Good Jesus!
Woooohooo!
SKKrreeeleee
WAAAooooooAAAoo

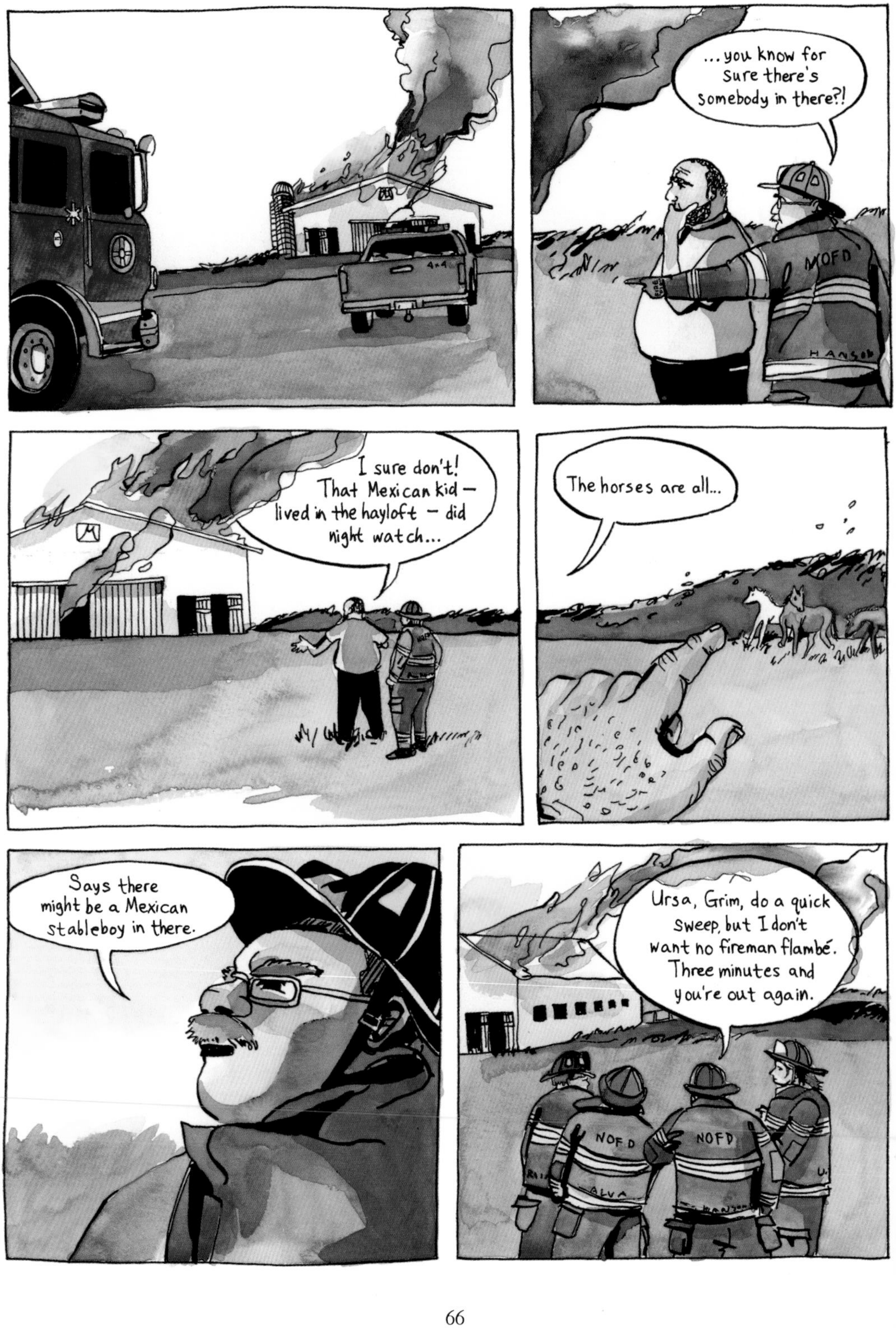
...you know for sure there's somebody in there?!
I sure don't! That Mexican kid — lived in the hayloft — did night watch...
The horses are all...
Says there might be a Mexican stableboy in there.
Ursa, Grim, do a quick sweep, but I don't want no fireman flambé. Three minutes and you're out again.

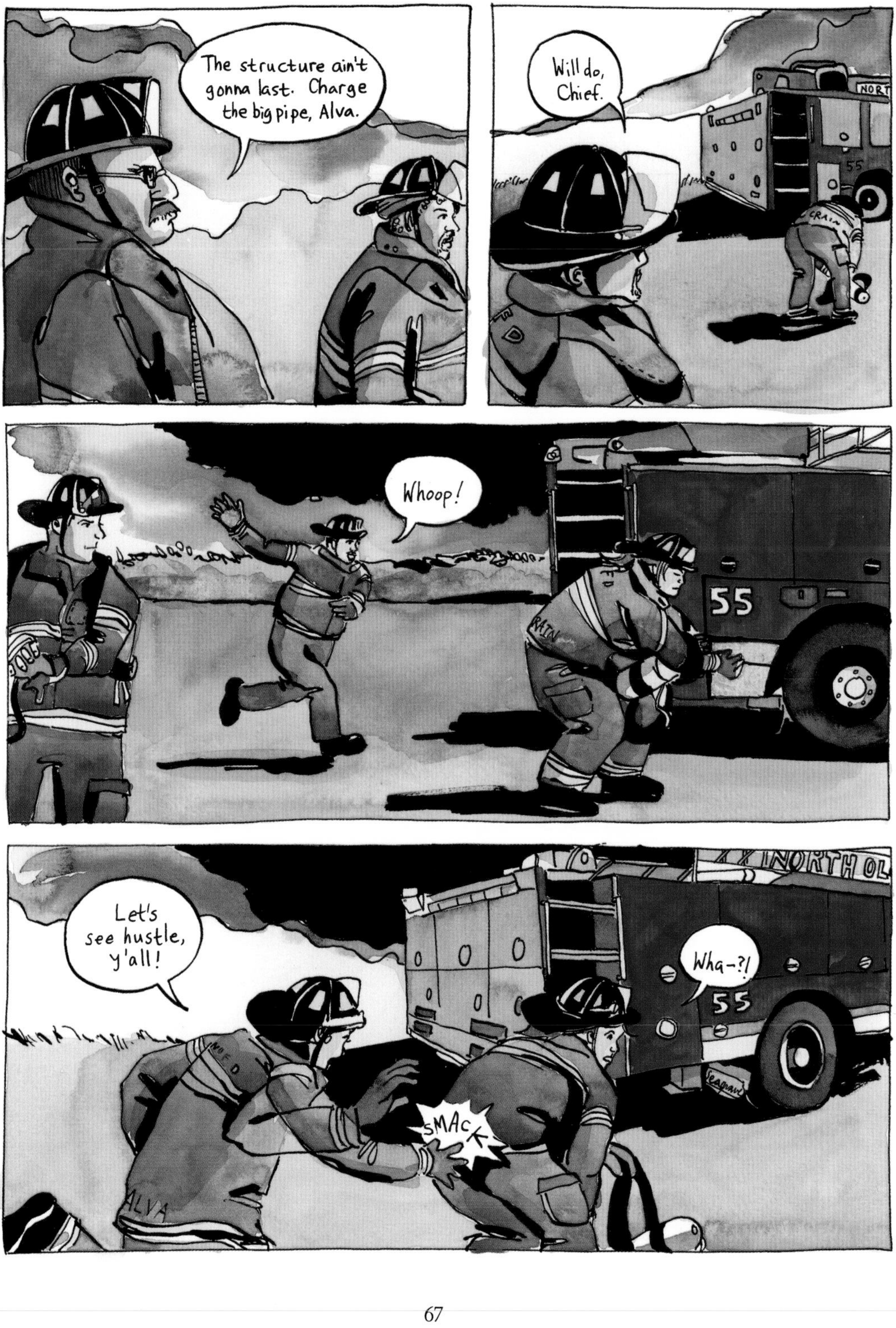

The structure ain't gonna last. Charge the big pipe, Alva.
Will do, Chief.
Whoop!
55
Let's see hustle, y'all!
Wha-?!
55
SMACK
ALVA

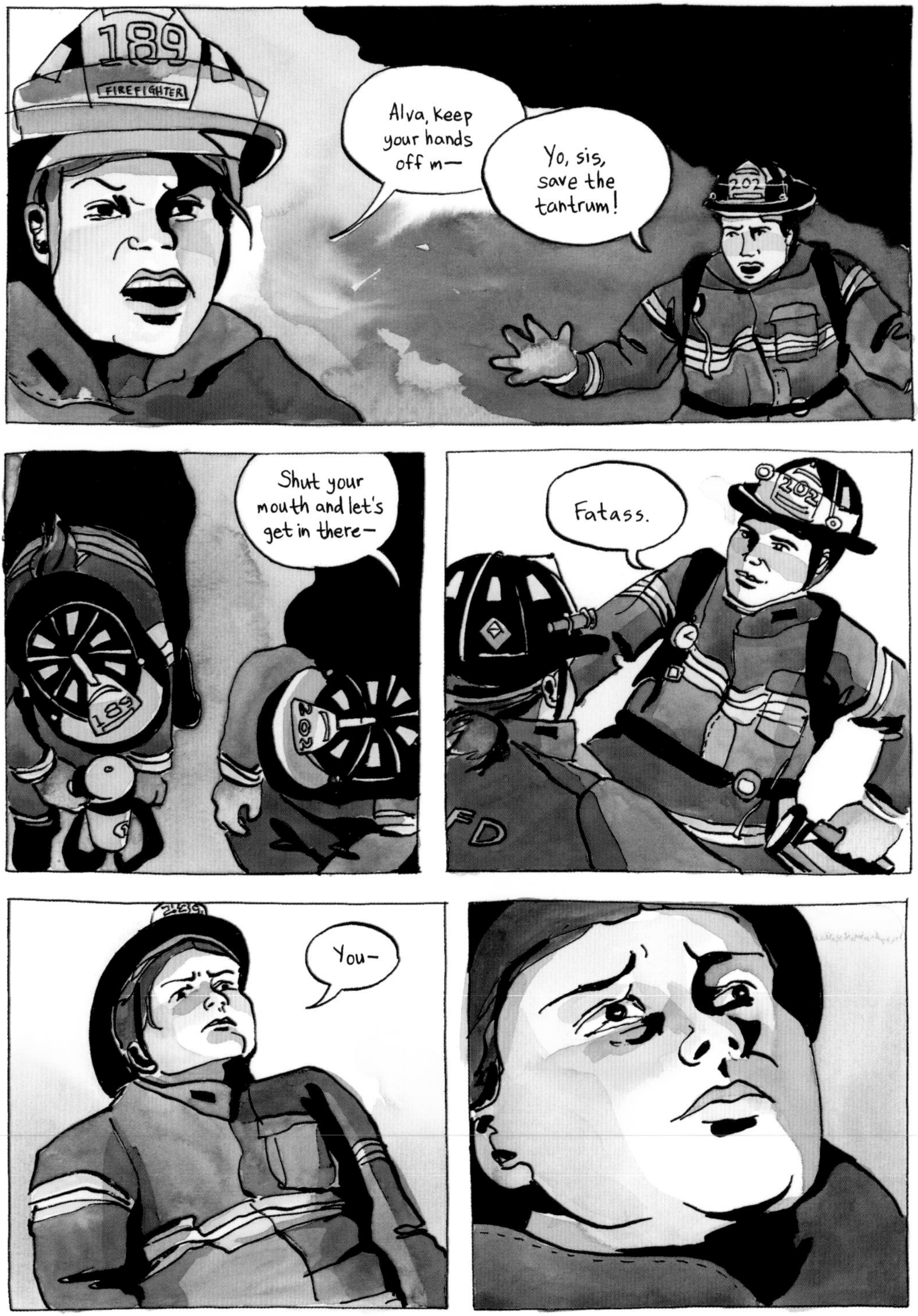
FIREFIGHTER
Alva, keep your hands off m—
Yo, sis, save the tantrum!
Shut your mouth and let's get in there—
Fatass.
You—

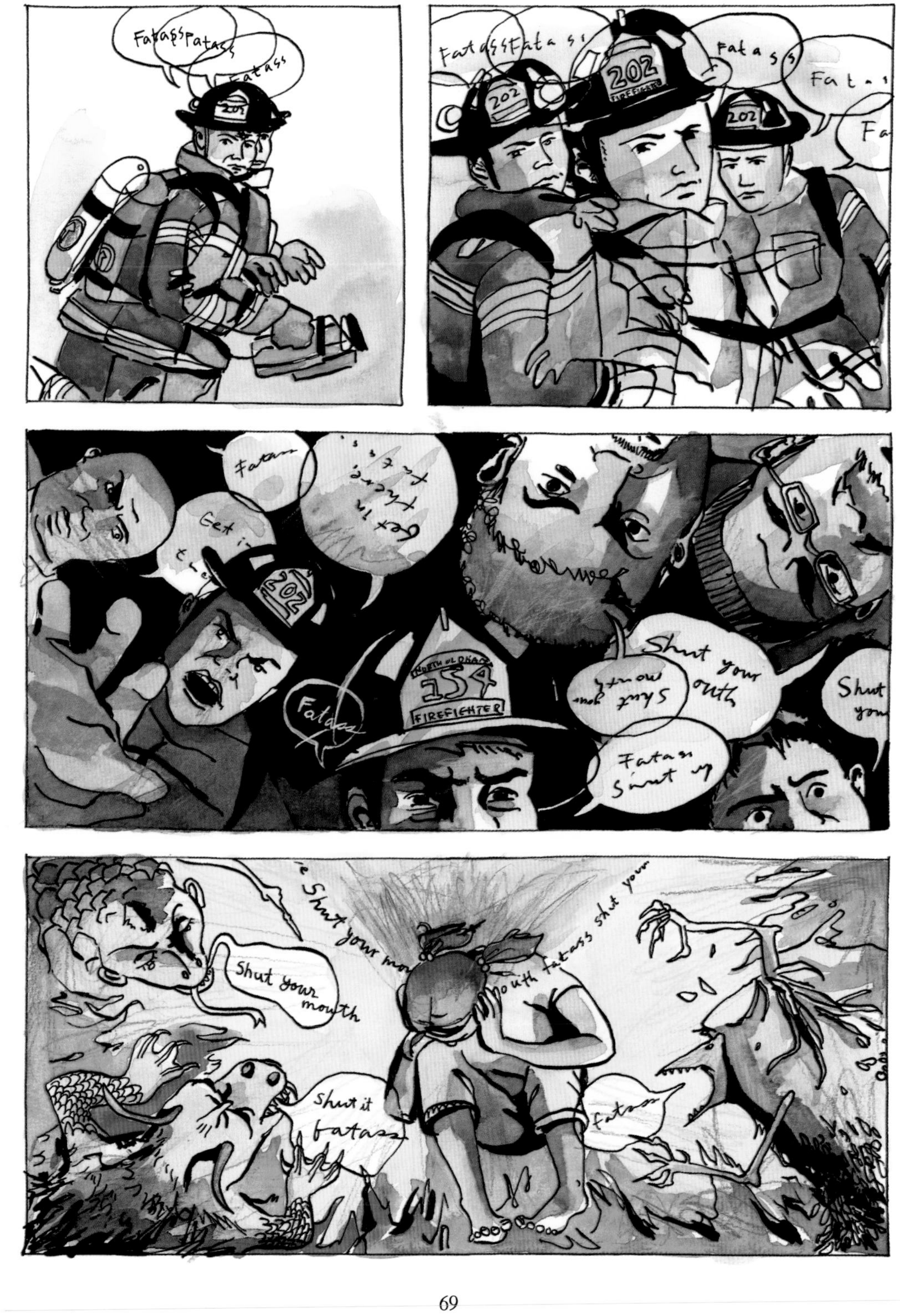
Fatass
Fatass
Fatass
Fatass
Fatass
Fatass
Fatass
Shut your mouth
Fatass
Shut up
Shut your mouth
Shut your mouth fatass shut your
Shut it fatass
Fatass

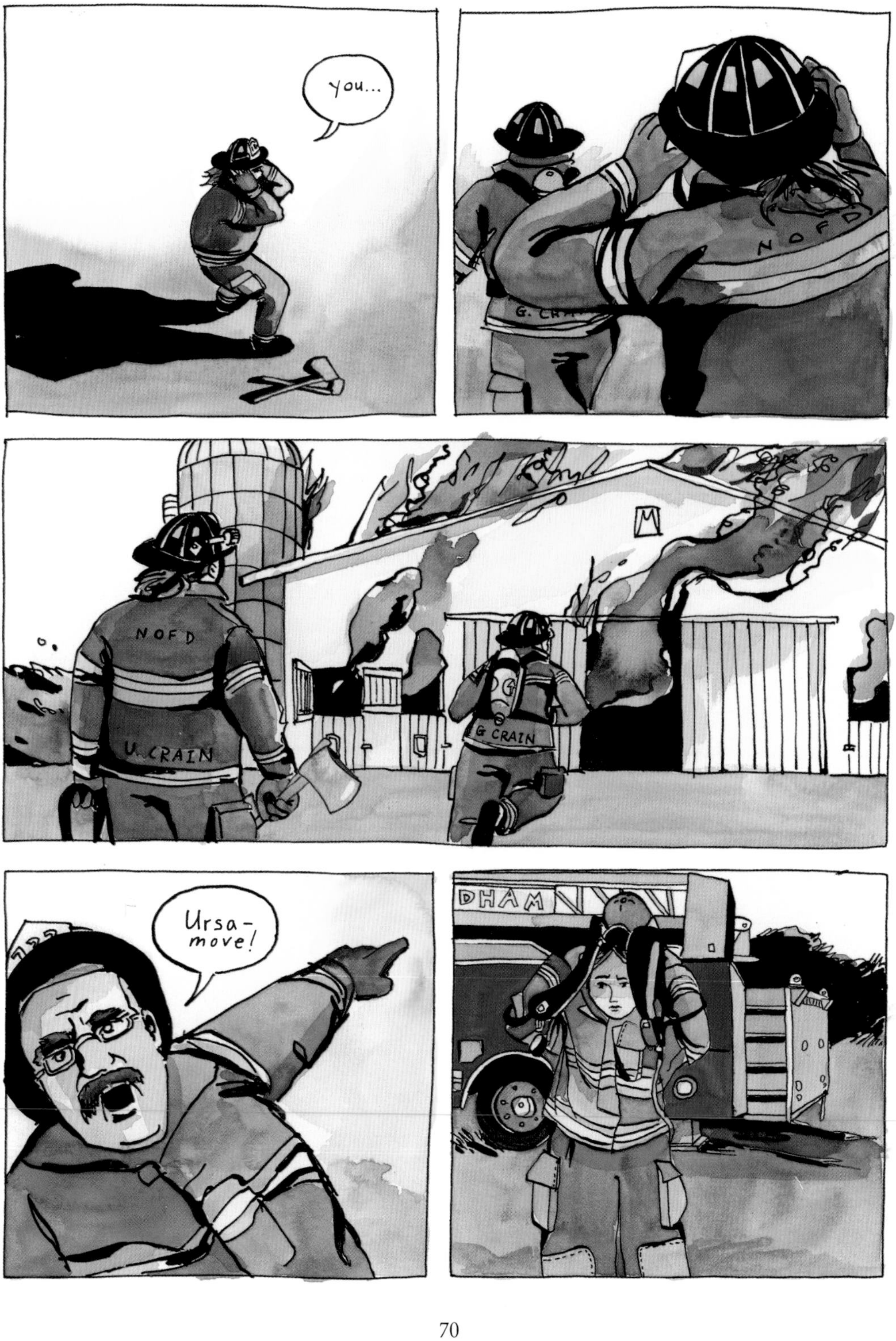
you...
N O F D
G. CRA
N O F D
U. CRAIN
G CRAIN
Ursa-
move!
DHAM

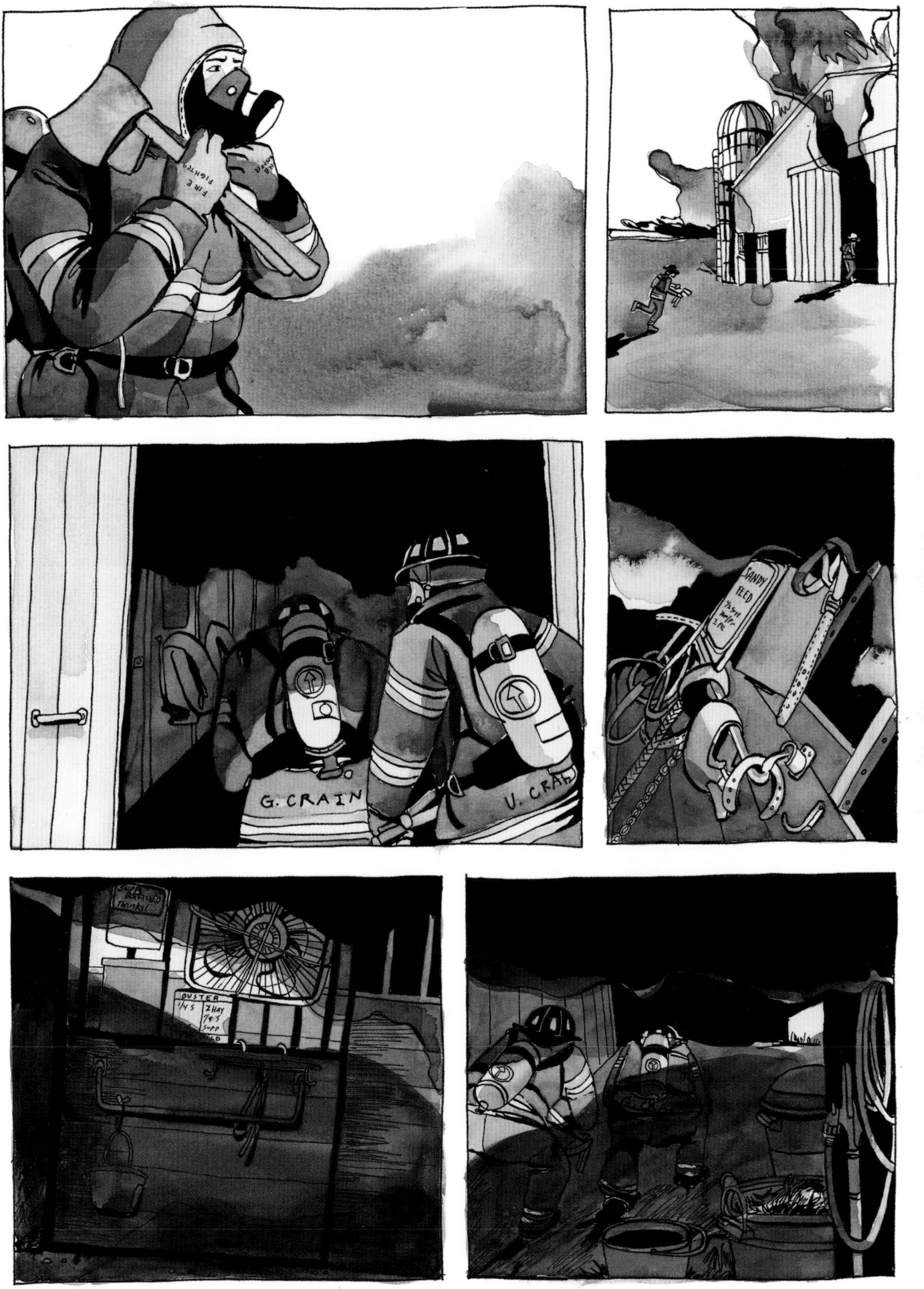
FIRE FIGHTER
G. CRAIN
SANDY FEED
BUSTER

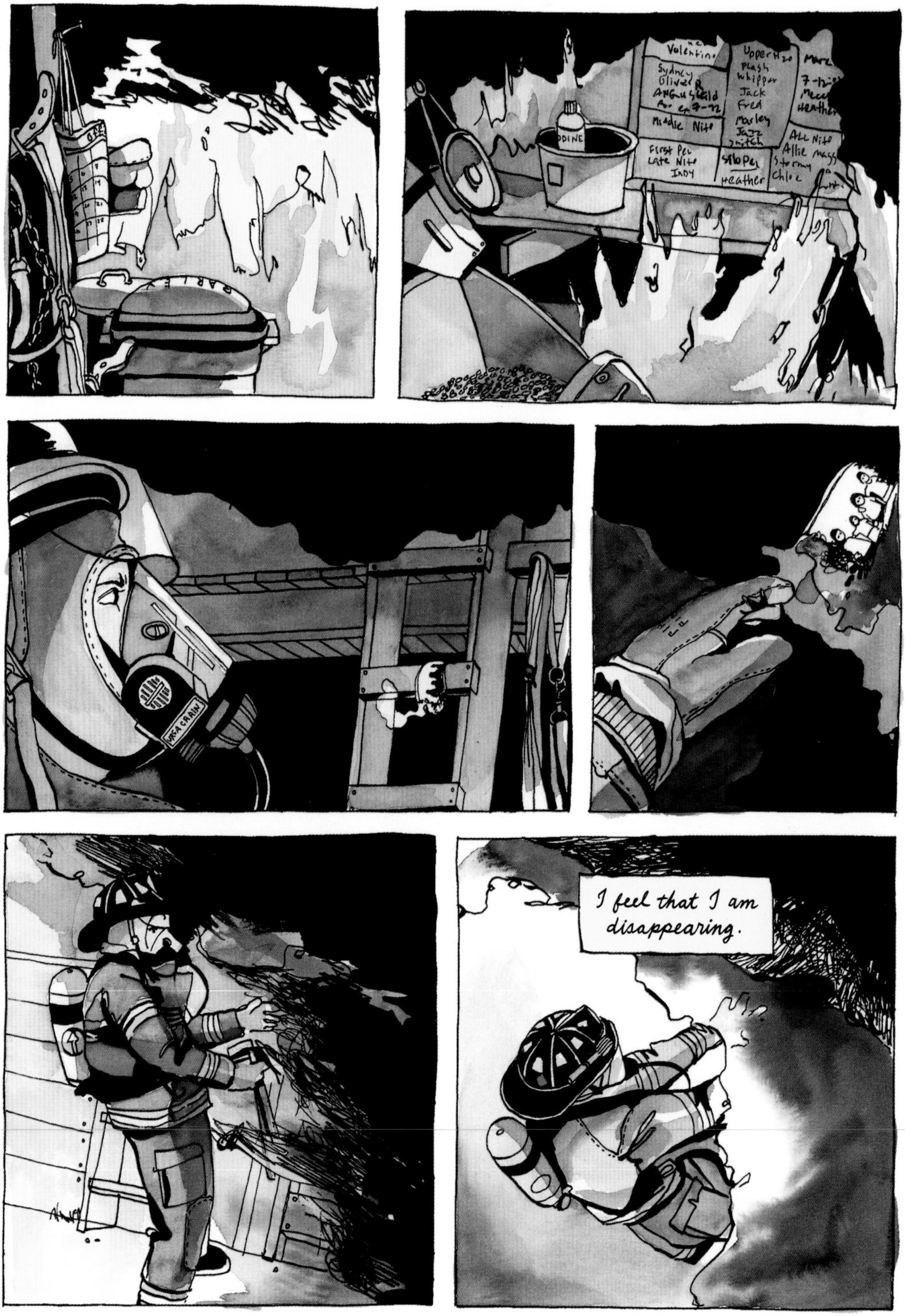
I feel that I am disappearing.

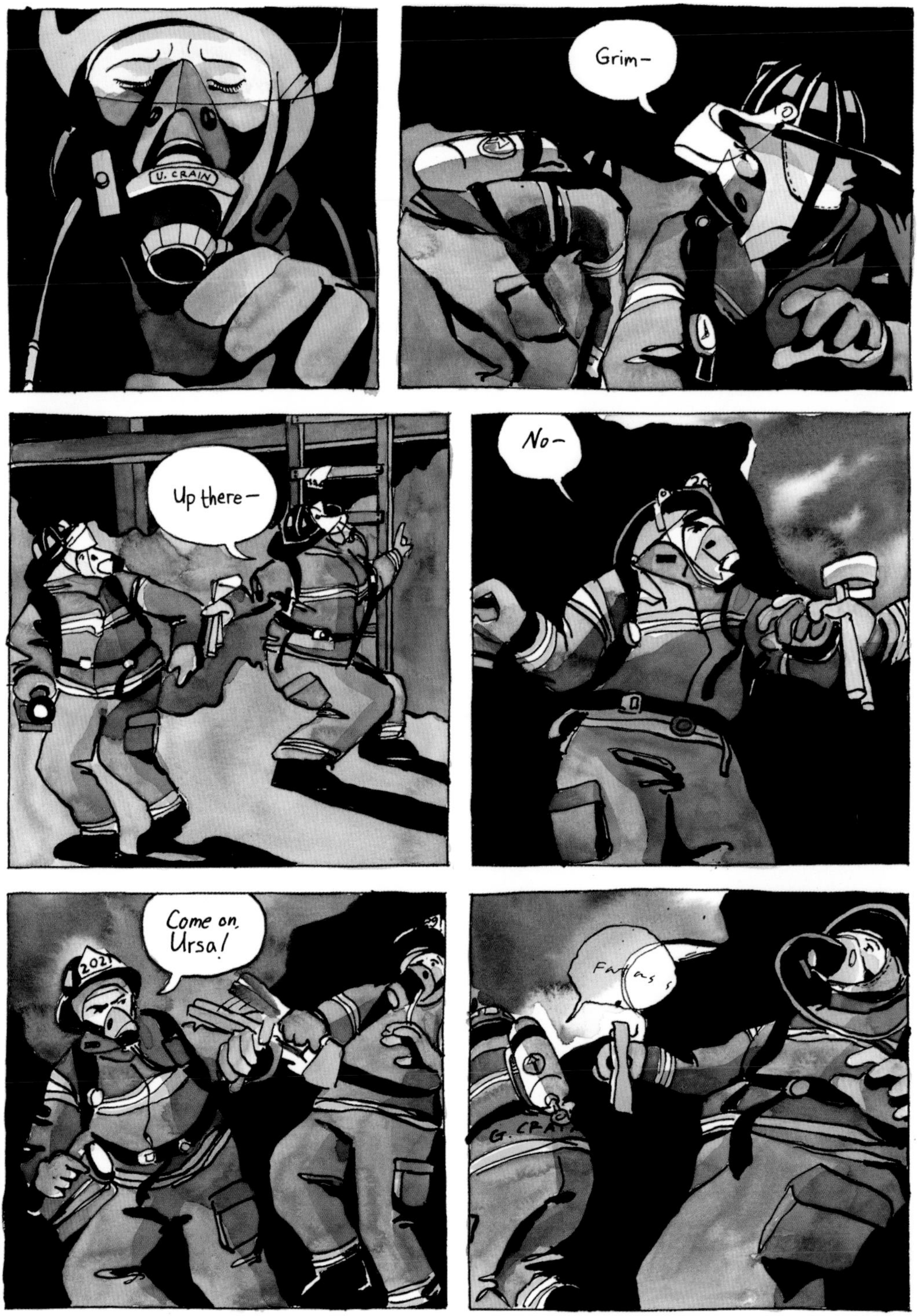
U. CRAIN
Grim–
Up there–
No–
Come on, Ursa!

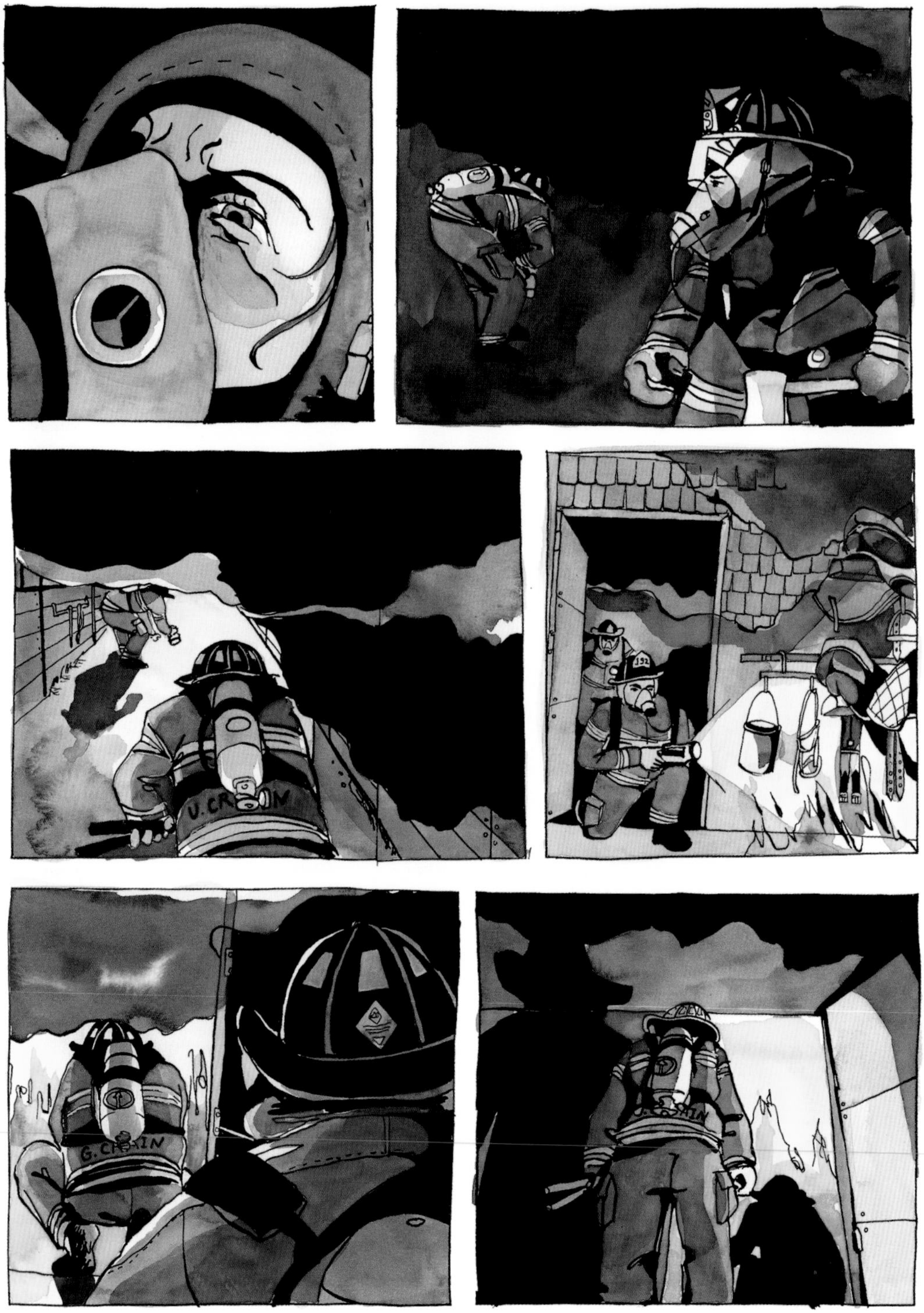

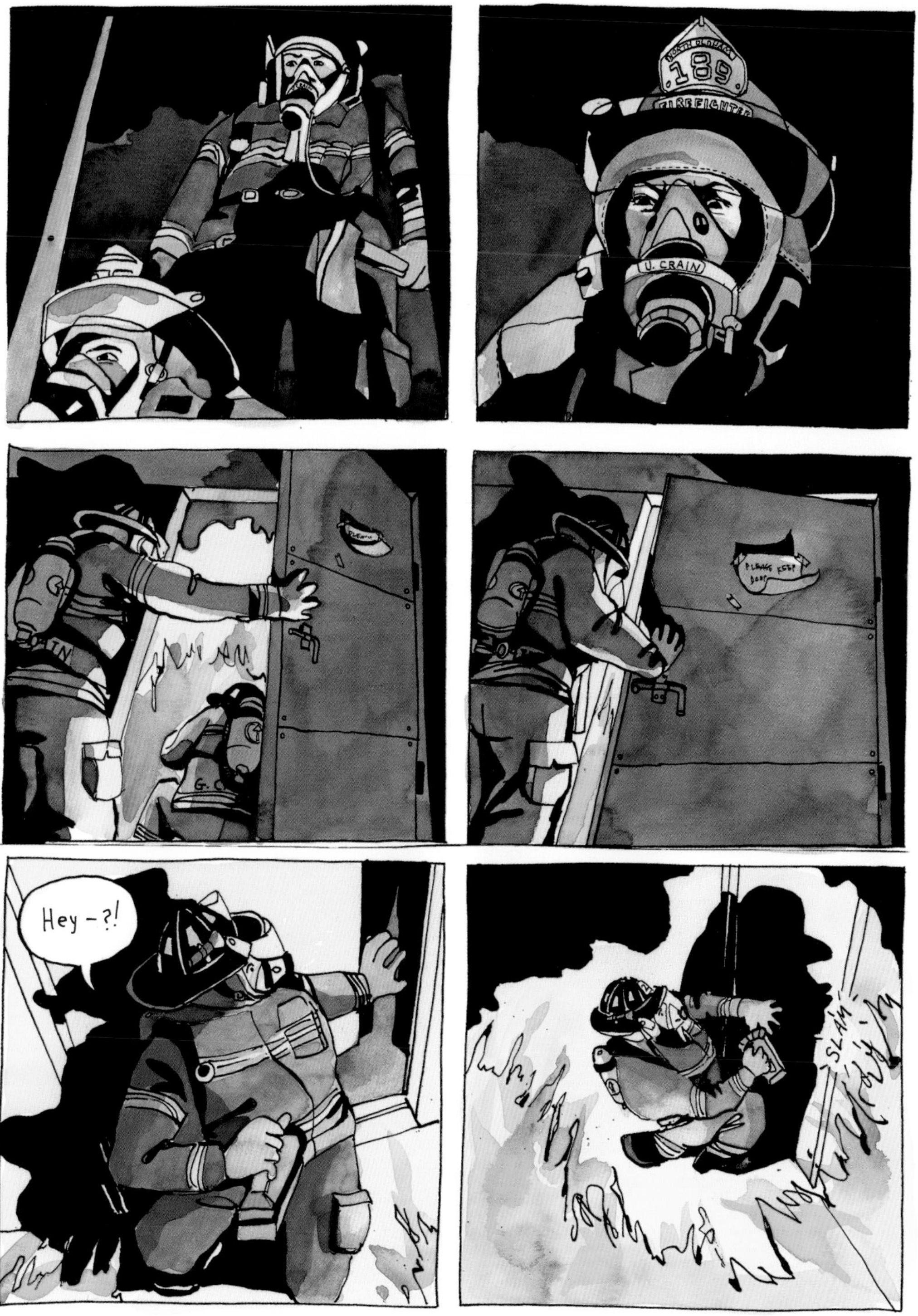
189
FIREFIGHTER
U. CRAIN
Hey – ?!
SLAM

Hey—
BANG
THUMP
KKFF
THUMP
BANG
CLACK
Ursa?! Help!
FIREFIGHTER
U. CRAIN
BANG
help
THUMP

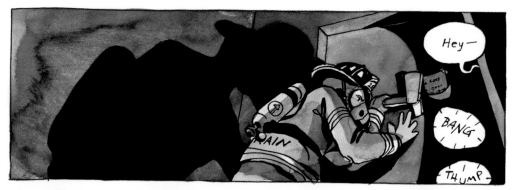

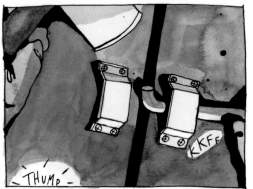

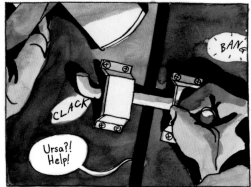

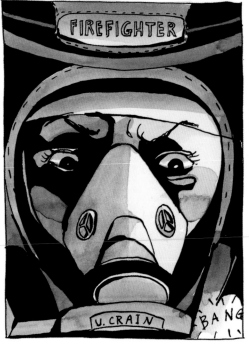

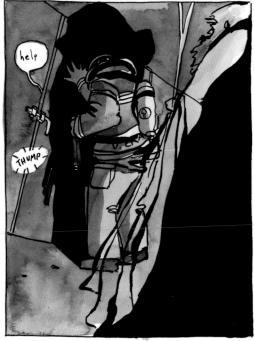

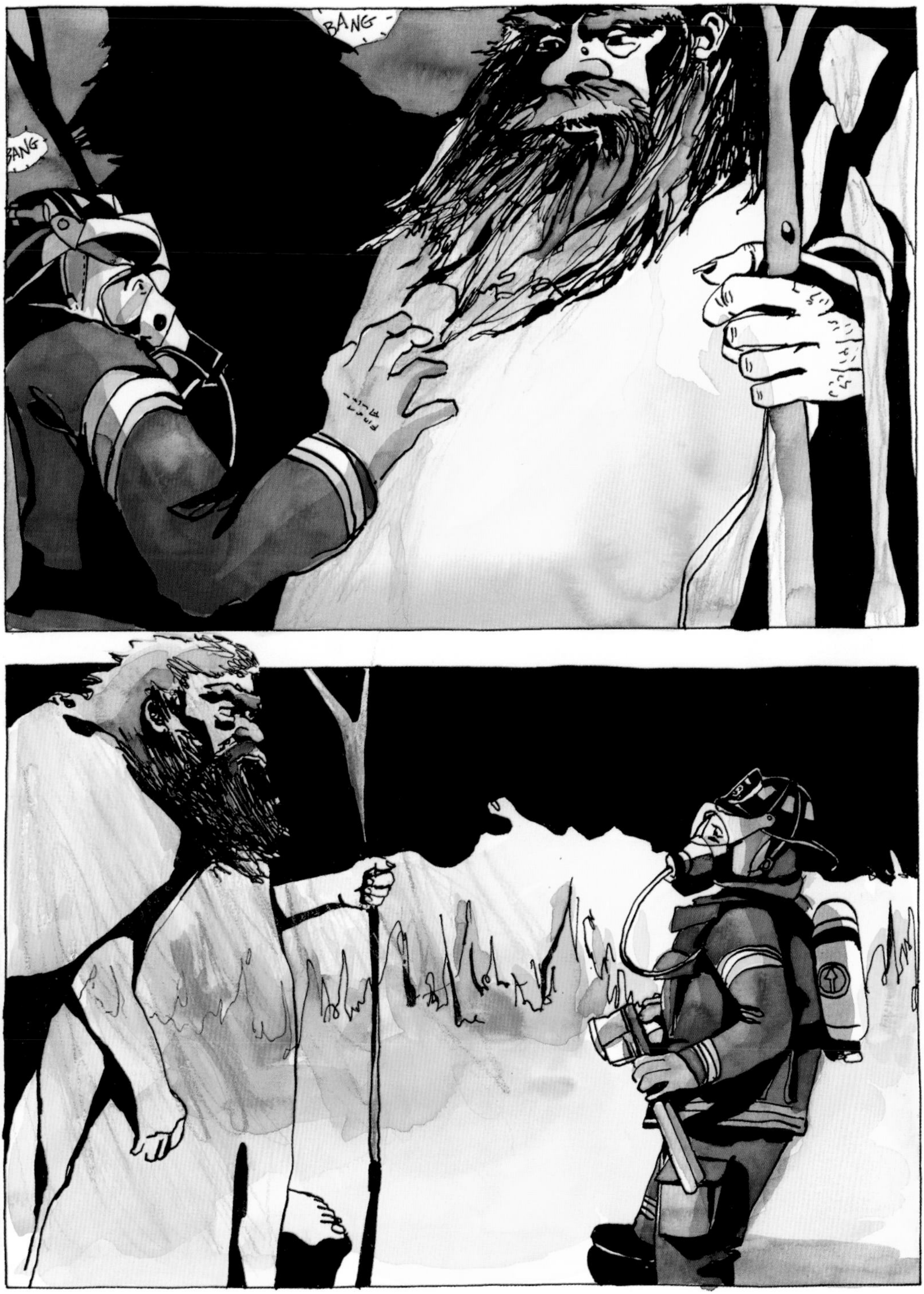
BANG
BANG

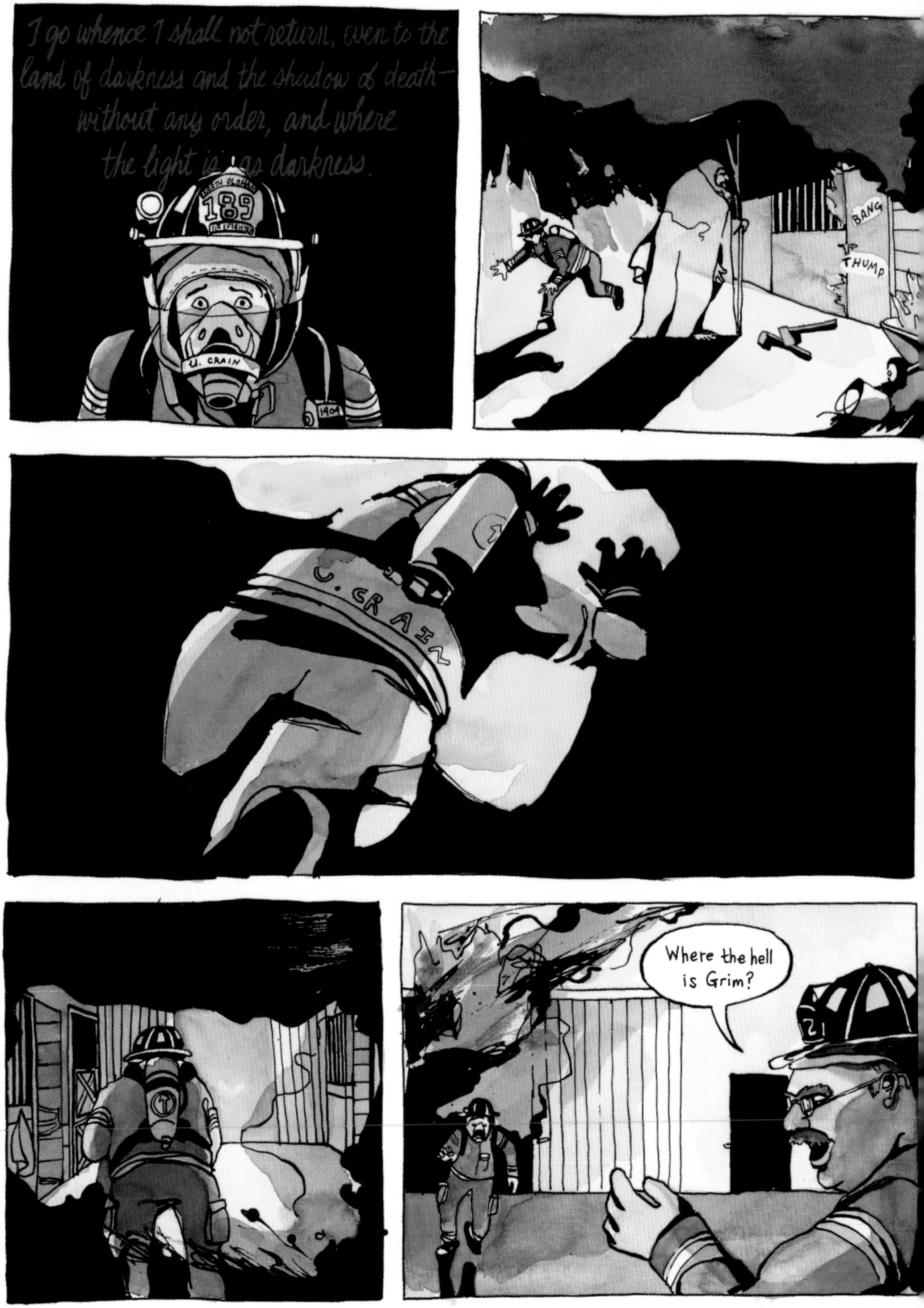
I go whence I shall not return, even to the land of darkness and the shadow of death— without any order, and where the light is as darkness.
189
U. CRAIN
BANG
THUMP
U. CRAIN
Where the hell is Grim?

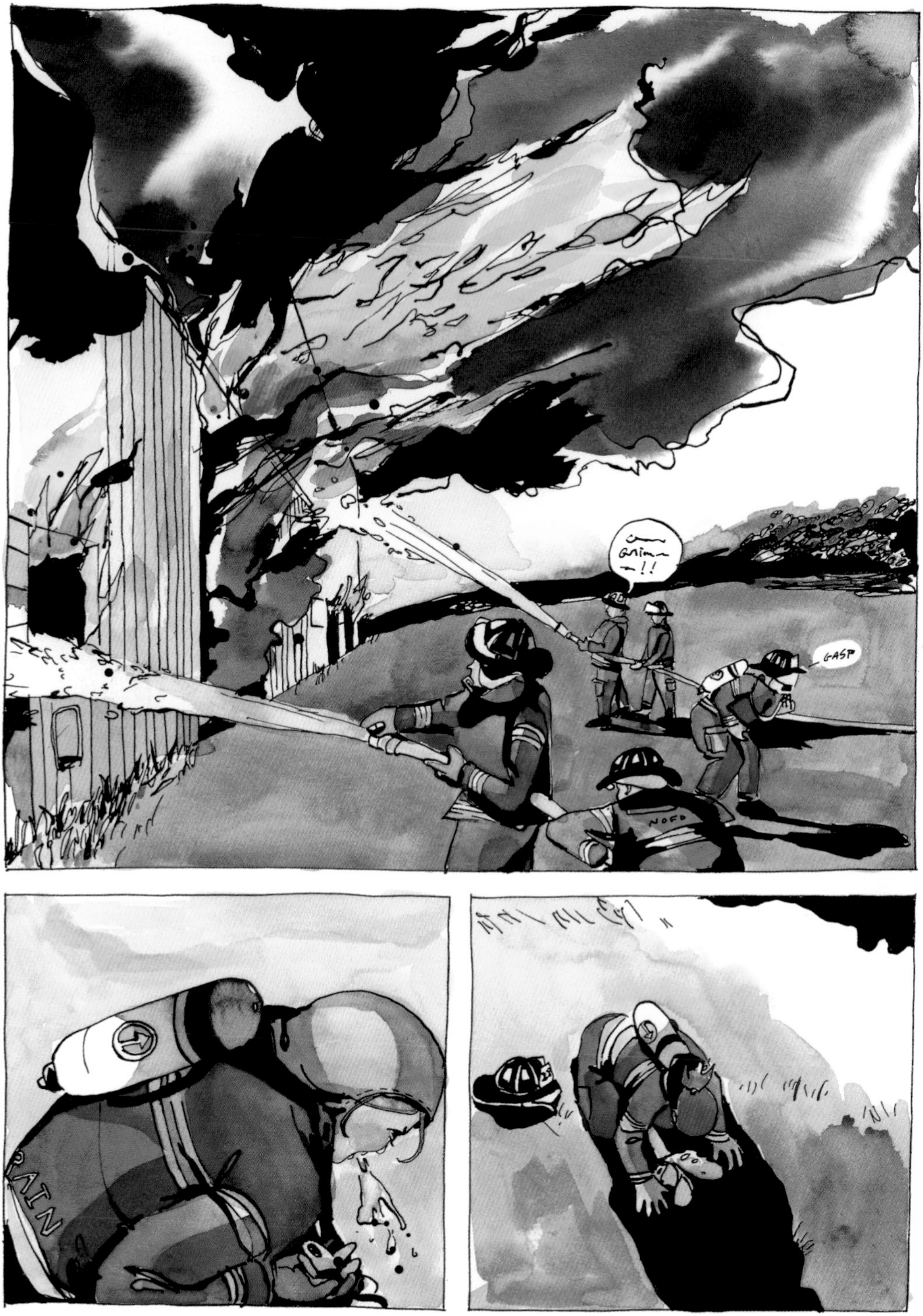
GASP
NOFD
RAIN

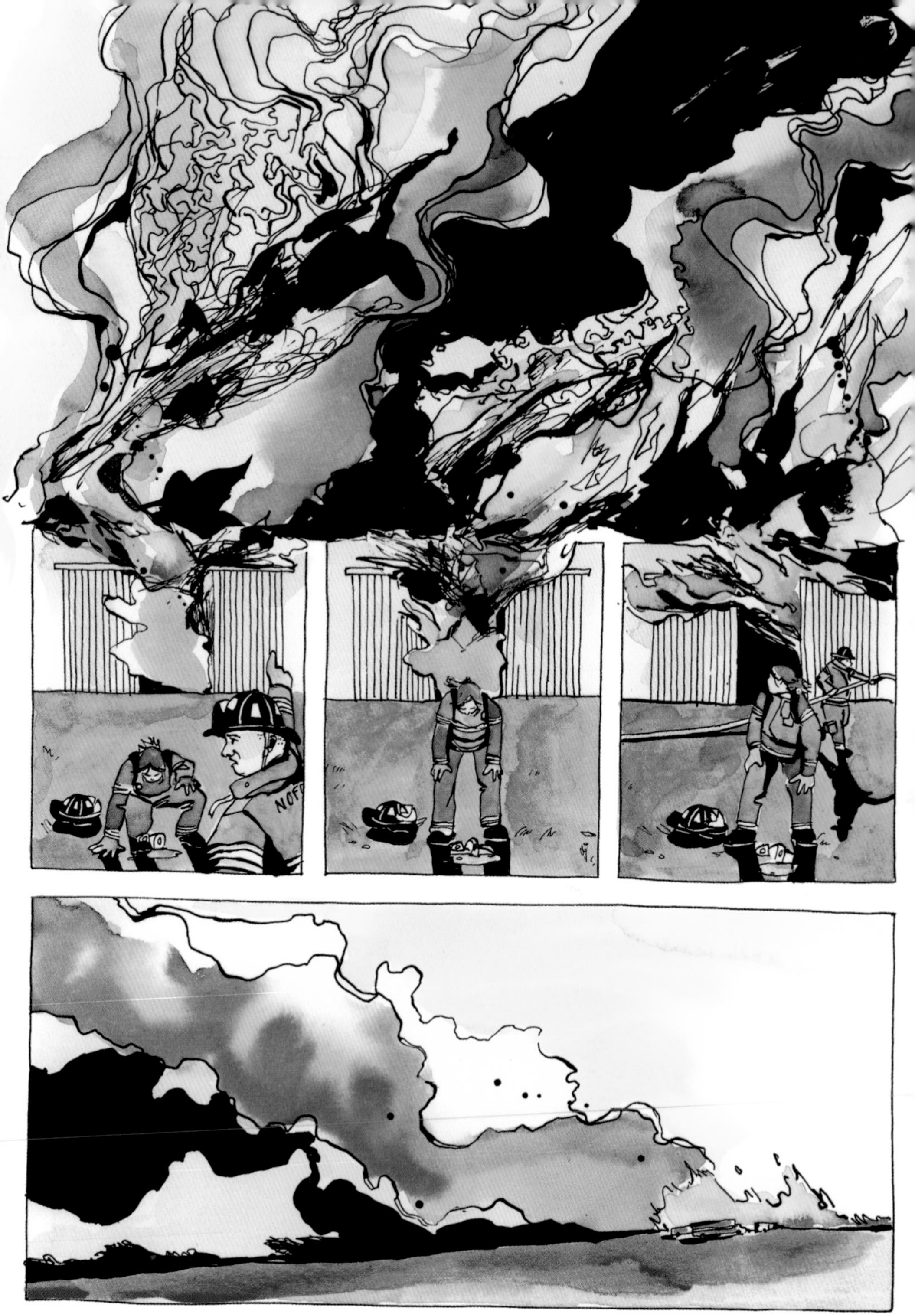

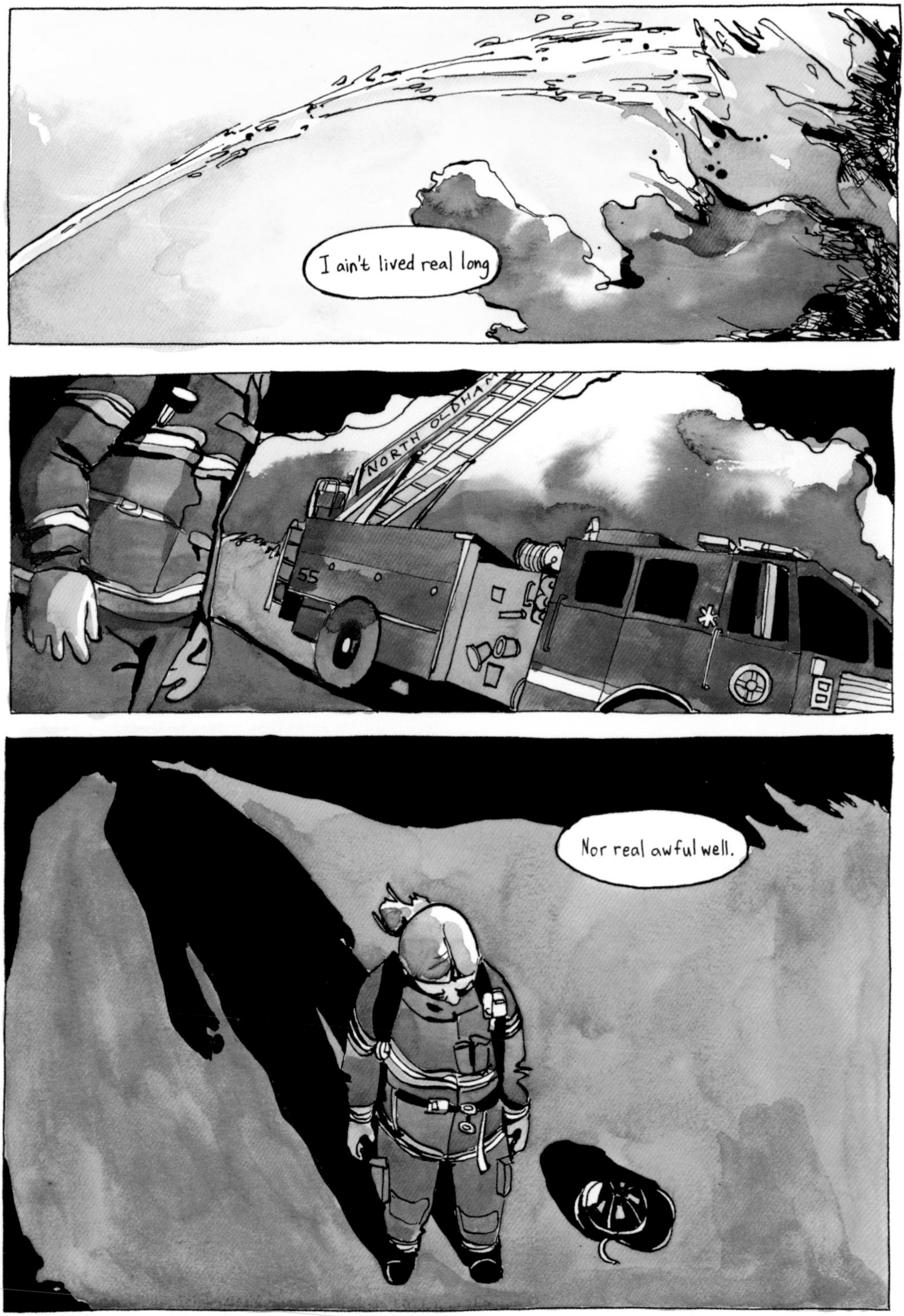
I ain't lived real long
NORTH OLDHA
55
Nor real awful well.

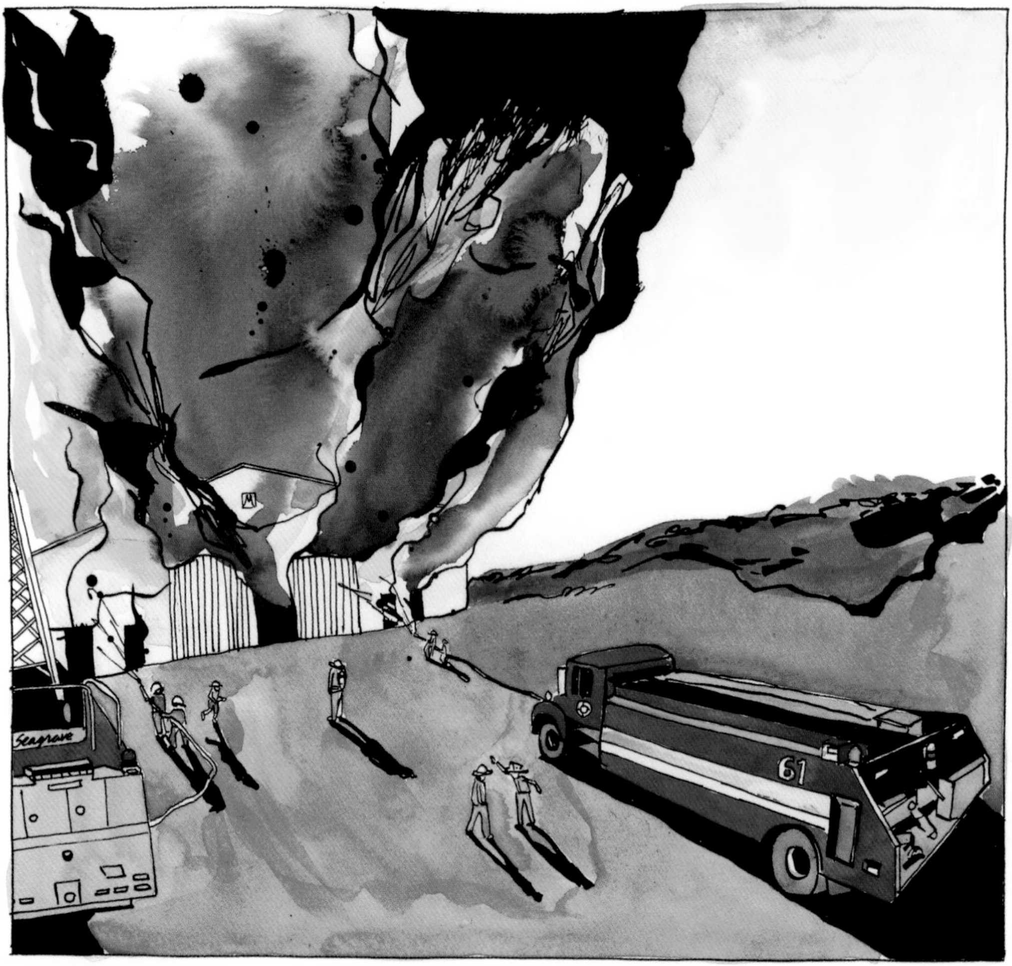
Seagrave
61

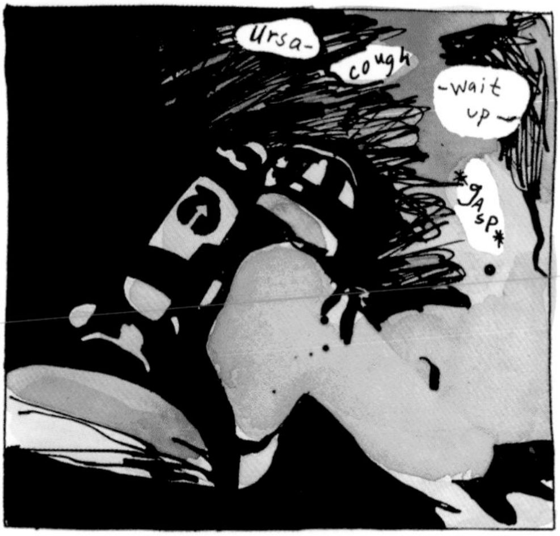
Ursa-
cough
-wait up-
gasp

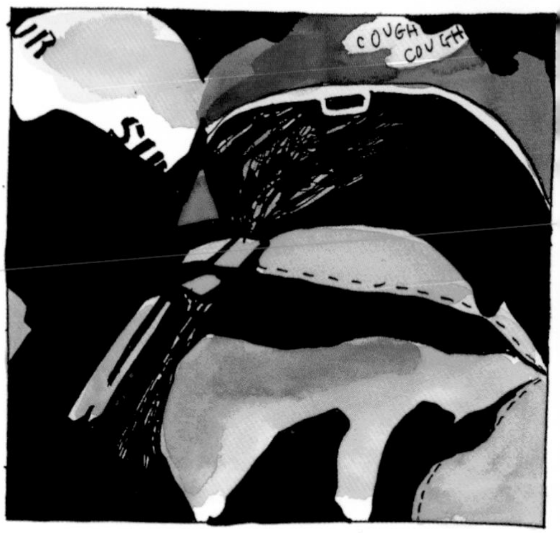
COUGH COUGH

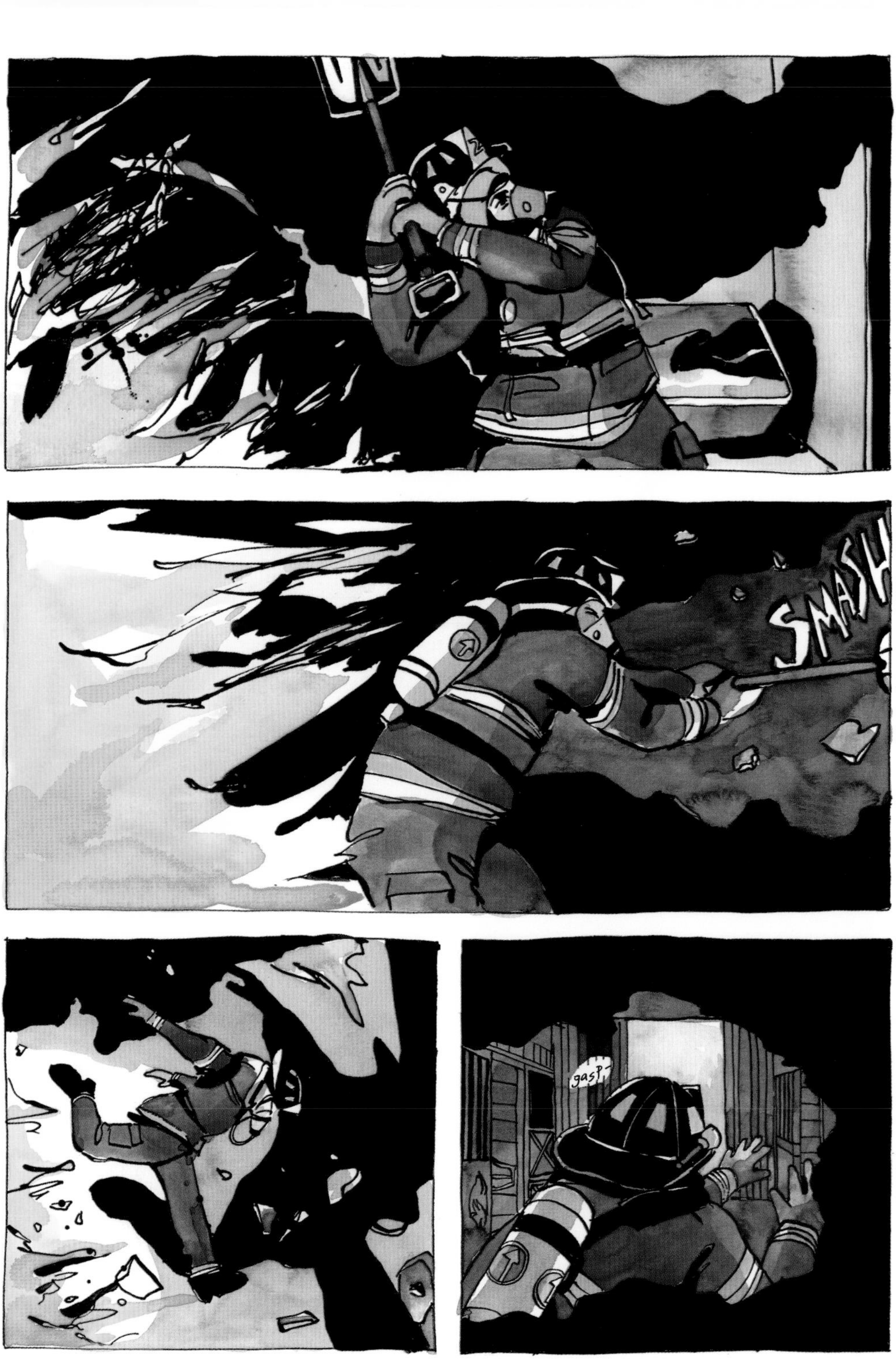
SMASH
gasp

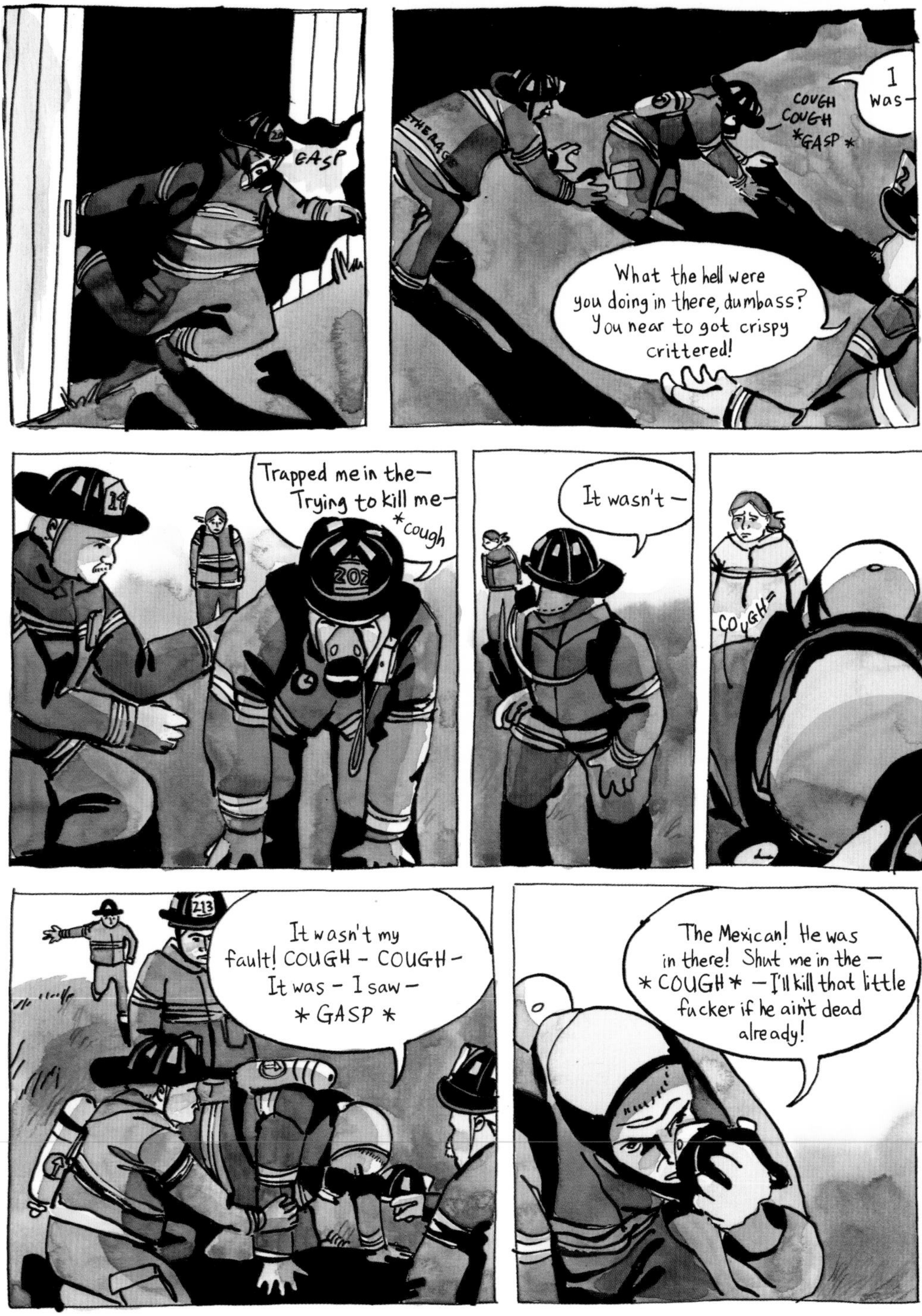
GASP
COUGH COUGH *GASP*
I Was–
What the hell were you doing in there, dumbass? You near to got crispy crittered!
Trapped me in the– Trying to kill me– *cough
It wasn't –
COUGH=
It wasn't my fault! COUGH – COUGH – It was – I saw – * GASP *
The Mexican! He was in there! Shut me in the – * COUGH * – I'll kill that little fucker if he ain't dead already!

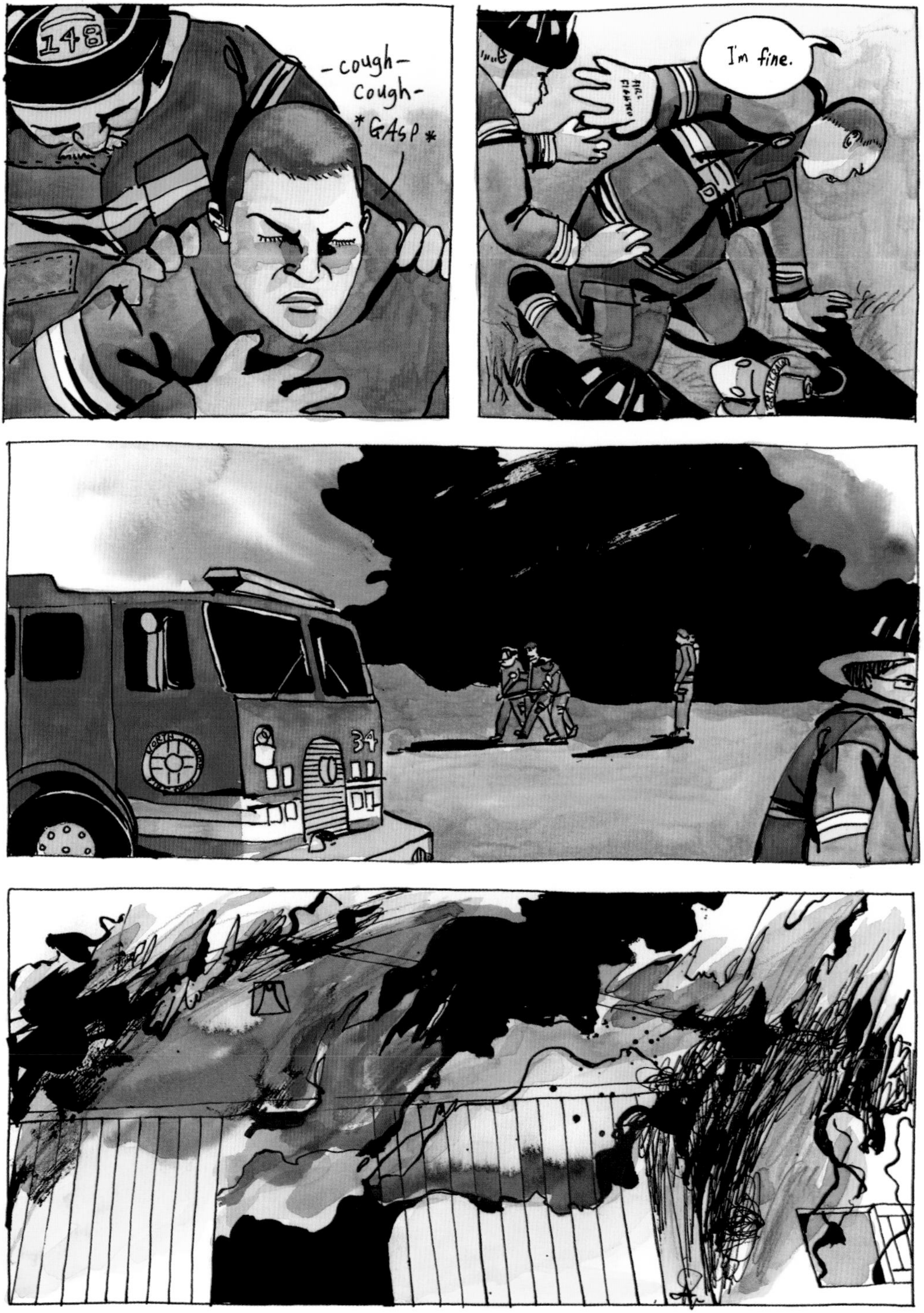
148
-cough-
cough-
GASP
I'm fine.
34

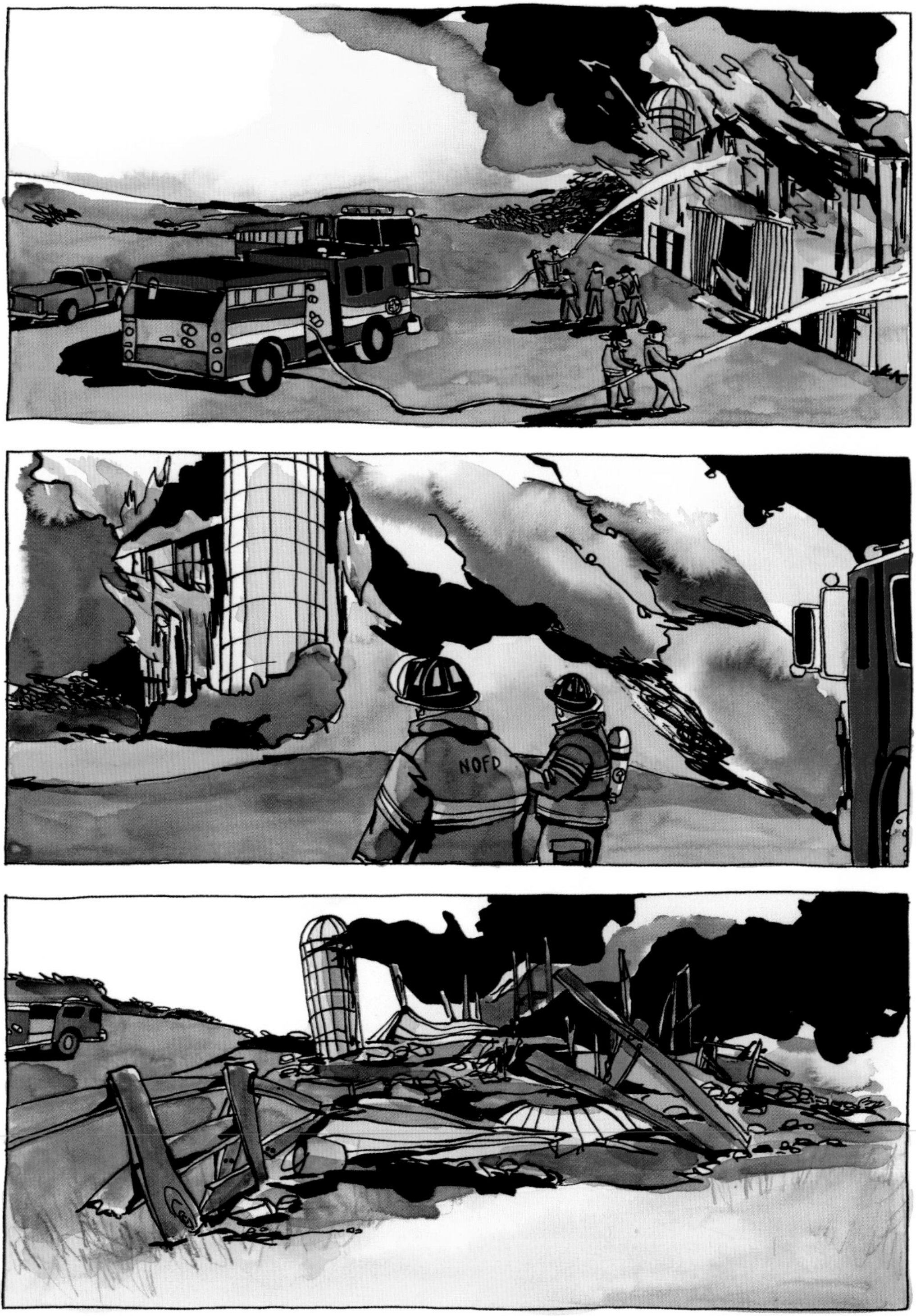
NOFD

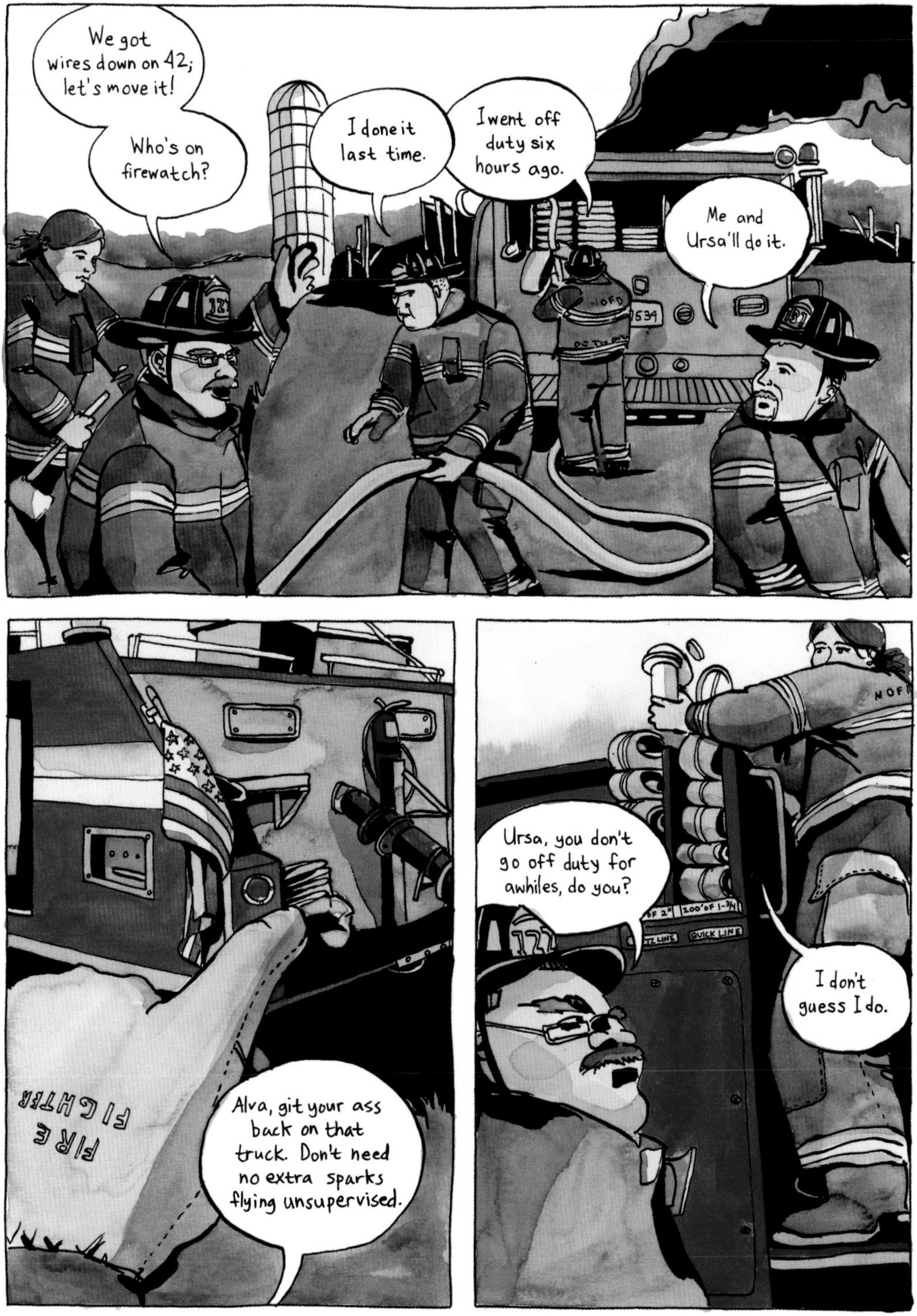
We got wires down on 42; let's move it!
Who's on firewatch?
I done it last time.
I went off duty six hours ago.
Me and Ursa'll do it.
Alva, git your ass back on that truck. Don't need no extra sparks flying unsupervised.
Ursa, you don't go off duty for awhiles, do you?
I don't guess I do.

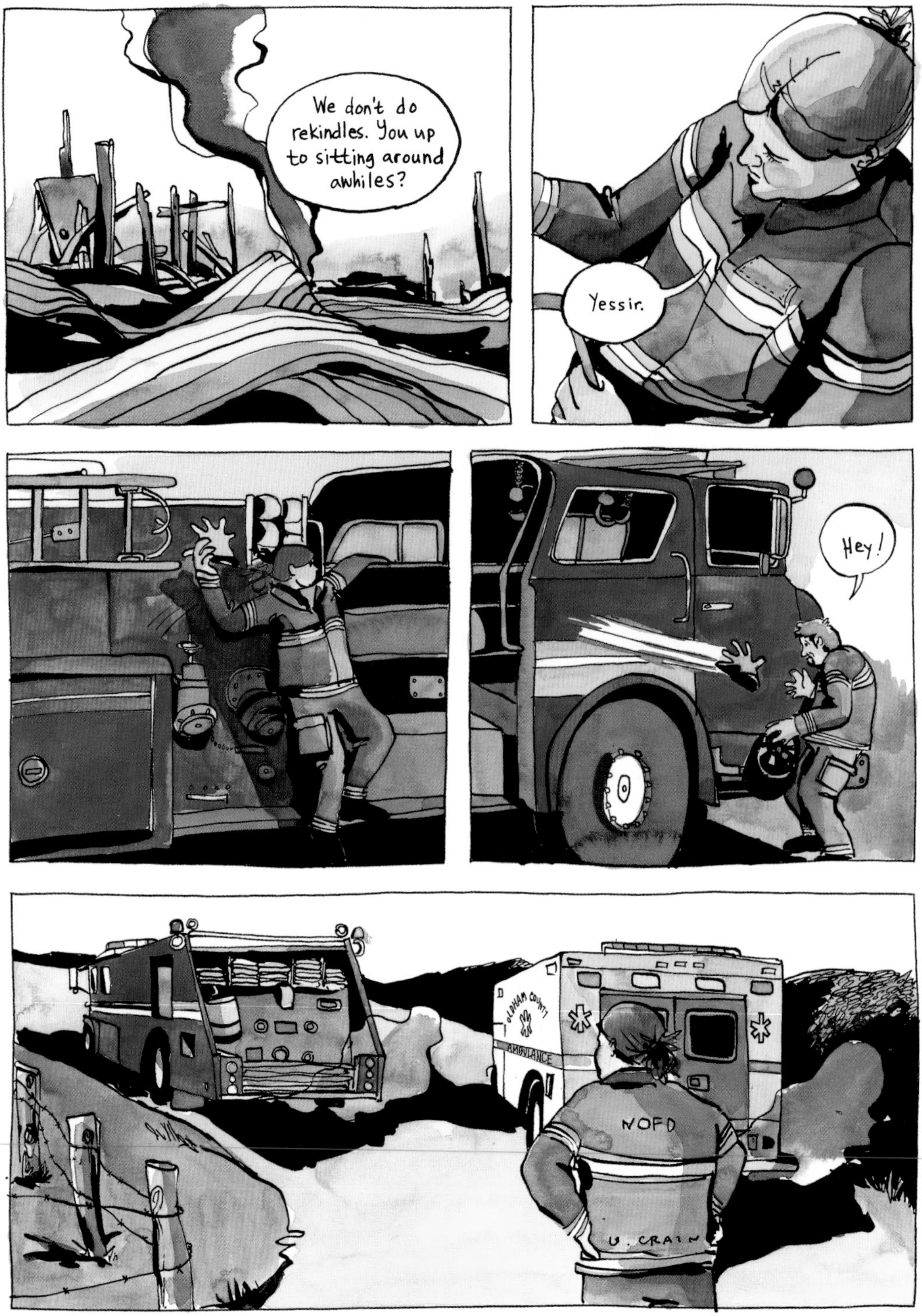
We don't do rekindles. You up to sitting around awhiles?
Yessir.
Hey!
OLDHAM COUNTY
AMBULANCE
NOFD
U. CRAIN

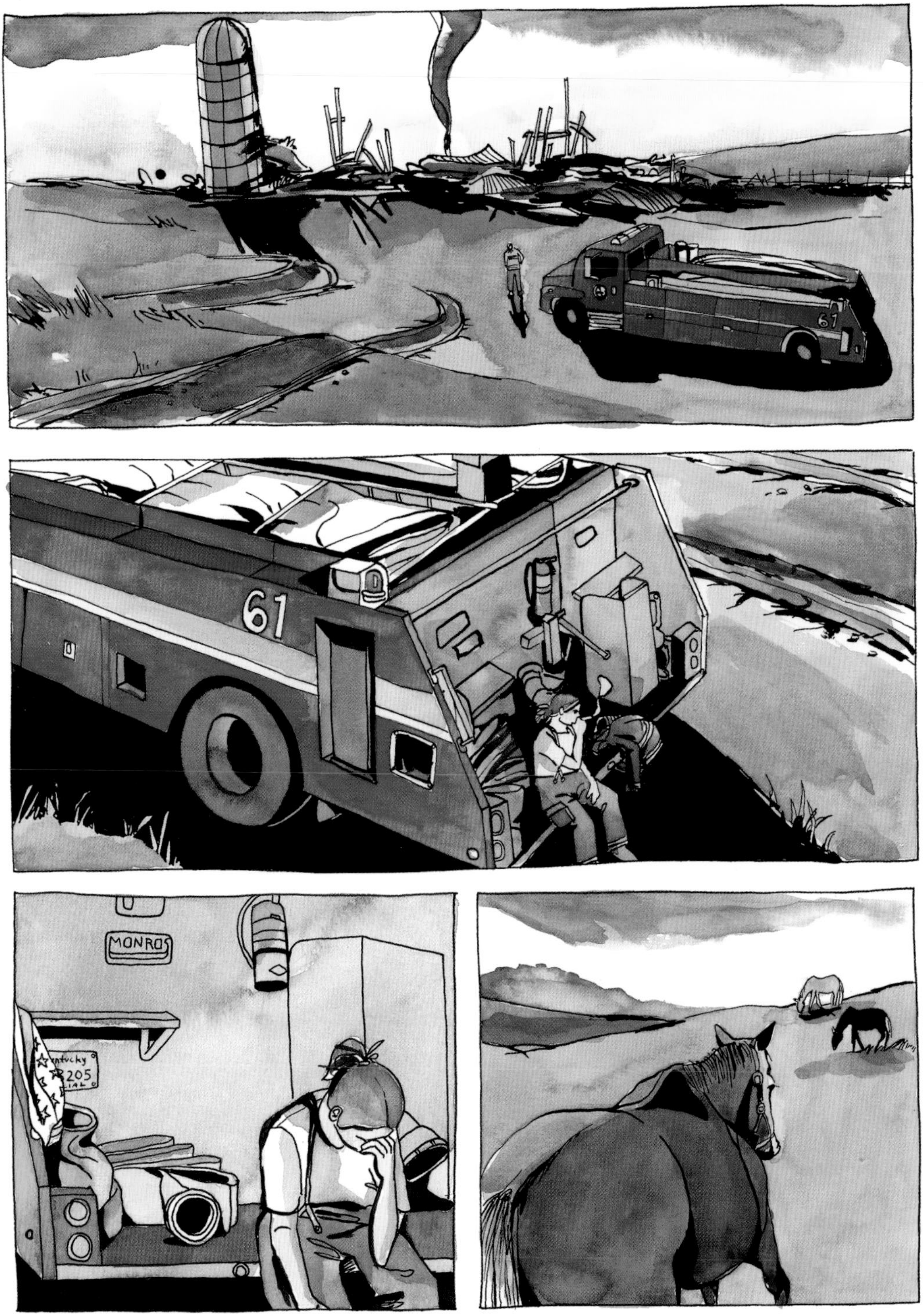
61
61
MONROE
entucky
205
IAL

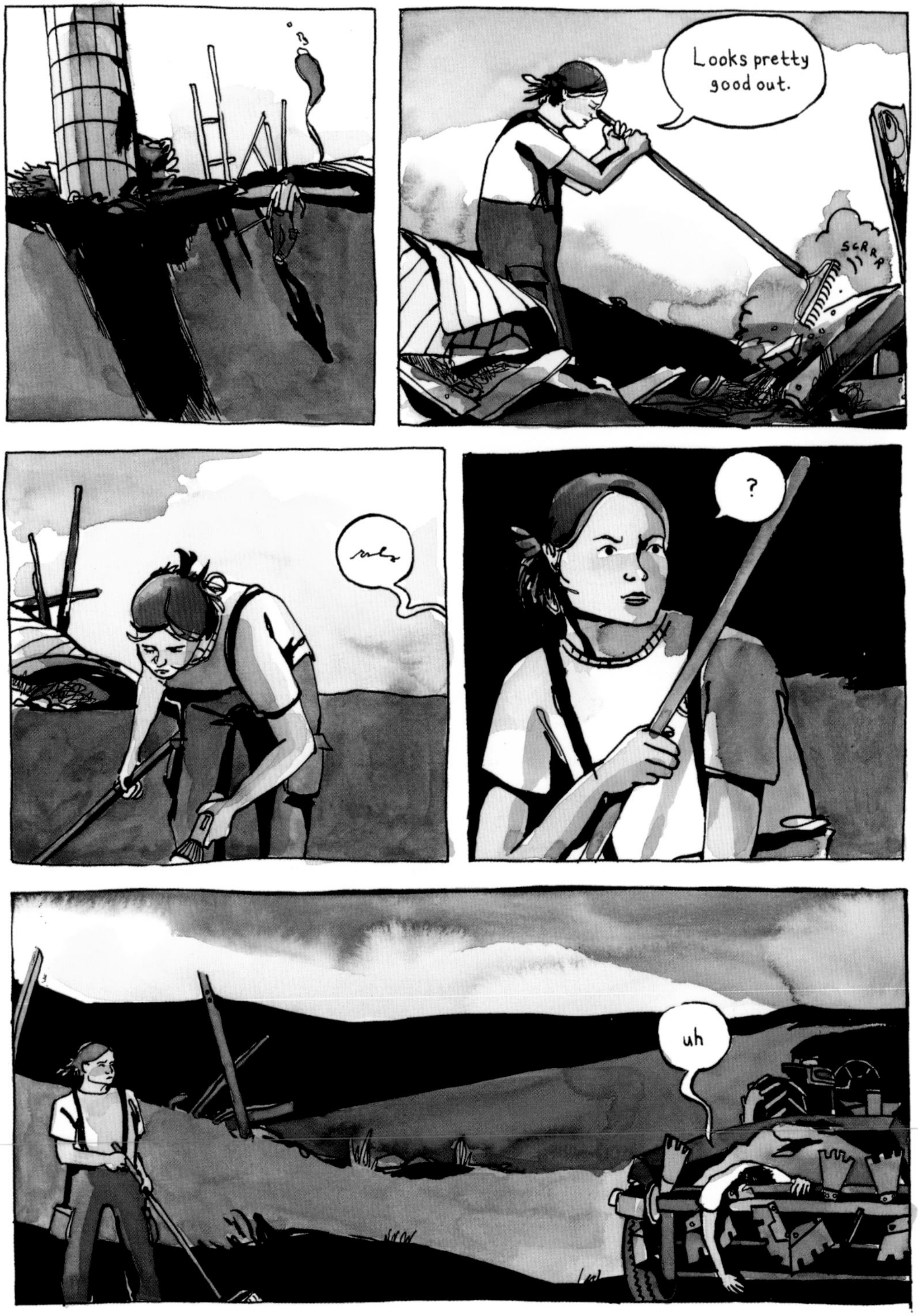
Looks pretty good out.
SCRRR
?
uh

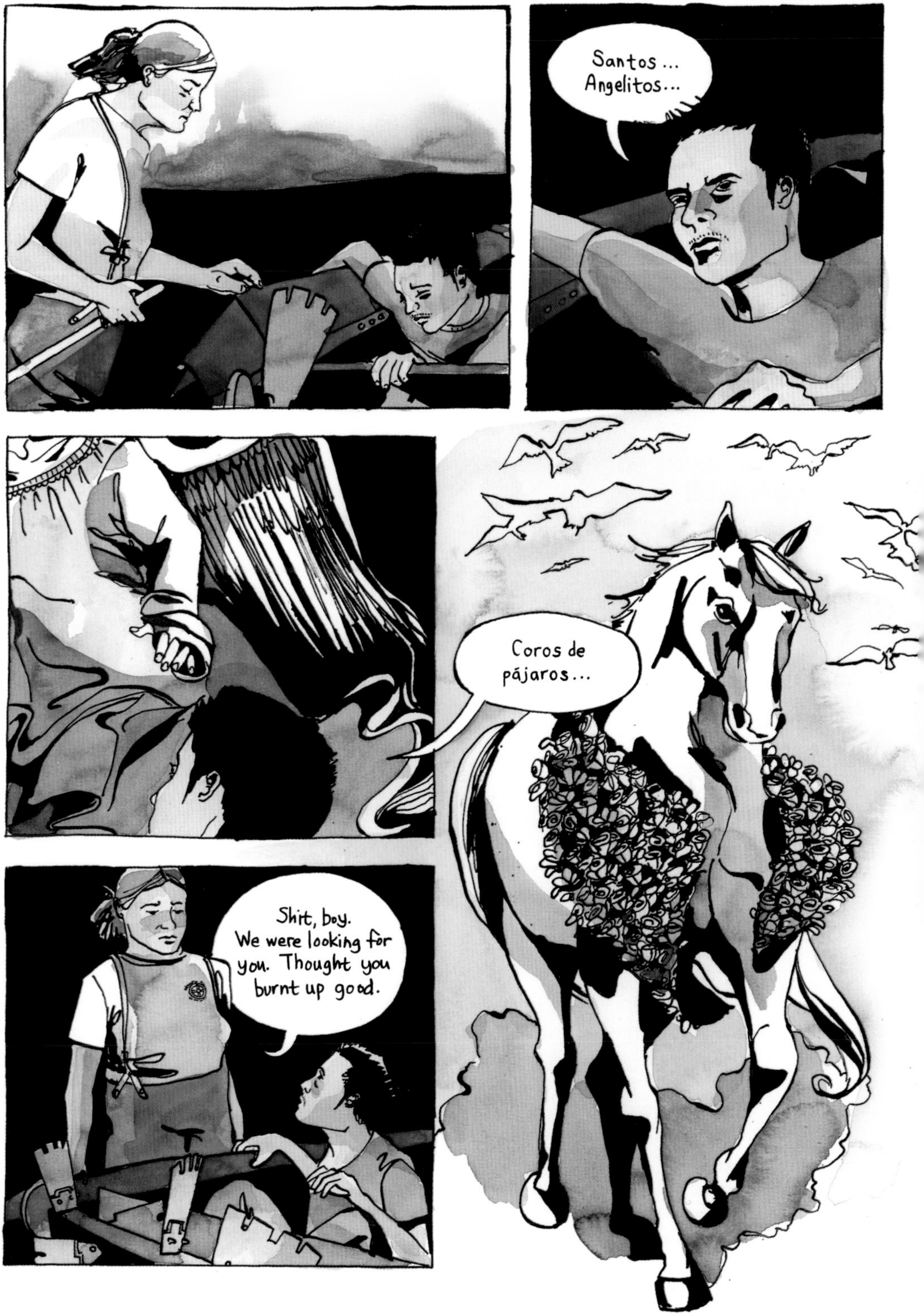
Santos ...
Angelitos...
Coros de pájaros...
Shit, boy. We were looking for you. Thought you burnt up good.

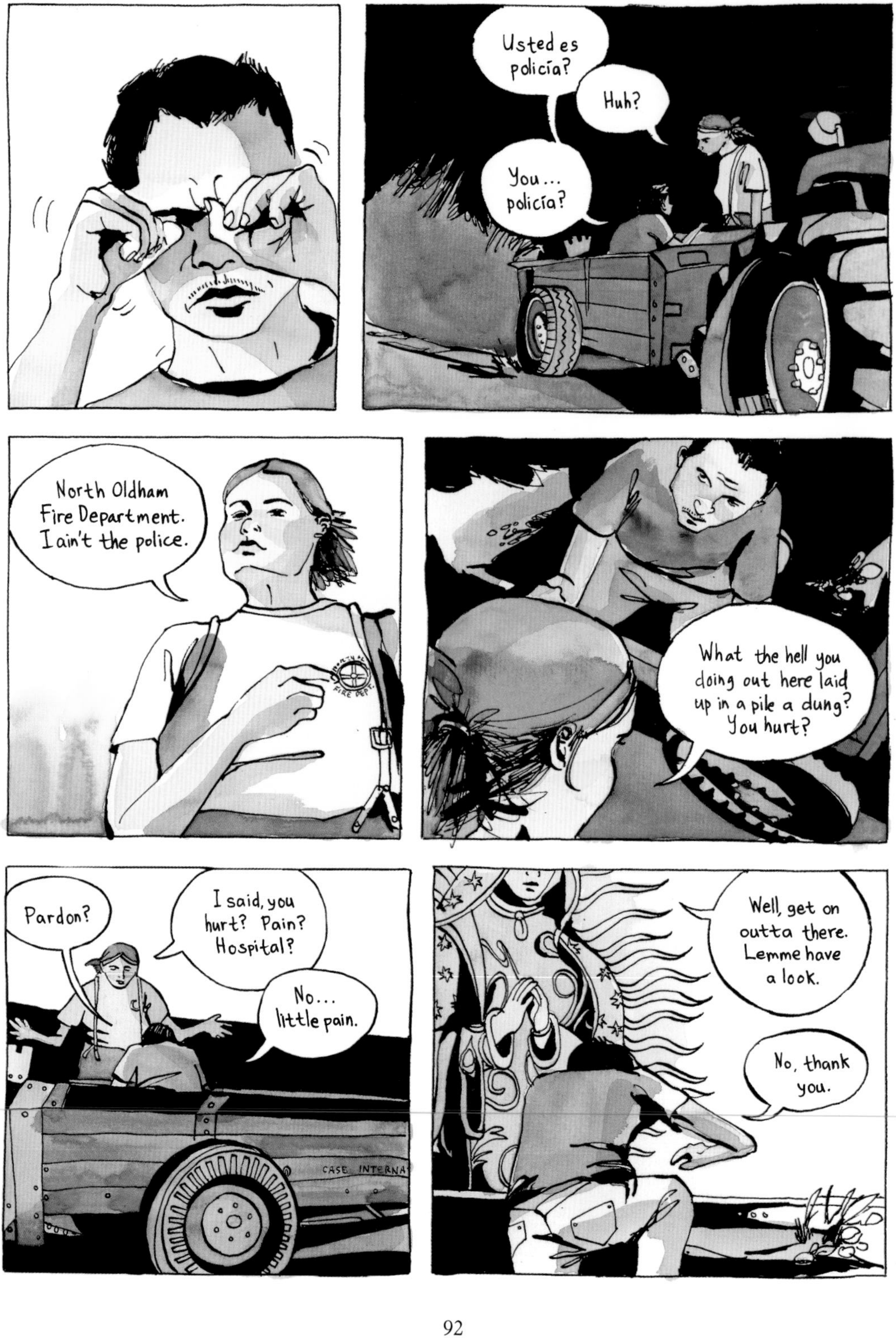
Usted es policía?
Huh?
You... policía?
North Oldham Fire Department. I ain't the police.
What the hell you doing out here laid up in a pile a dung? You hurt?
Pardon?
I said, you hurt? Pain? Hospital?
No... little pain.
CASE INTERNA
Well, get on outta there. Lemme have a look.
No, thank you.

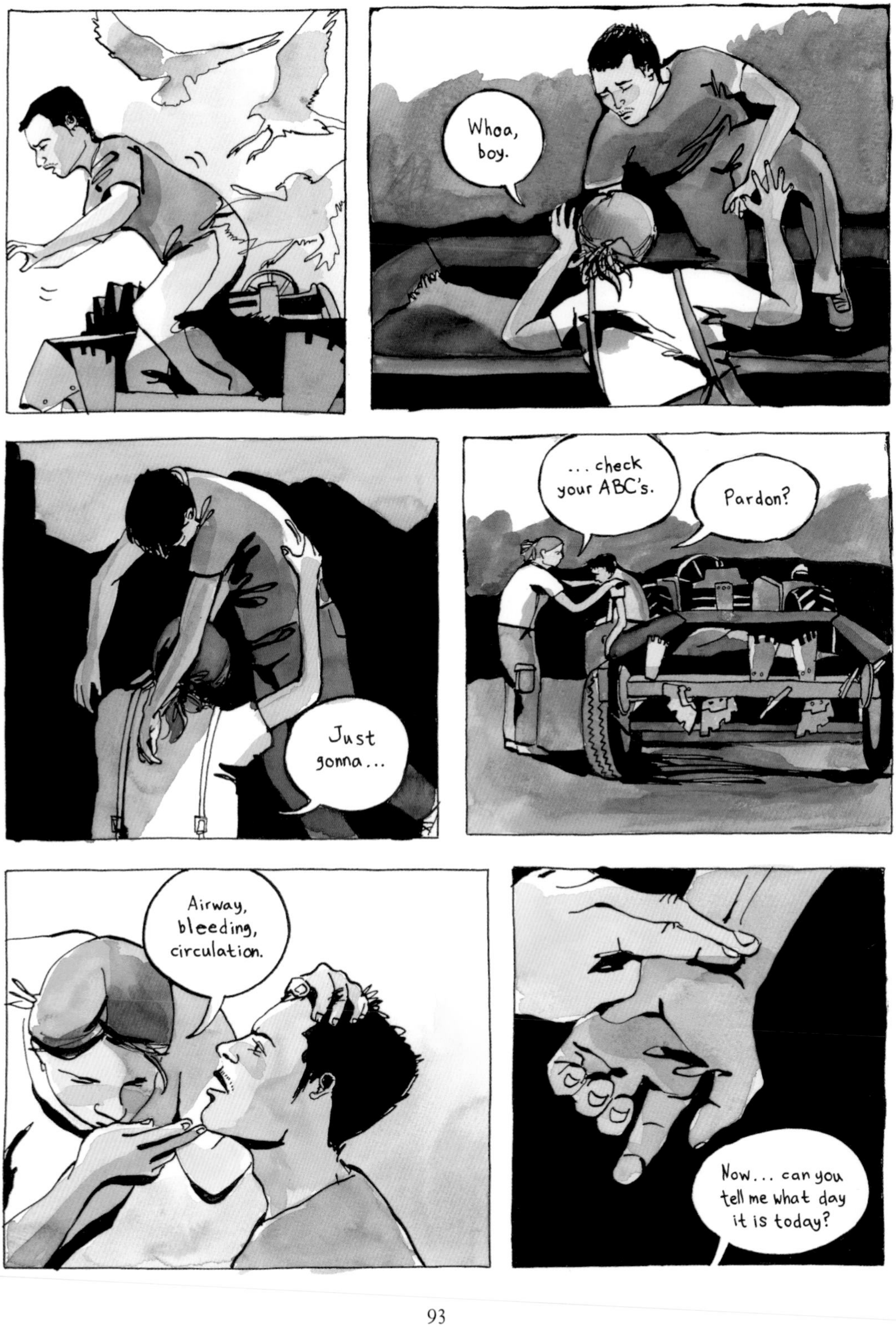
Whoa, boy.
Just gonna...
...check your ABC's.
Pardon?
Airway, bleeding, circulation.
Now... can you tell me what day it is today?

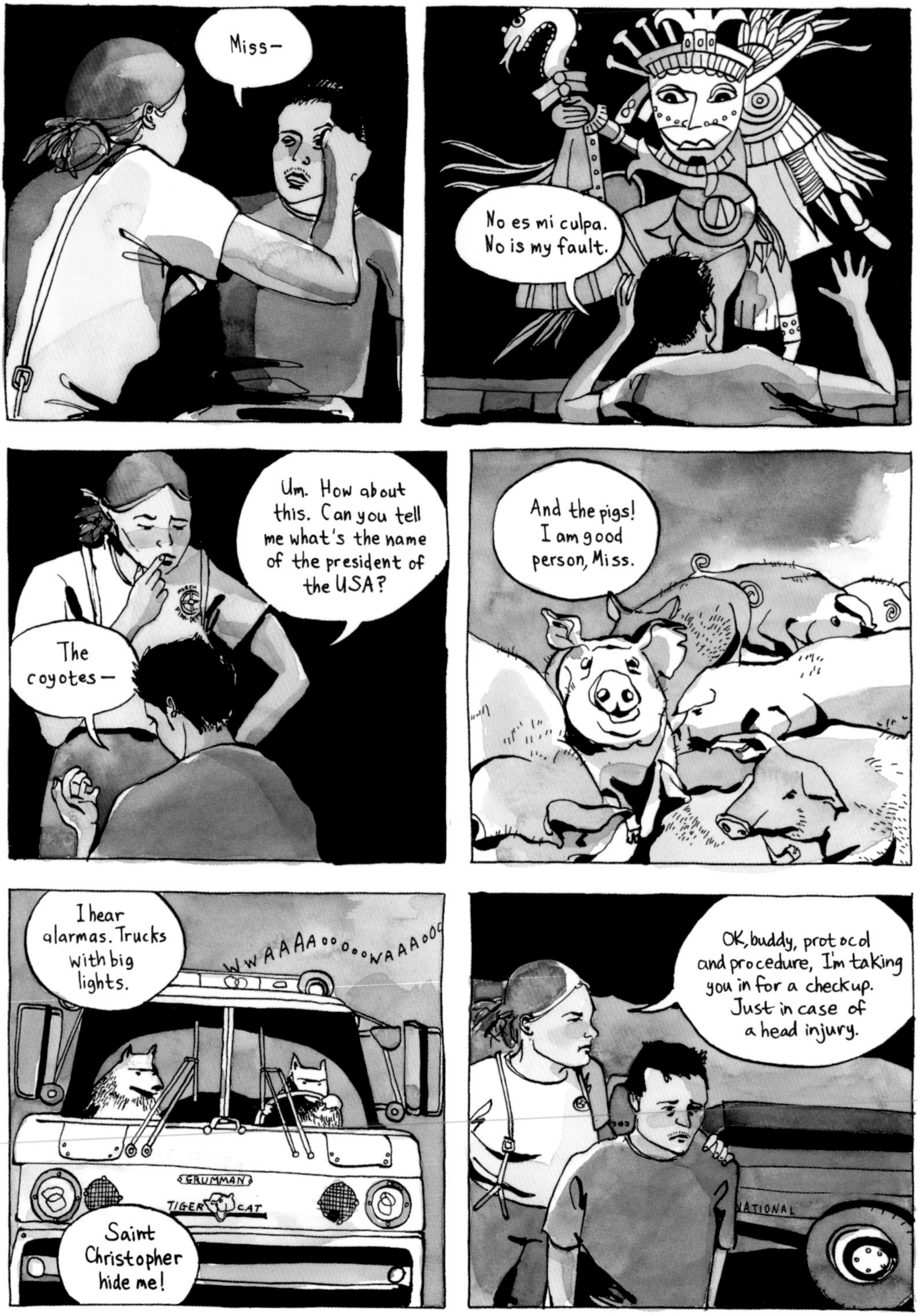
Miss–
No es mi culpa. No is my fault.
Um. How about this. Can you tell me what's the name of the president of the USA?
The coyotes–
And the pigs! I am good person, Miss.
I hear alarmas. Trucks with big lights.
WWAAAAoooooWAAAOO
GRUMMAN
TIGER CAT
Saint Christopher hide me!
OK, buddy, protocol and procedure, I'm taking you in for a checkup. Just in case of a head injury.
NATIONAL

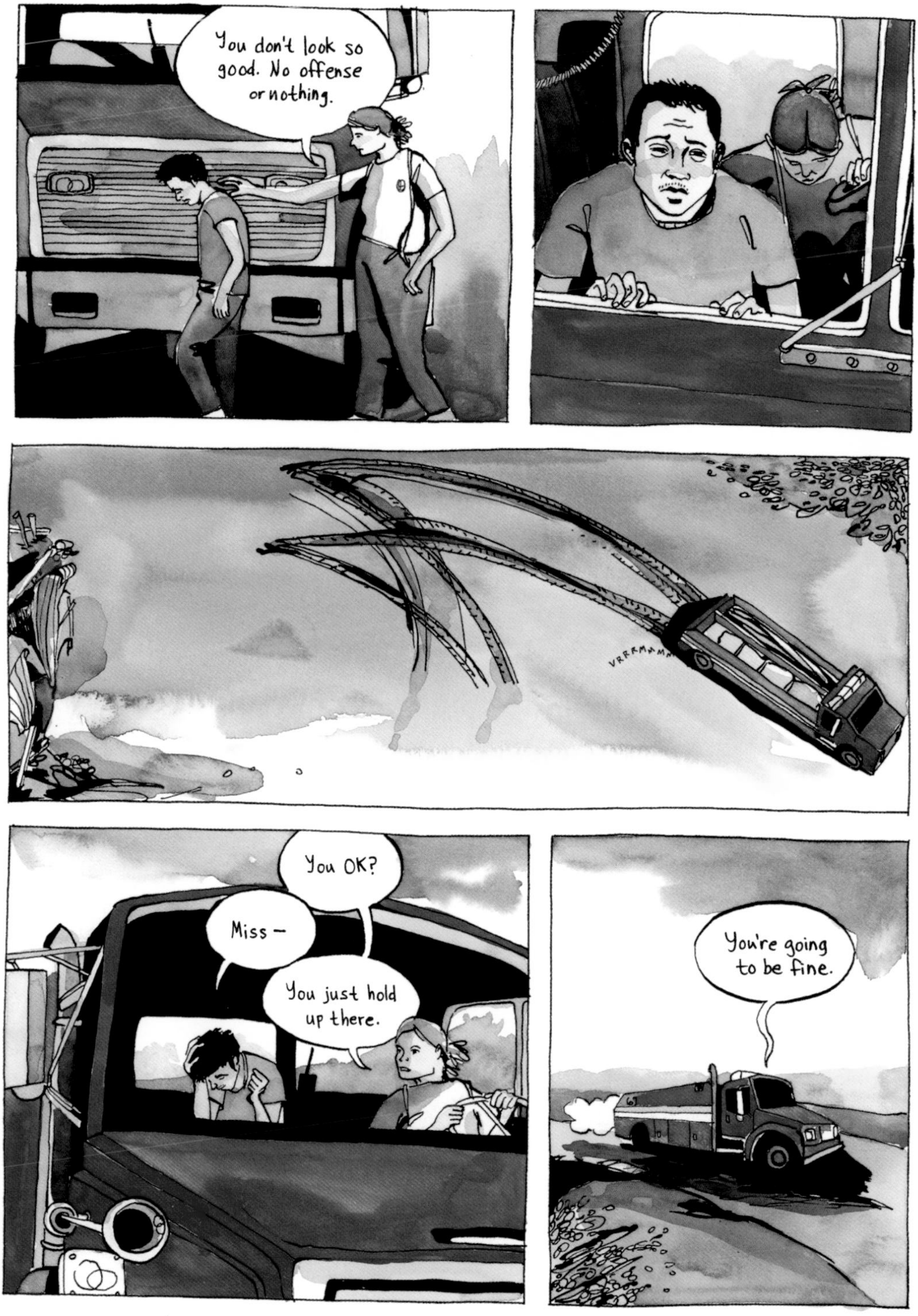
You don't look so good. No offense or nothing.
VRRRMMMM
You OK?
Miss –
You just hold up there.
You're going to be fine.

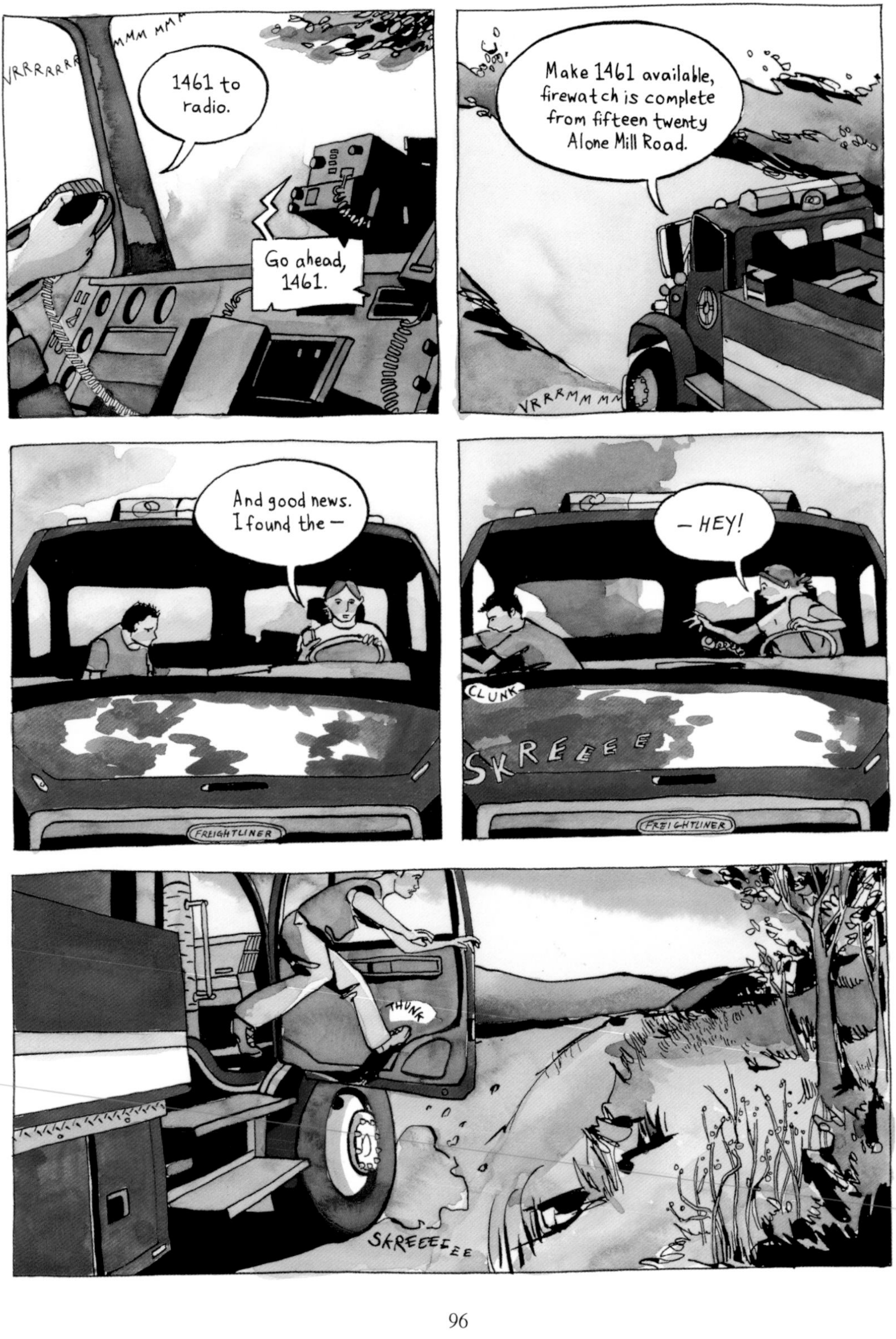
VRRRRRRR
MMM MM
1461 to radio.
Go ahead, 1461.
Make 1461 available, firewatch is complete from fifteen twenty Alone Mill Road.
VRRRMM MM
And good news. I found the —
FREIGHTLINER
— HEY!
CLUNK
SKREEEEE
FREIGHTLINER
THUNK
SKREEEEEE

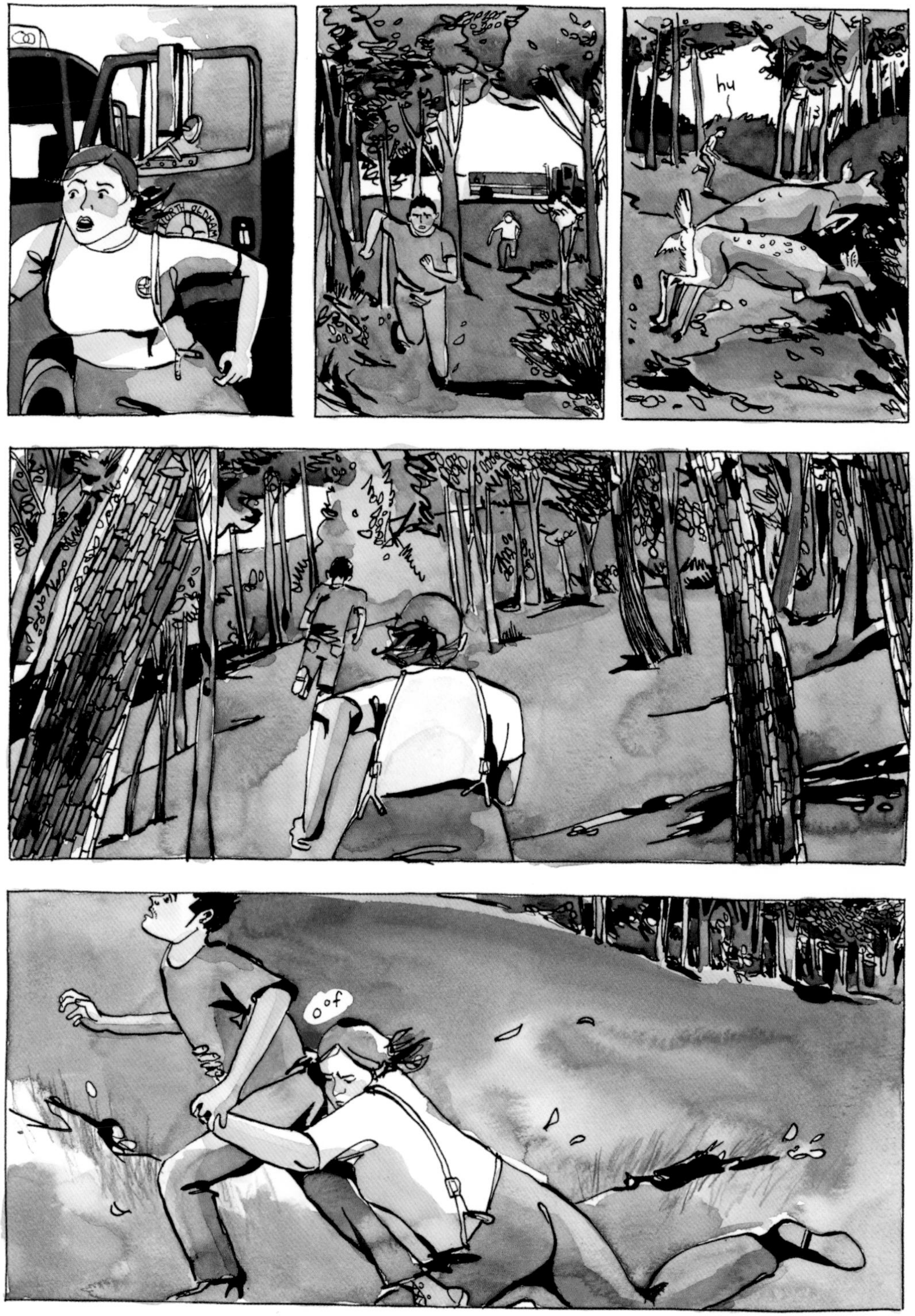
NORTH OLDHAM
hu
oof

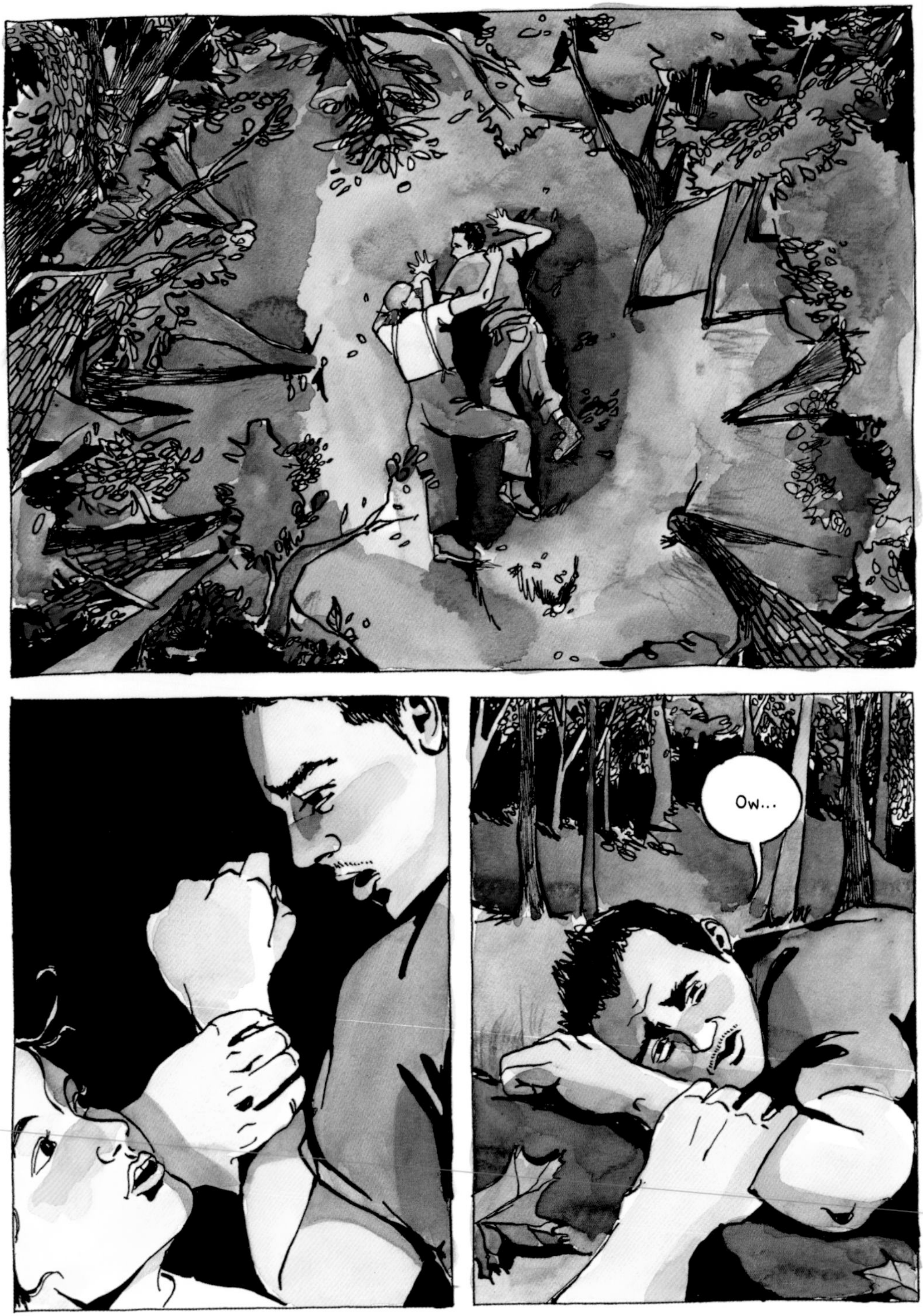
Ow...

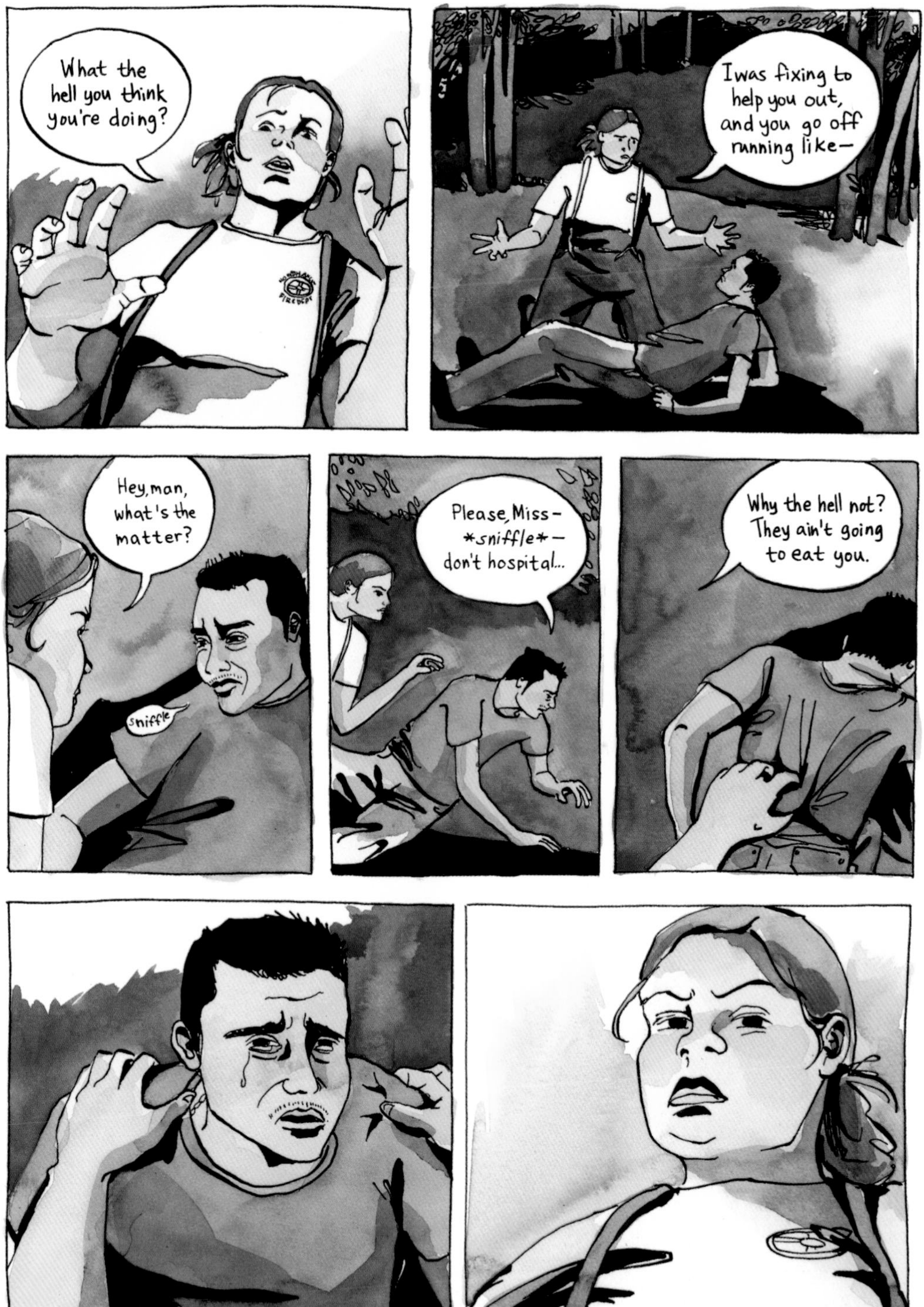

What the hell you think you're doing?
I was fixing to help you out, and you go off running like—
Hey, man, what's the matter?
sniffle
Please, Miss— *sniffle*— don't hospital...
Why the hell not? They ain't going to eat you.

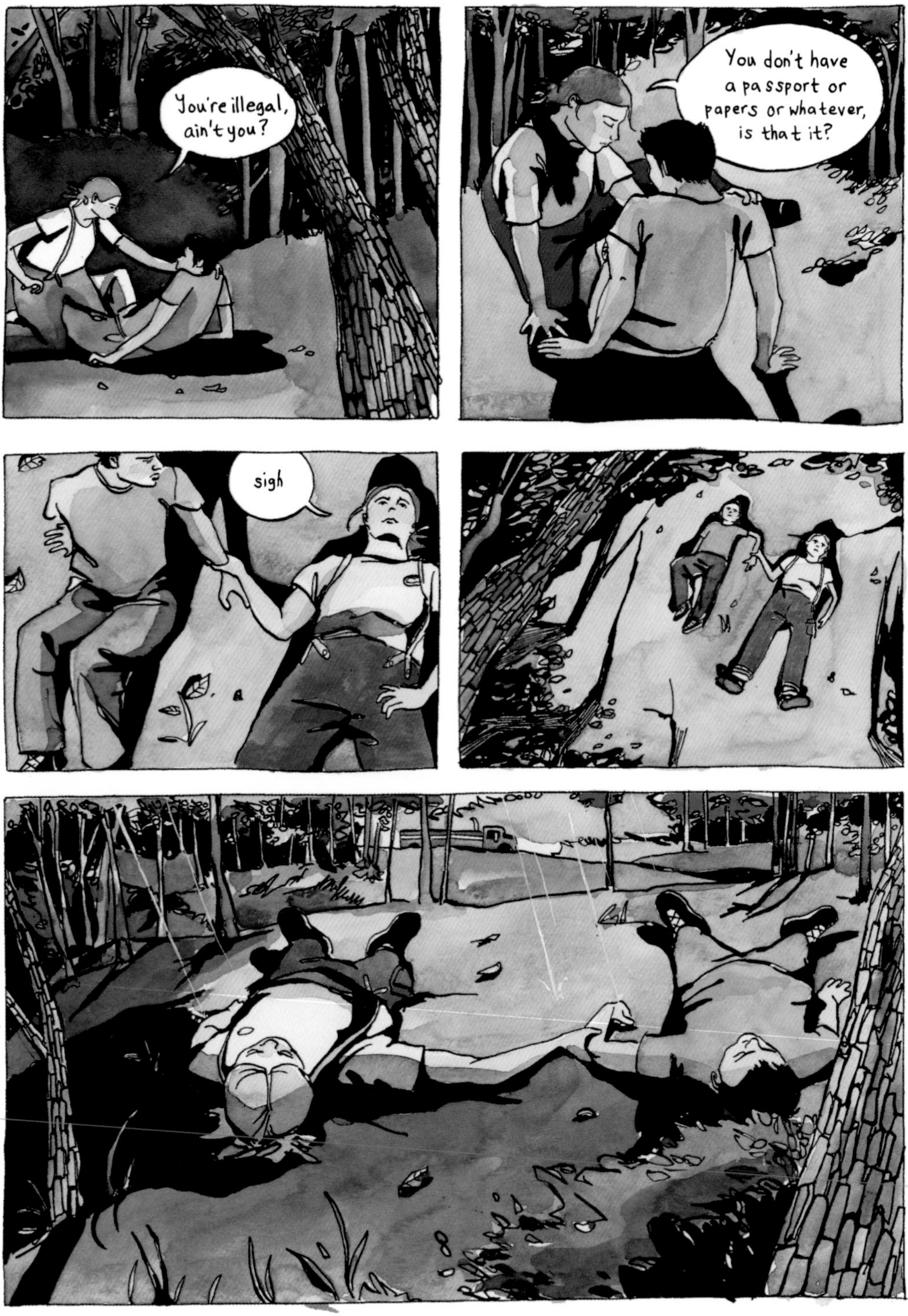
You're illegal, ain't you?
You don't have a passport or papers or whatever, is that it?
sigh

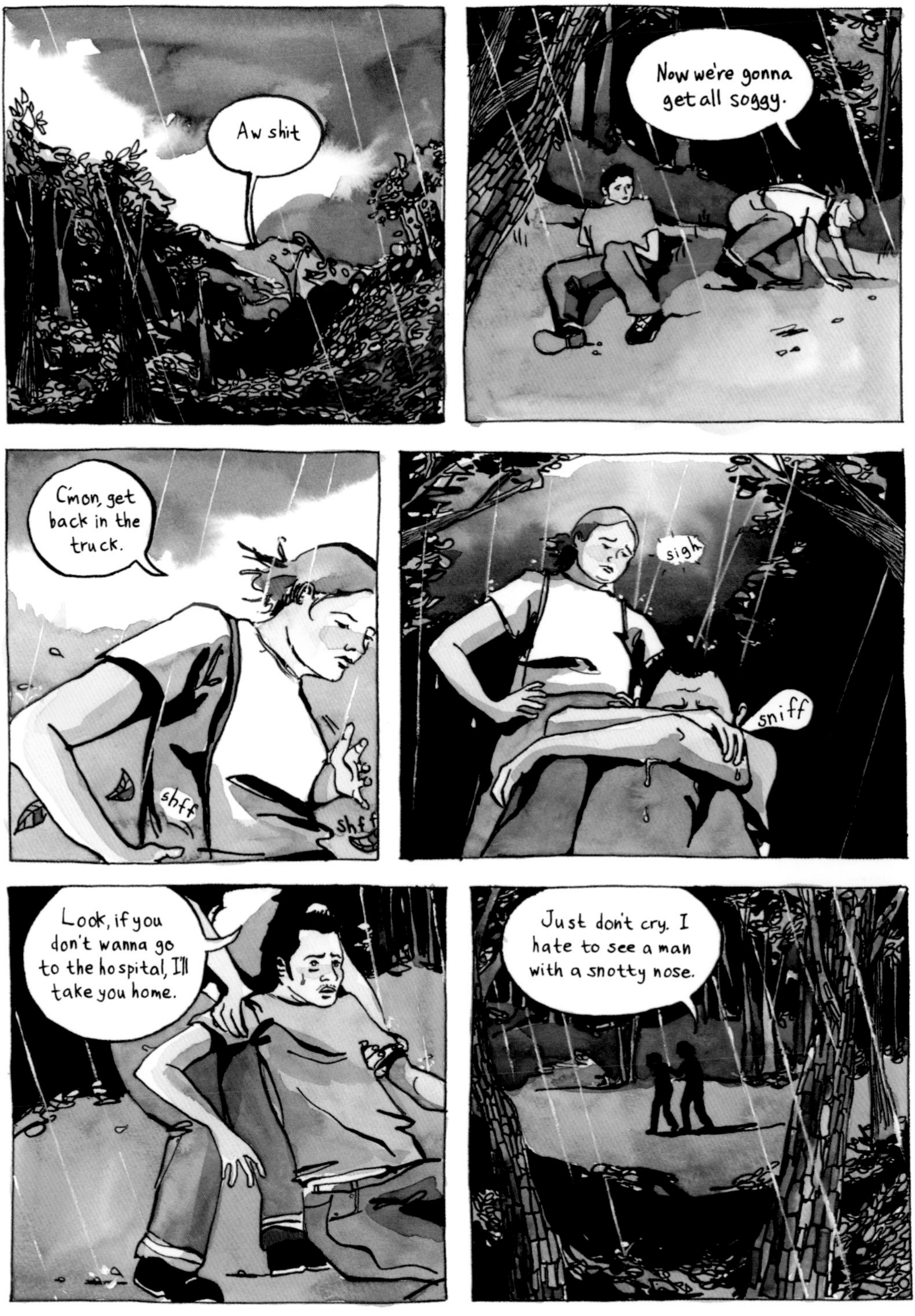
Aw shit
Now we're gonna get all soggy.
C'mon, get back in the truck.
shff
shff
sigh
sniff
Look, if you don't wanna go to the hospital, I'll take you home.
Just don't cry. I hate to see a man with a snotty nose.

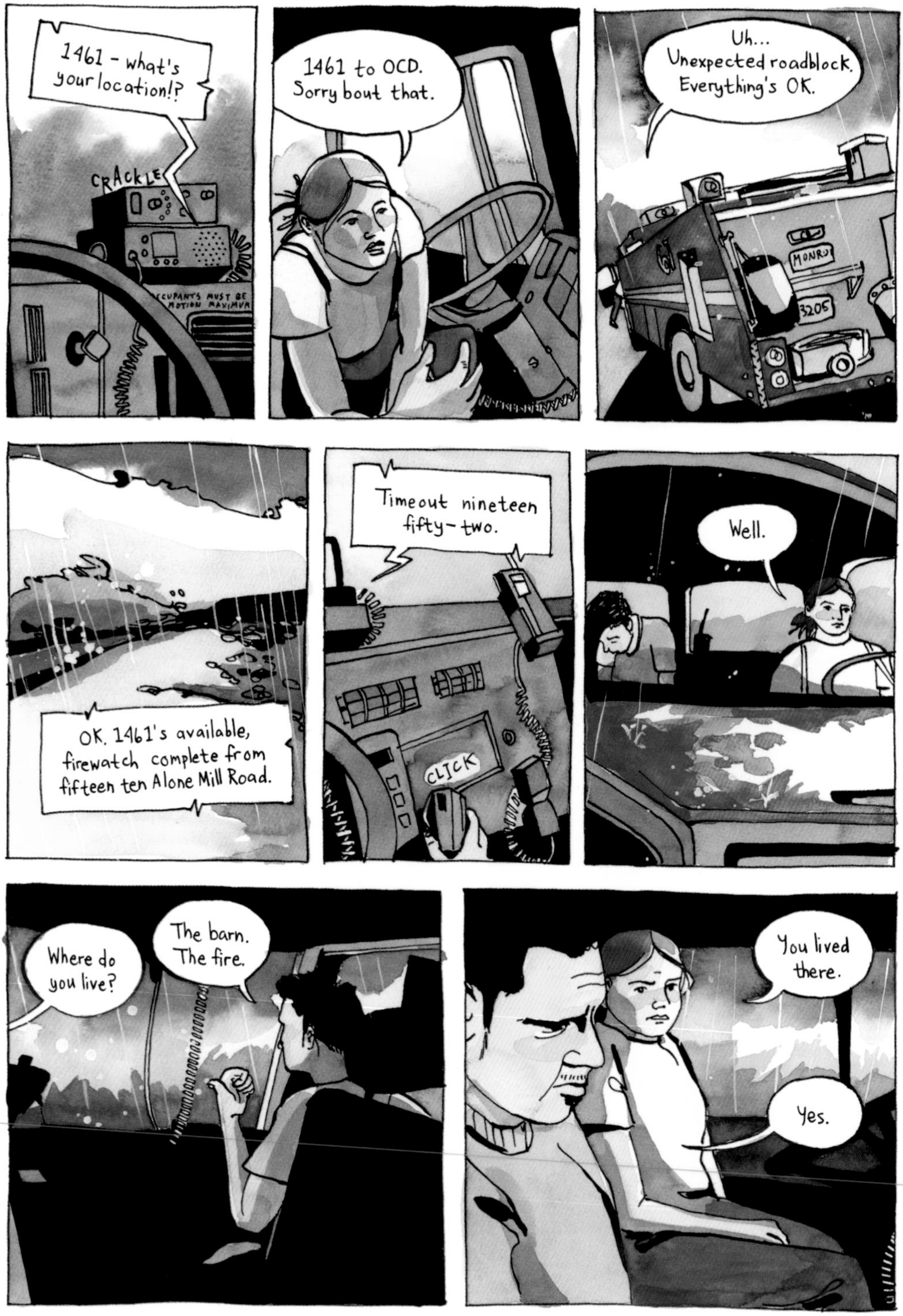
1461 - what's your location!?
CRACKLE
1461 to OCD. Sorry bout that.
Uh... Unexpected roadblock. Everything's OK.
OK. 1461's available, firewatch complete from fifteen ten Alone Mill Road.
Timeout nineteen fifty-two.
CLICK
Well.
Where do you live?
The barn. The fire.
You lived there.
Yes.

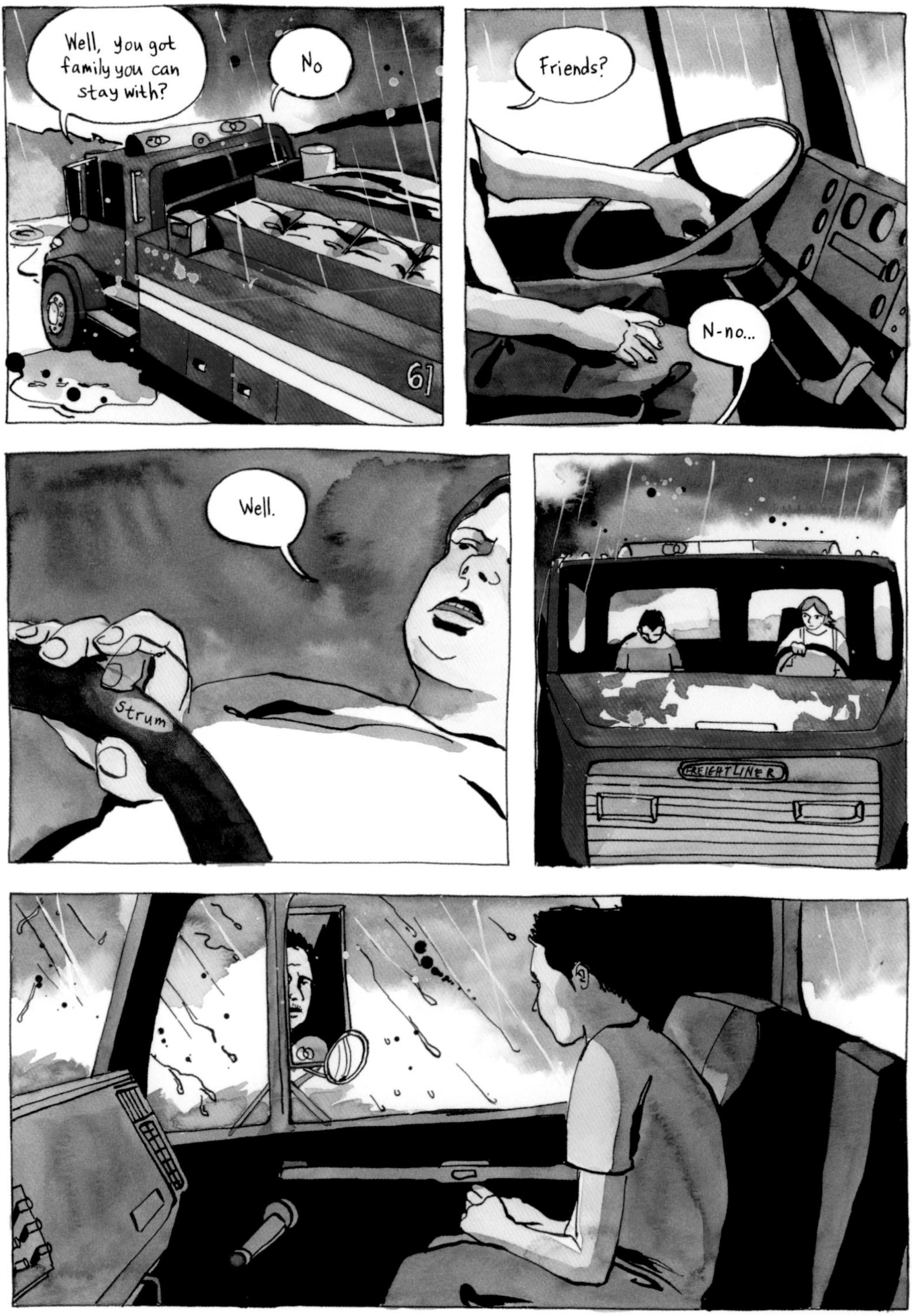
Well, you got family you can stay with?
No
Friends?
N-no...
Well.
Strum
FREIGHTLINER

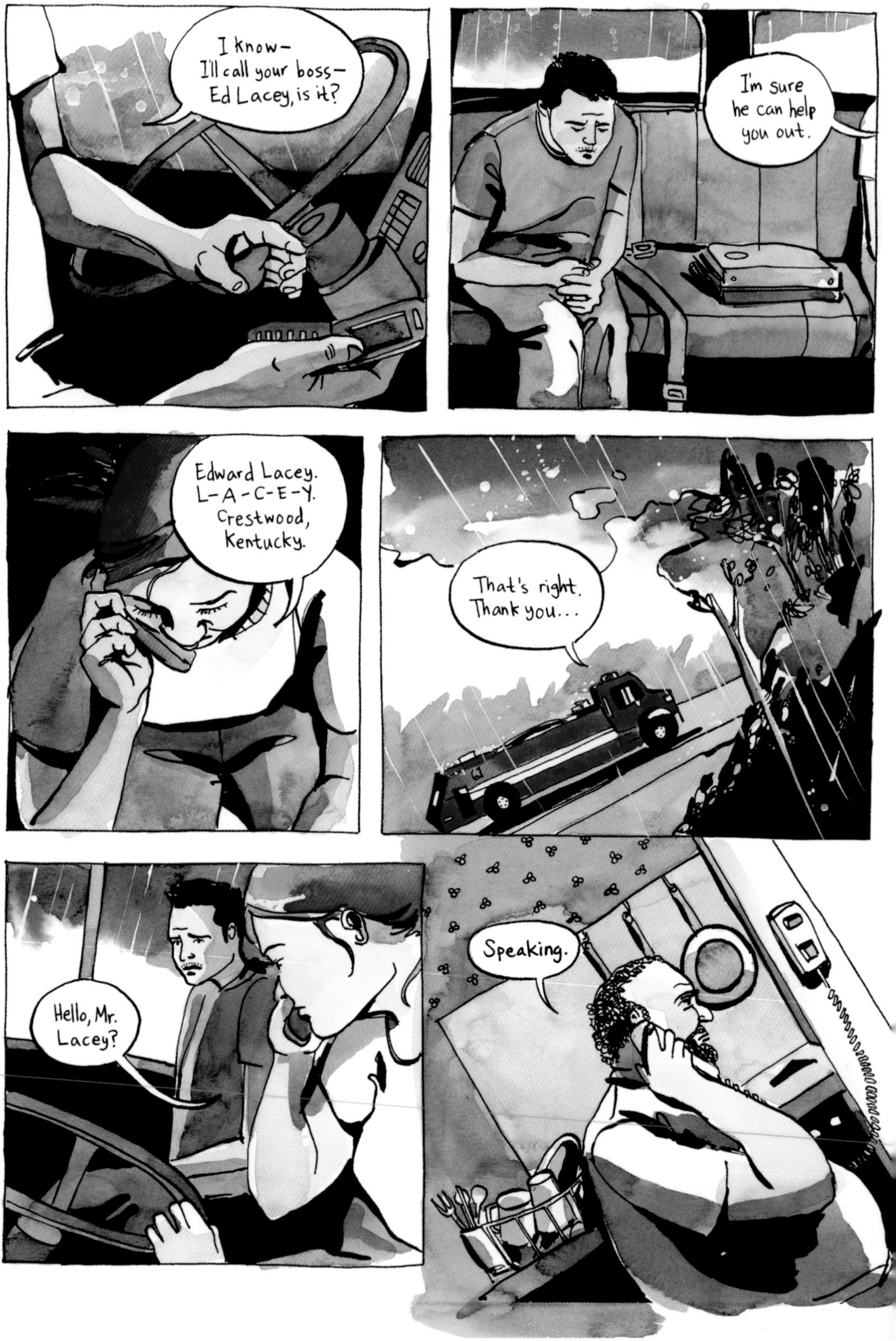
I know— I'll call your boss— Ed Lacey, is it?
I'm sure he can help you out.
Edward Lacey. L-A-C-E-Y. Crestwood, Kentucky.
That's right. Thank you...
Hello, Mr. Lacey?
Speaking.

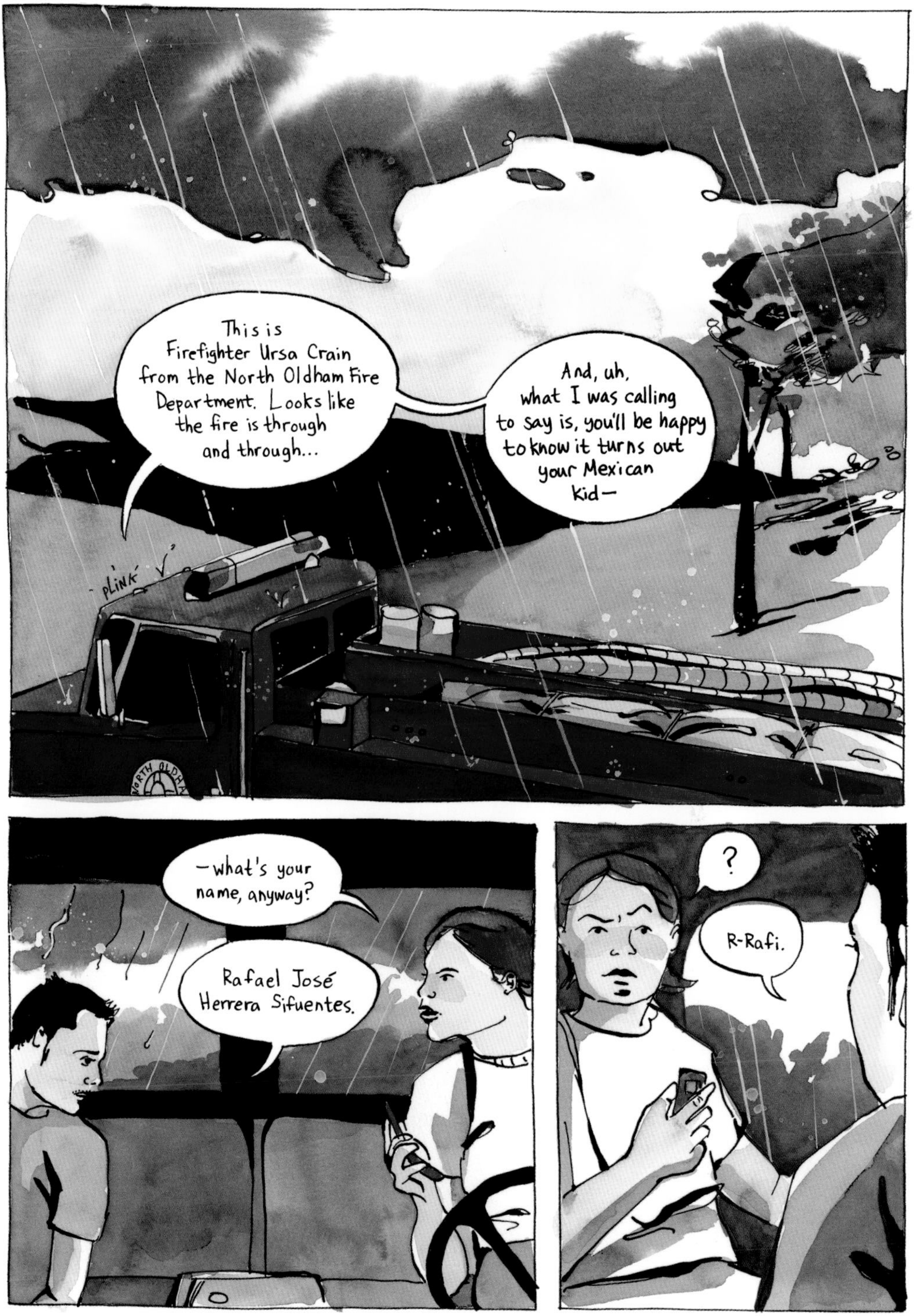
This is Firefighter Ursa Crain from the North Oldham Fire Department. Looks like the fire is through and through...
And, uh, what I was calling to say is, you'll be happy to know it turns out your Mexican kid—
PLINK
—what's your name, anyway?
Rafael José Herrera Sifuentes.
?
R-Rafi.

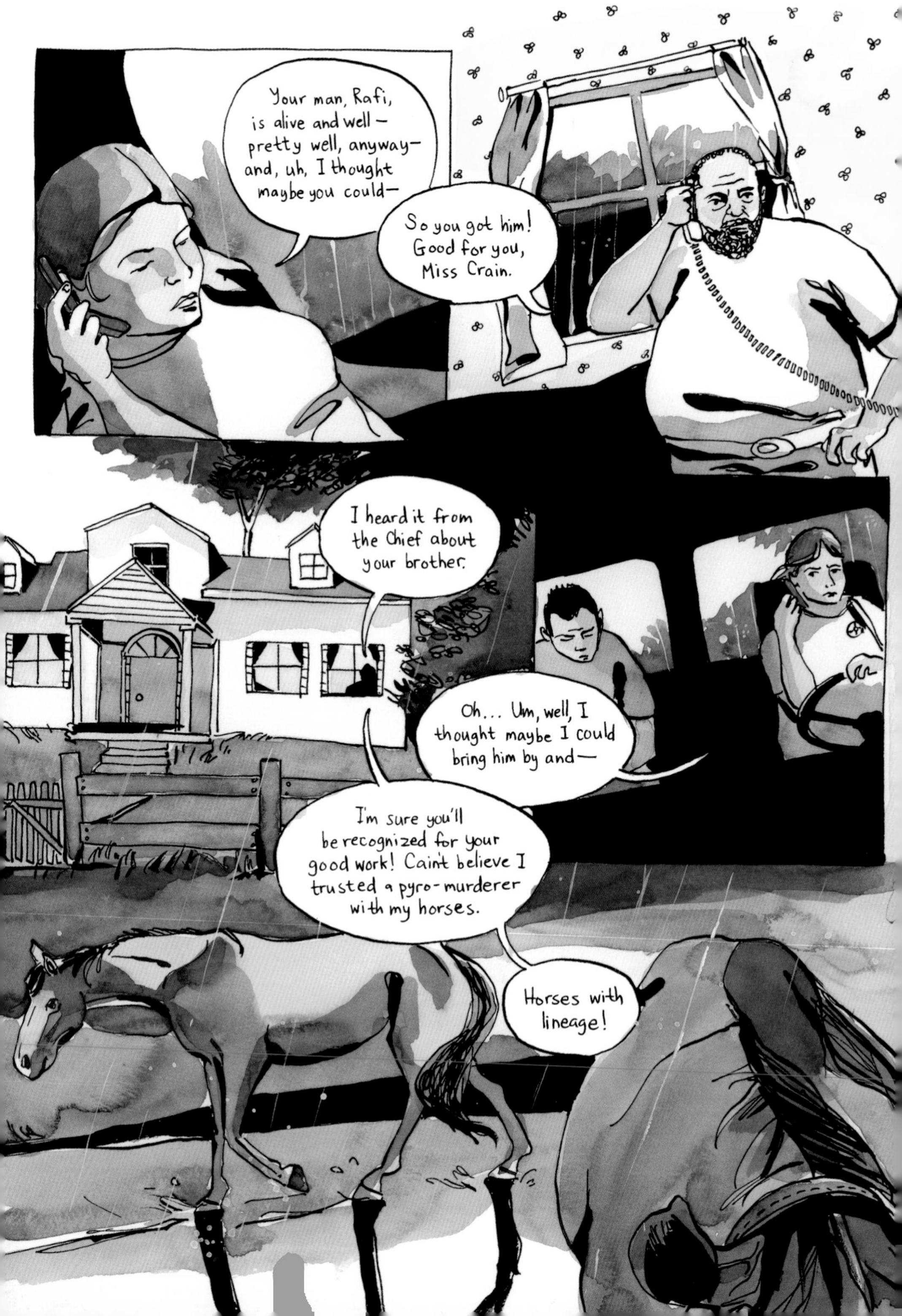

Your man, Rafi, is alive and well — pretty well, anyway— and, uh, I thought maybe you could—
So you got him! Good for you, Miss Crain.
I heard it from the Chief about your brother.
Oh... Um, well, I thought maybe I could bring him by and—
I'm sure you'll be recognized for your good work! Cain't believe I trusted a pyro-murderer with my horses.
Horses with lineage!

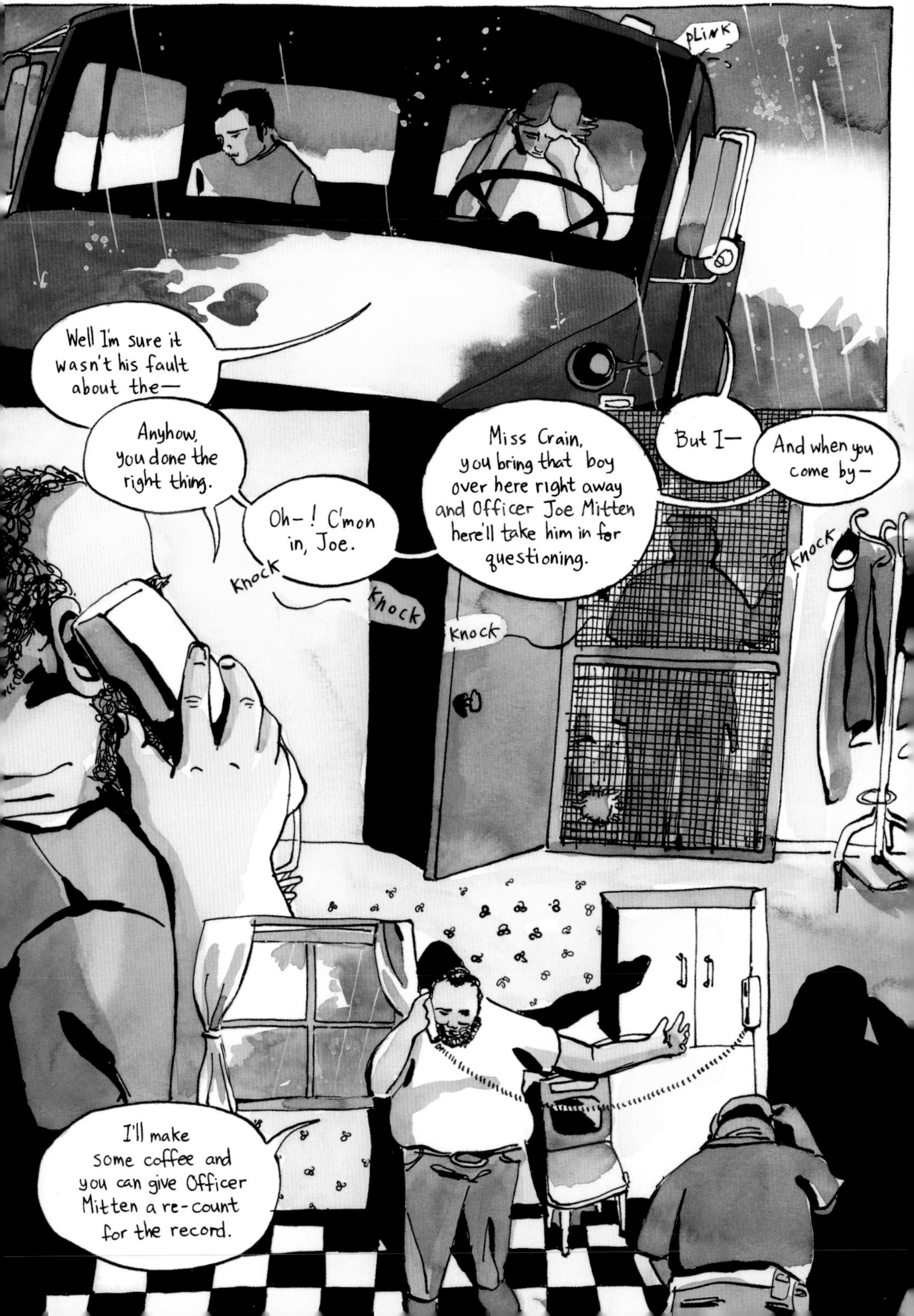

PLINK
Well I'm sure it wasn't his fault about the—
Anyhow, you done the right thing.
Oh–! C'mon in, Joe.
Miss Crain, you bring that boy over here right away and Officer Joe Mitten here'll take him in for questioning.
But I—
And when you come by–
KNOCK
KNOCK
KNOCK
KNOCK
I'll make some coffee and you can give Officer Mitten a re-count for the record.

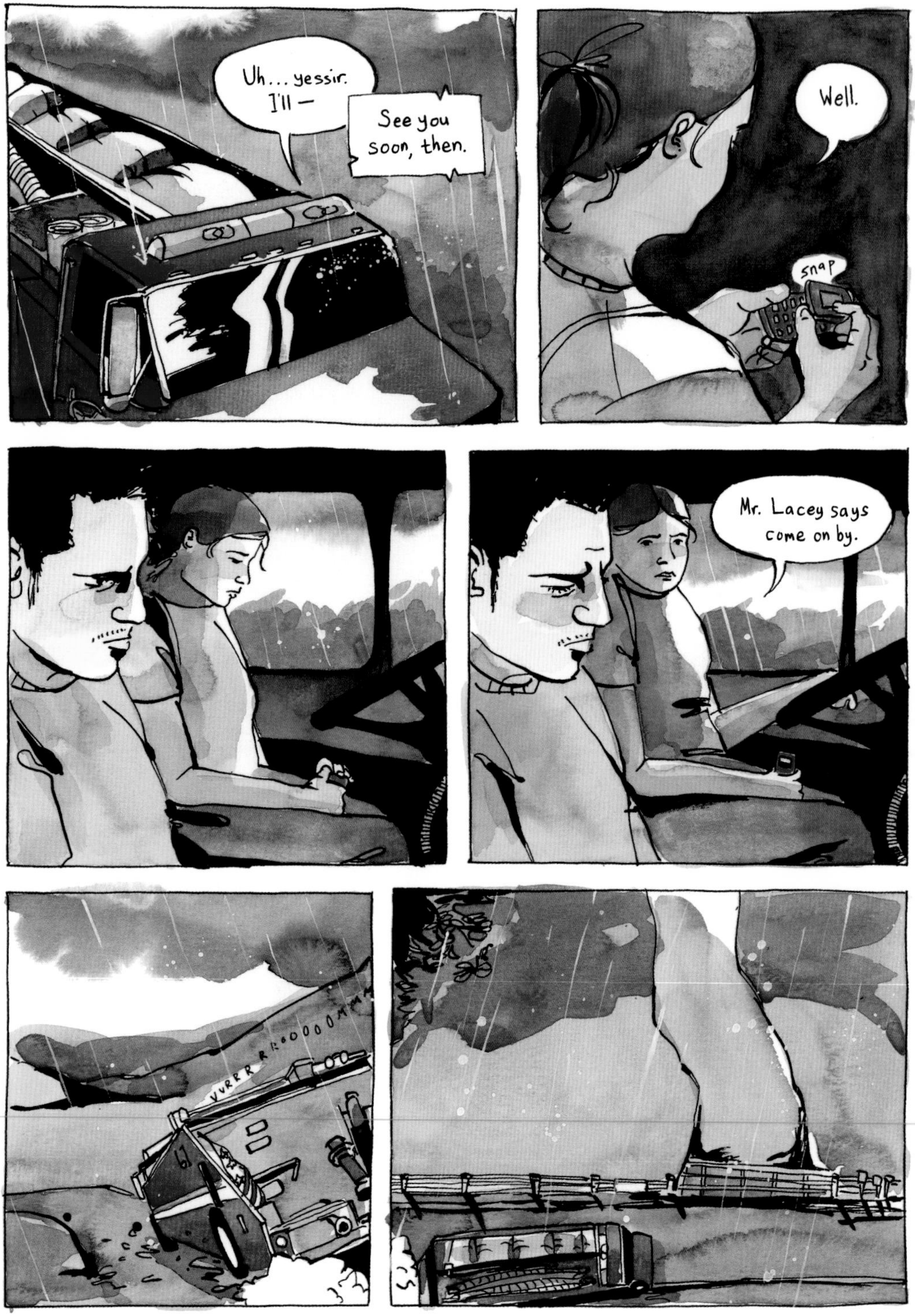
Uh... yessir. I'll —
See you soon, then.
Well.
snap
Mr. Lacey says come on by.
VURRR RRoooooOMMM

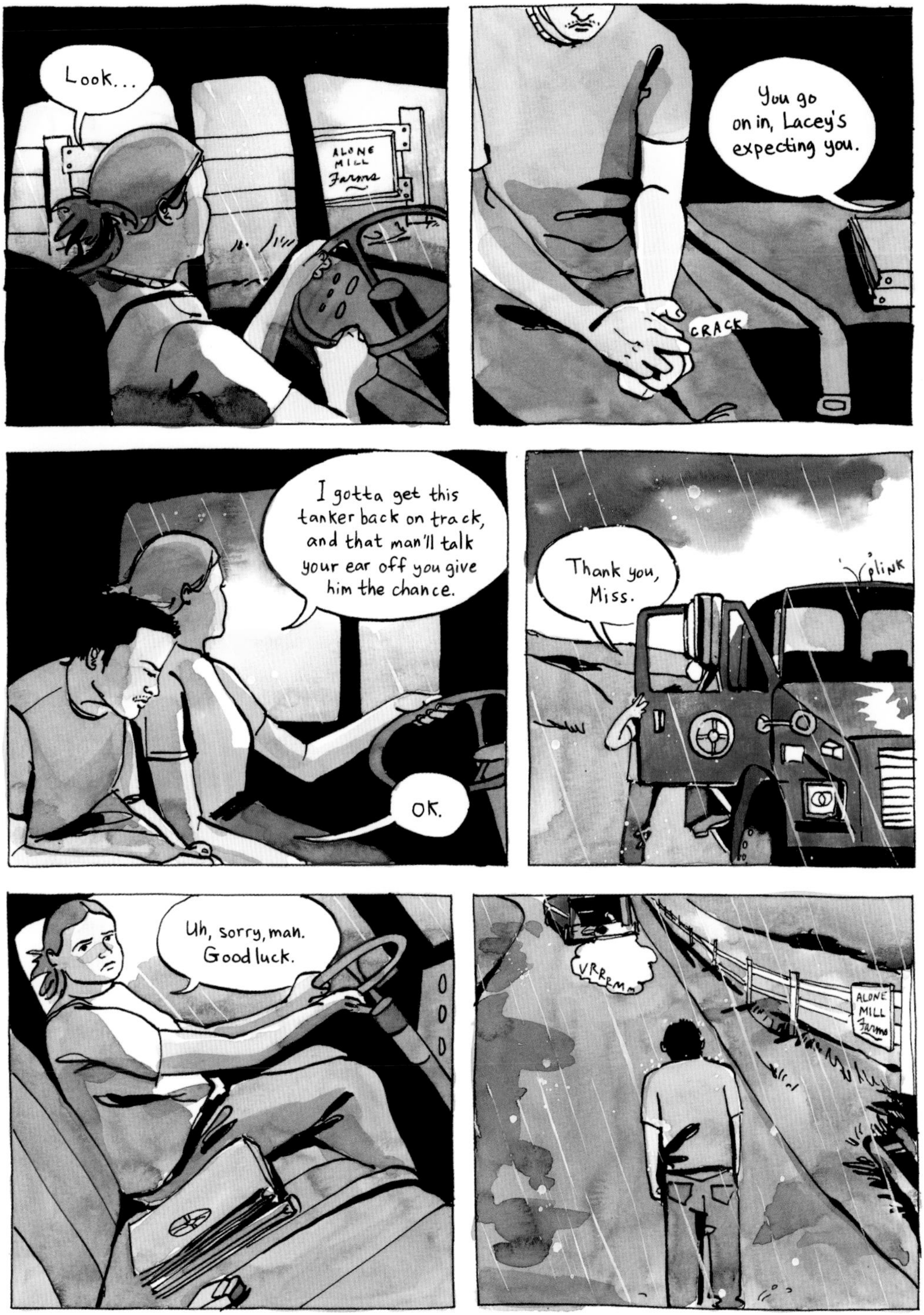
Look...
ALONE MILL Farms
You go on in, Lacey's expecting you.
CRACK
I gotta get this tanker back on track, and that man'll talk your ear off you give him the chance.
OK.
Thank you, Miss.
plink
Uh, sorry, man. Good luck.
VRRRMM
ALONE MILL Farms

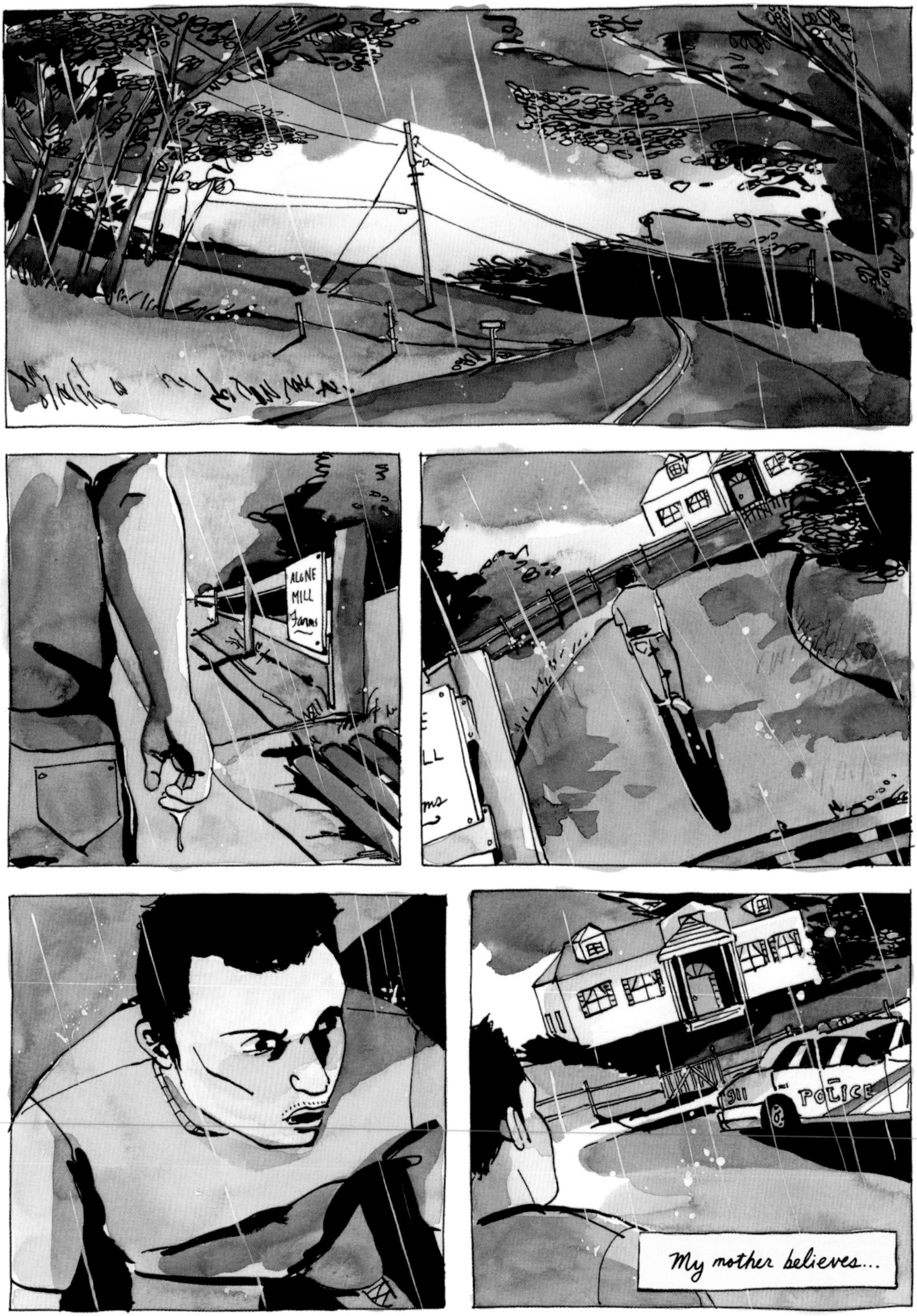
ALONE
MILL
Farms
POLICE
911
My mother believes...

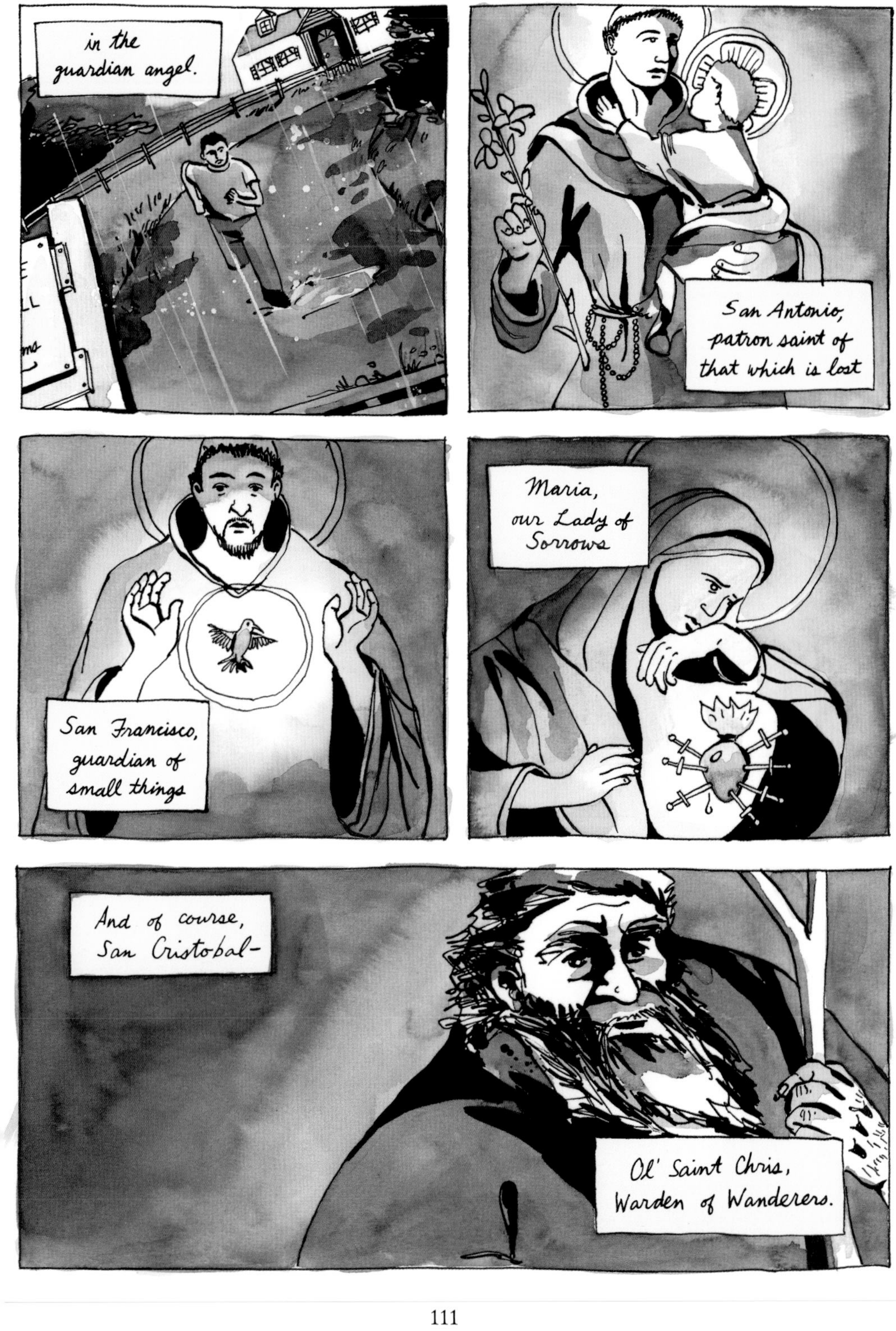
in the guardian angel.
San Antonio, patron saint of that which is lost
San Francisco, guardian of small things
Maria, our Lady of Sorrows
And of course, San Cristobal-
Ol' Saint Chris, Warden of Wanderers.

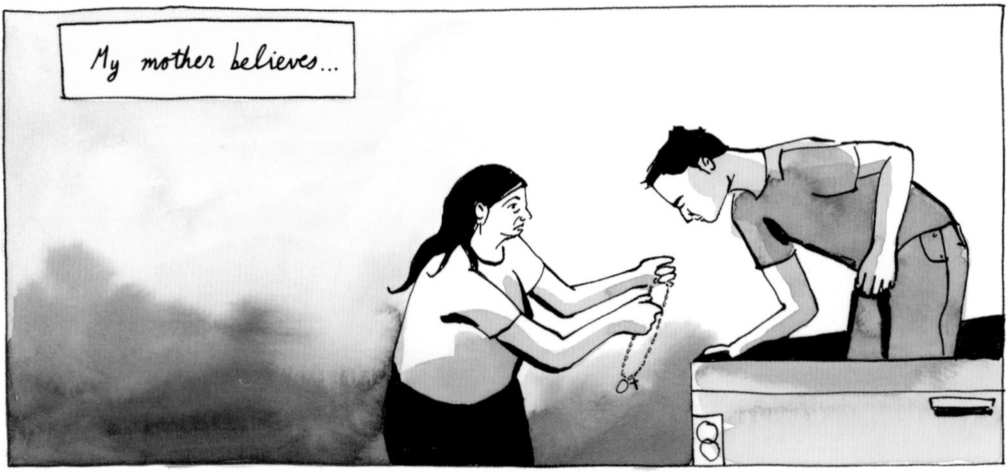
My mother believes...

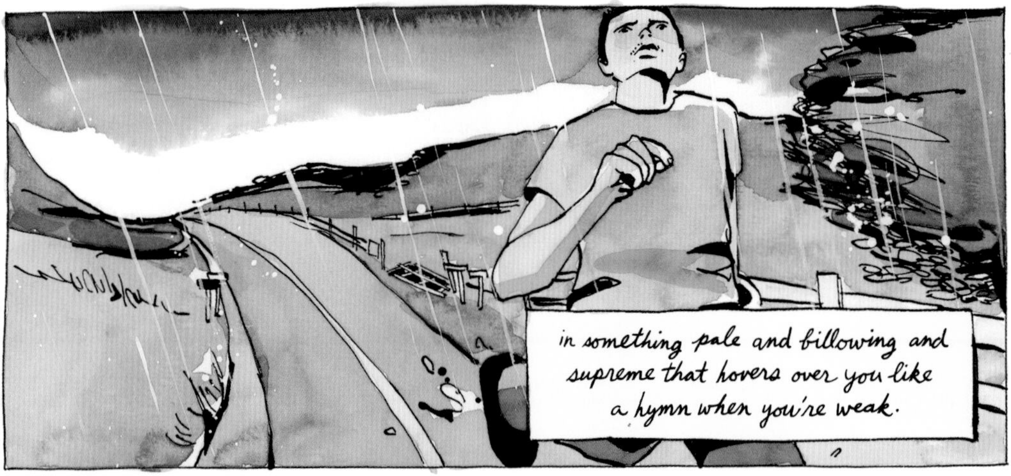
in something pale and billowing and supreme that hovers over you like a hymn when you're weak.

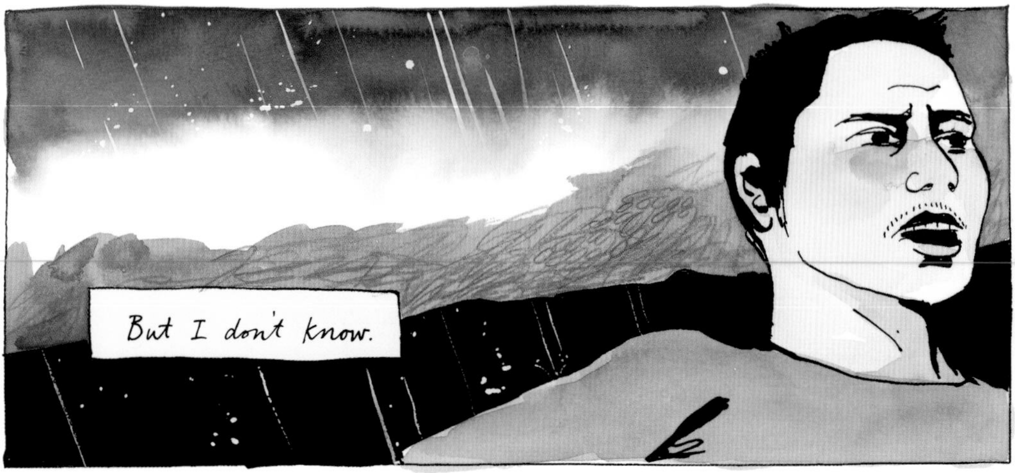
But I don't know.

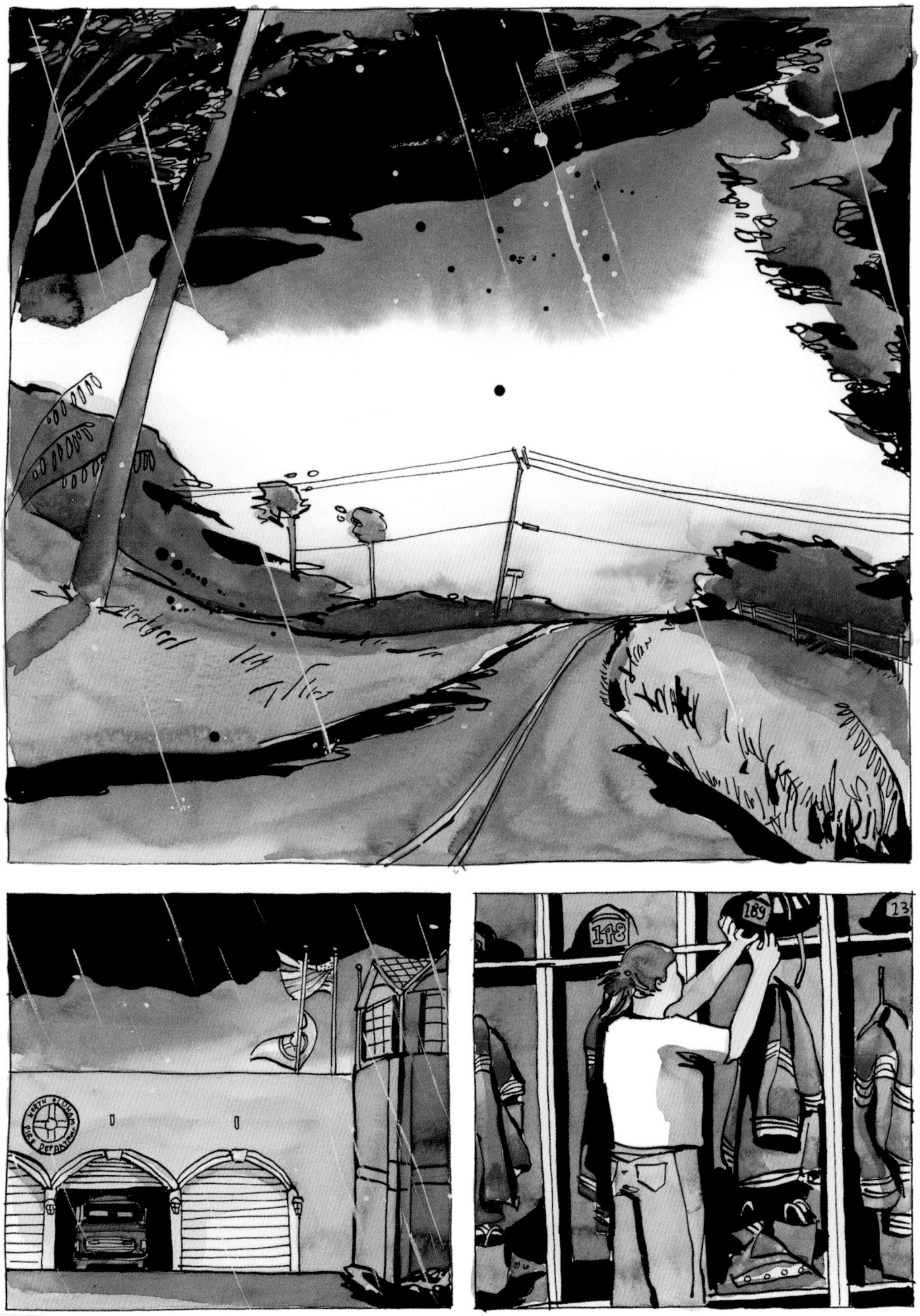
148
189

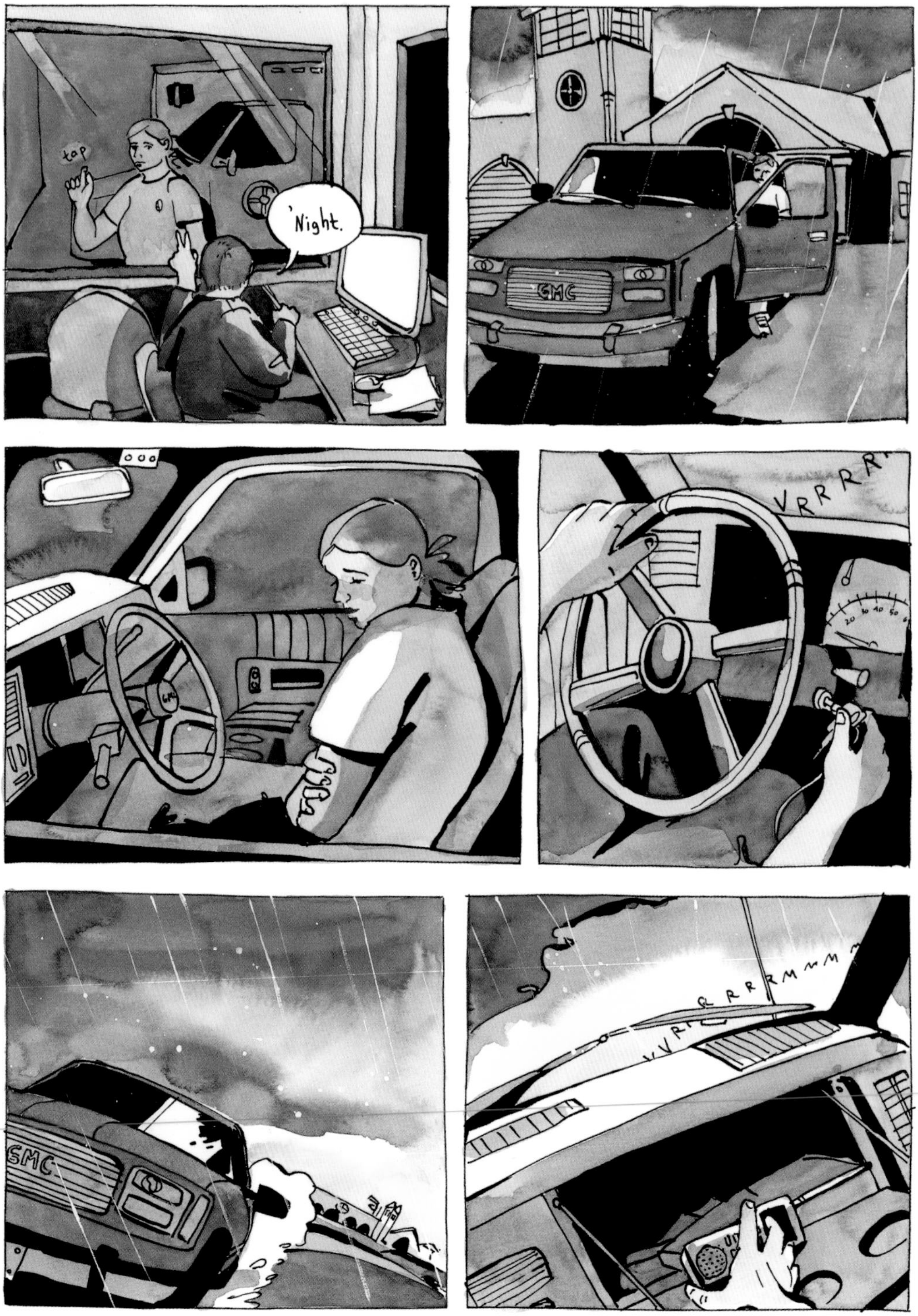
tap
'Night.
VRRRR
VVRRRRRRMMMMM

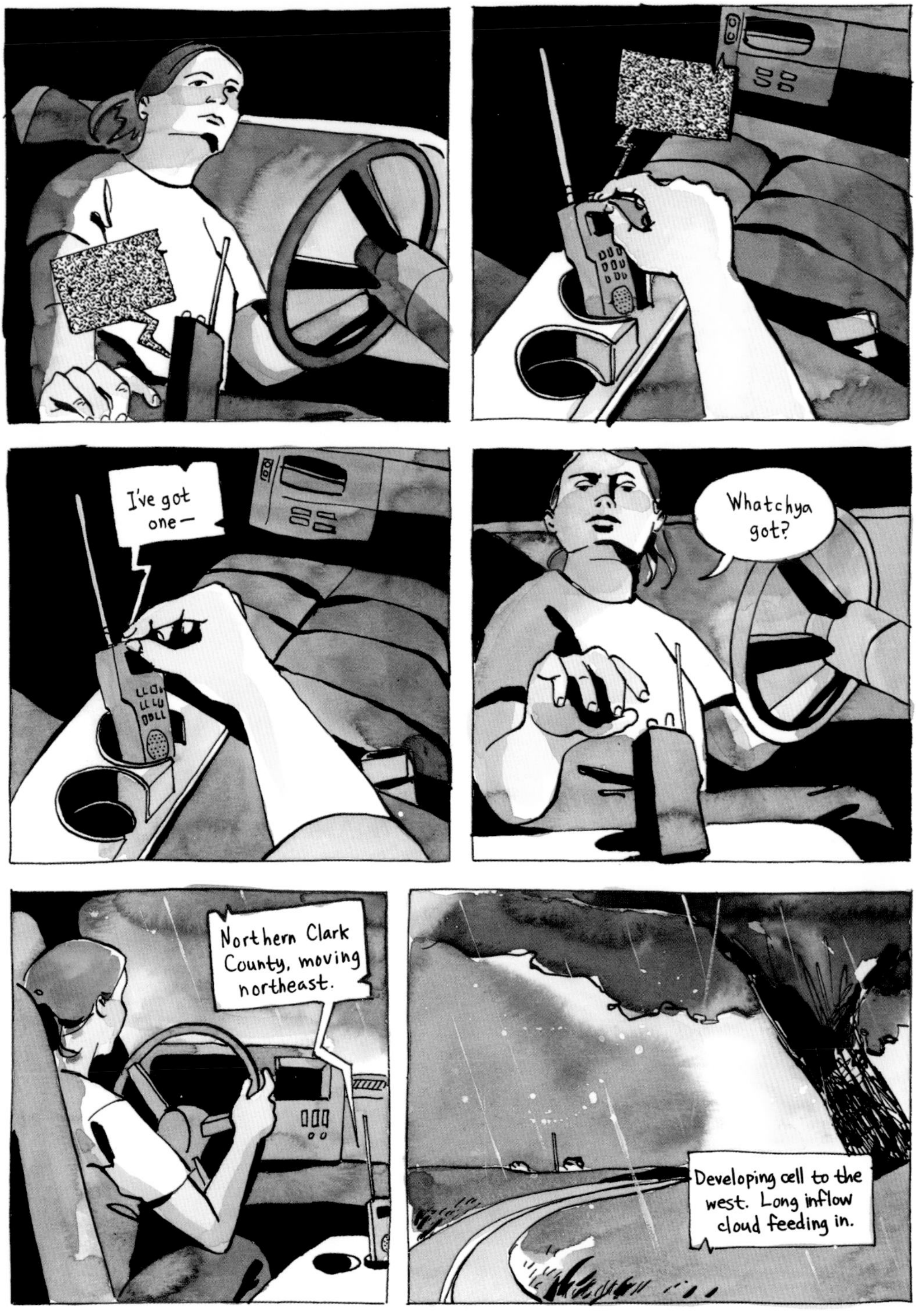
I've got one—
Whatchya got?
Northern Clark County, moving northeast.
Developing cell to the west. Long inflow cloud feeding in.

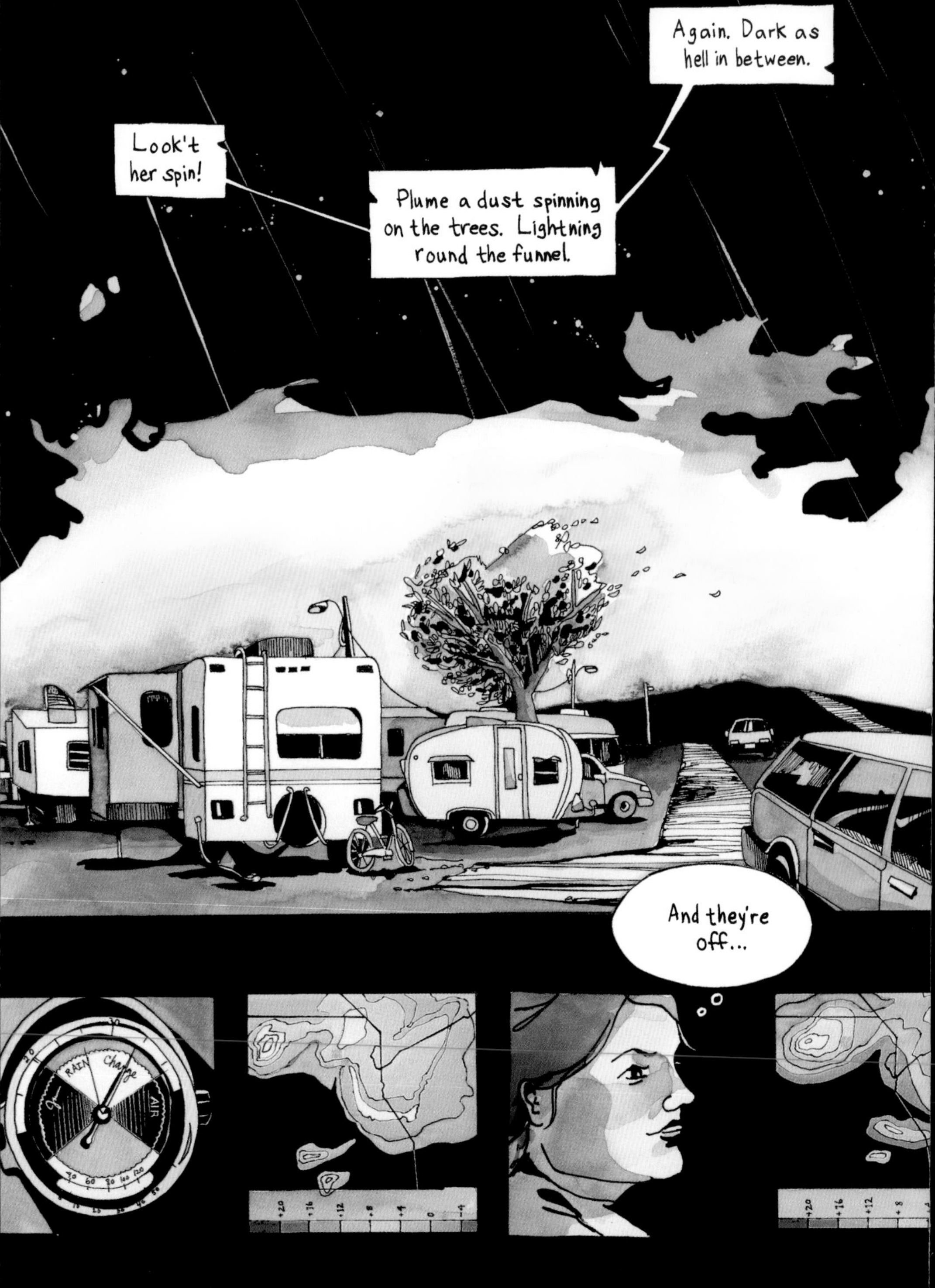
Look't her spin!
Plume a dust spinning on the trees. Lightning round the funnel.
Again. Dark as hell in between.
And they're off...
RAIN
Change
AIR

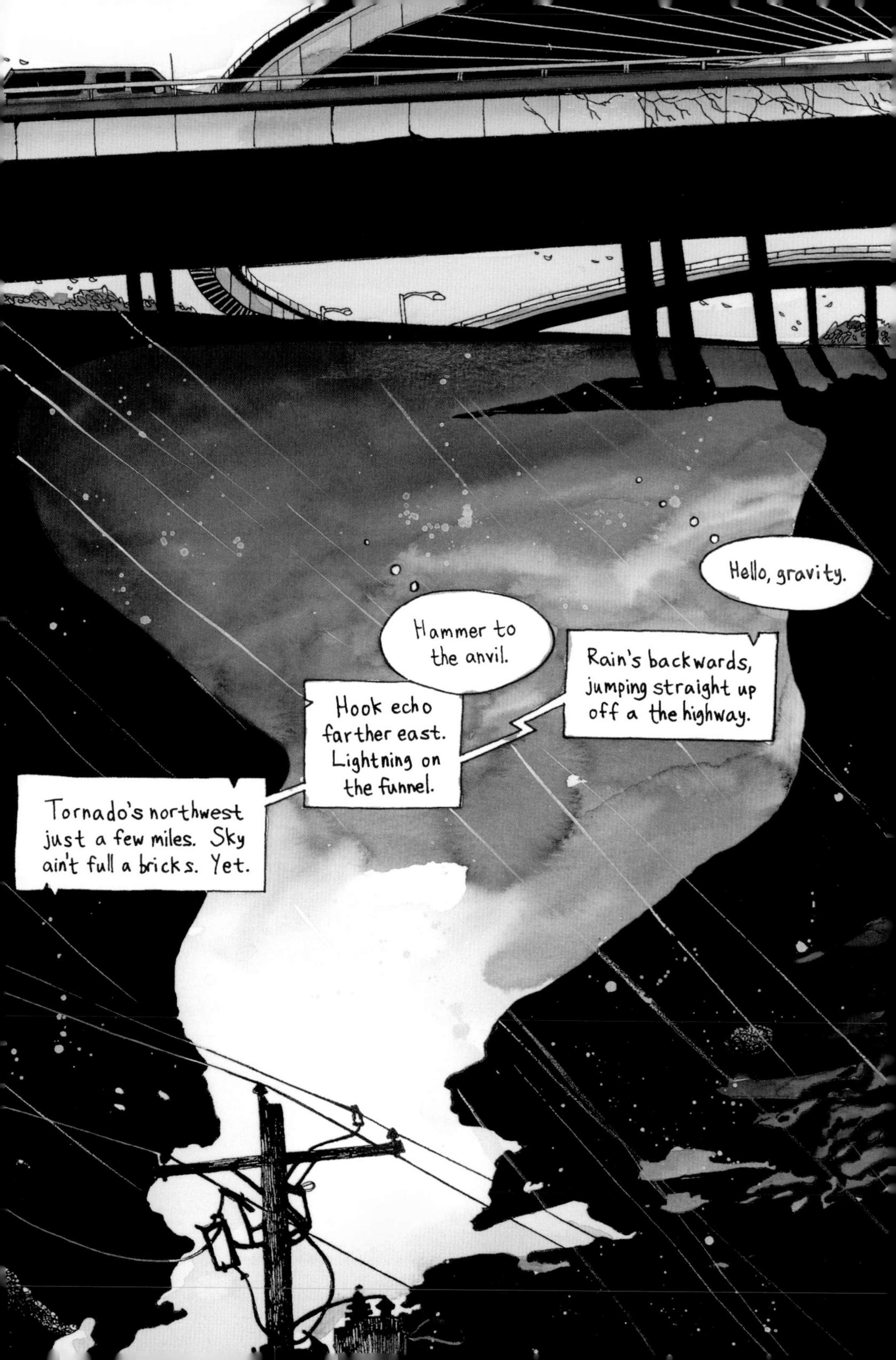
Tornado's northwest just a few miles. Sky ain't full a bricks. Yet.
Hook echo farther east. Lightning on the funnel.
Rain's backwards, jumping straight up off a the highway.
Hammer to the anvil.
Hello, gravity.

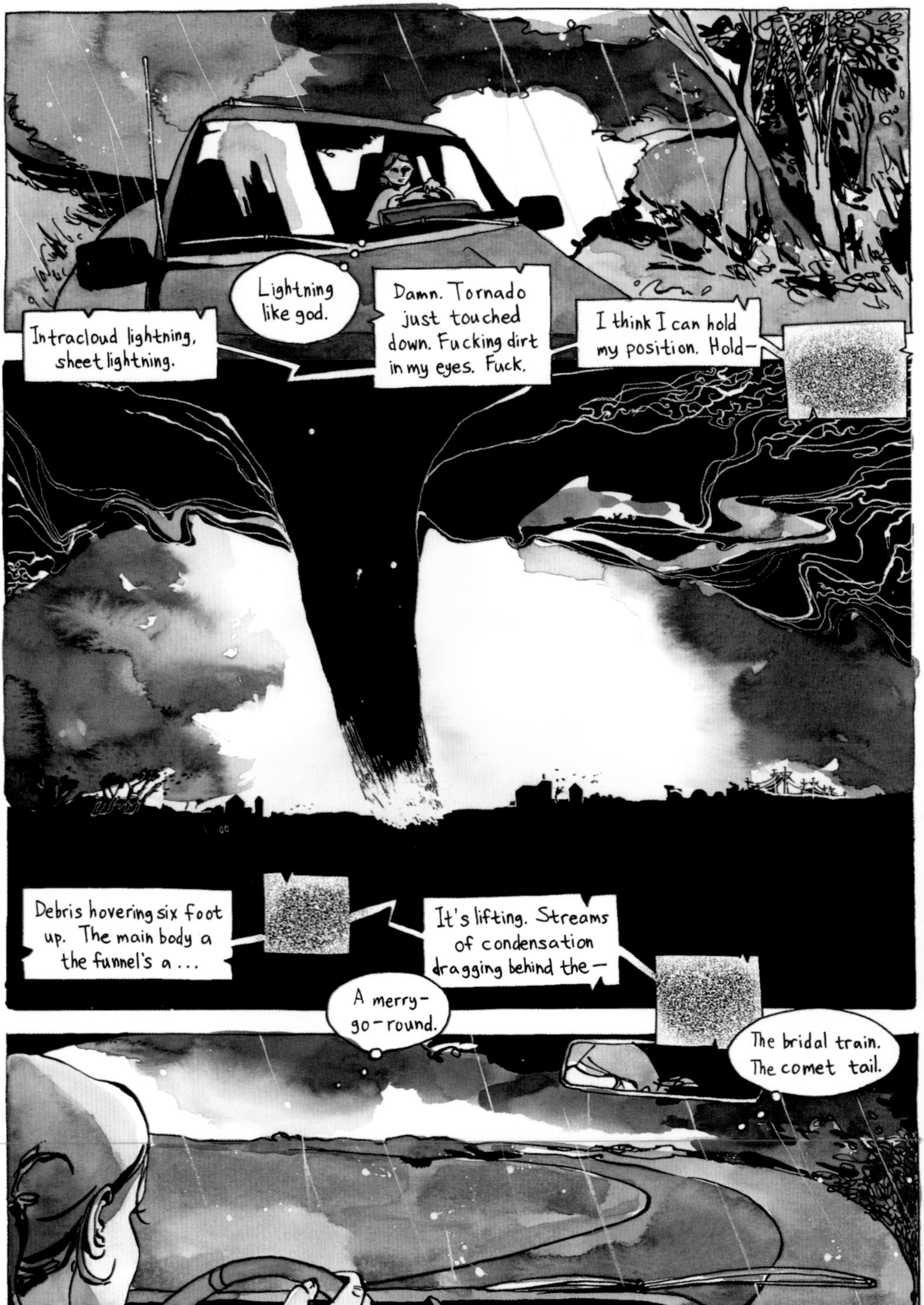
Intracloud lightning, sheet lightning.
Lightning like god.
Damn. Tornado just touched down. Fucking dirt in my eyes. Fuck.
I think I can hold my position. Hold–
Debris hovering six foot up. The main body a the funnel's a . . .
It's lifting. Streams of condensation dragging behind the–
A merry-go-round.
The bridal train. The comet tail.

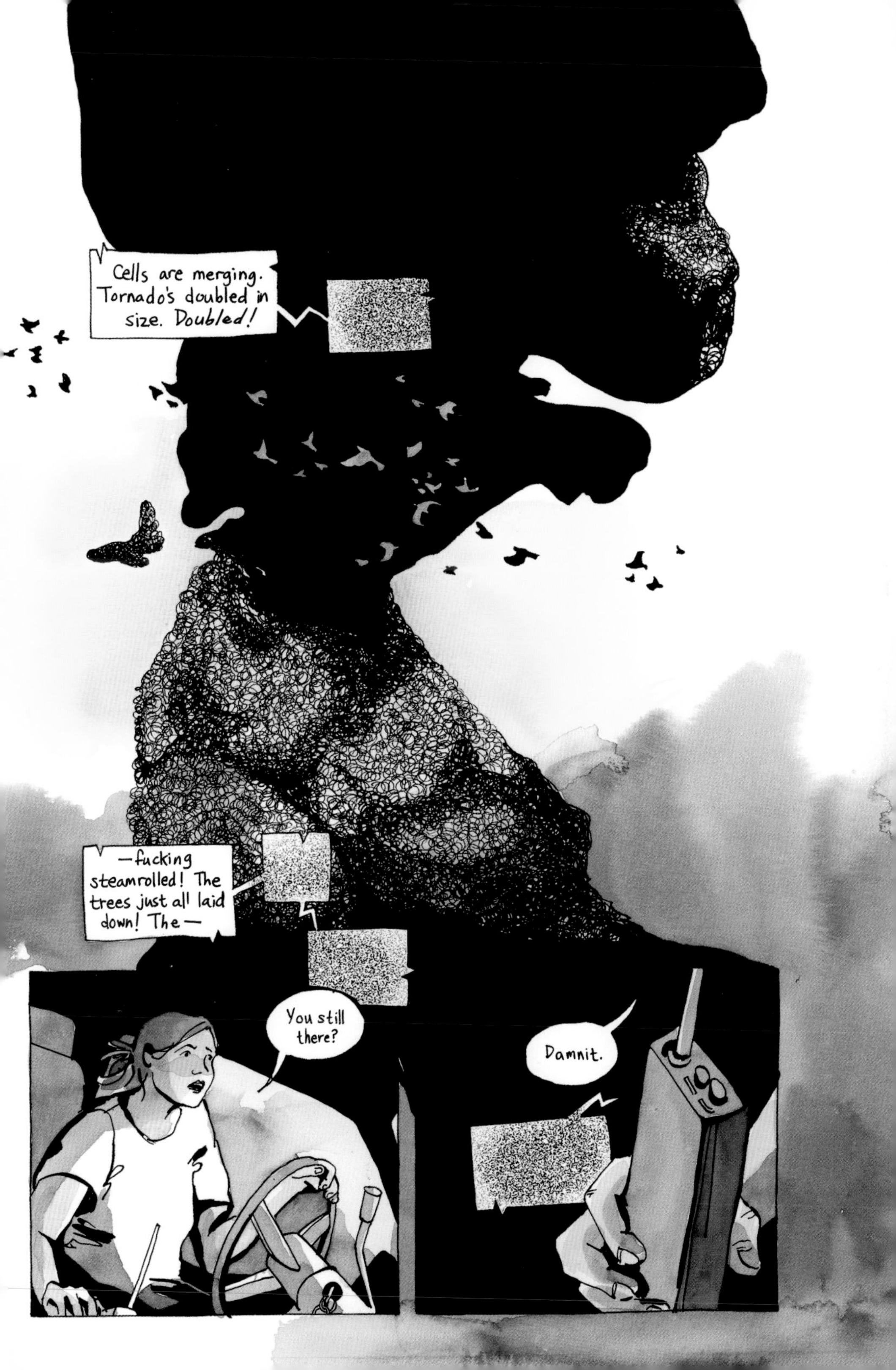
Cells are merging. Tornado's doubled in size. Doubled!
—fucking steamrolled! The trees just all laid down! The—
You still there?
Damnit.

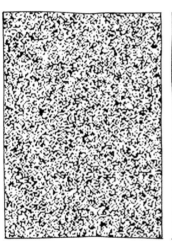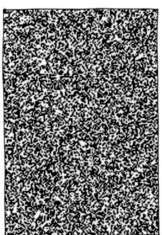

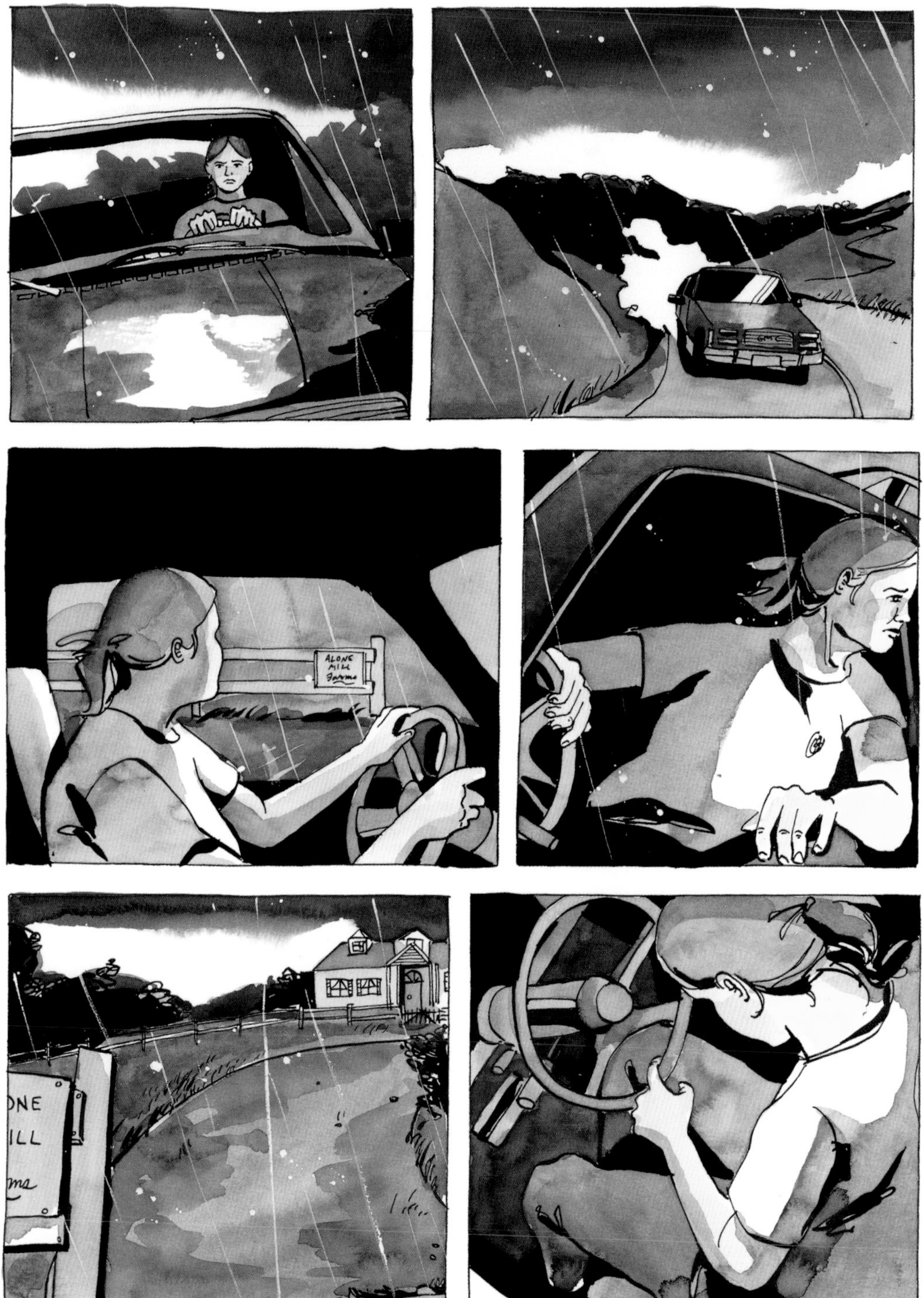
GMC
ALONE
MILL
Farms
ONE
ILL
ms

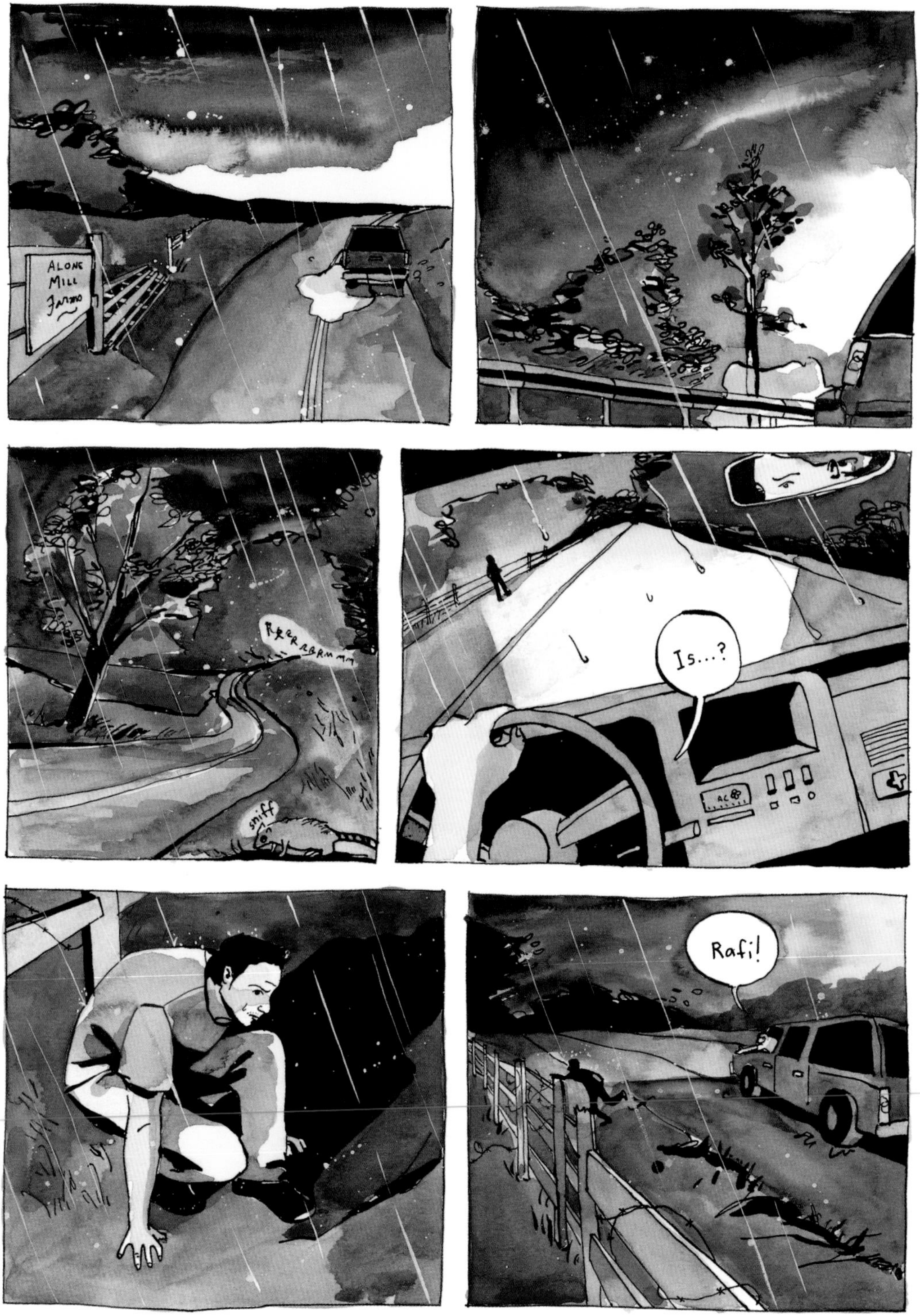
ALONE
MILL
Farms
RRRRRRRRMMM
sniff
Is...?
Rafi!

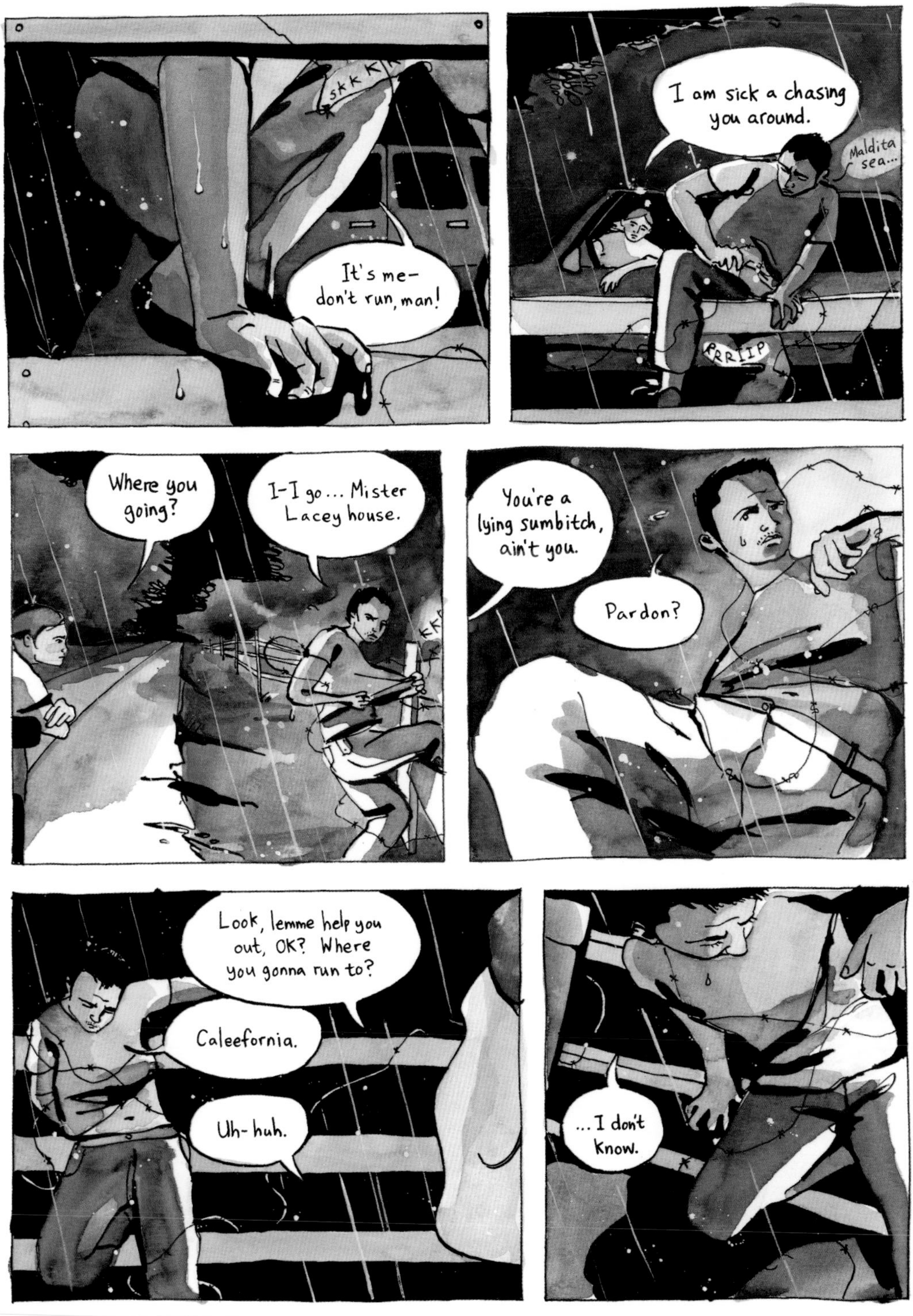
SKKK
It's me- don't run, man!
I am sick a chasing you around.
Maldita sea...
RRRIIP
Where you going?
I-I go... Mister Lacey house.
You're a lying sumbitch, ain't you.
Pardon?
Look, lemme help you out, OK? Where you gonna run to?
Caleefornia.
Uh-huh.
...I don't know.

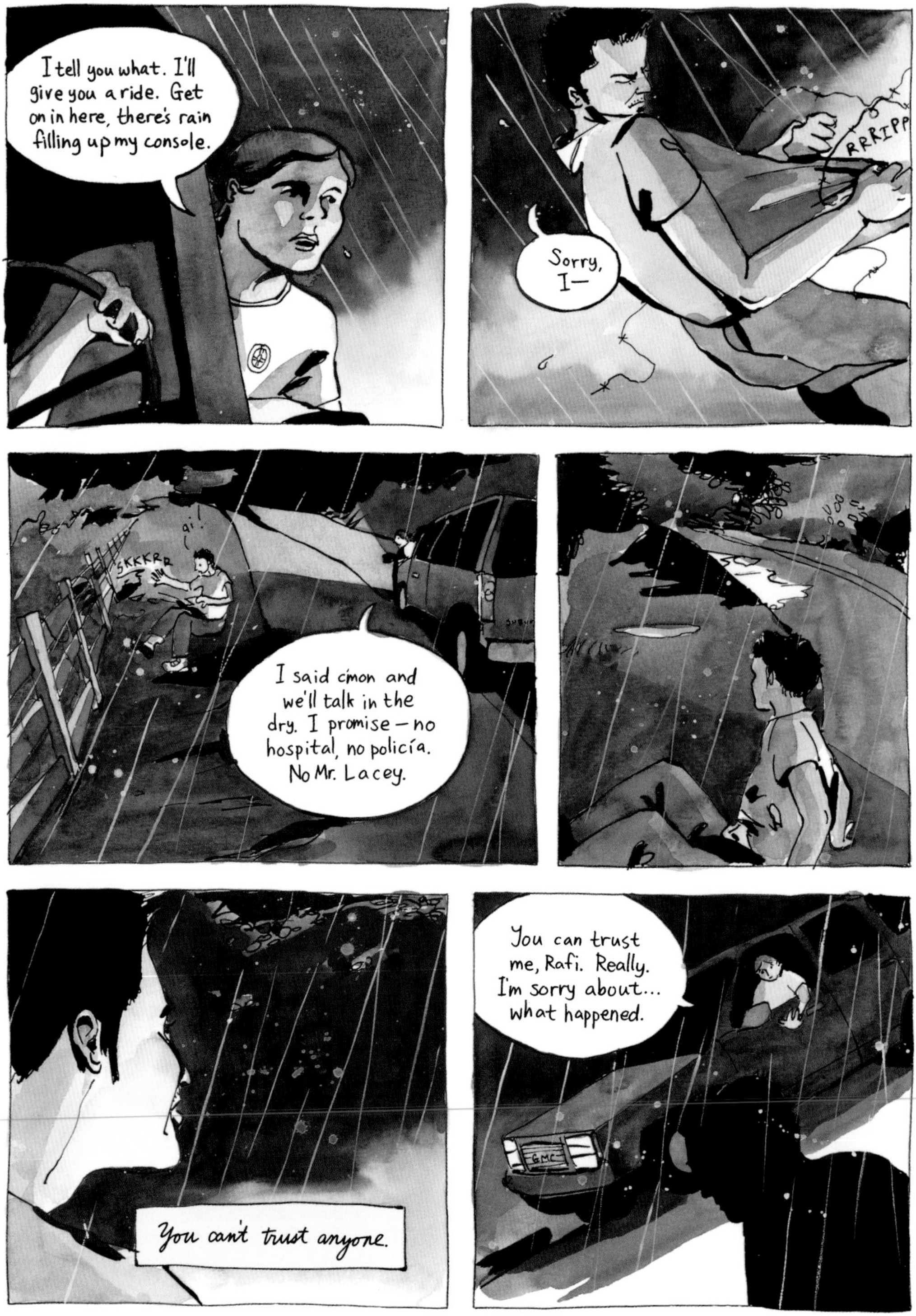
I tell you what. I'll give you a ride. Get on in here, there's rain filling up my console.
RRRIPP
Sorry, I—
ai!
SKKKRR
I said c'mon and we'll talk in the dry. I promise—no hospital, no policía. No Mr. Lacey.
You can't trust anyone.
You can trust me, Rafi. Really. I'm sorry about... what happened.
GMC

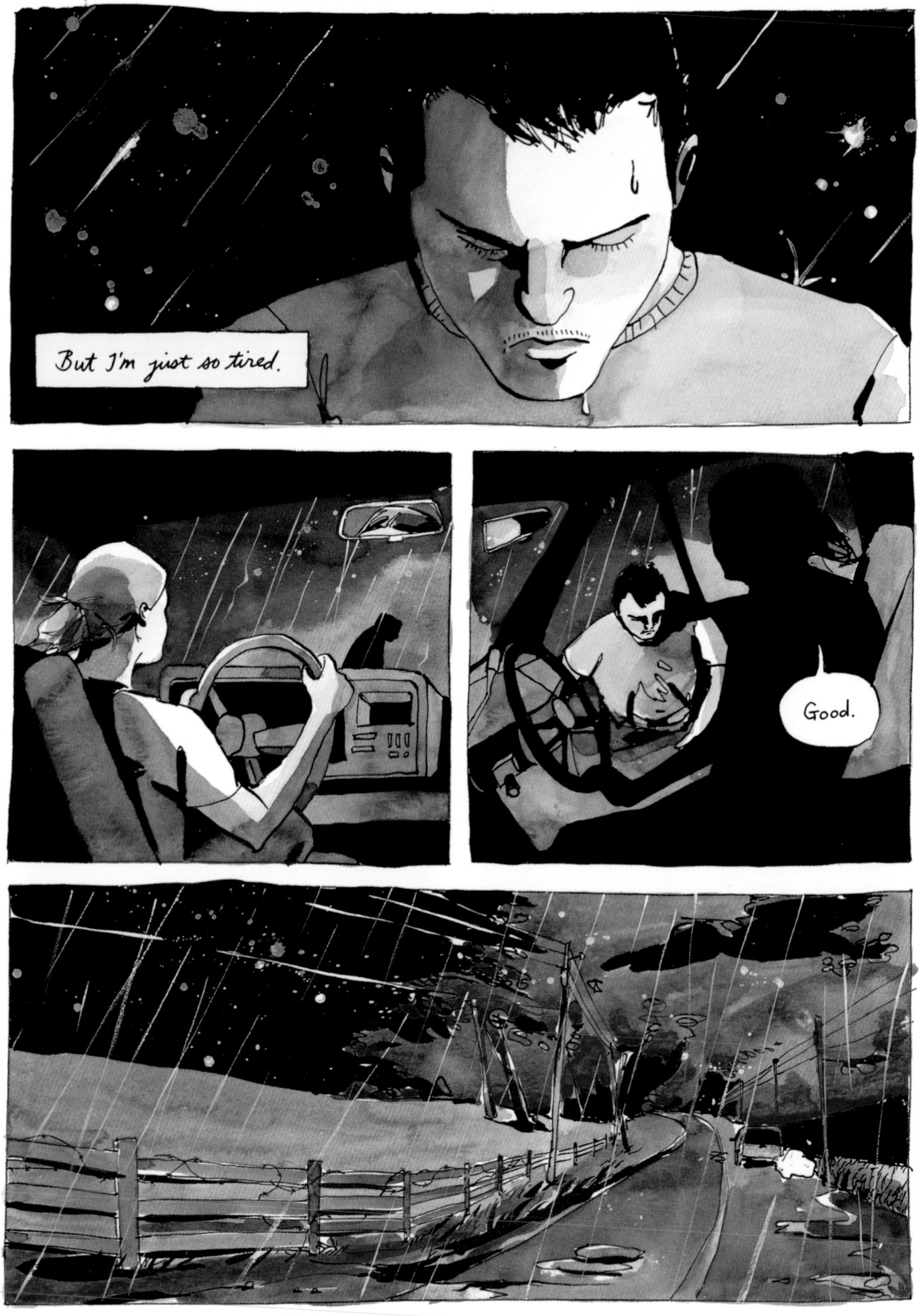
But I'm just so tired.
Good.

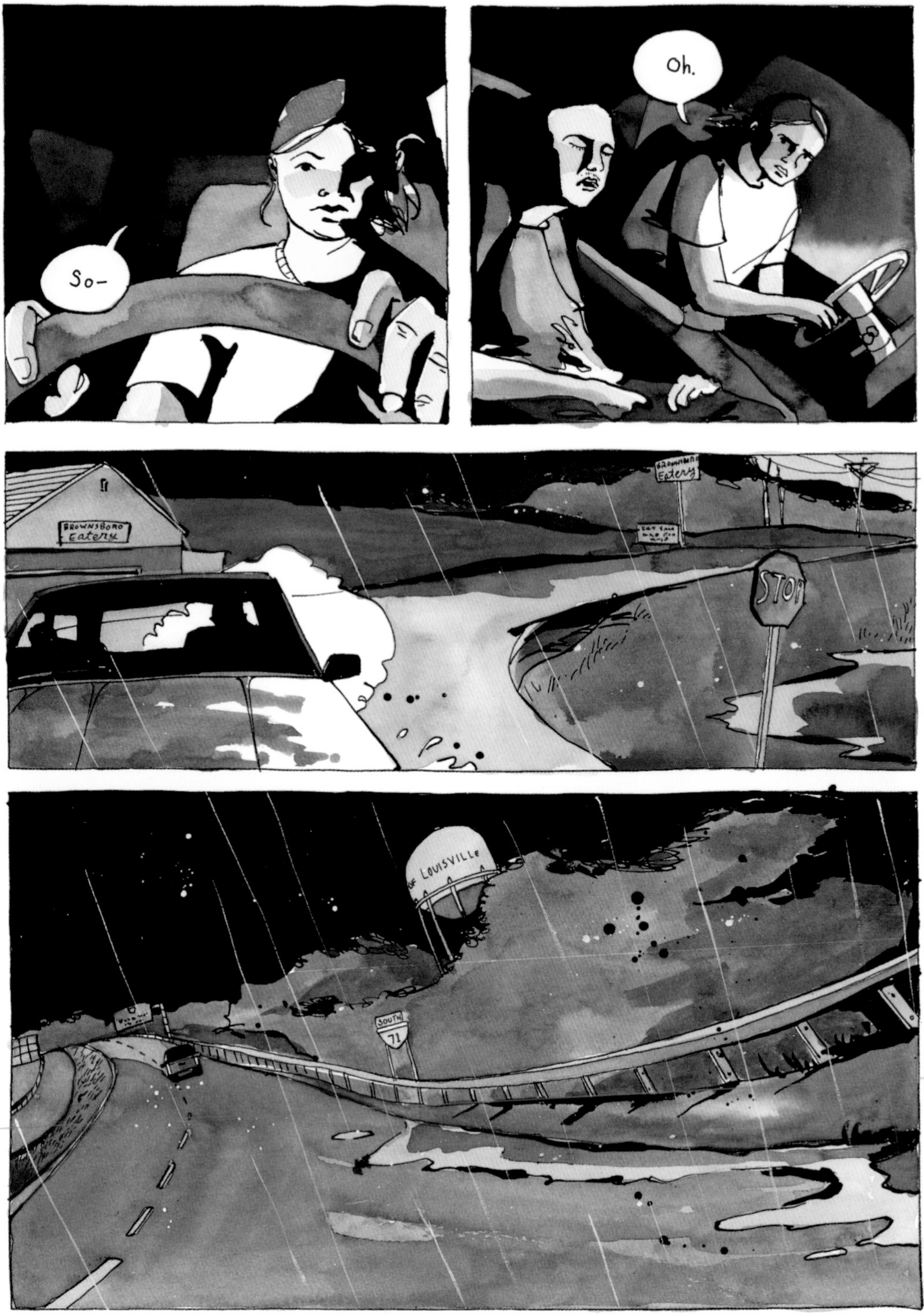
So-
Oh.
BROWNSBORO Eatery
Eatery
STOP
LOUISVILLE
SOUTH
71

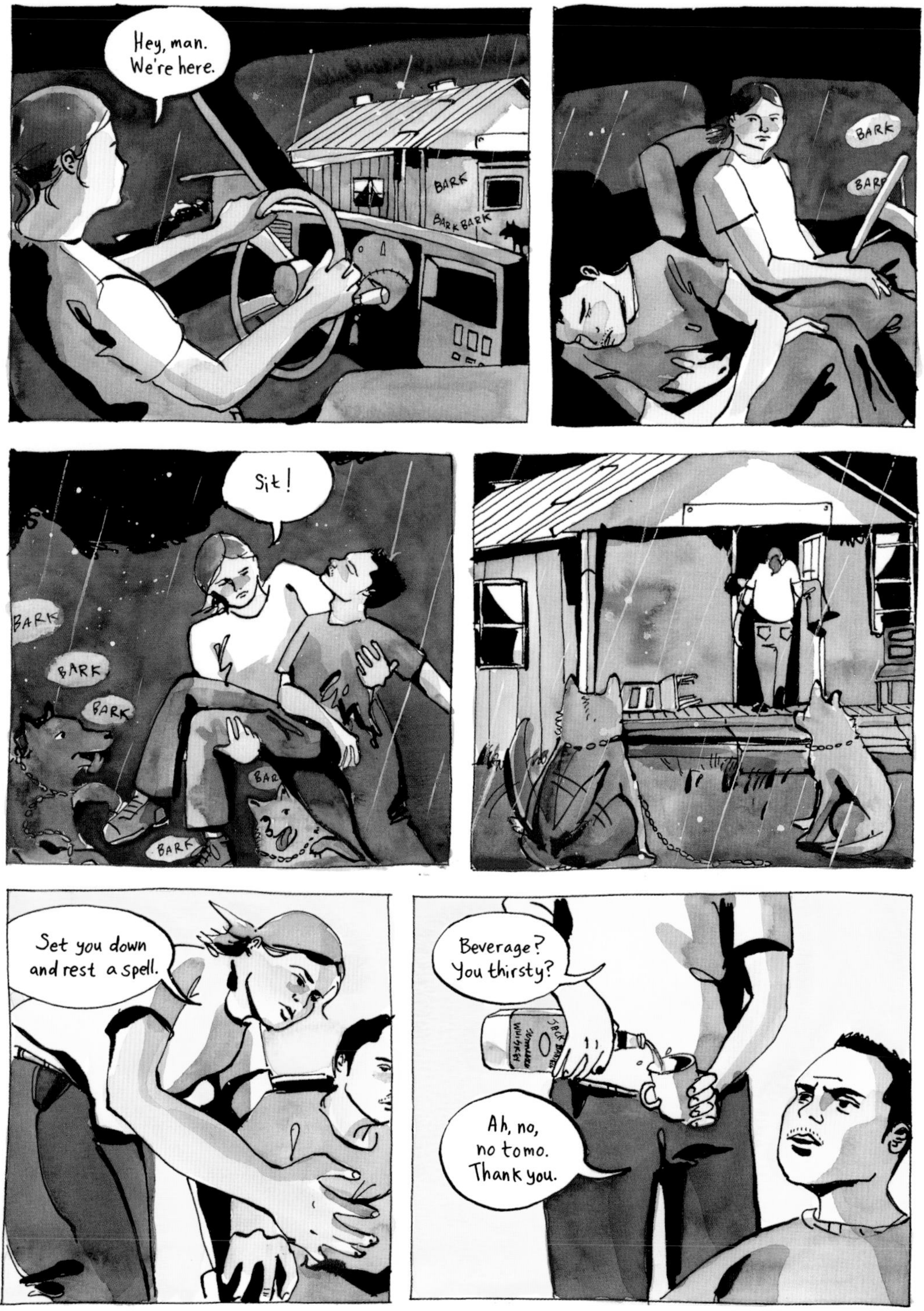
Hey, man.
We're here.
BARK
BARK BARK
BARK
BARK
Sit!
BARK
BARK
BARK
BARK
BARK
Set you down
and rest a spell.
Beverage?
You thirsty?
Ah, no,
no tomo.
Thank you.

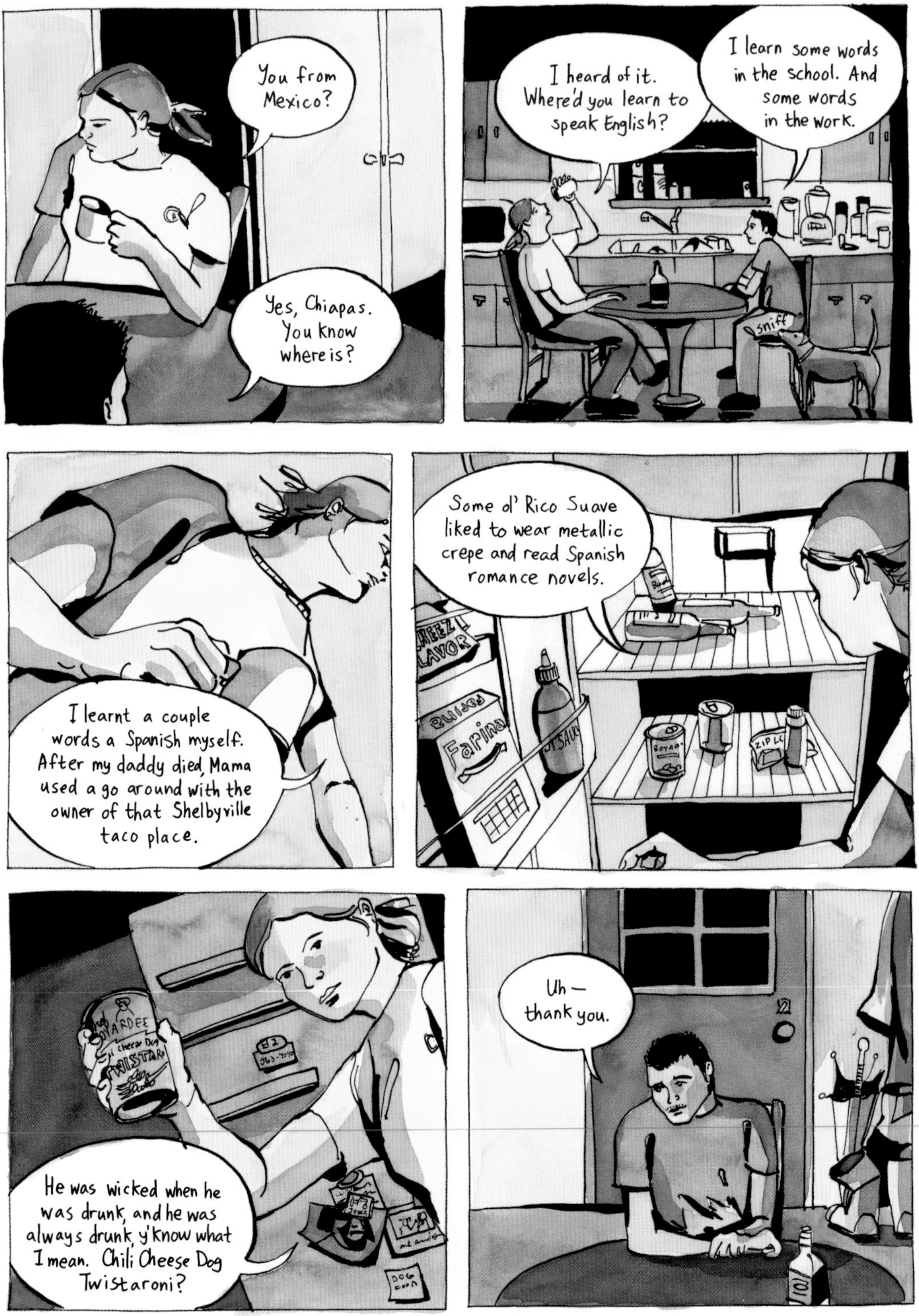
You from Mexico?
Yes, Chiapas. You know where is?
I heard of it. Where'd you learn to speak English?
I learn some words in the school. And some words in the work.
sniff
I learnt a couple words a Spanish myself. After my daddy died, Mama used a go around with the owner of that Shelbyville taco place.
Some ol' Rico Suave liked to wear metallic crepe and read Spanish romance novels.
Farina
He was wicked when he was drunk, and he was always drunk, y'know what I mean. Chili Cheese Dog Twistaroni?
Uh — thank you.

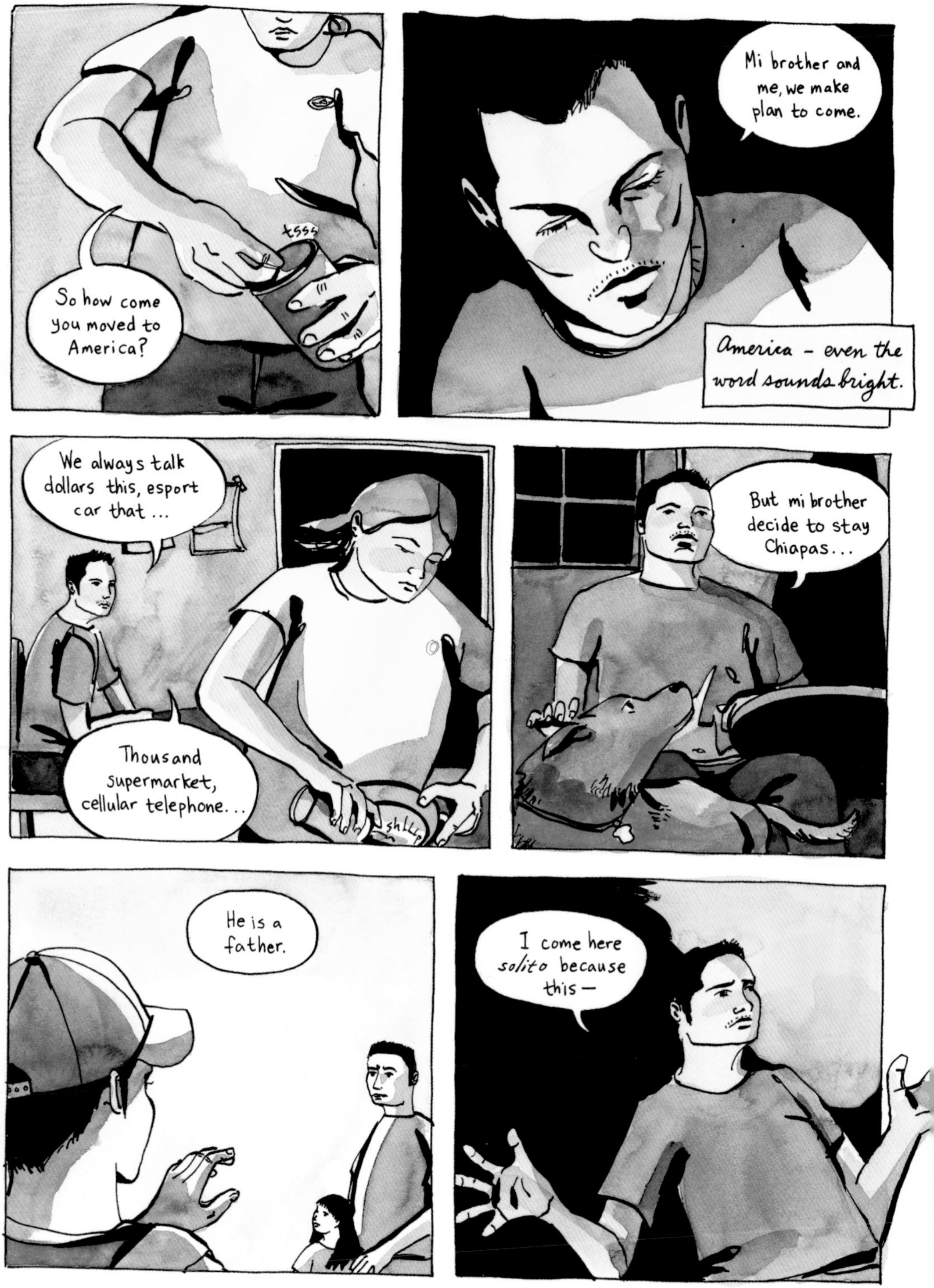
So how come you moved to America?
tsss
Mi brother and me, we make plan to come.
America - even the word sounds bright.
We always talk dollars this, esport car that...
Thousand supermarket, cellular telephone...
shlllp
But mi brother decide to stay Chiapas...
He is a father.
I come here *solito* because this—

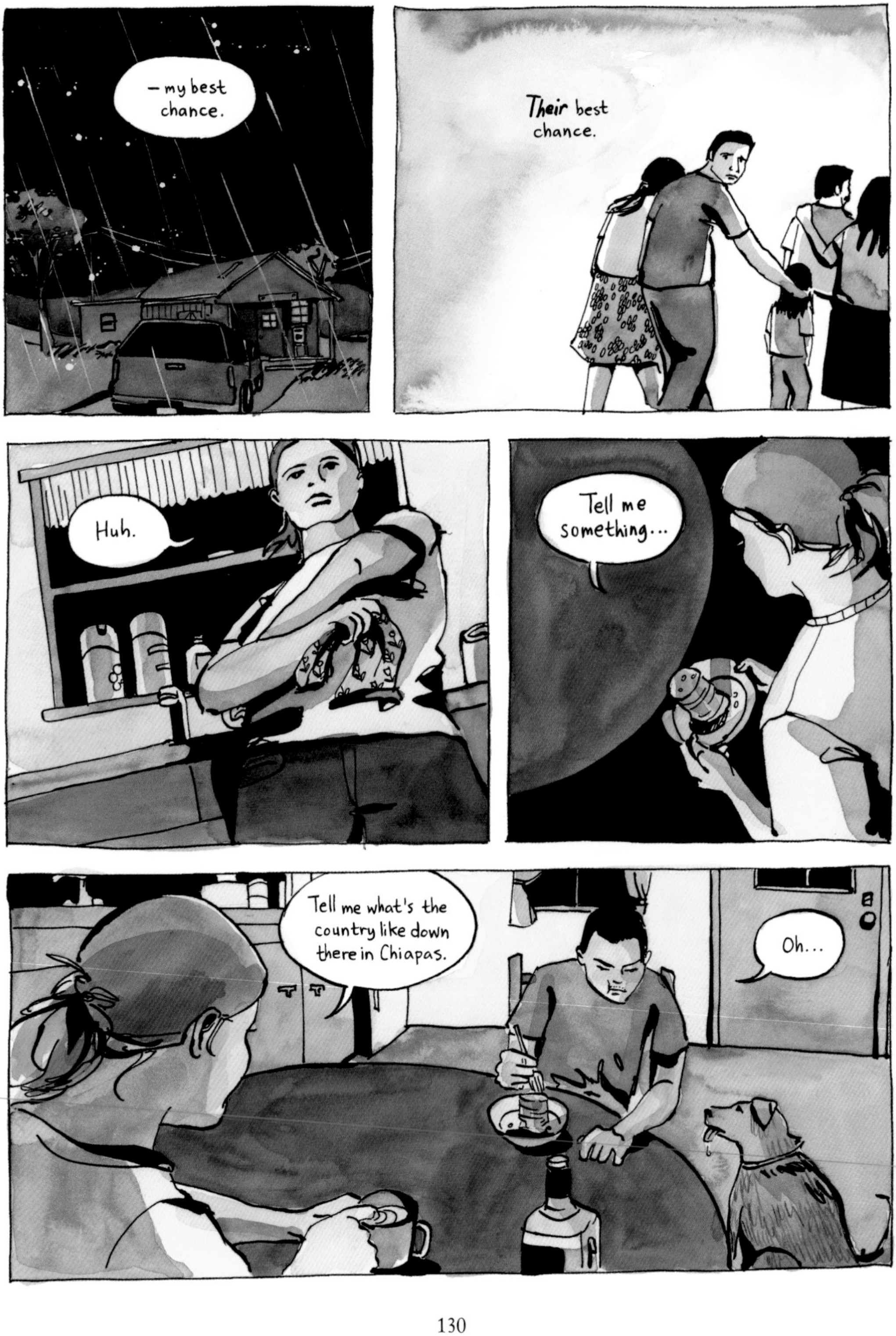
– my best chance.
Their best chance.
Huh.
Tell me something...
Tell me what's the country like down there in Chiapas.
Oh...

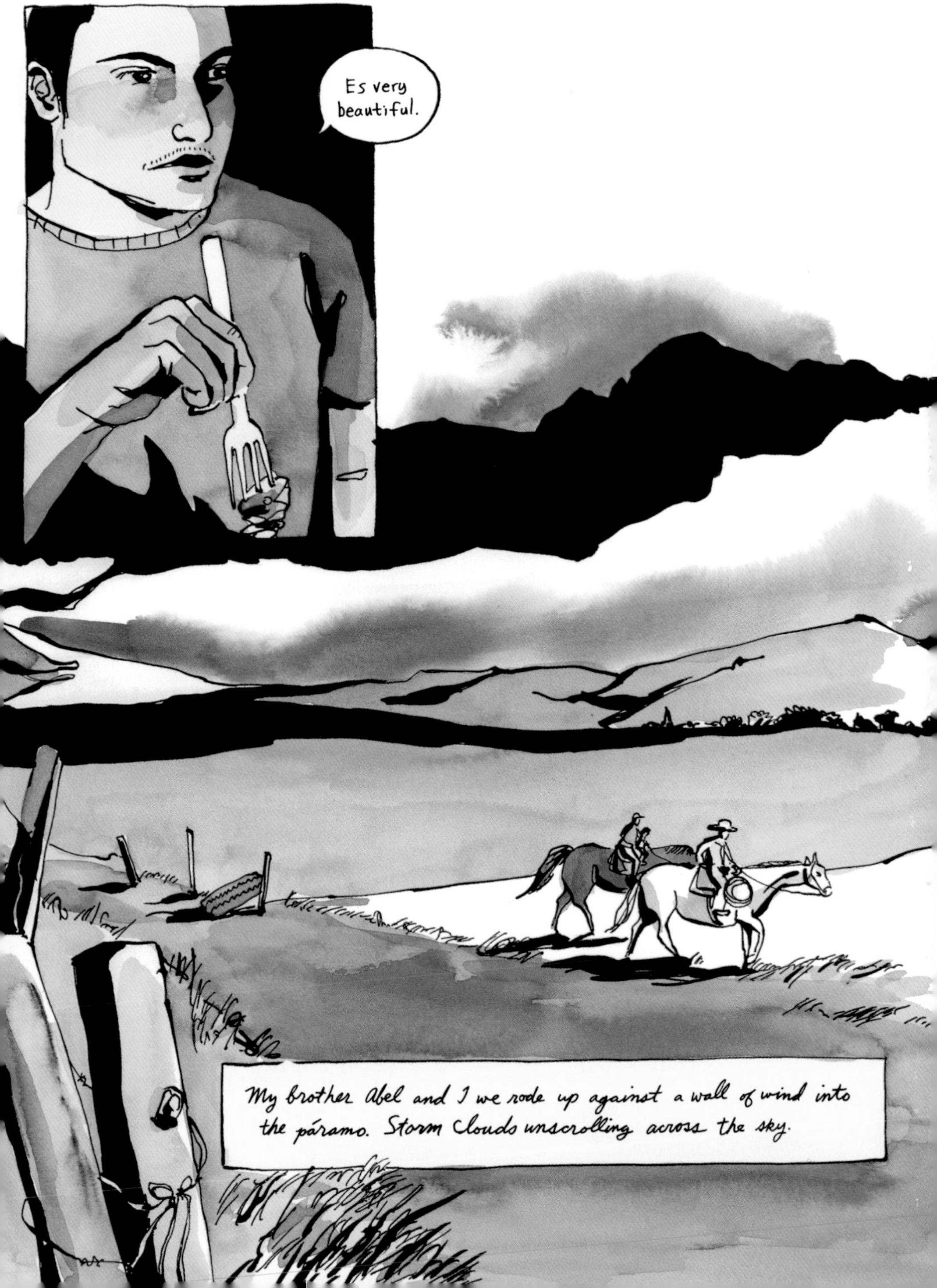
Es very beautiful.
My brother Abel and I we rode up against a wall of wind into the páramo. Storm Clouds unscrolling across the sky.

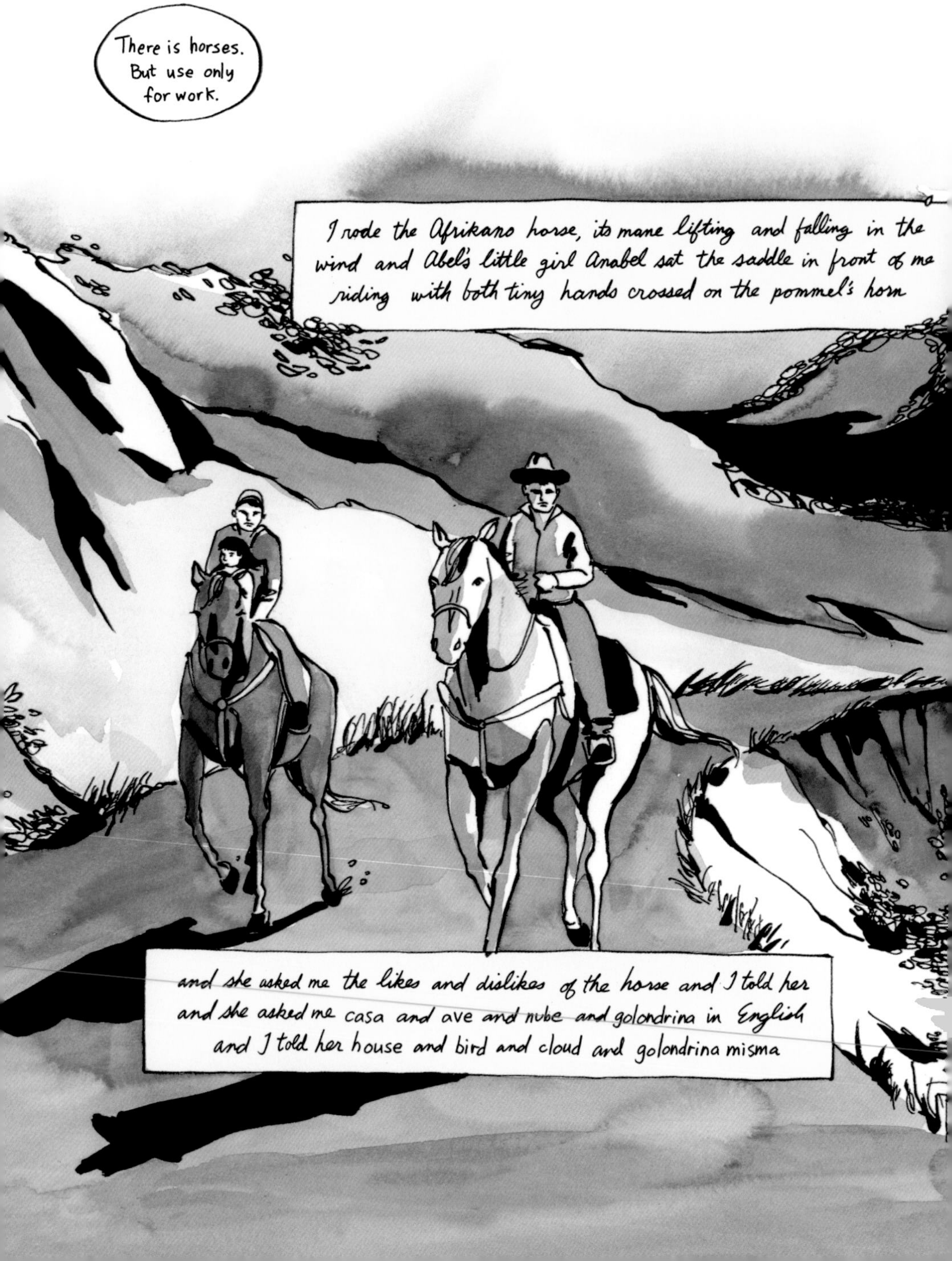
There is horses. But use only for work.
I rode the Afrikano horse, its mane lifting and falling in the wind and Abel's little girl Anabel sat the saddle in front of me riding with both tiny hands crossed on the pommel's horn
and she asked me the likes and dislikes of the horse and I told her and she asked me casa and ave and nube and golondrina in English and I told her house and bird and cloud and golondrina misma

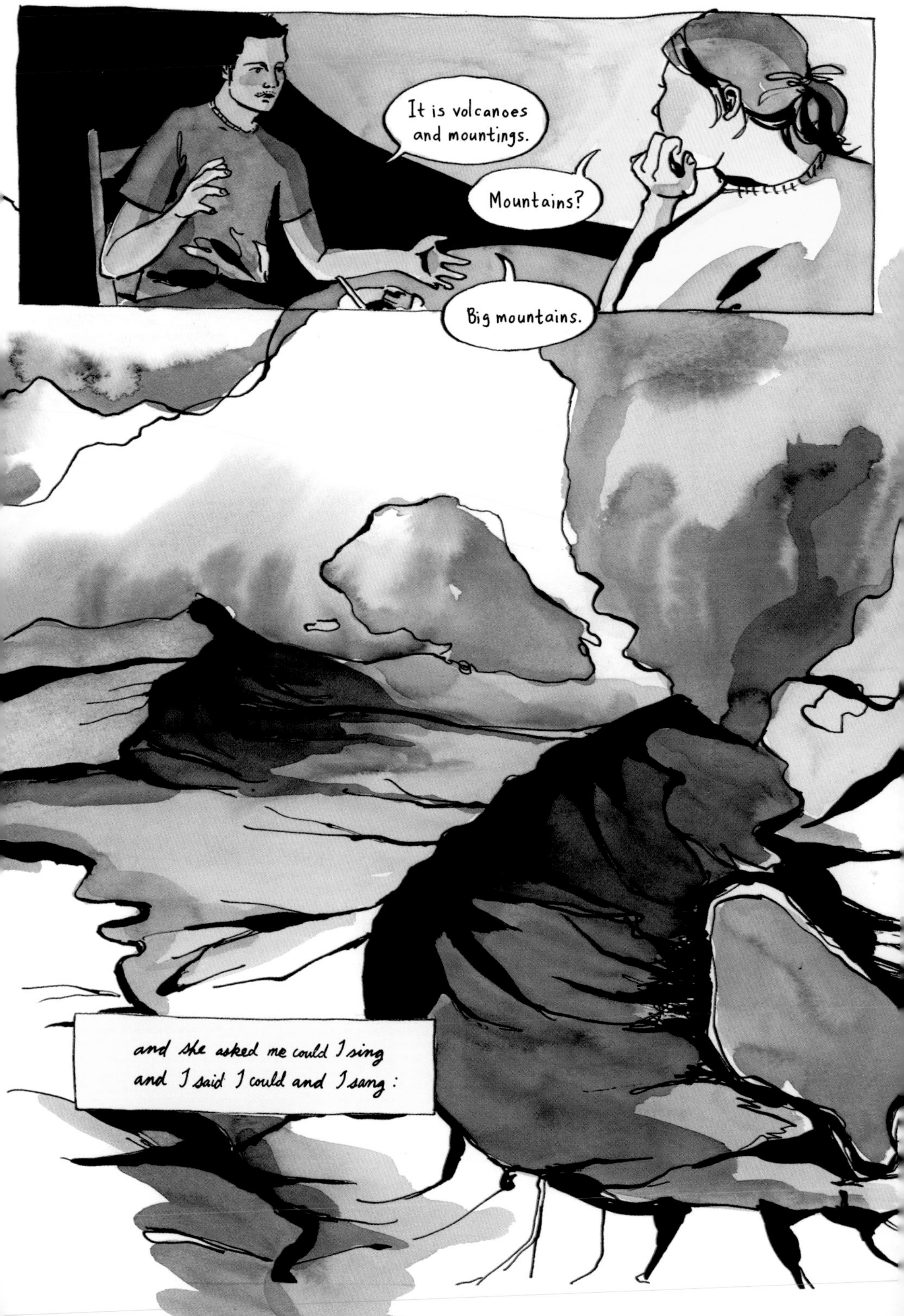
It is volcanoes and mountings.
Mountains?
Big mountains.
and she asked me could I sing and I said I could and I sang:

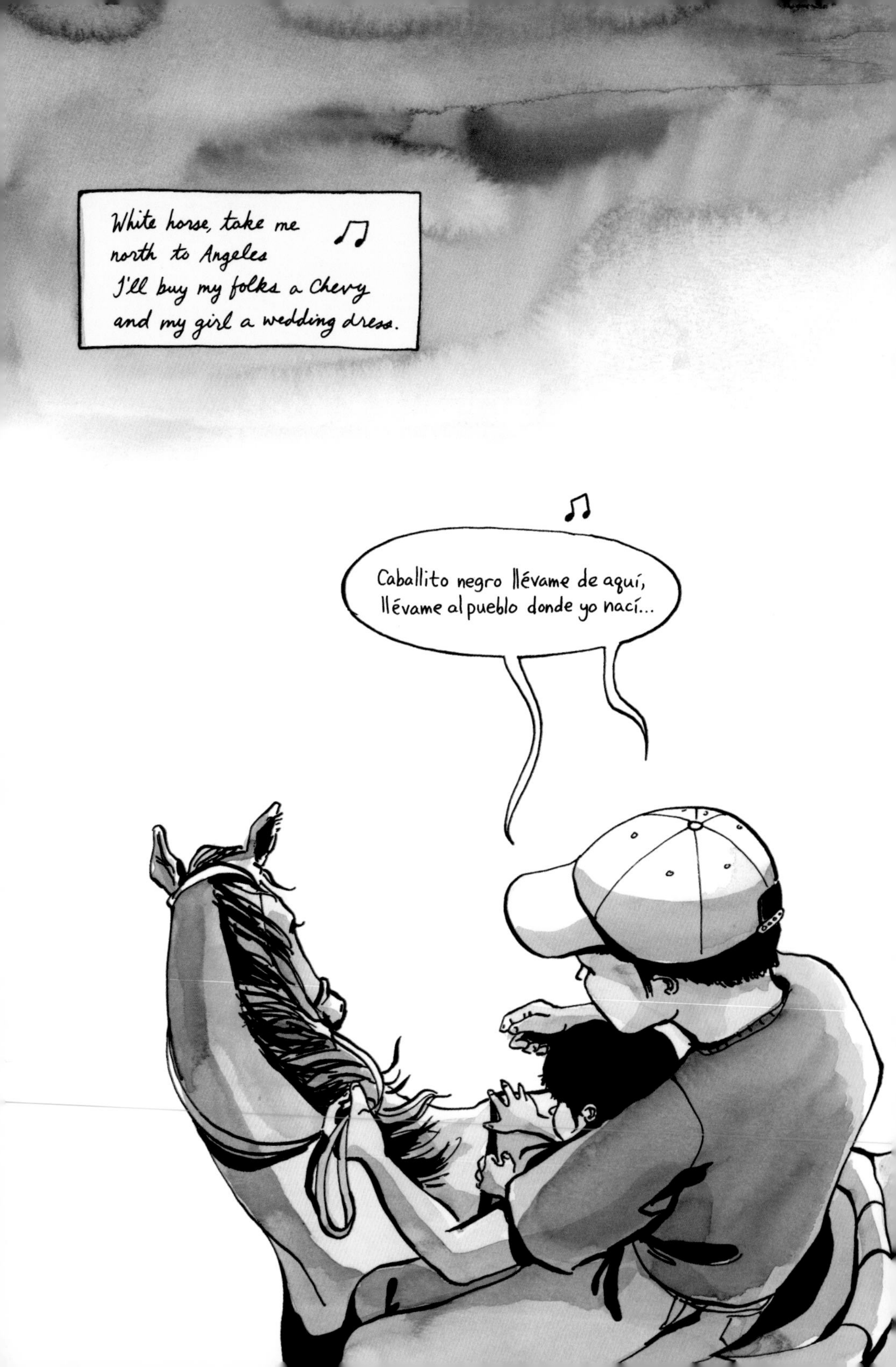
White horse, take me north to Angeles I'll buy my folks a Chevy and my girl a wedding dress.
Caballito negro llévame de aquí, llévame al pueblo donde yo nací...

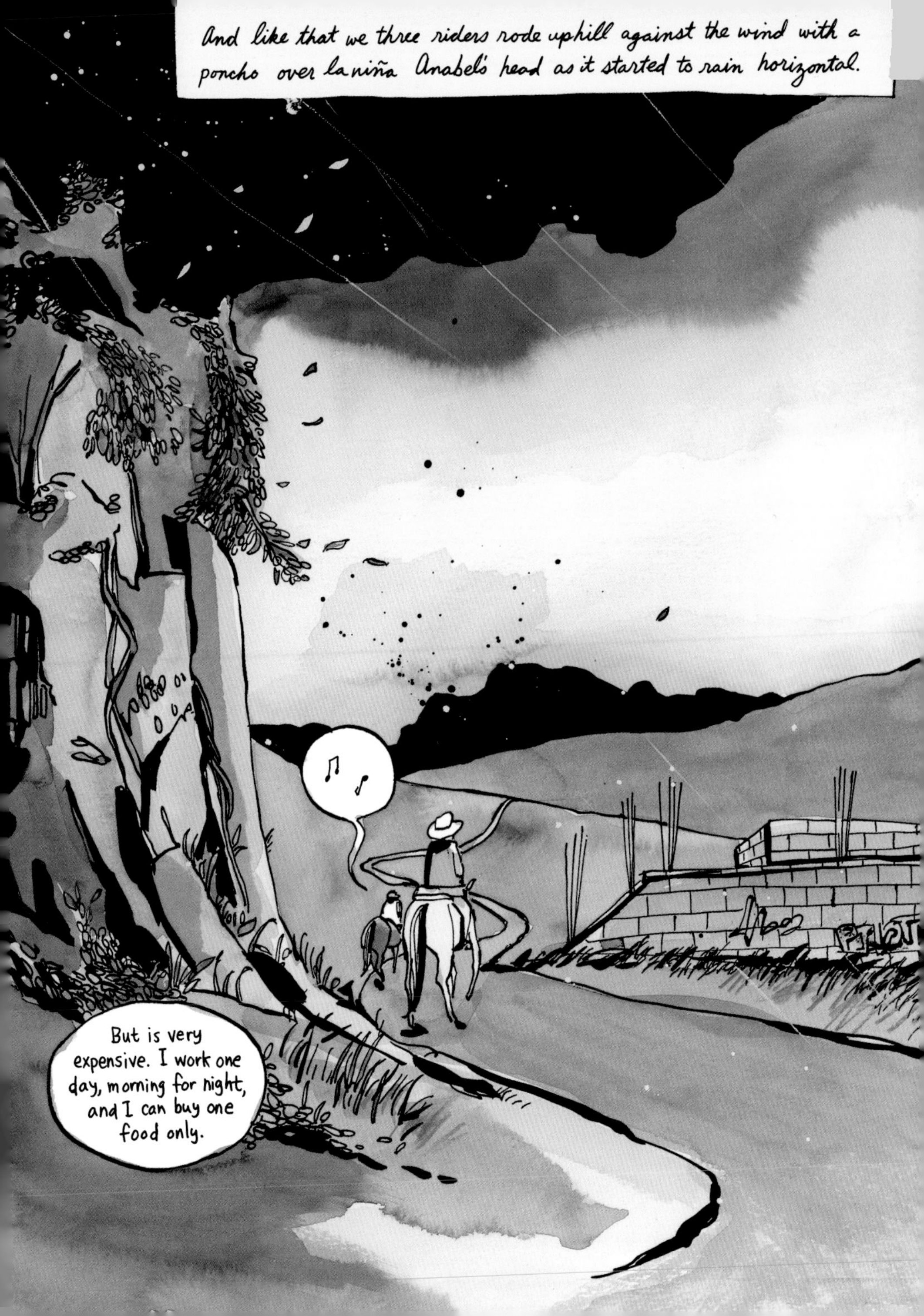
And like that we three riders rode uphill against the wind with a poncho over la niña Anabel's head as it started to rain horizontal.
But is very expensive. I work one day, morning for night, and I can buy one food only.

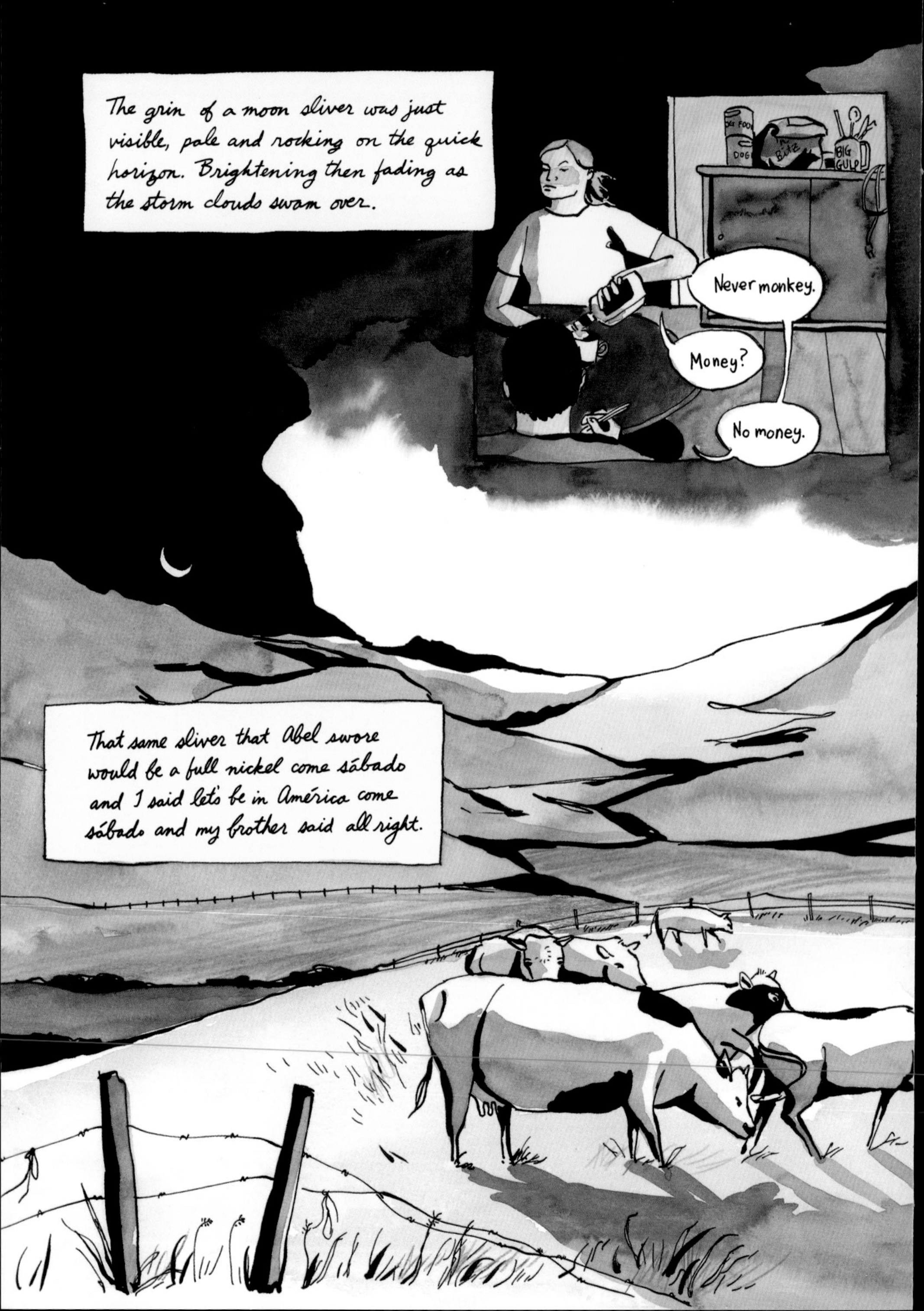
The grin of a moon sliver was just visible, pale and rocking on the quick horizon. Brightening then fading as the storm clouds swam over.
DOG FOOD
BITE
BIG GULP
Never monkey.
Money?
No money.
That same sliver that Abel swore would be a full nickel come sábado and I said let's be in América come sábado and my brother said all right.

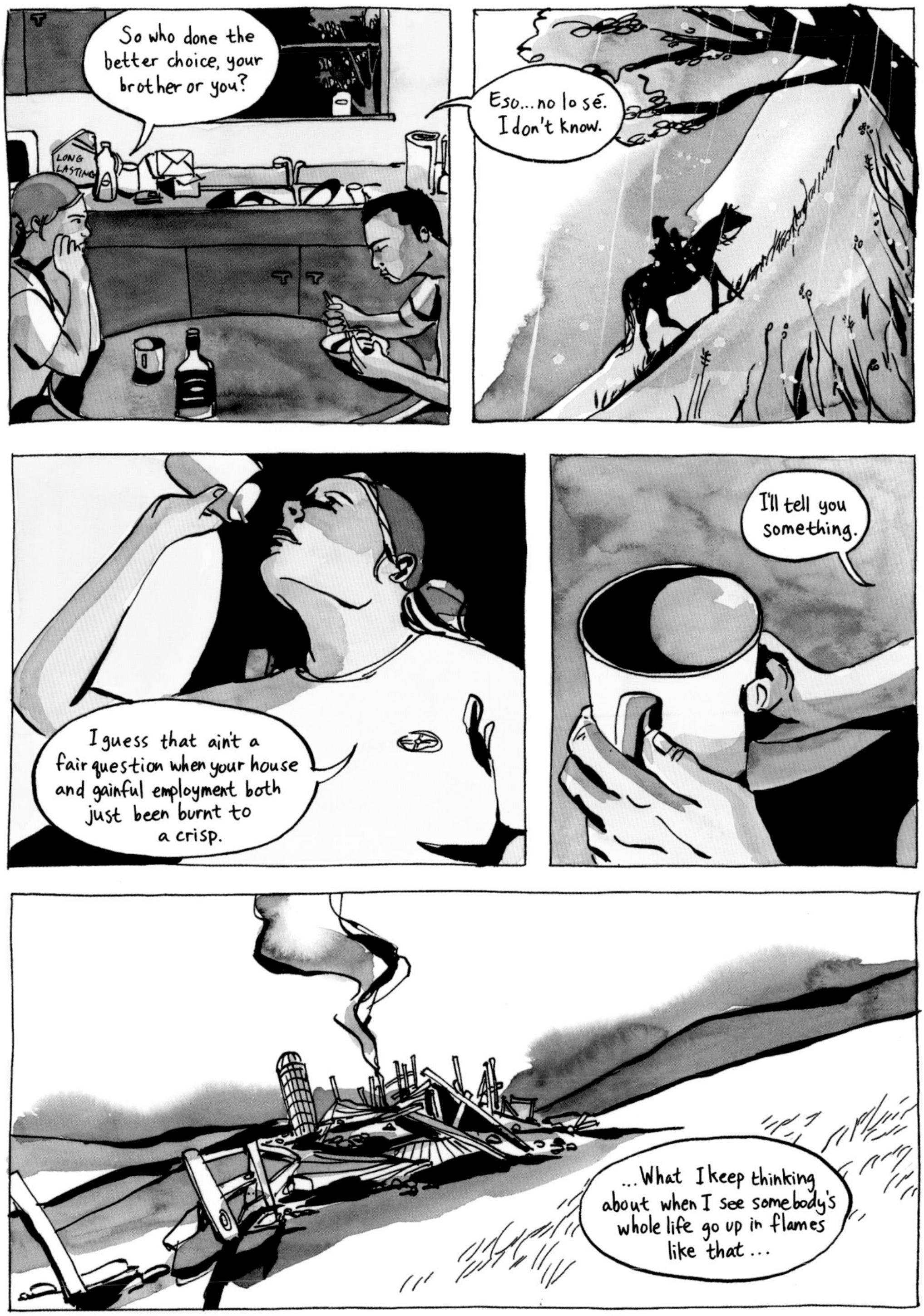
So who done the better choice, your brother or you?
LONG LASTING
Eso... no lo sé. I don't know.
I guess that ain't a fair question when your house and gainful employment both just been burnt to a crisp.
I'll tell you something.
...What I keep thinking about when I see somebody's whole life go up in flames like that...

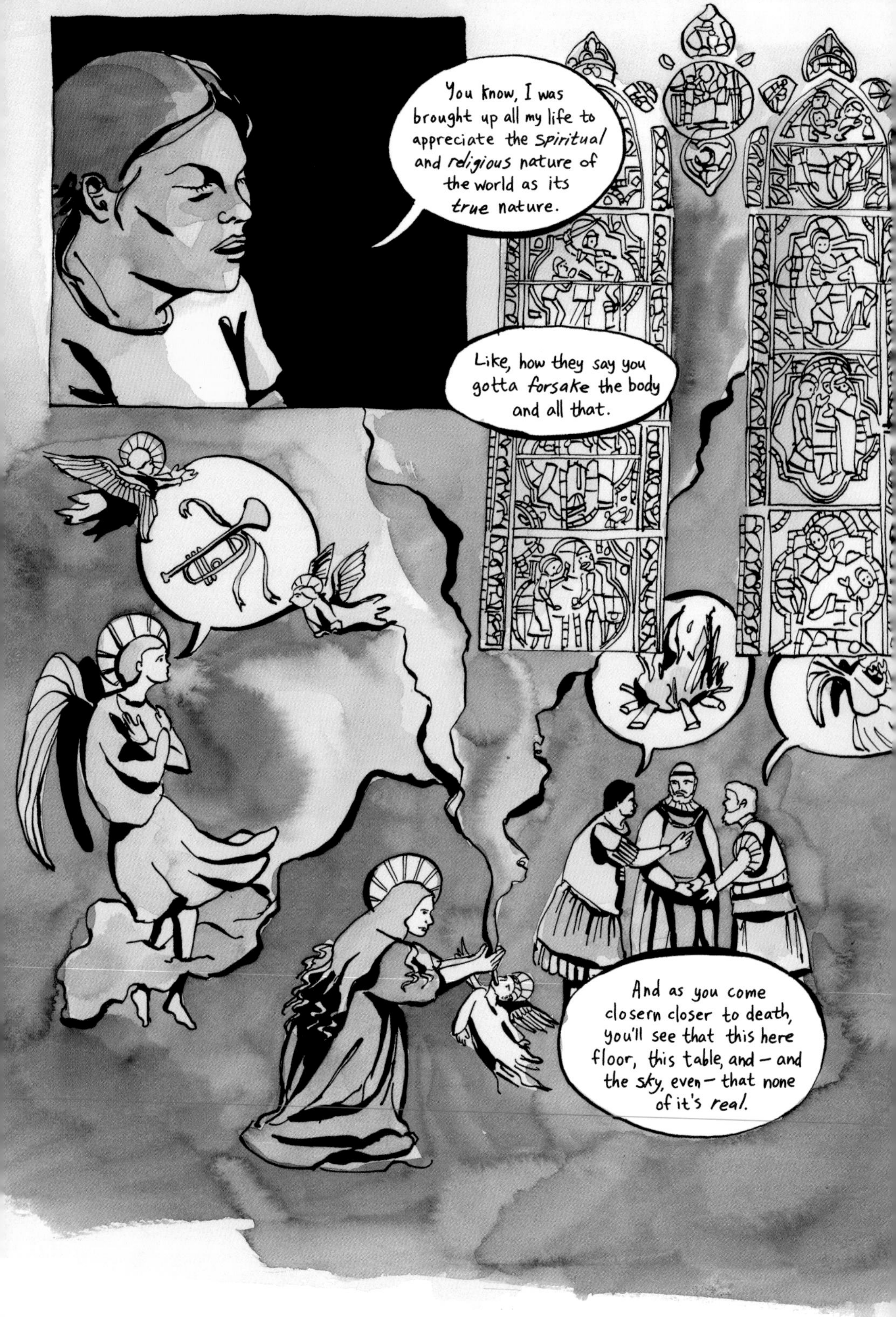
You know, I was brought up all my life to appreciate the *spiritual* and *religious* nature of the world as its *true* nature.
Like, how they say you gotta *forsake* the body and all that.
And as you come closer and closer to death, you'll see that this here floor, this table, and — and the *sky*, even — that none of it's *real*.

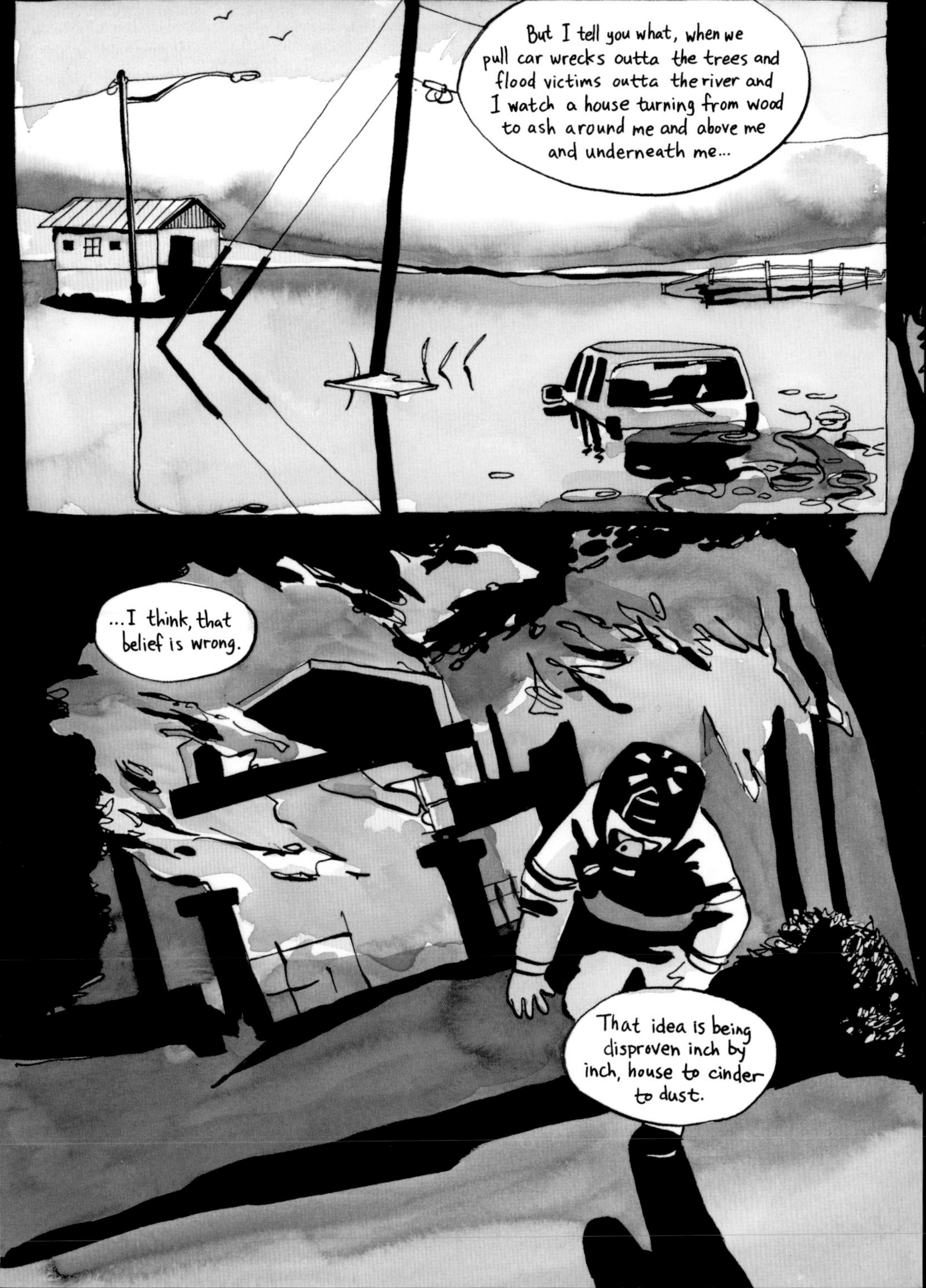
But I tell you what, when we pull car wrecks outta the trees and flood victims outta the river and I watch a house turning from wood to ash around me and above me and underneath me...
...I think, that belief is wrong.
That idea is being disproven inch by inch, house to cinder to dust.

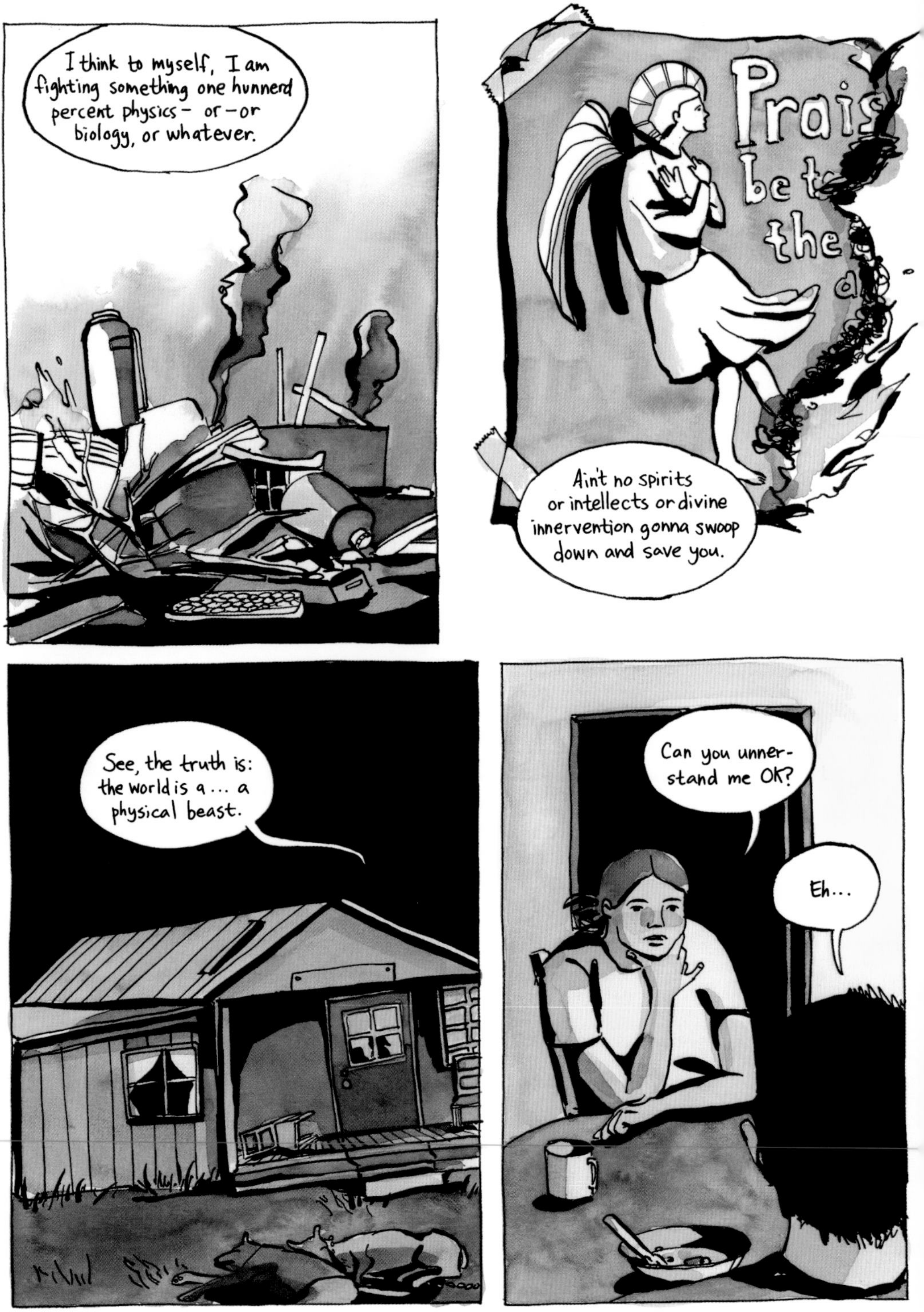
I think to myself, I am fighting something one hunnerd percent physics – or – or biology, or whatever.
Prais be t the a
Ain't no spirits or intellects or divine innervention gonna swoop down and save you.
See, the truth is: the world is a… a physical beast.
Can you unner-stand me OK?
Eh…

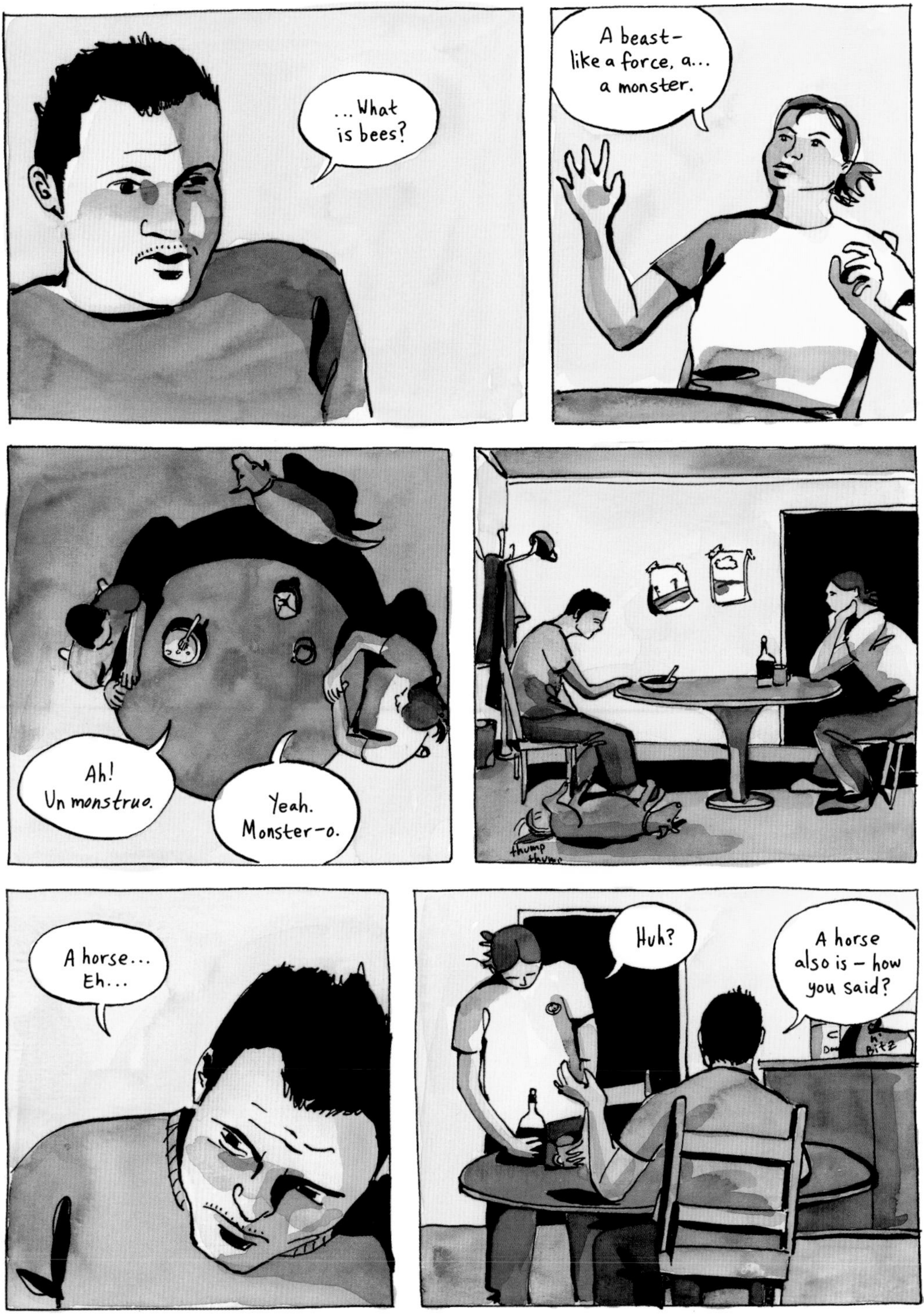
...What is bees?
A beast- like a force, a... a monster.
Ah! Un monstruo.
Yeah. Monster-o.
thump
A horse... Eh...
Huh?
A horse also is – how you said?

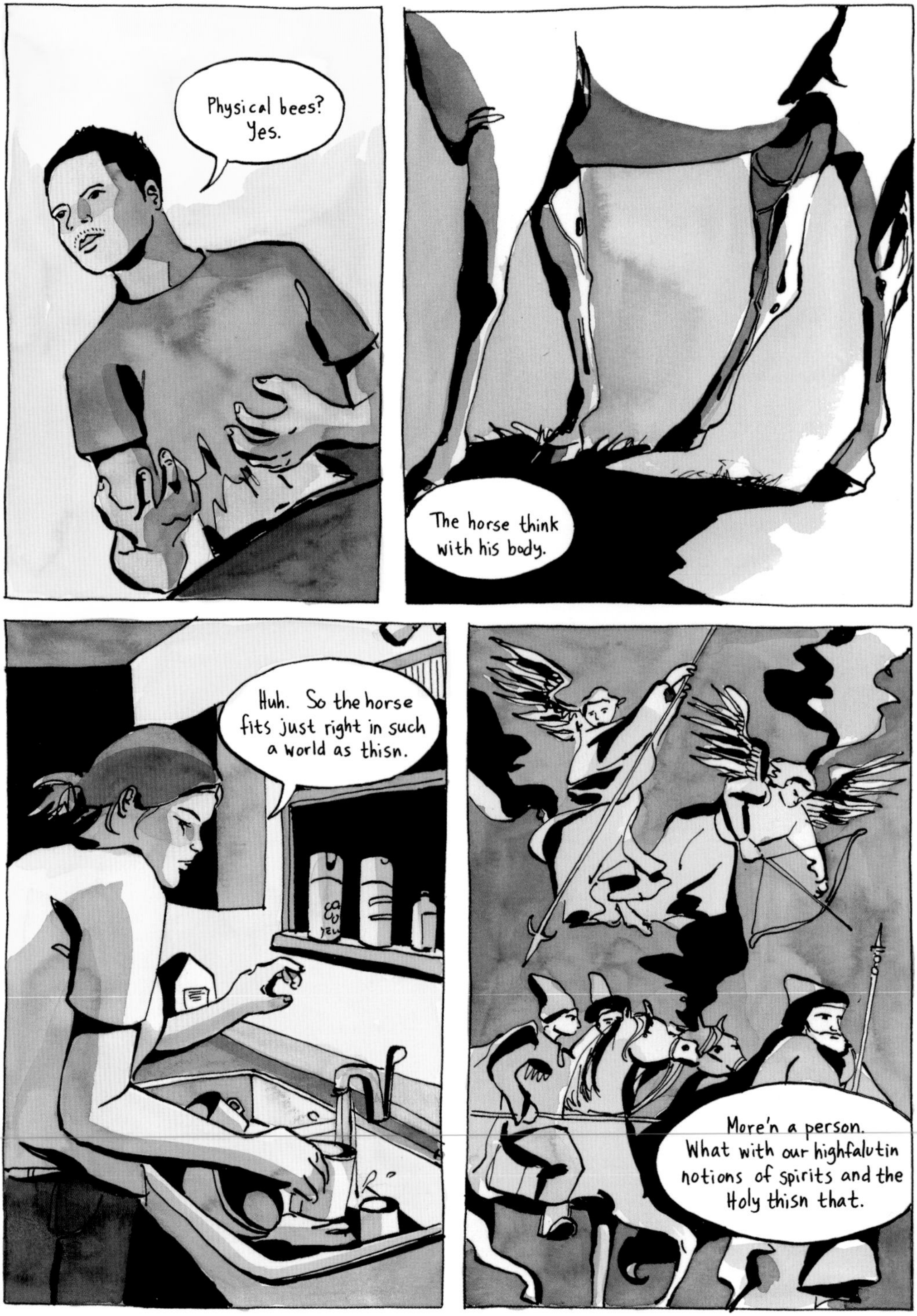
Physical bees? Yes.
The horse think with his body.
Huh. So the horse fits just right in such a world as thisn.
More'n a person. What with our highfalutin notions of spirits and the Holy thisn that.

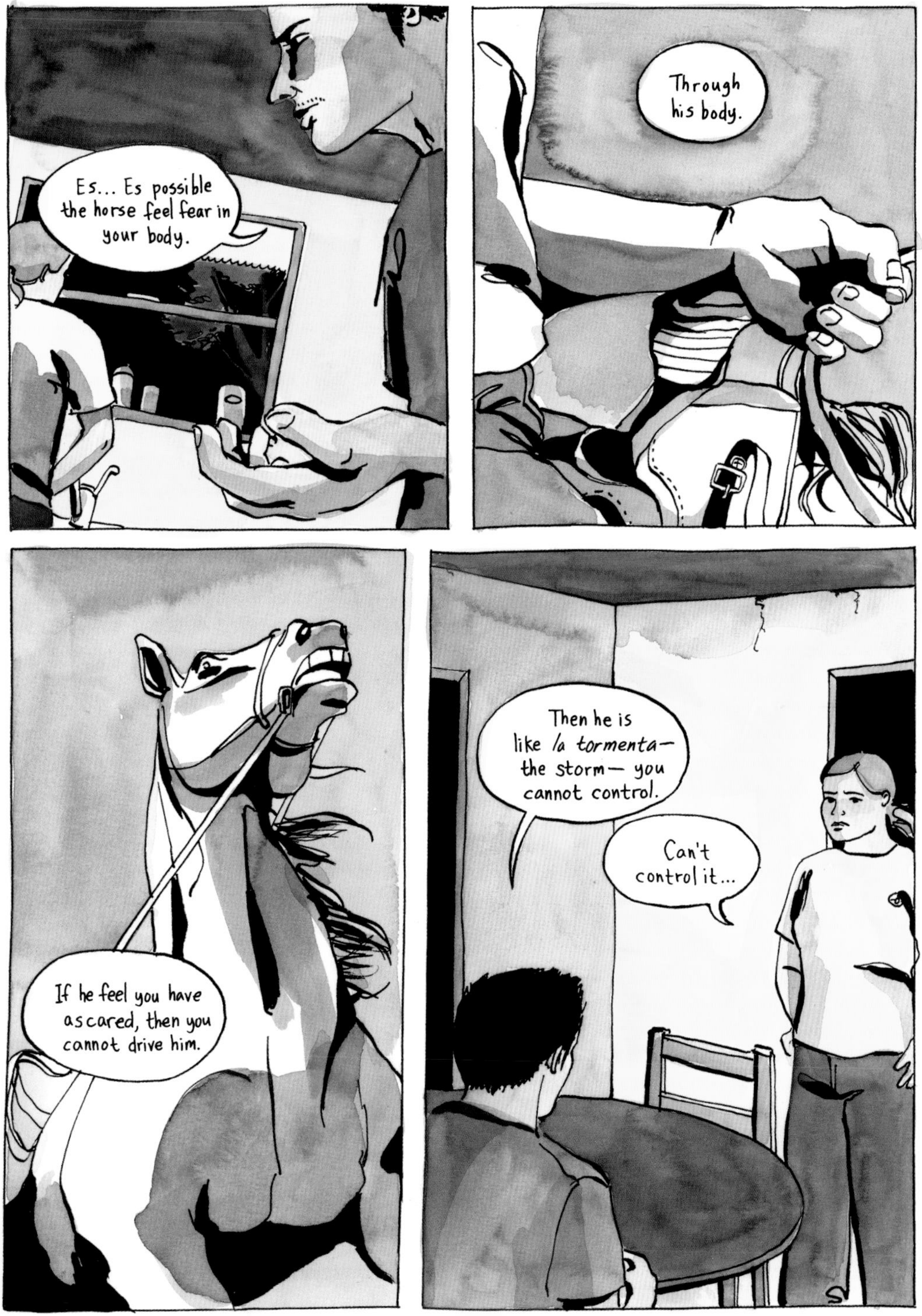
Es... Es possible the horse feel fear in your body.
Through his body.
If he feel you have ascared, then you cannot drive him.
Then he is like *la tormenta*— the storm— you cannot control.
Can't control it...

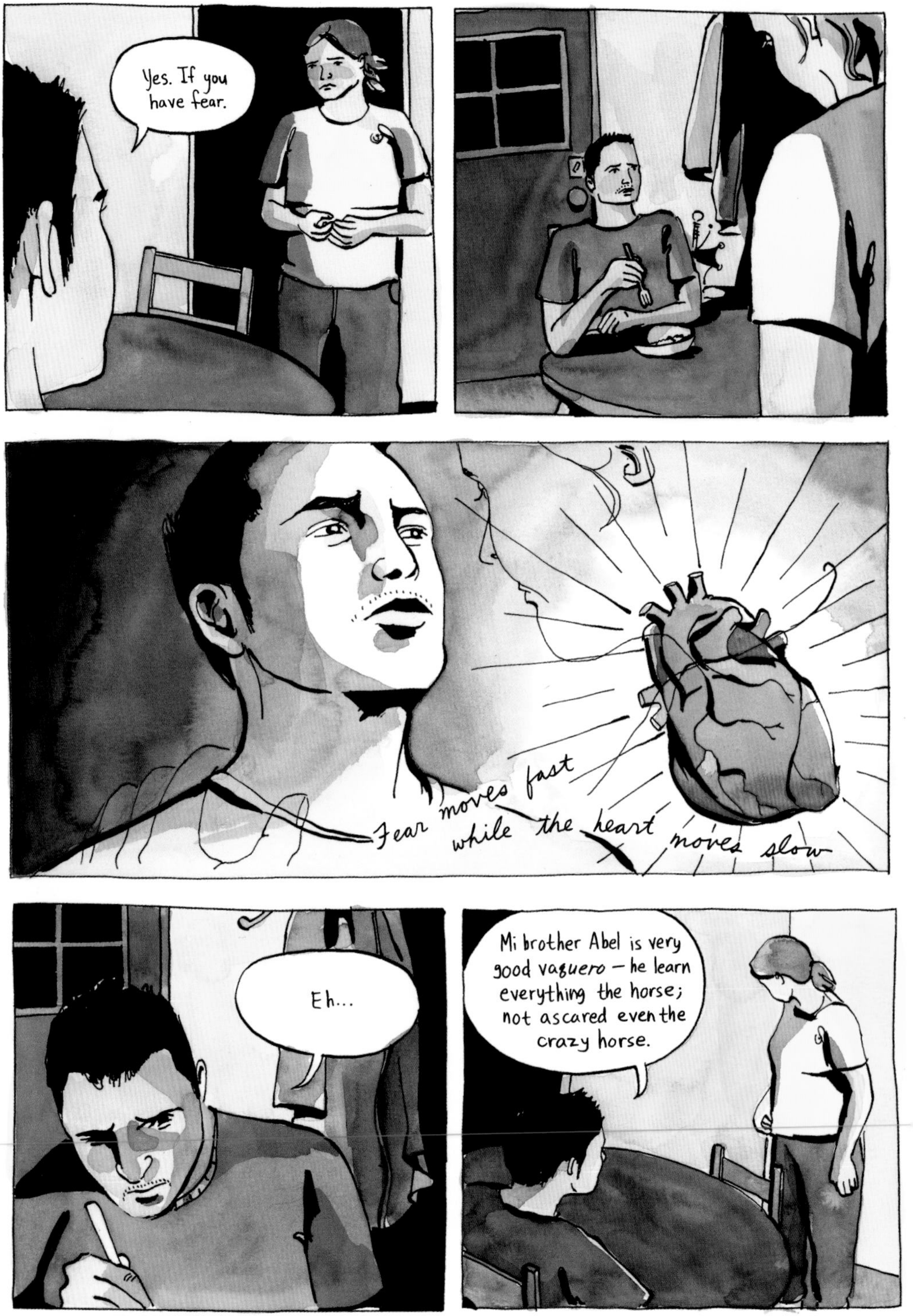
Yes. If you have fear.
Fear moves fast while the heart moves slow
Eh...
Mi brother Abel is very good vaguero – he learn everything the horse; not ascared even the crazy horse.

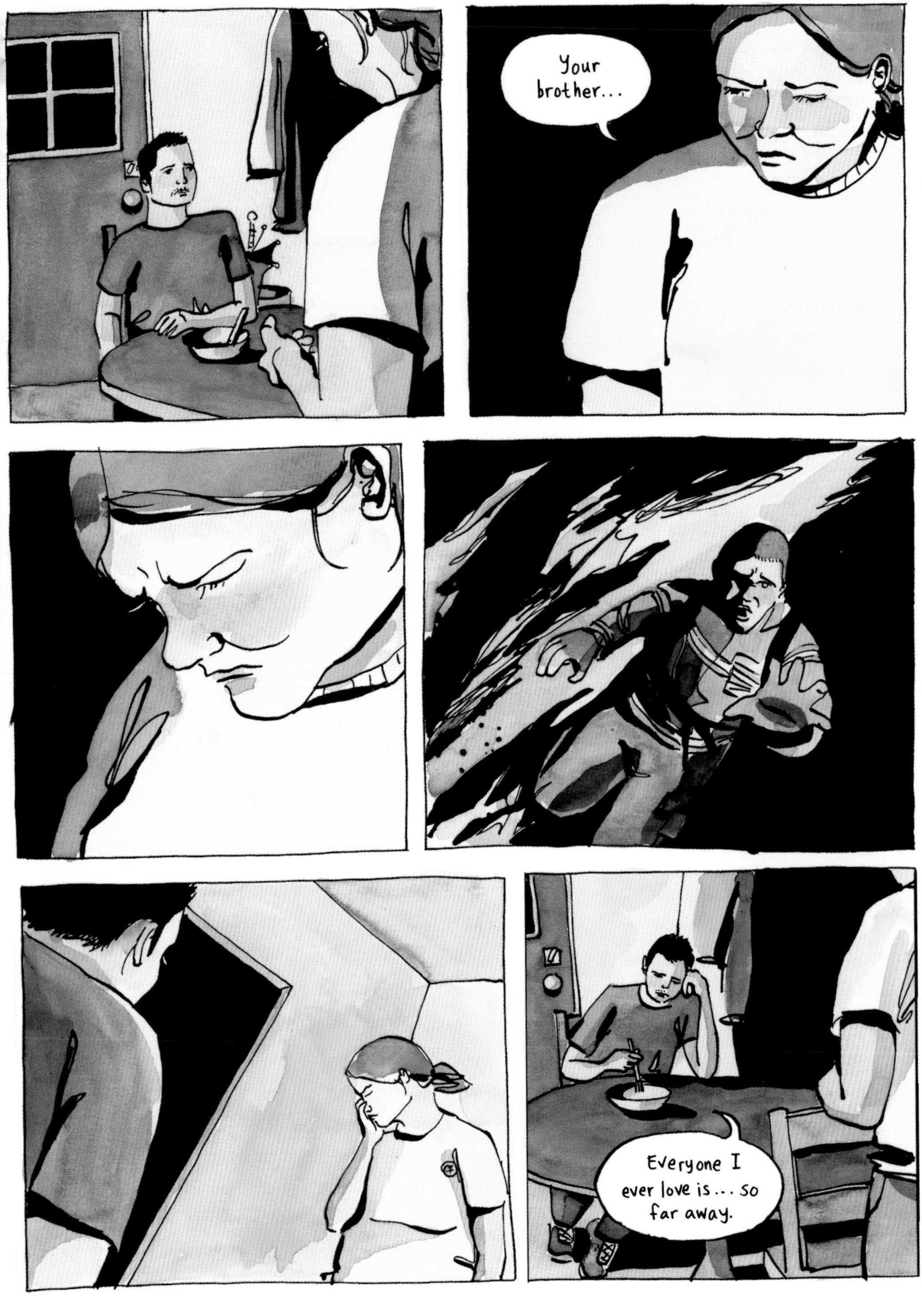
Your brother...
Everyone I ever love is... so far away.

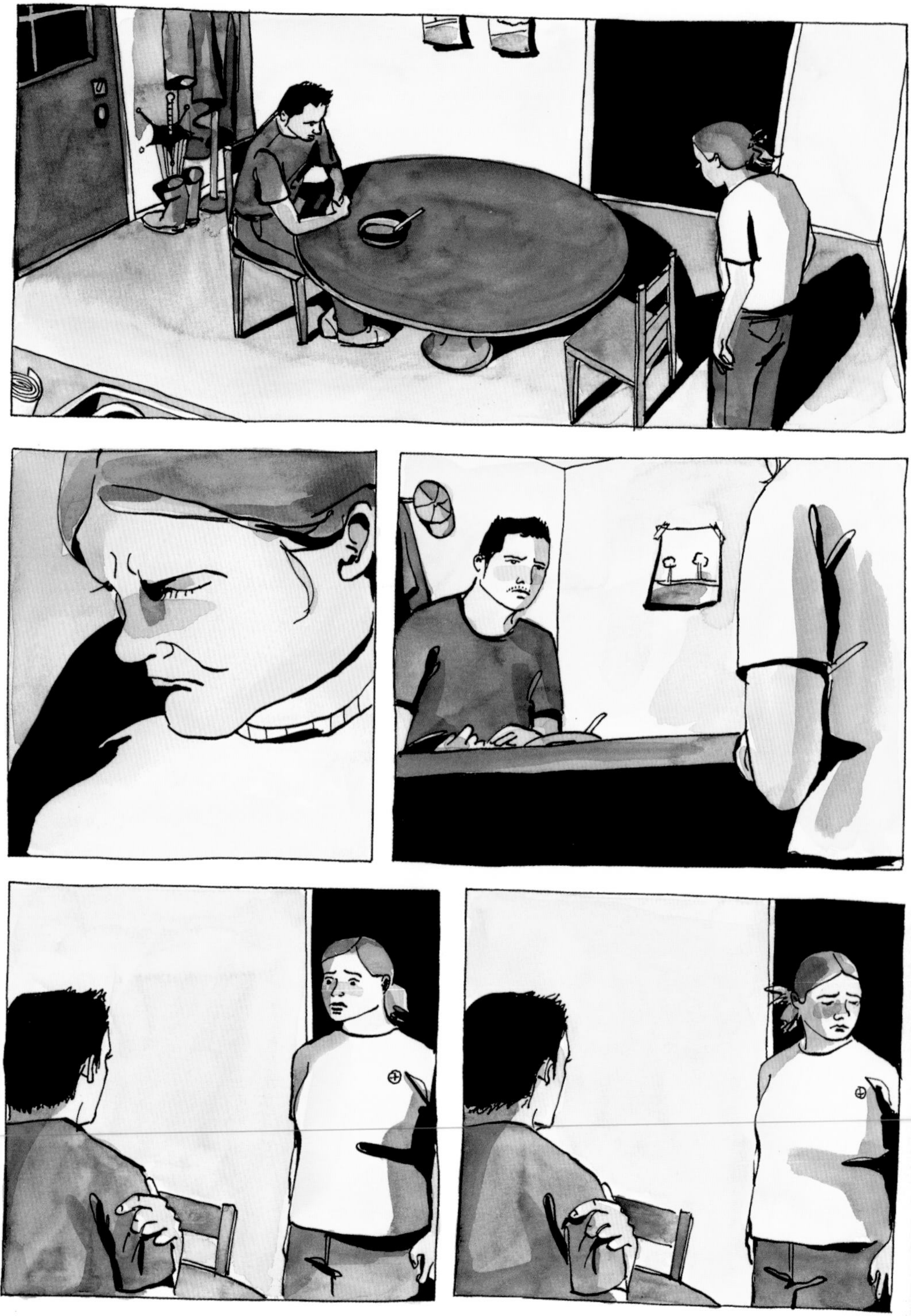

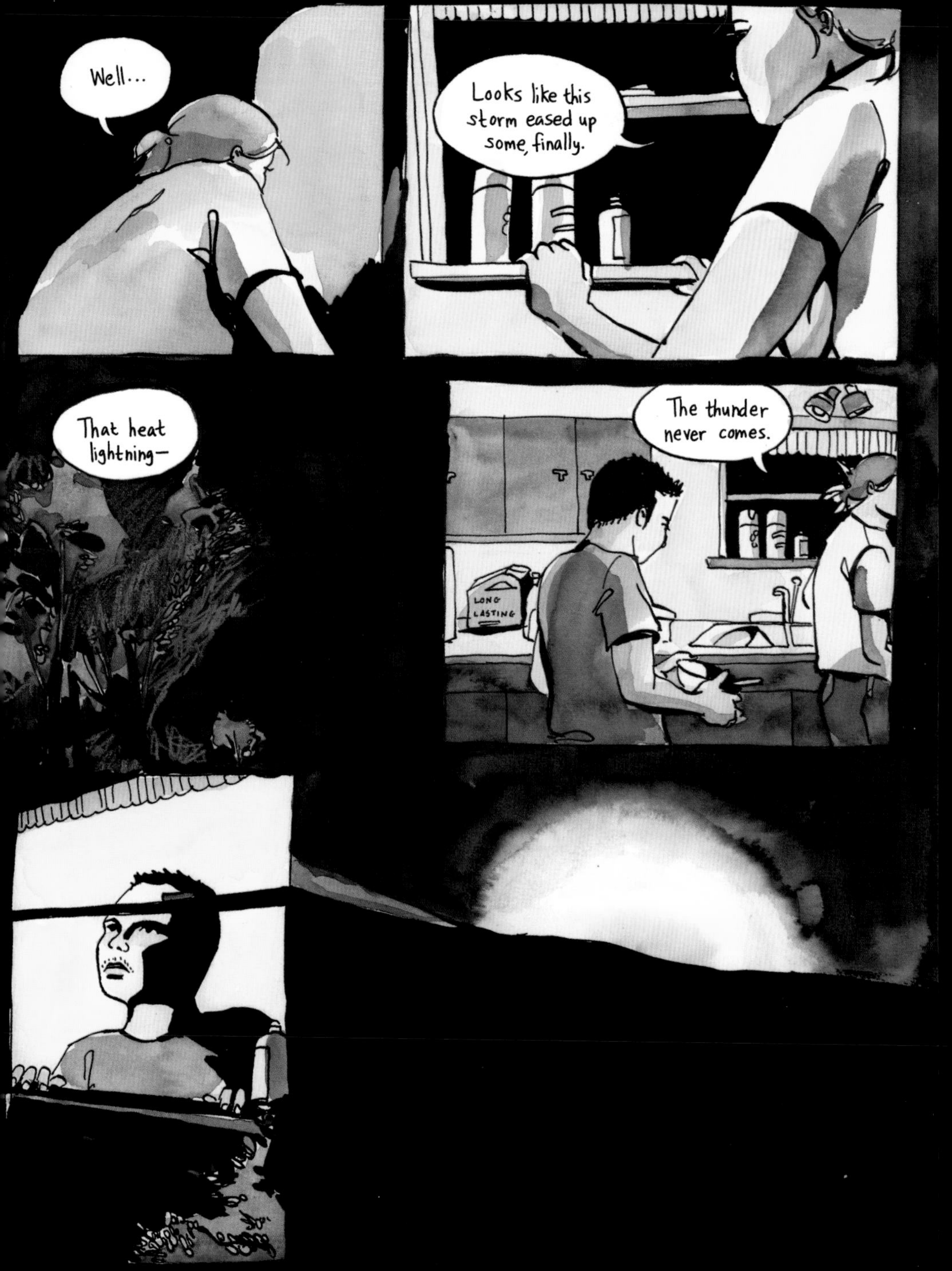
Well...
Looks like this storm eased up some, finally.
That heat lightning—
The thunder never comes.
LONG LASTING

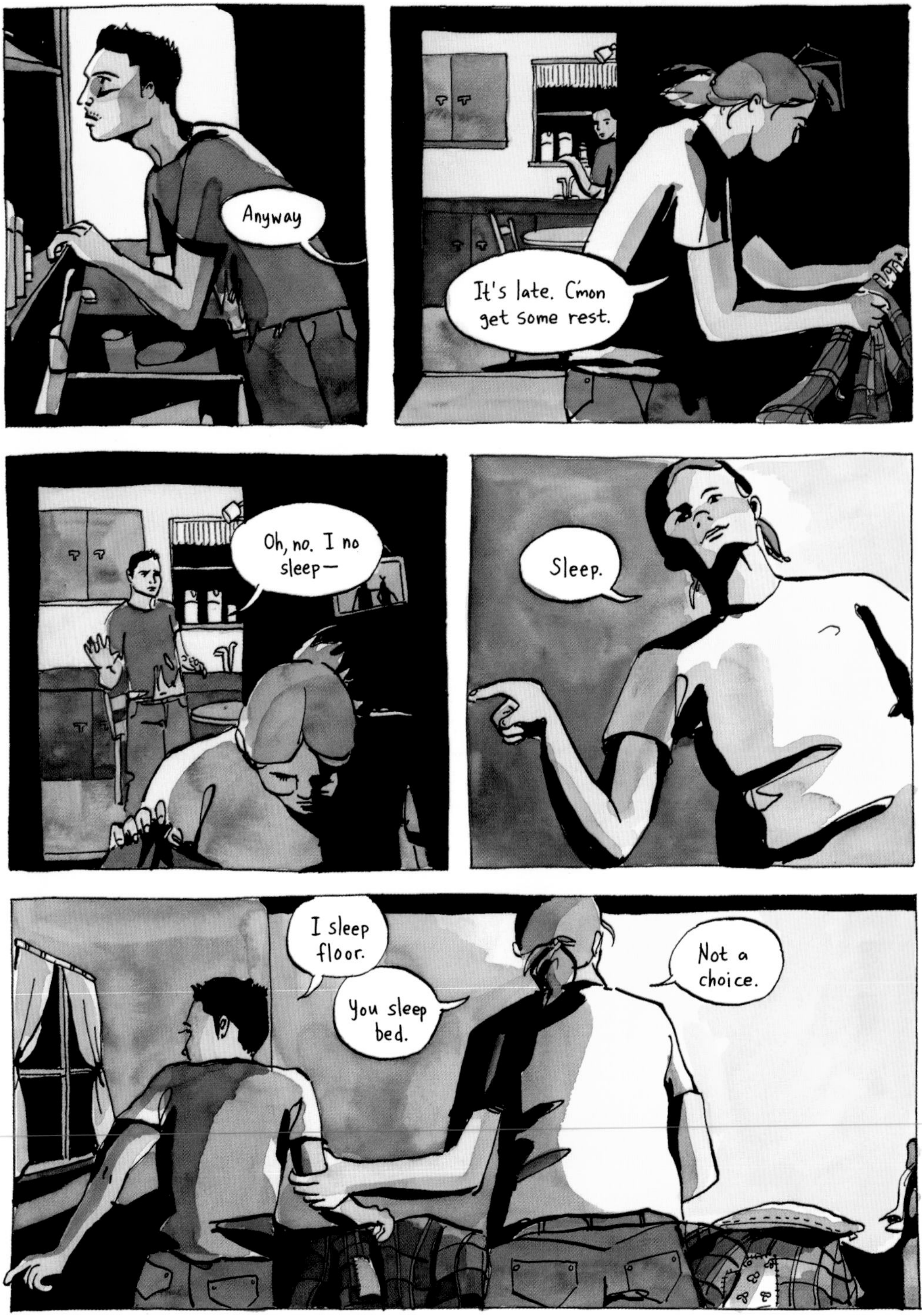
Anyway
It's late. C'mon get some rest.
Oh, no. I no sleep—
Sleep.
I sleep floor.
You sleep bed.
Not a choice.

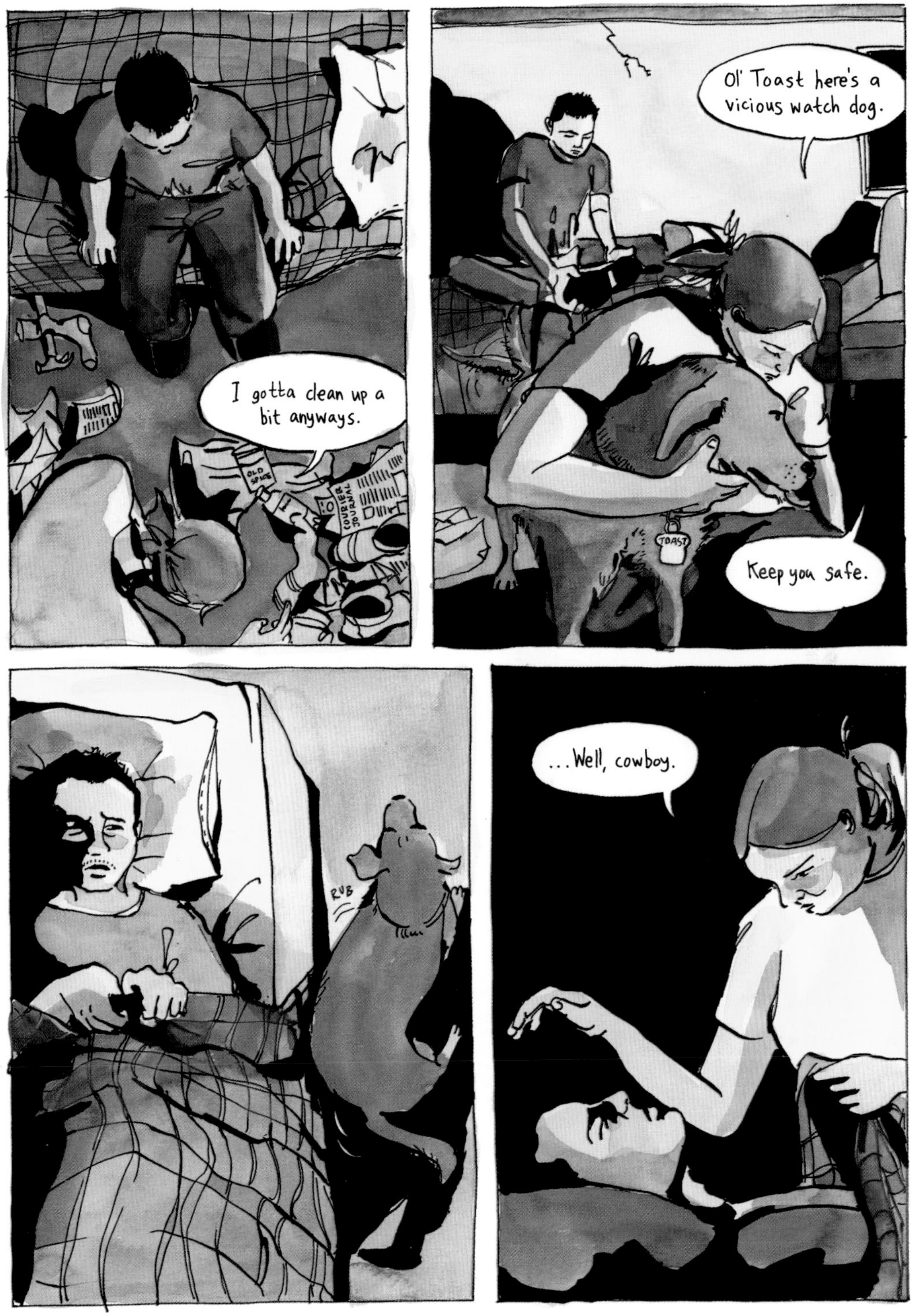
I gotta clean up a bit anyways.
OLD SPICE
COURIER JOURNAL
Ol' Toast here's a vicious watch dog.
TOAST
Keep you safe.
RUB
...Well, cowboy.

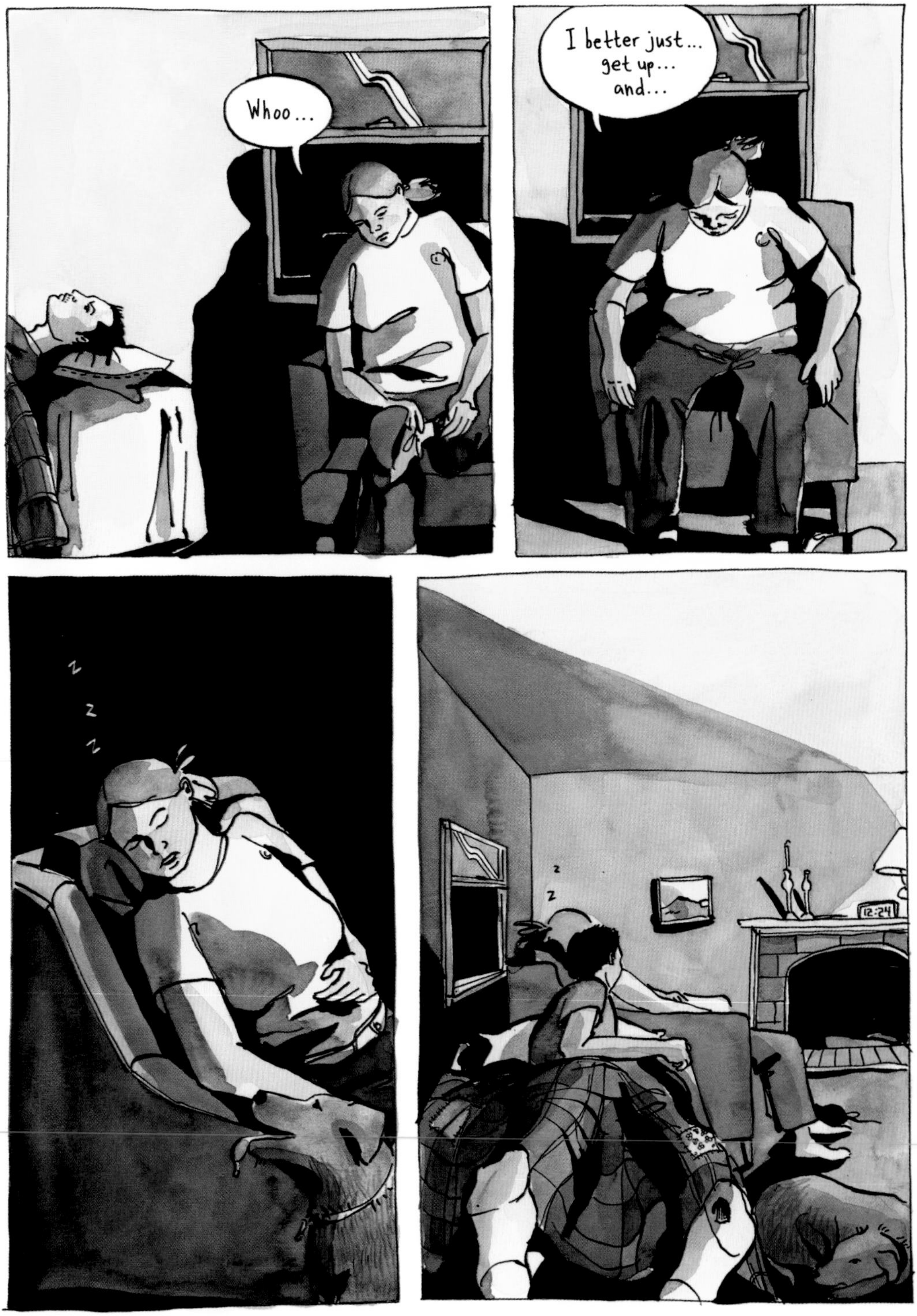
Whoo...
I better just... get up... and...
12:24

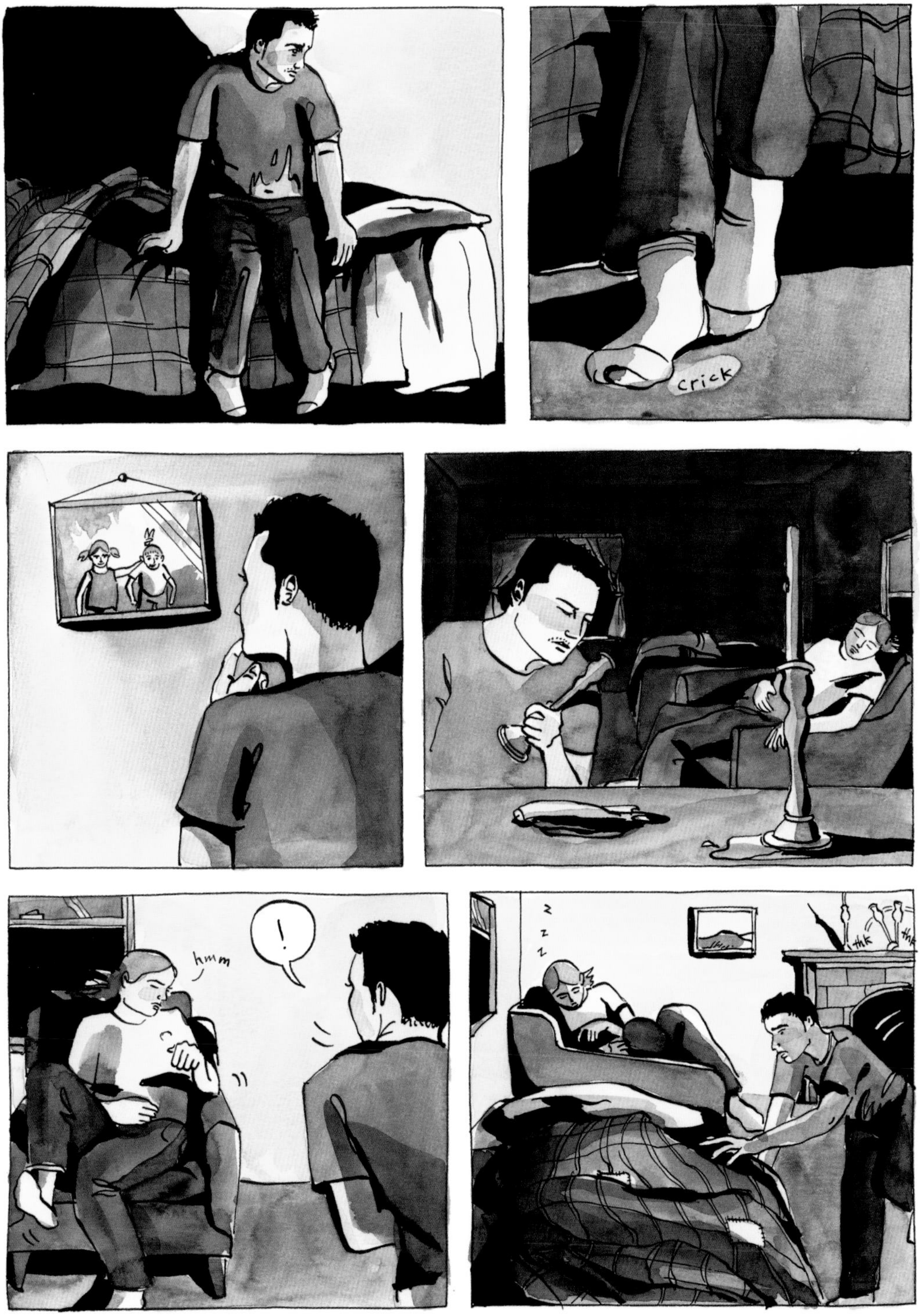
crick
hmm
!
z
z
z
thk
thk

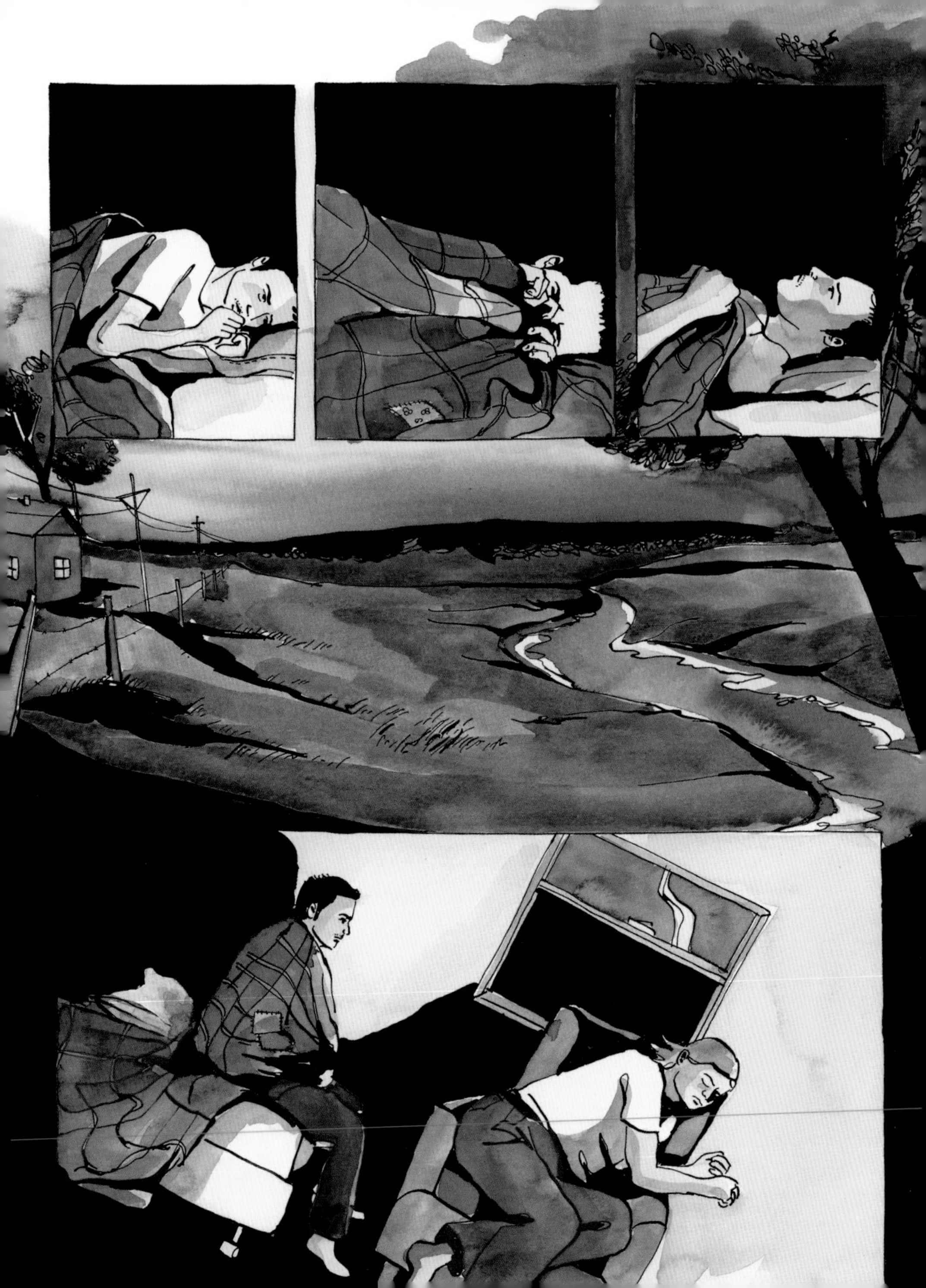

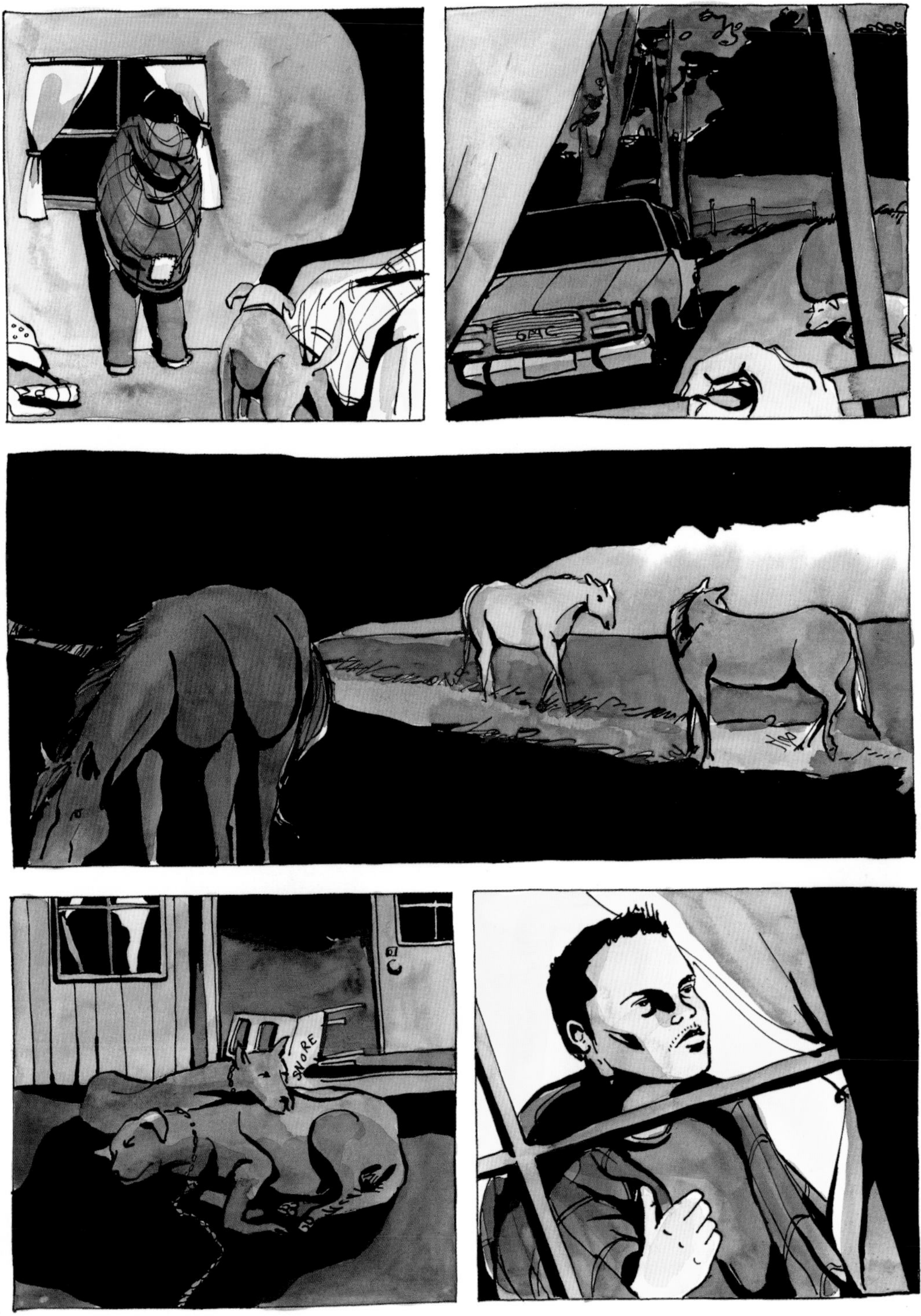
GMC
SNORE

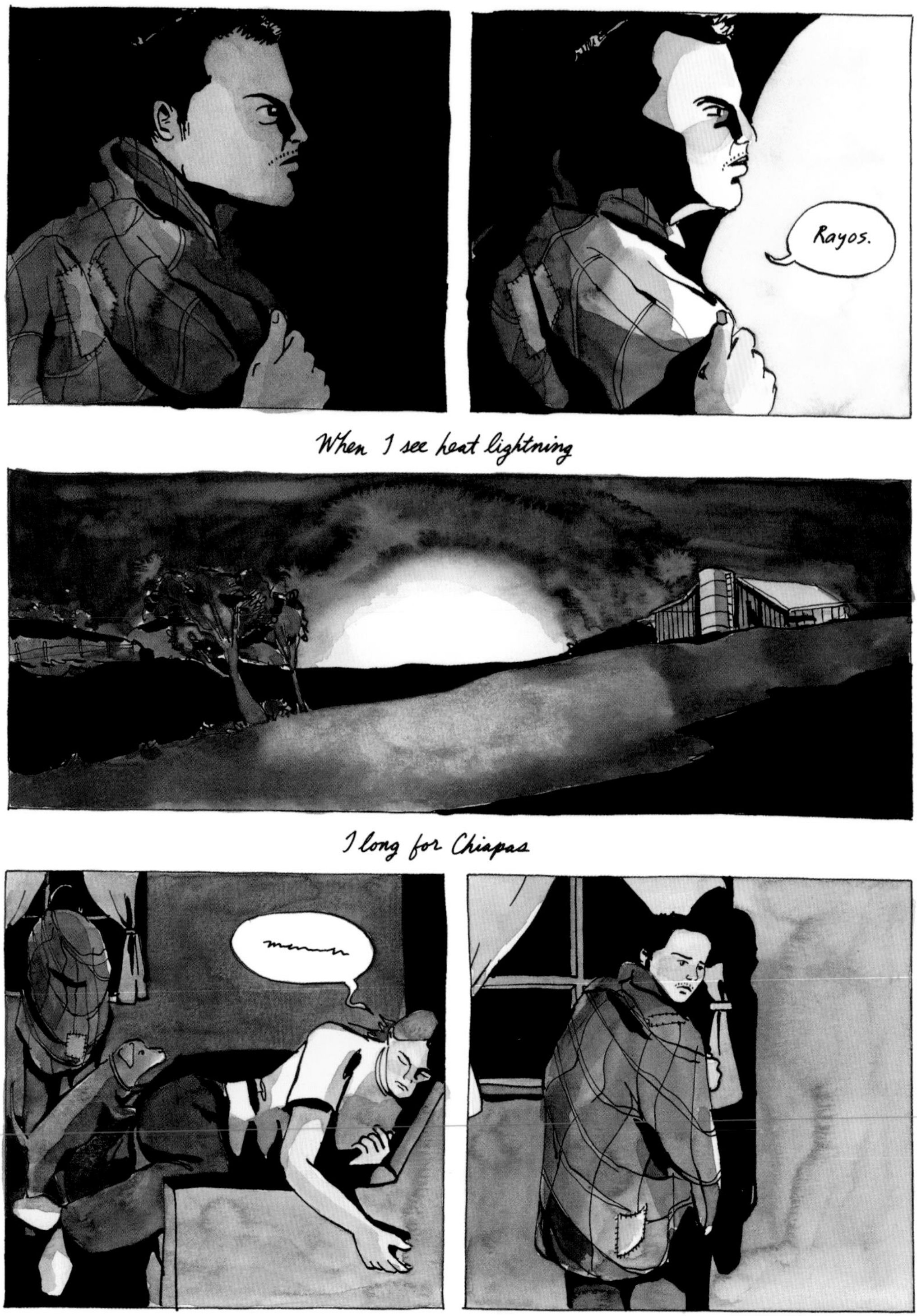
Rayos.
When I see heat lightning
I long for Chiapas

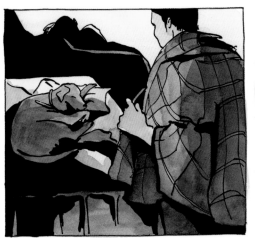

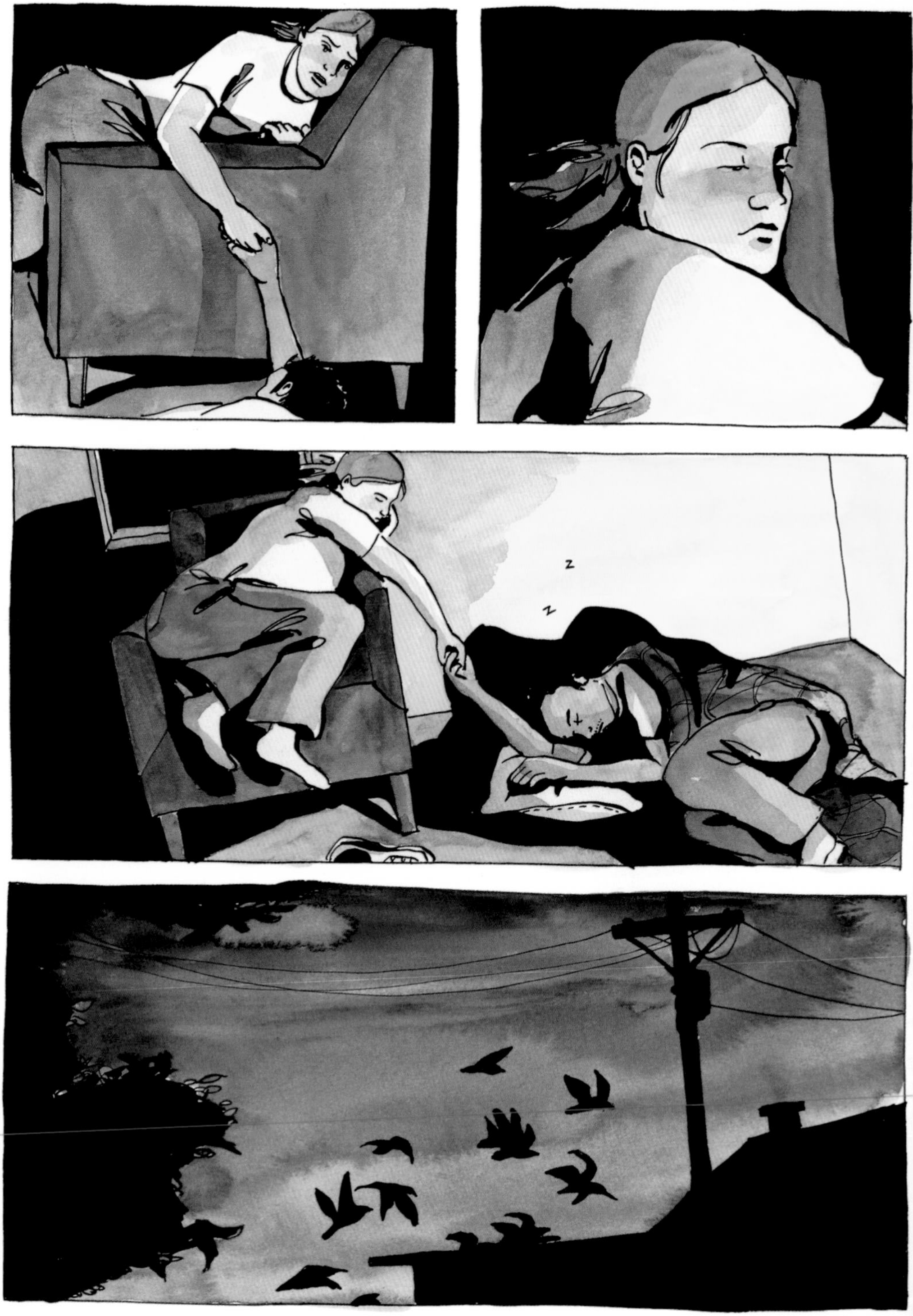
Z
Z

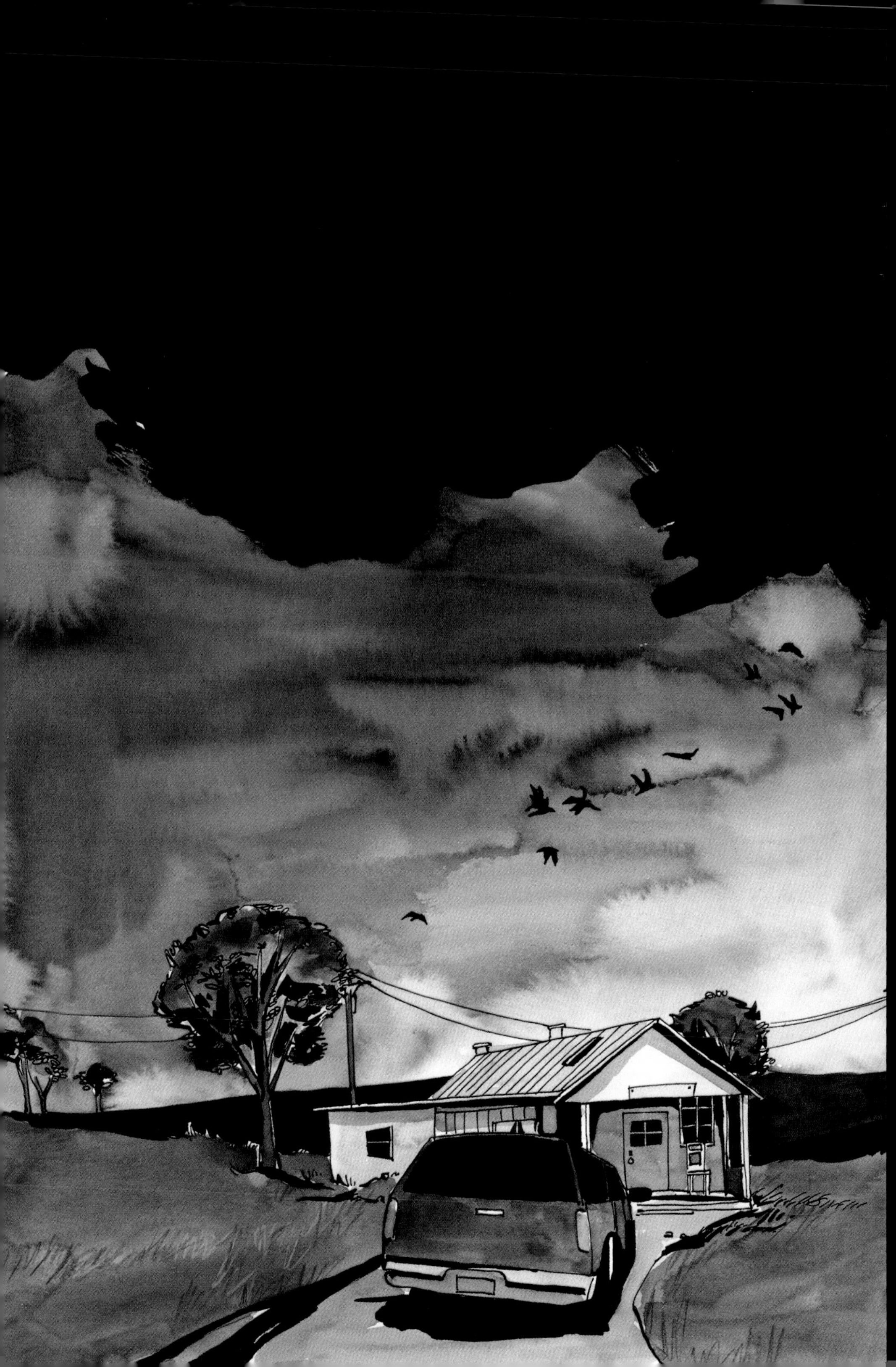

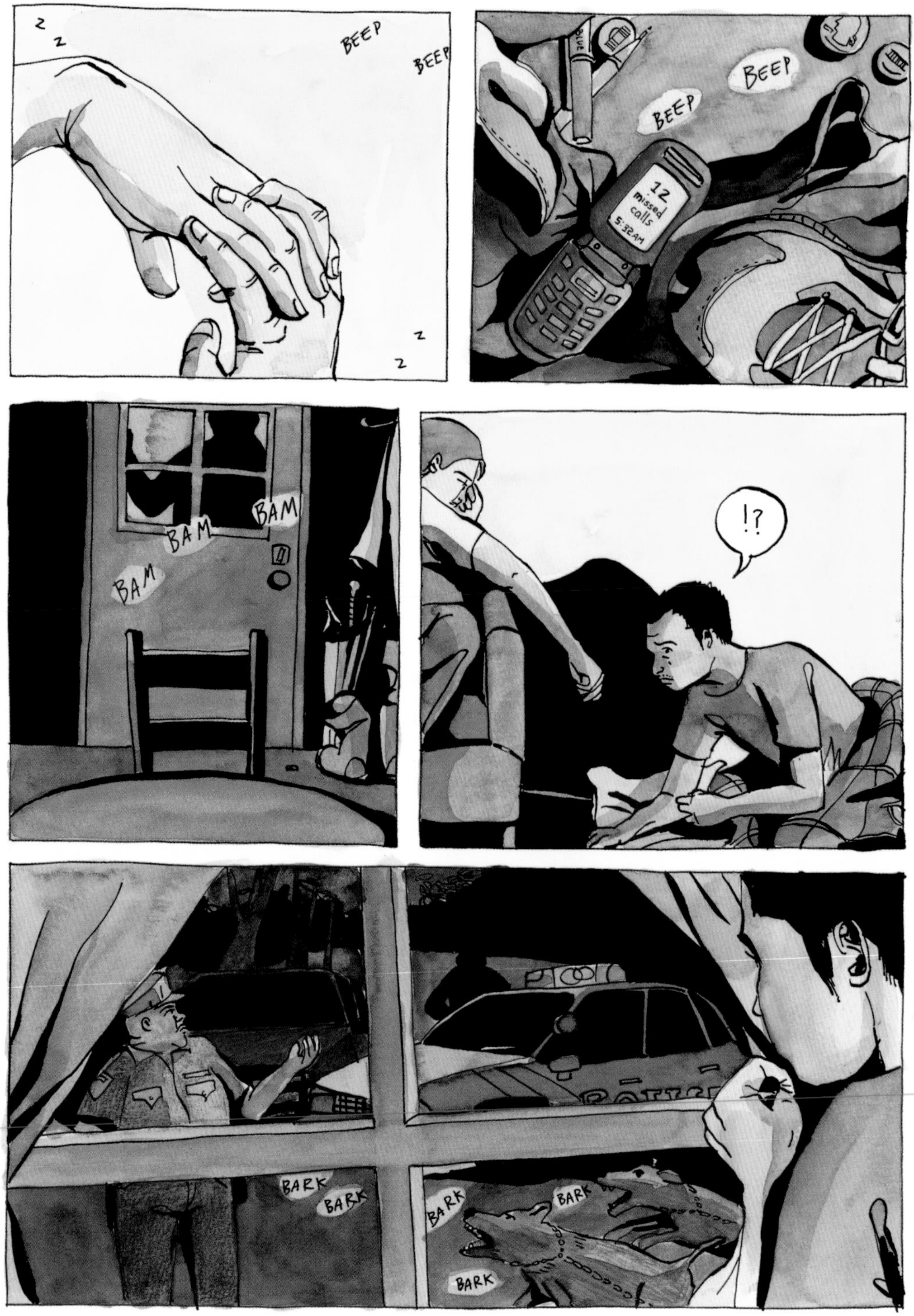
Z
Z
BEEP
BEEP
Z
Z
BEEP
BEEP
12
missed
calls
5:32AM
BAM
BAM
BAM
!?
BARK
BARK
BARK
BARK
BARK

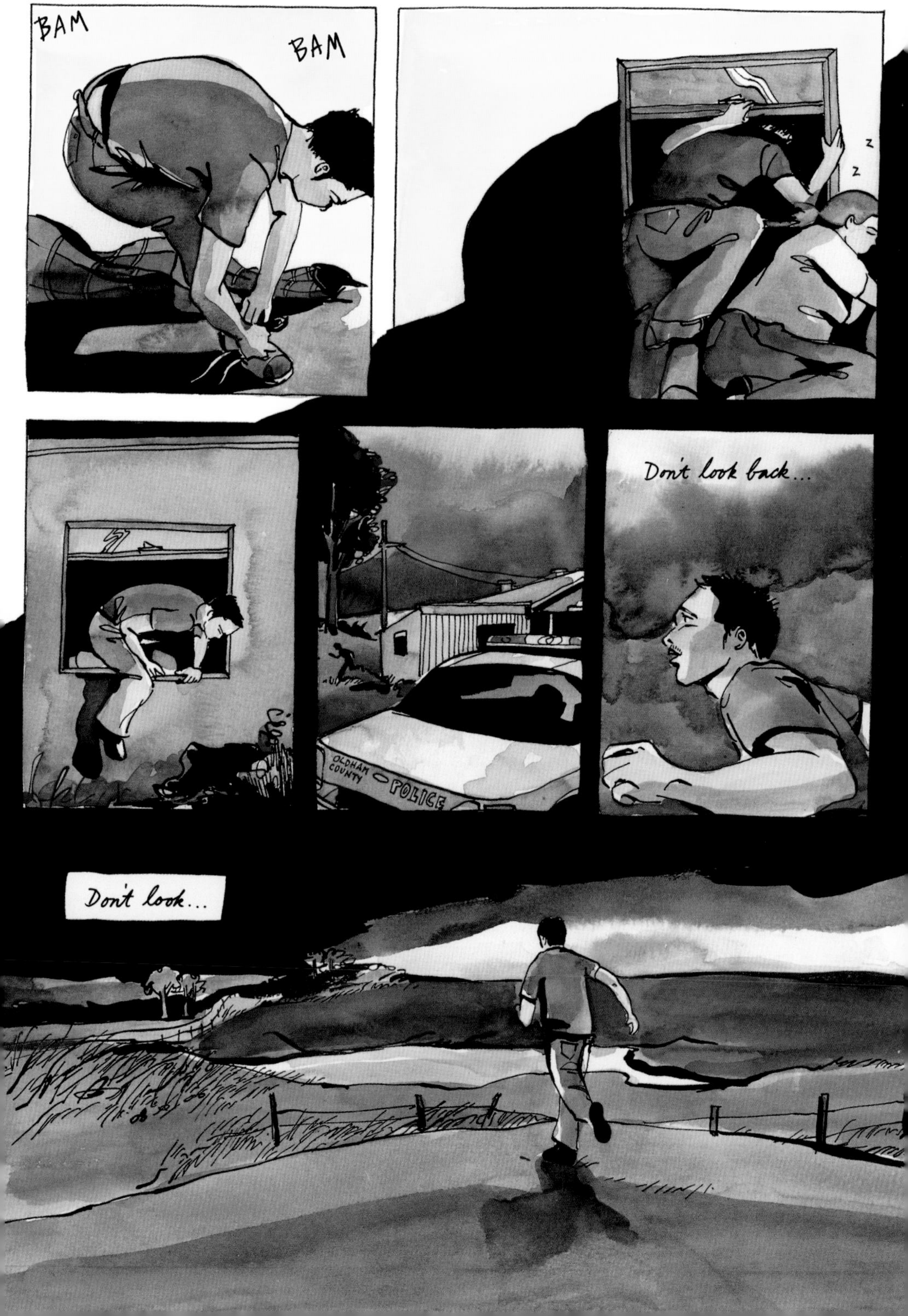
BAM
BAM
Z
Z
OLDHAM COUNTY POLICE
Don't look back...
Don't look...

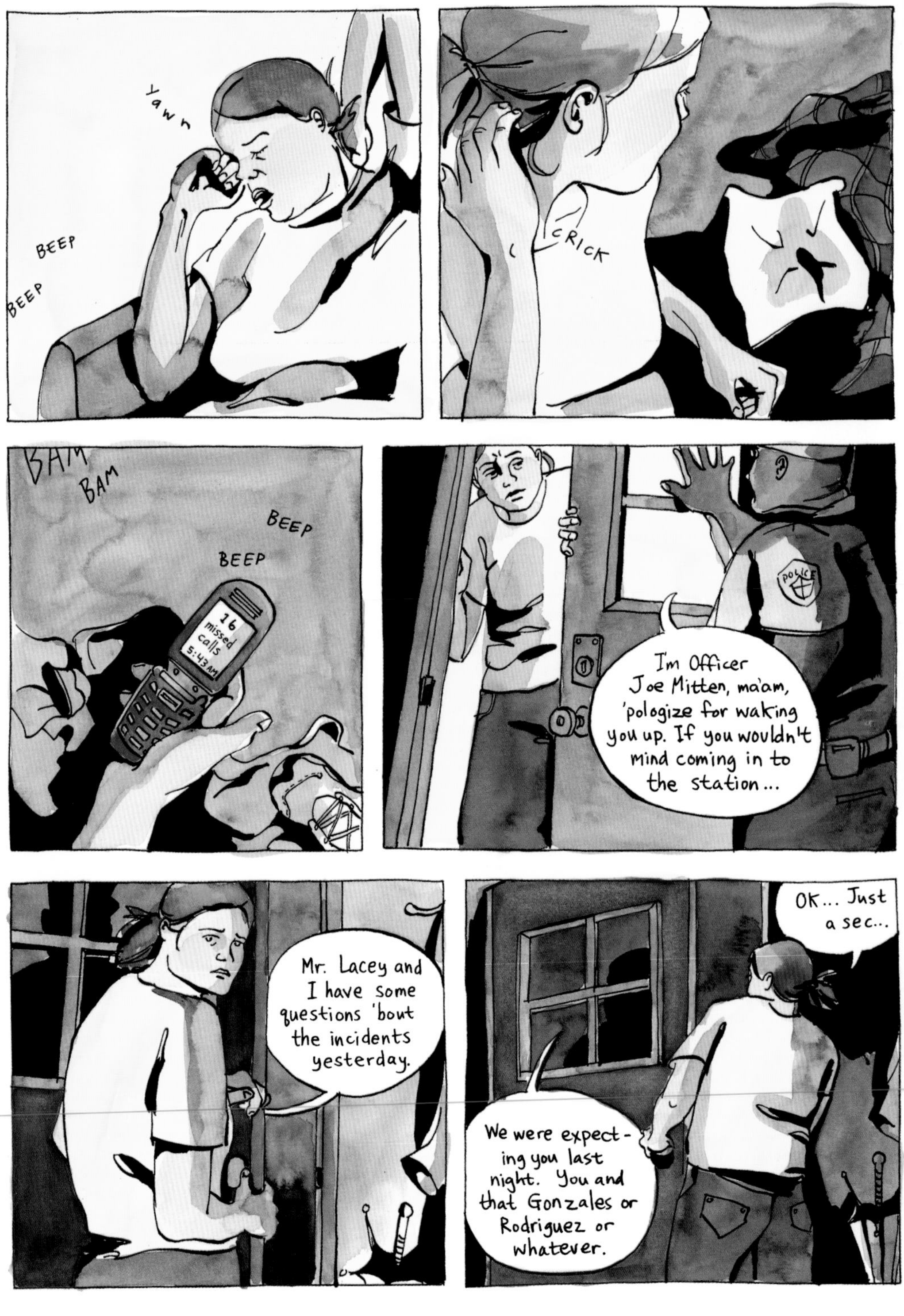
yawn
BEEP
BEEP
CRICK
BAM
BAM
BEEP
BEEP
16 missed calls 5:43AM
I'm Officer Joe Mitten, ma'am, 'pologize for waking you up. If you wouldn't mind coming in to the station...
POLICE
Mr. Lacey and I have some questions 'bout the incidents yesterday.
OK... Just a sec...
We were expecting you last night. You and that Gonzales or Rodriguez or whatever.

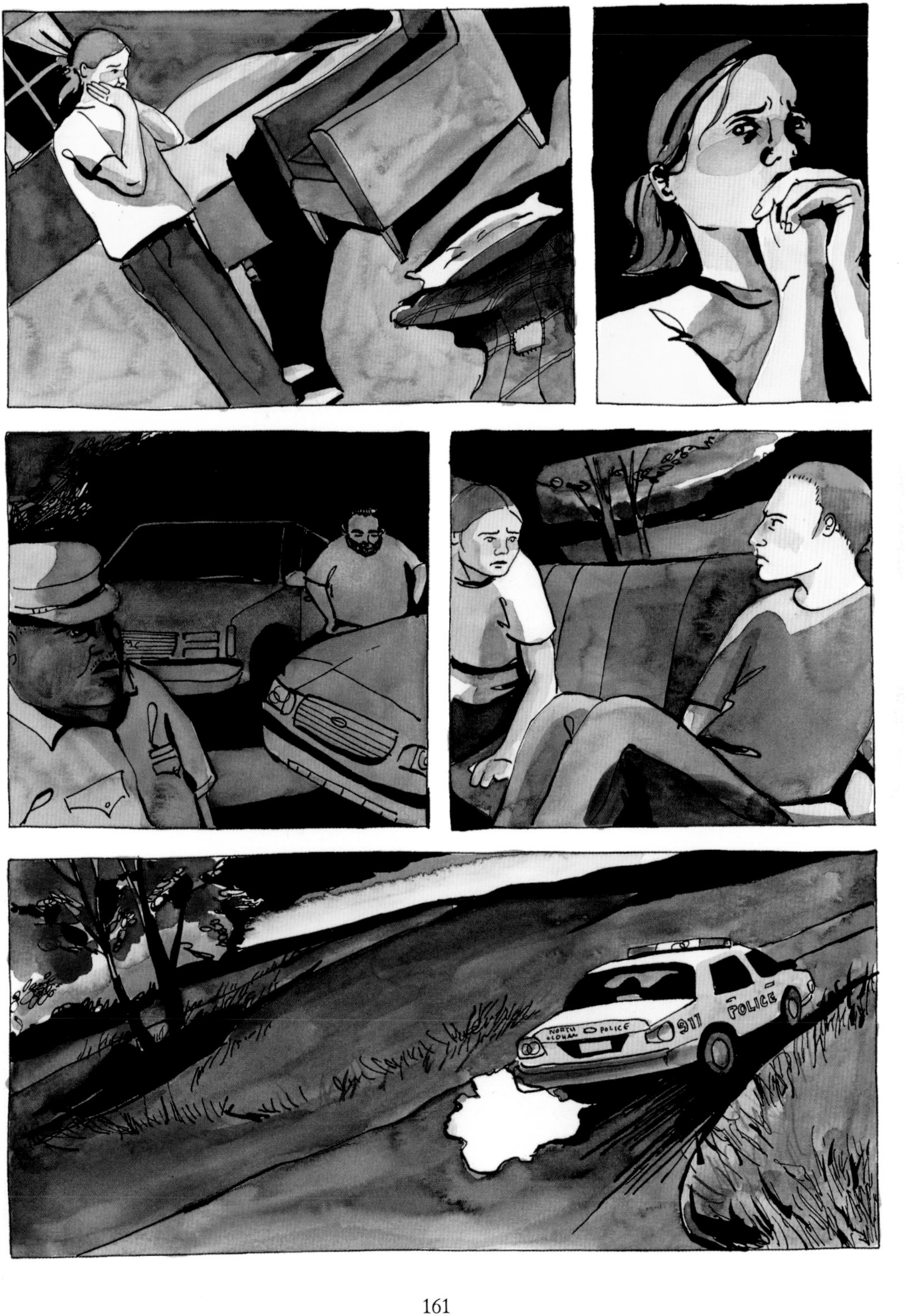
POLICE
311
POLICE

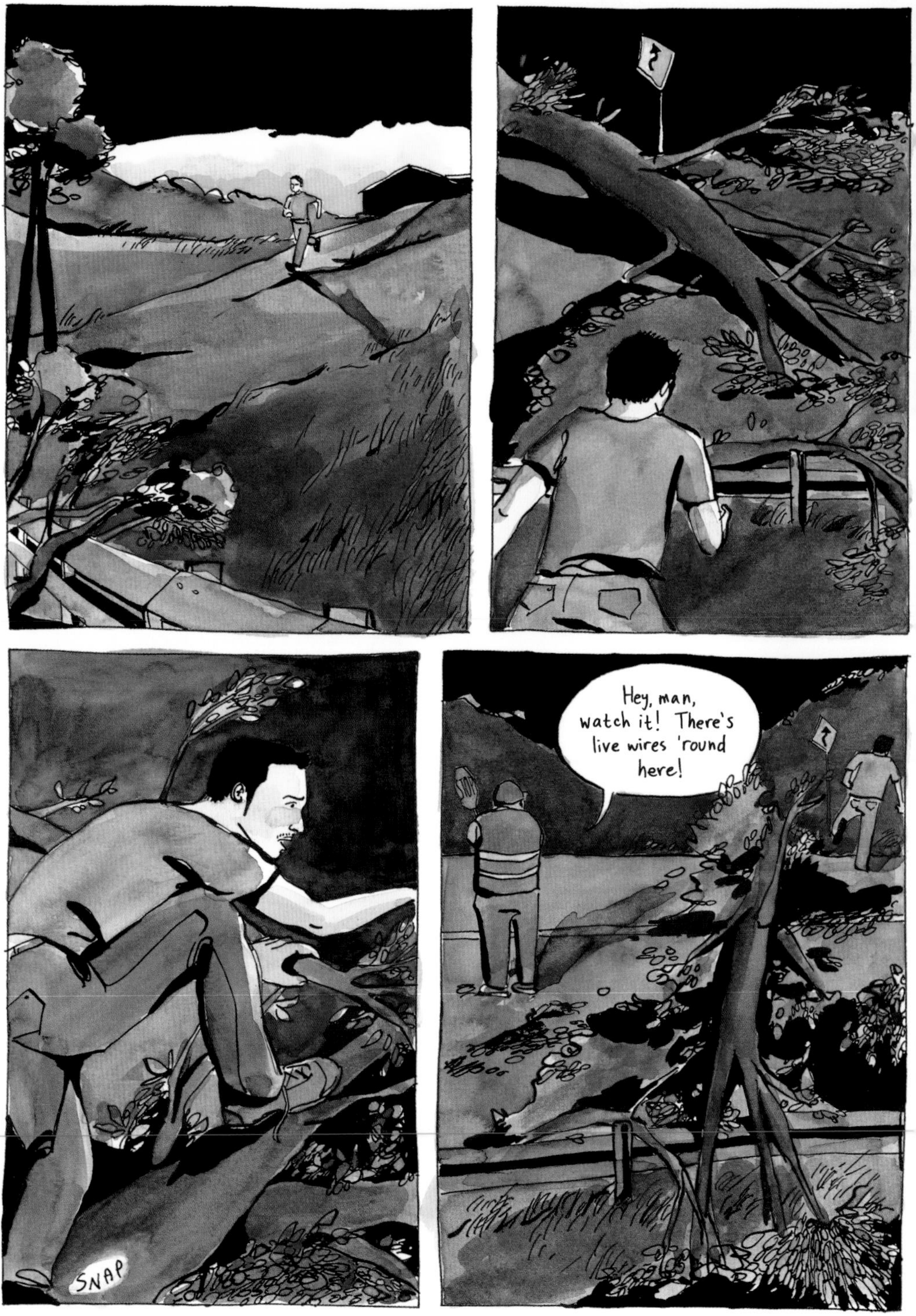
Hey, man, watch it! There's live wires 'round here!
SNAP

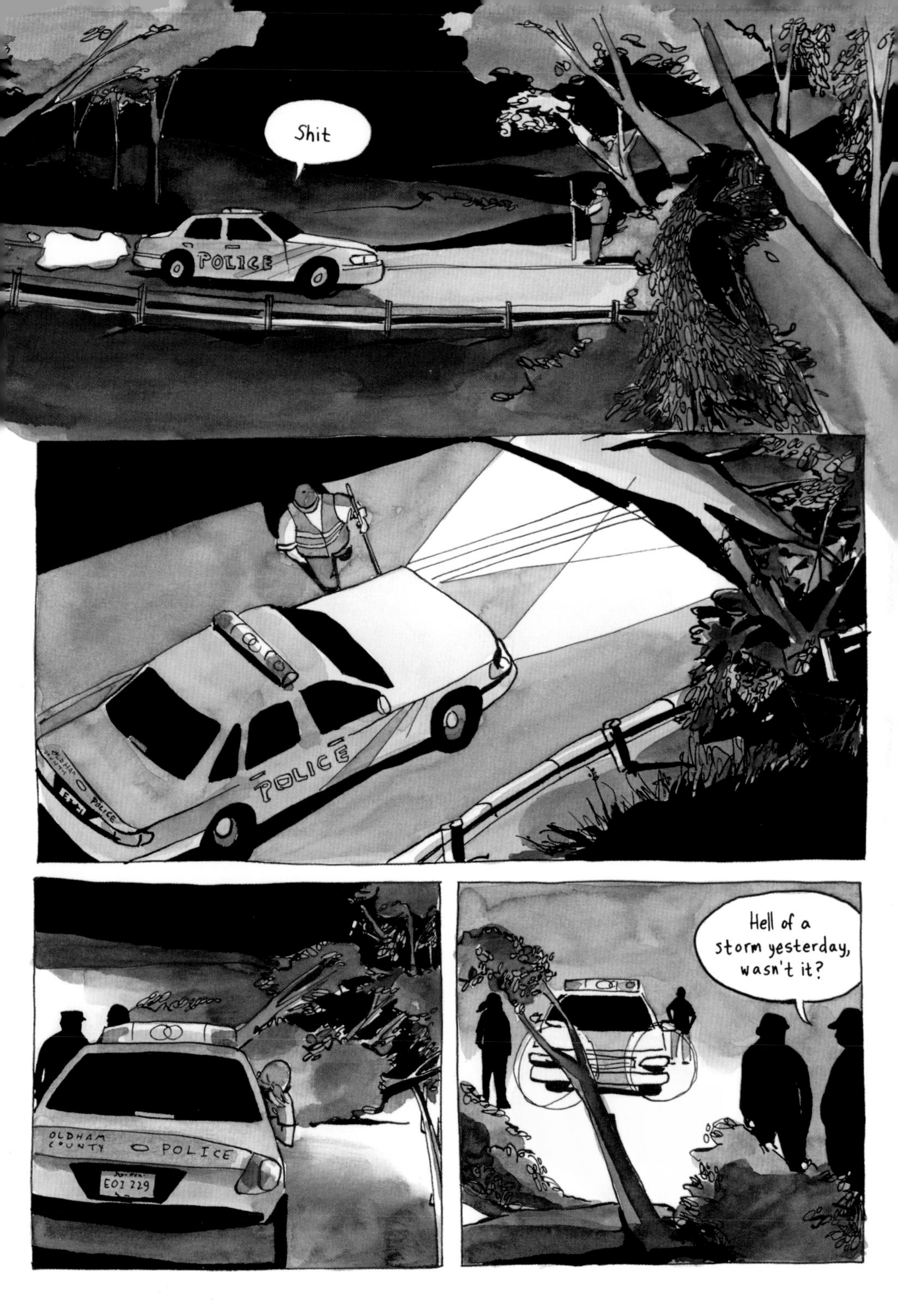
Shit
POLICE
POLICE
OLDHAM COUNTY
POLICE
Hell of a storm yesterday, wasn't it?

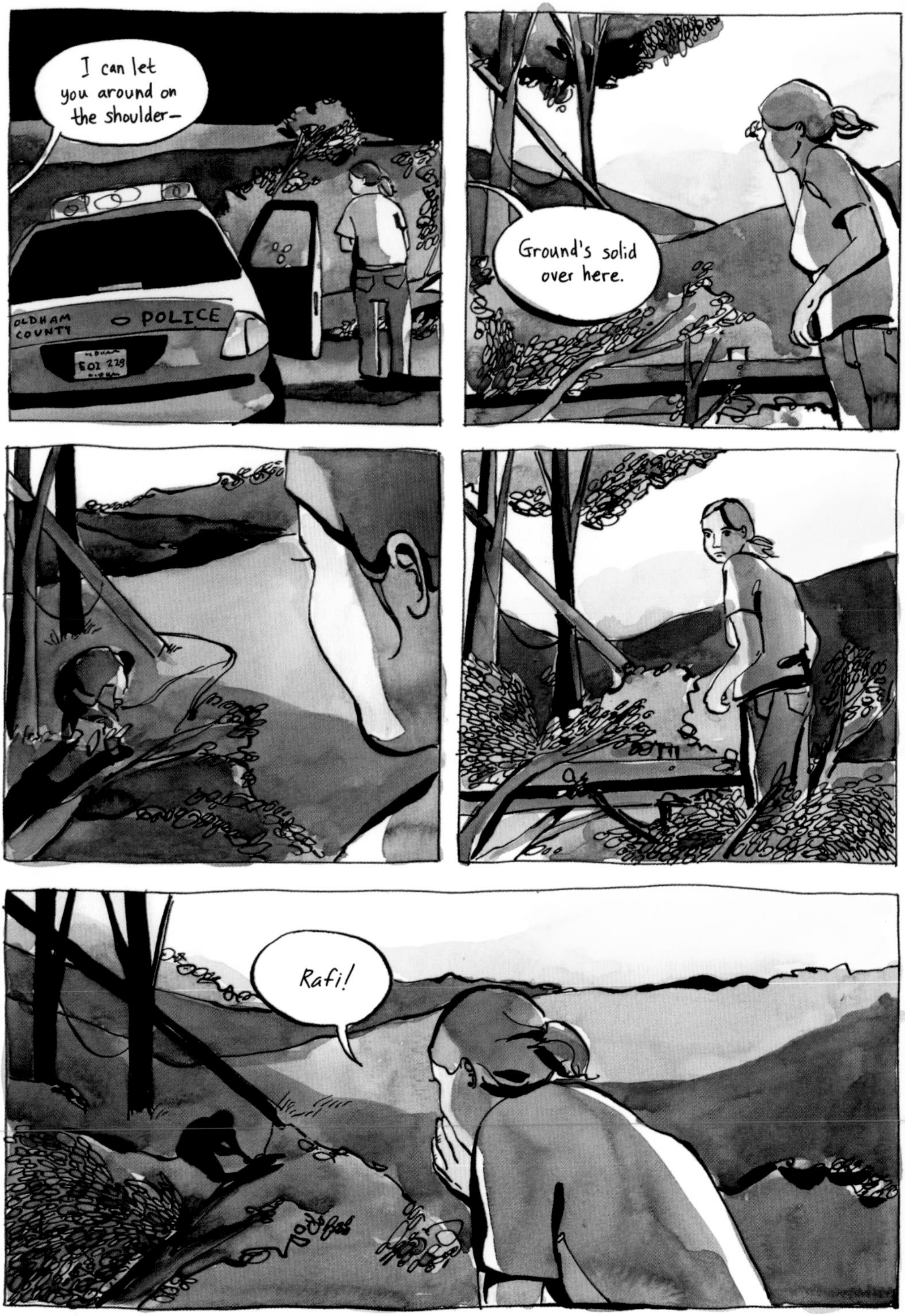
I can let you around on the shoulder—
OLDHAM COUNTY
POLICE
Ground's solid over here.
Rafi!

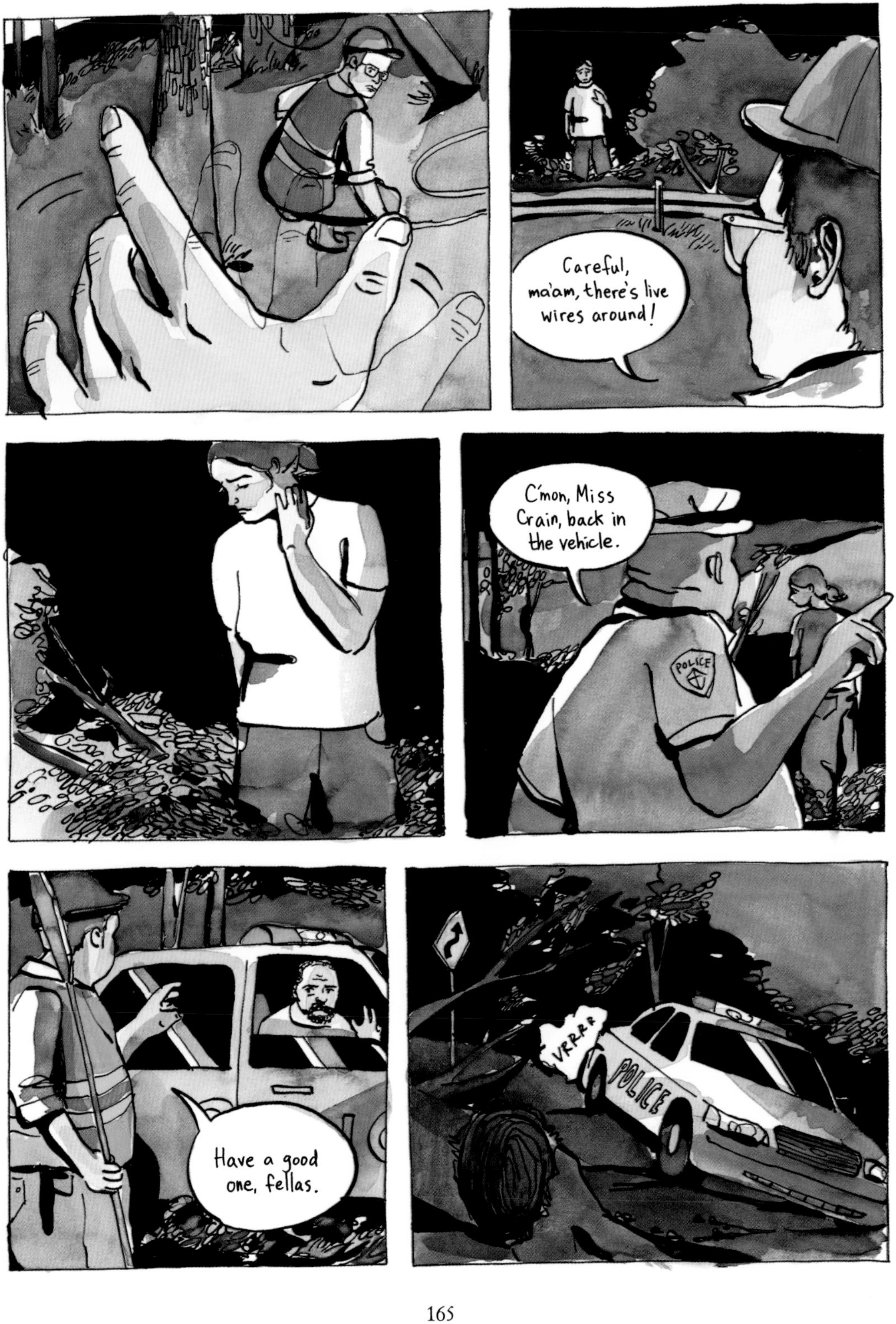
Careful, ma'am, there's live wires around!
C'mon, Miss Crain, back in the vehicle.
POLICE
Have a good one, fellas.
VRRRR
POLICE

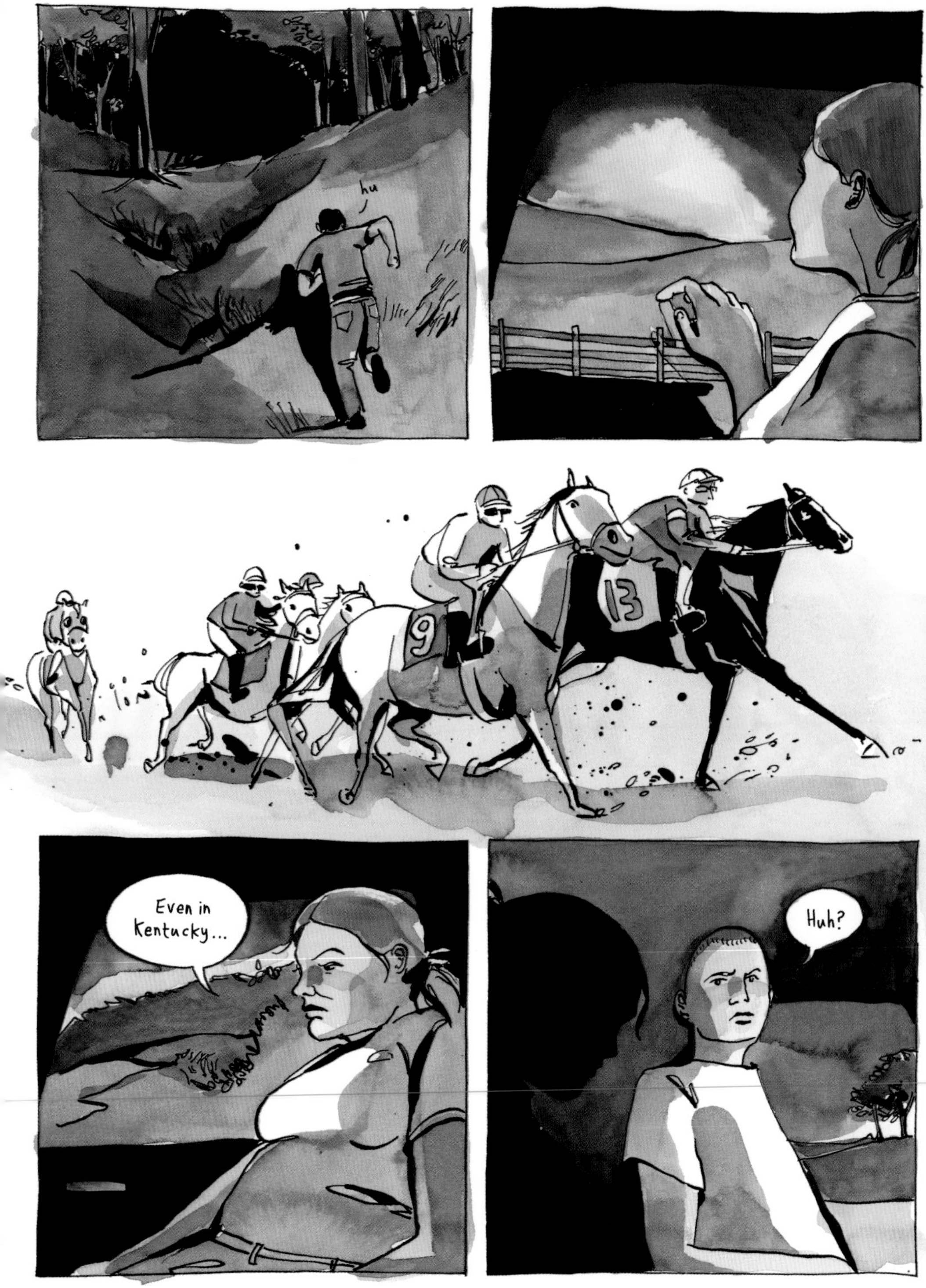
hu
13
9
Even in Kentucky...
Huh?

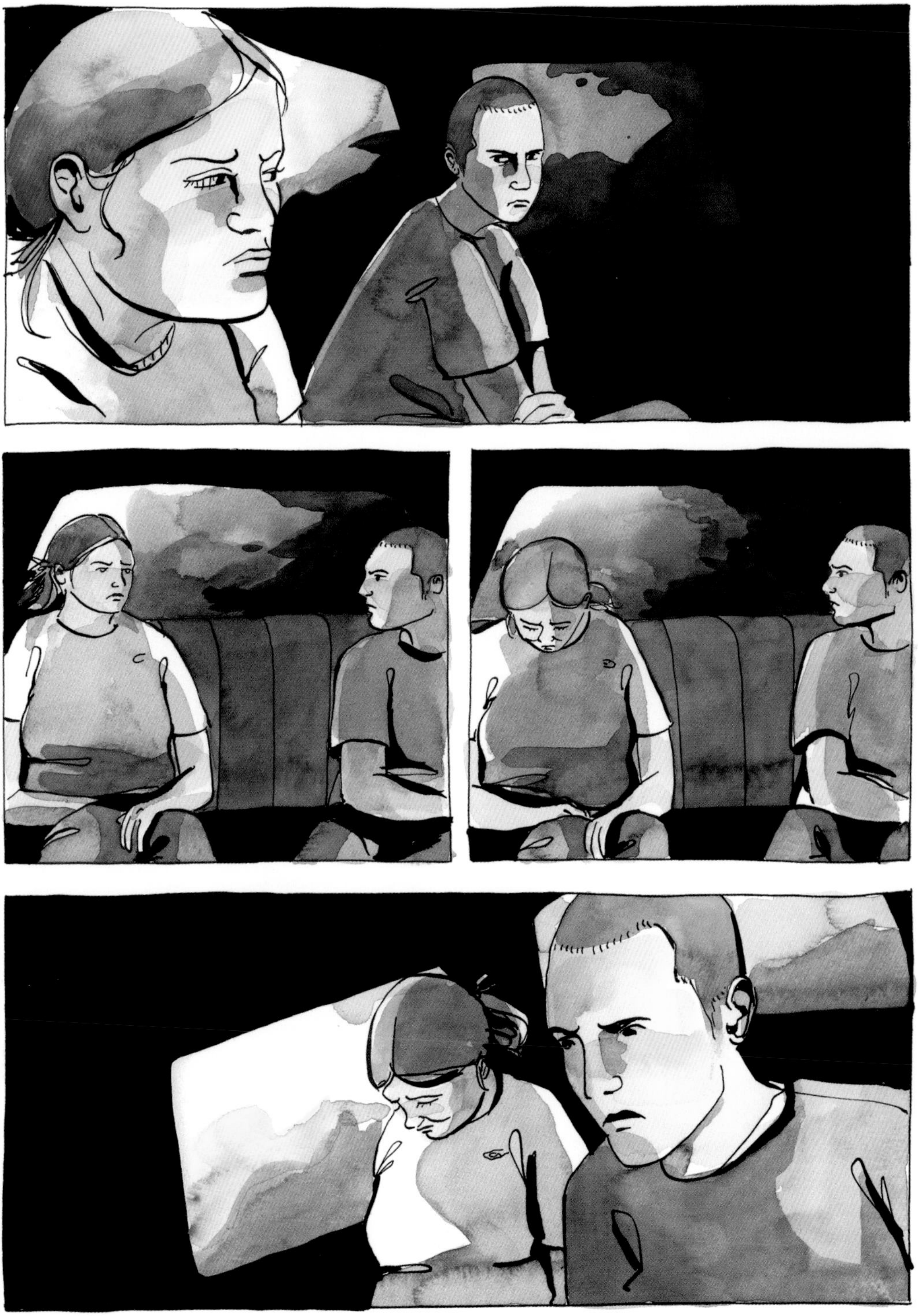

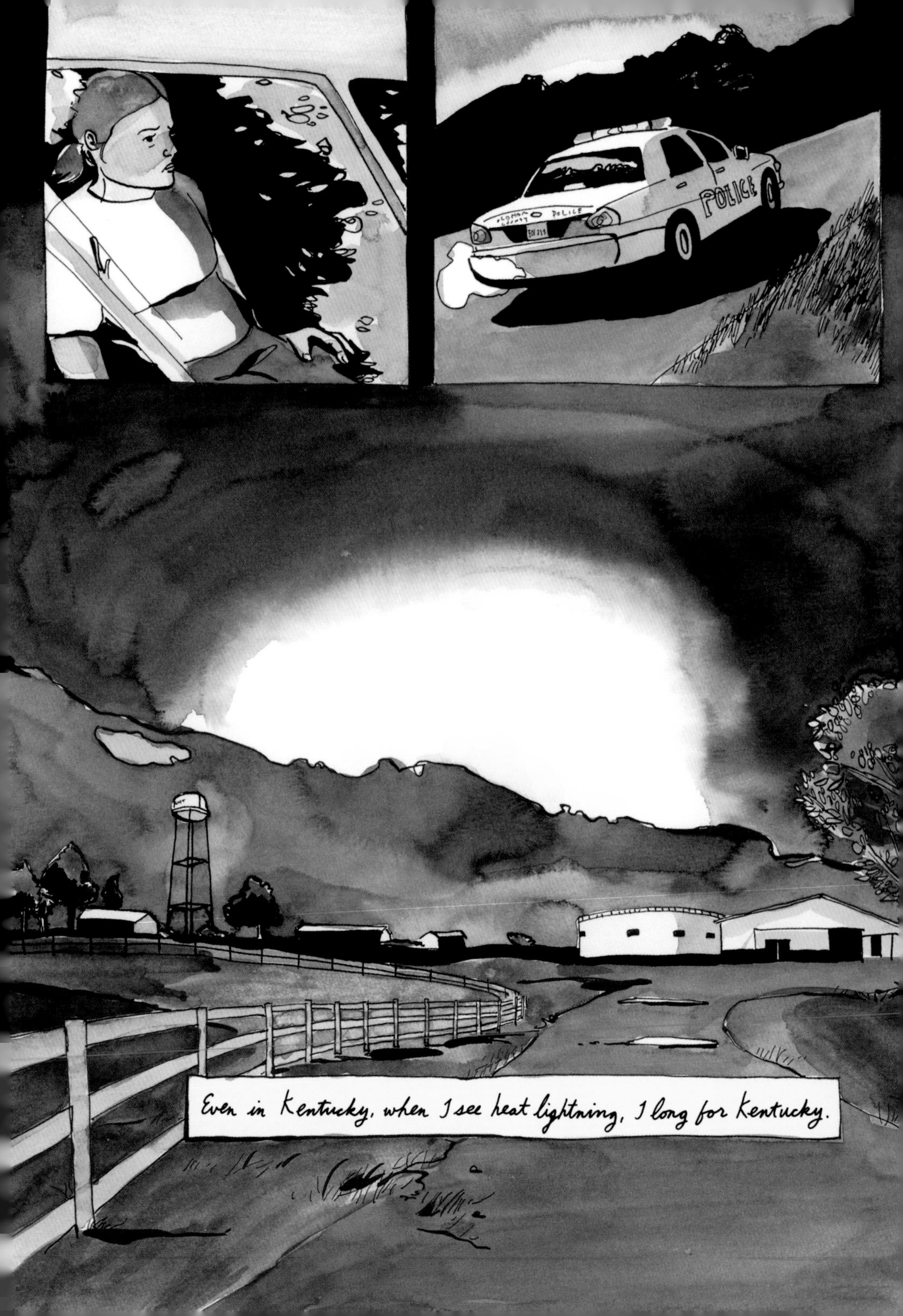
POLICE
Even in Kentucky, when I see heat lightning, I long for Kentucky.

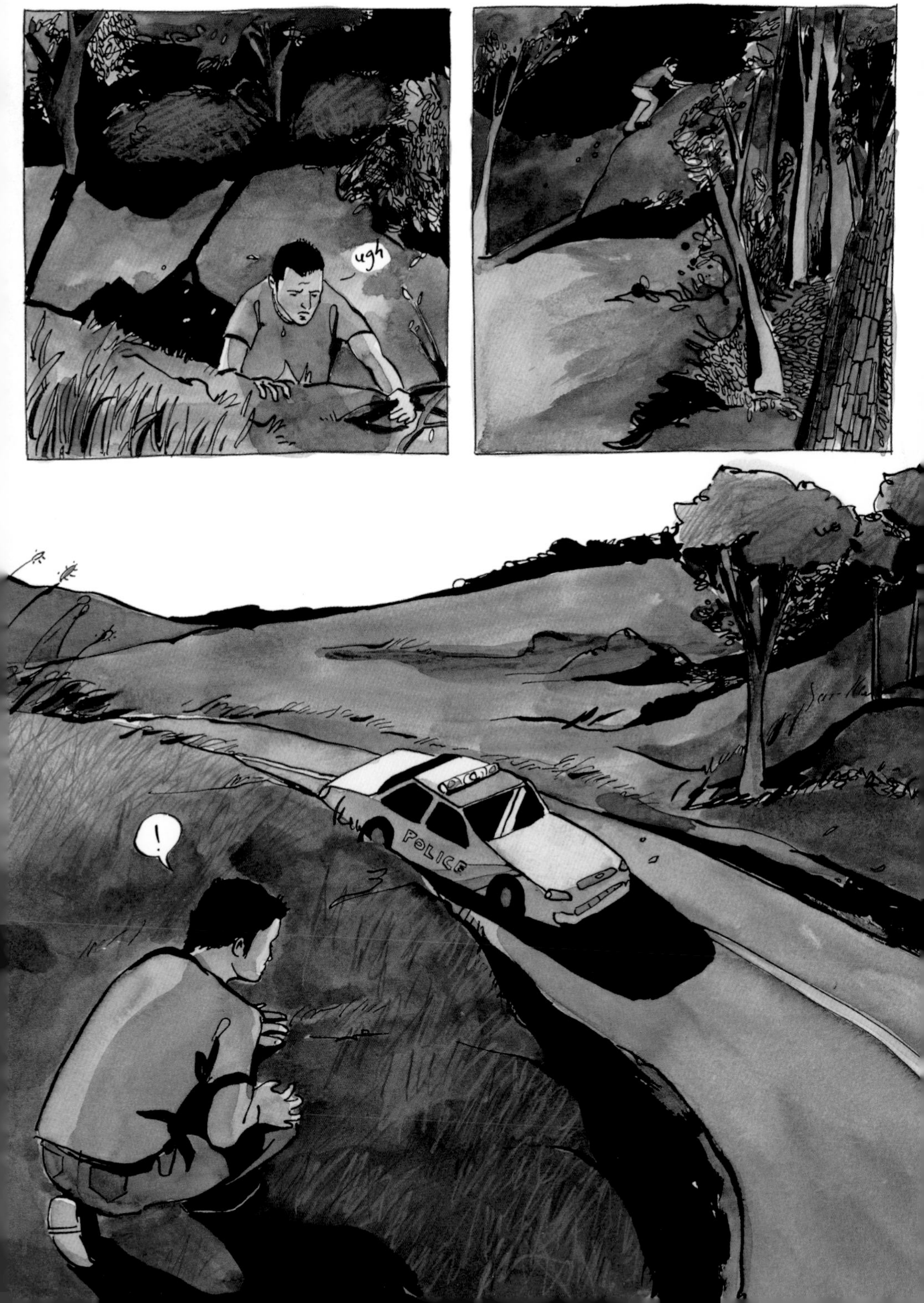
ugh
!
POLICE

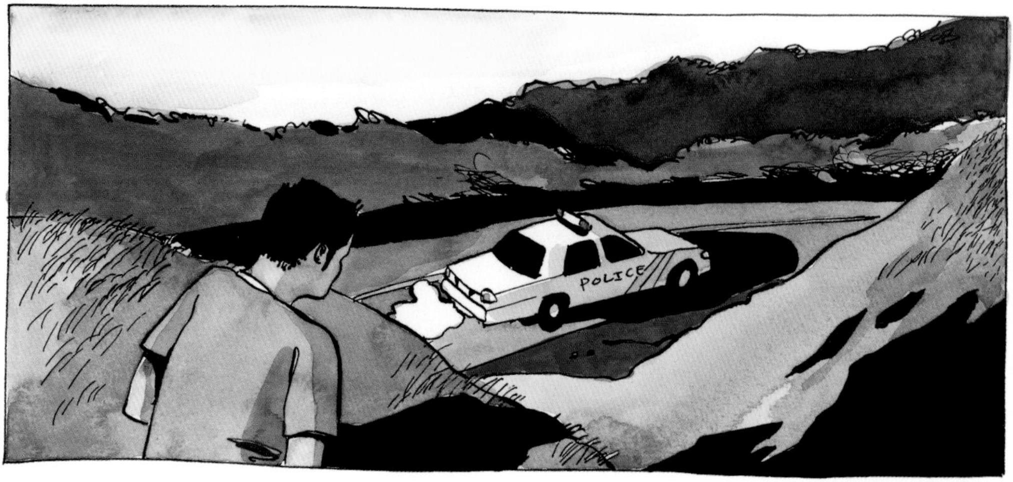
POLICE

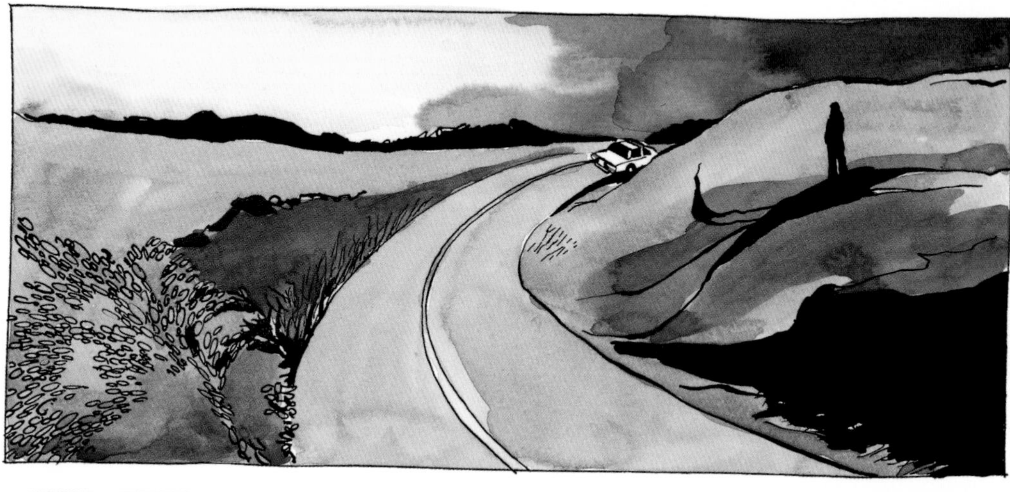

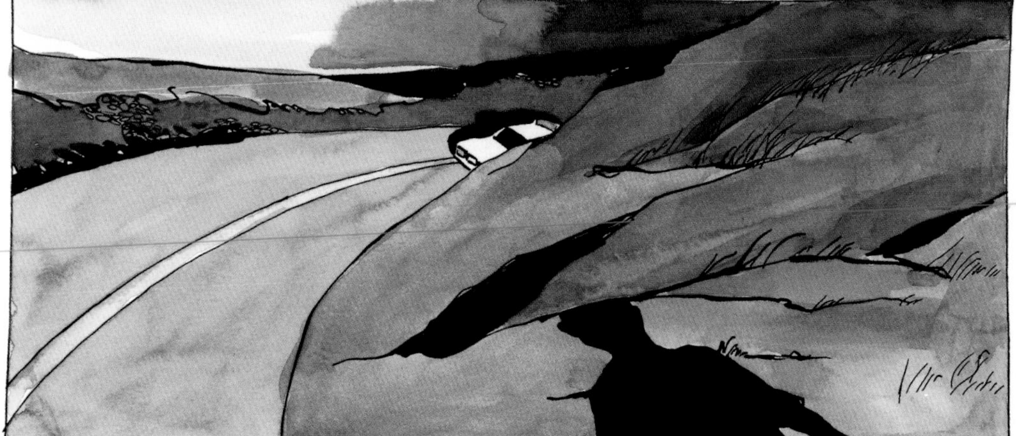

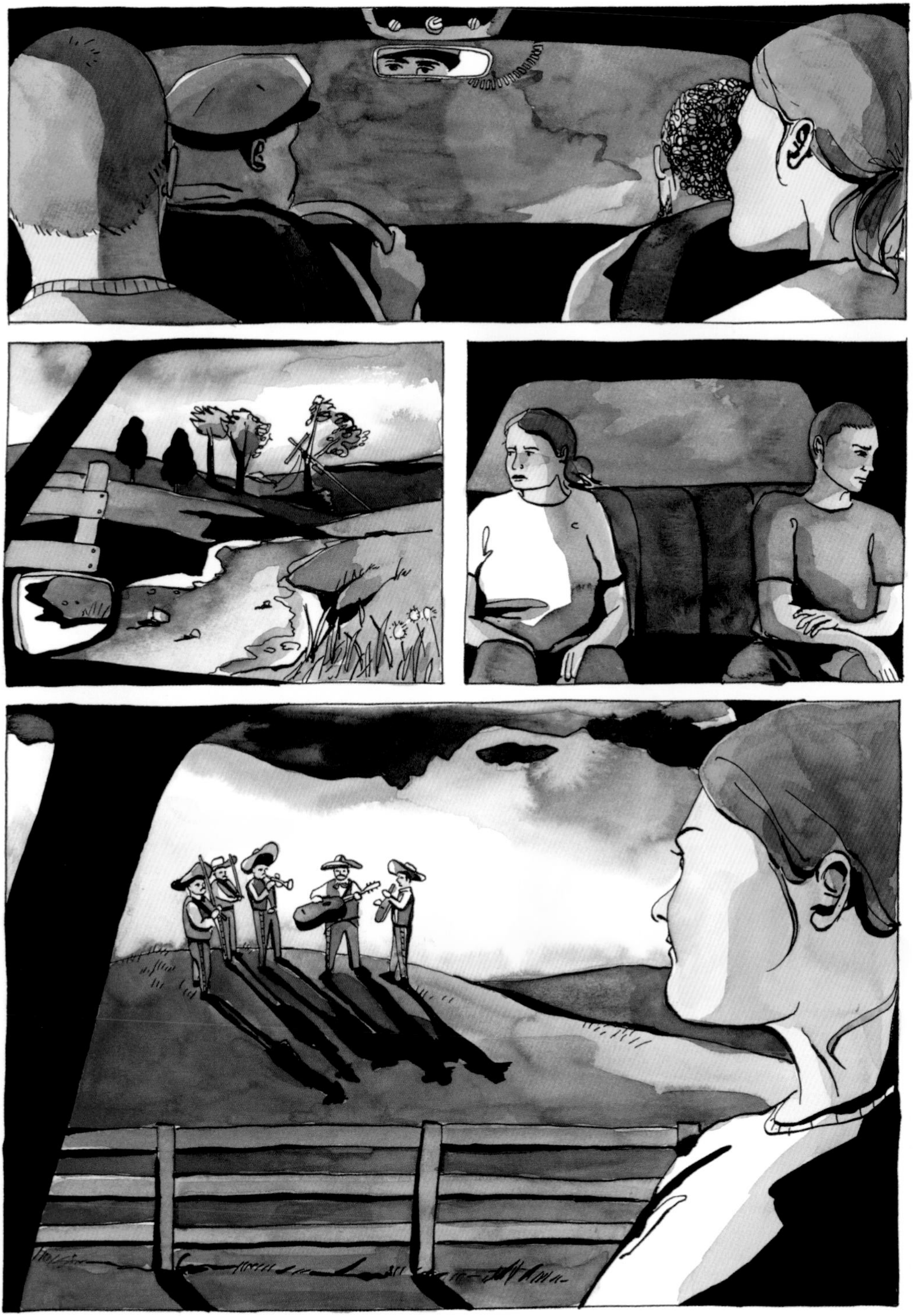

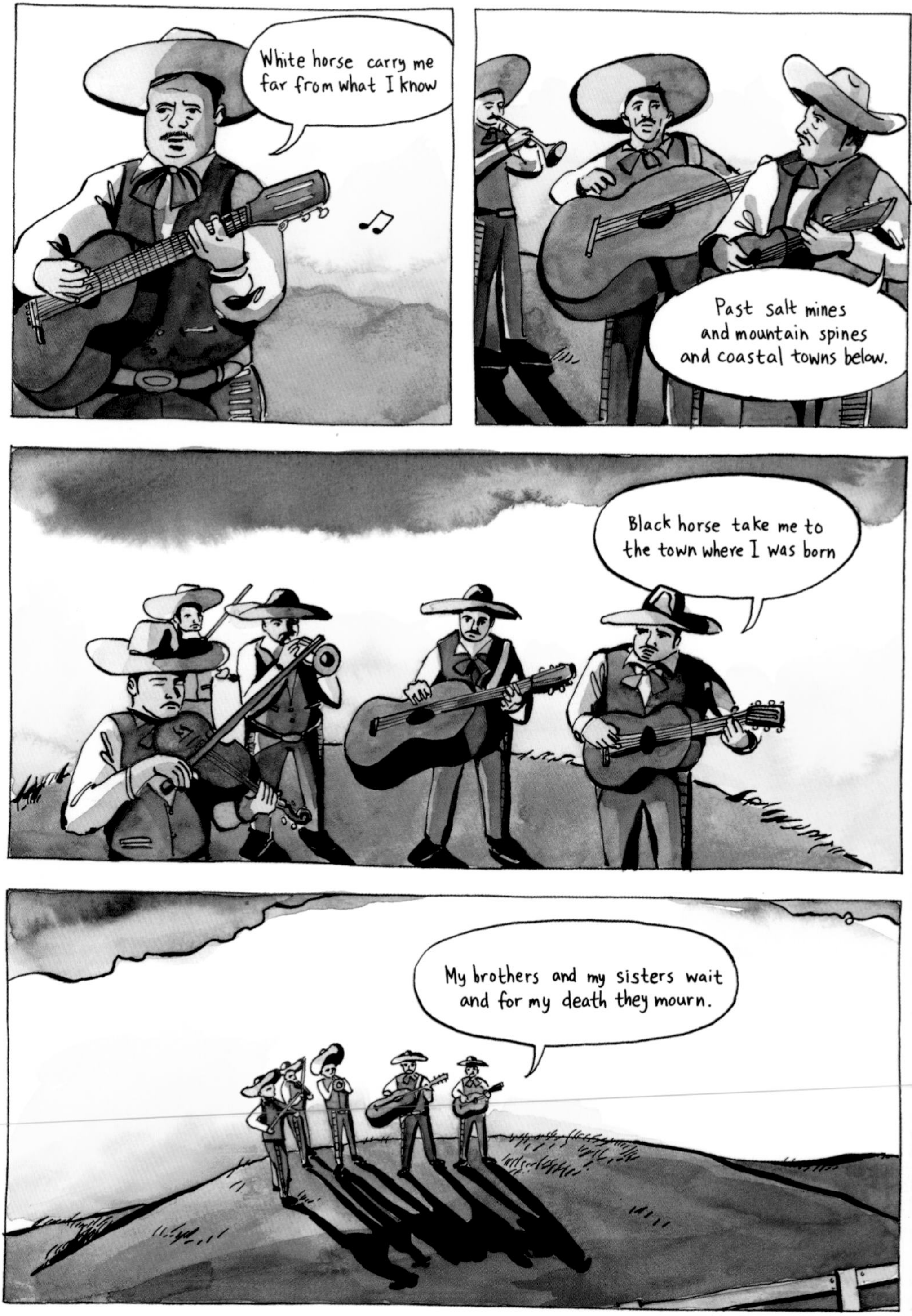
White horse carry me far from what I know
Past salt mines and mountain spines and coastal towns below.
Black horse take me to the town where I was born
My brothers and my sisters wait and for my death they mourn.

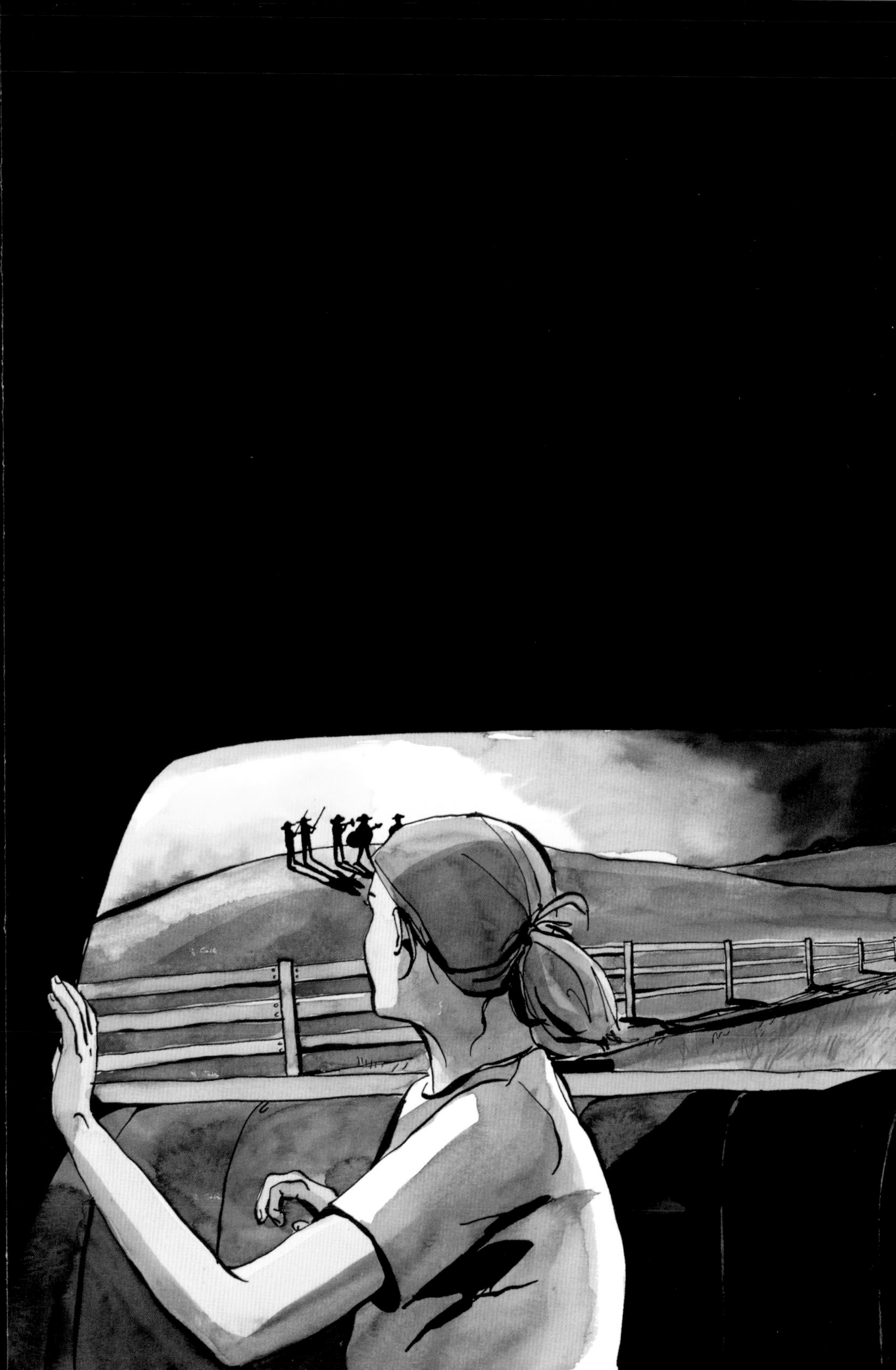

To Mom & Dad

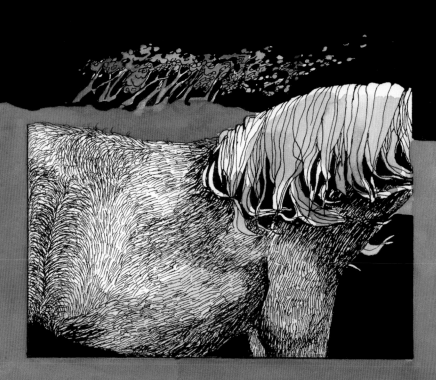

Many, many thanks to John Detherage, Tanya McKinnon, and Mark Siegel. Thanks also to Tim Smith, Kat Kopit, Gina Gagliano, Linda Rosenbury, Will Garner, Abel Pérez, Matthew Stadelmann, and Dawn Landes.

First Second
New York & London

Copyright © 2008 by Danica Novgorodoff

Published by First Second
First Second is an imprint of Roaring Brook Press,
a division of Holtzbrinck Publishing Holdings Limited Partnership
175 Fifth Avenue, New York, NY 10010

Distributed in Canada by H. B. Fenn and Company Ltd.
Distributed in the United Kingdom by Macmillan Children's Books, a division of Pan Macmillan.

Design by Danica Novgorodoff

Library of Congress Cataloging-in-Publication Data

Novgorodoff, Danica.
Slow storm / by Danica Novgorodoff. – 1st ed.
p. cm.
ISBN-13: 978-1-59643-250-5
ISBN-10: 1-59643-250-0
1. Graphic novels. I. Title.
PN6727.N68S56 2008
741.5'973–dc22

2007046202

First Second books are available for special promotions and premiums.
For details, contact: Director of Special Markets, Holtzbrinck Publishers.

First Edition September 2008
Printed in China

10 9 8 7 6 5 4 3 2 1